BRIGHT LIGHT CITY

CultureAmerica

Erika Doss
Philip J. Deloria
Series Editors

Karal Ann Marling
Editor Emerita

BRIGHT LIGHT CITY

LAS VEGAS
in Popular Culture

LARRY GRAGG

UNIVERSITY PRESS OF KANSAS

© 2013 by the University Press of Kansas
All rights reserved

Published by the University Press of Kansas (Lawrence, Kansas
66045), which was organized by the Kansas Board of Regents and is
operated and funded by Emporia State University, Fort Hays State
University, Kansas State University, Pittsburg State University, the
University of Kansas, and Wichita State University

Library of Congress Cataloging-in-Publication Data

Gragg, Larry Dale, 1950–
Bright light city : Las Vegas in popular culture / Larry Gragg.
pages cm. — (CultureAmerica)
Includes bibliographical references and index.
ISBN 978-0-7006-1903-0 (cloth : alk. paper)
1. Las Vegas (Nev.)—Social life and customs. 2. Las Vegas (Nev.)—
History. I. Title.
F849.L35G275 2013
979.3'135—dc23

2012044370

British Library Cataloguing-in-Publication Data is available.

Printed in the United States of America

10 9 8 7 6 5 4 3 2 1

The paper used in this publication is recycled and contains 30
percent postconsumer waste. It is acid free and meets the minimum
requirements of the American National Standard for Permanence
of Paper for Printed Library Materials z39.48-1992.

CHANGING FIRST IMPRESSIONS OF LAS VEGAS

Ours was the first and doubtless will be the last party of whites to visit this profitless locality.

U.S. Army Lt. Joseph Ives, 1857

I thought it was the crummiest little place I'd been in.

John Beville, 1929

It was the hottest damn place in the world! It was hotter than hell.

Robert Kaltenborn, 1932

Las Vegas . . . is an ugly little town where gambling dens and saloons and prostitution run wide open day and night.

Harold L. Ickes, 1939

Las Vegas was still a small town with more dirt roads than sidewalks, replete with swinging-door saloons, blanketed Indians, bearded prospectors and burros.

Hank Greenspun, 1946

There were two hotels, the El Rancho and the Last Frontier. And across the street was just desert for centipedes and scorpions.

Herb McDonald, 1946

It was really something to see. You come out of the dark desert and you come in to all these lights.

Carl Barschdorf, 1952

It was a wild place where the attitude was "anything goes!"

Tony Bennett, 1952

There was magic in this place. It was like stepping back into the frontier.

Steve Wynn, 1952

The first impression was magic.

Peter Graves, ca. 1954

This is a fabulous madhouse.

Noel Coward, 1955

That's the key word for Vegas. Excitement. Then and now. Flashing neon in the middle of a sandpile. A flame in the desert that drew moths.

Jimmy the Greek, 1956

It was a very exciting place.

Helen Morelli, 1957

There were more glittering lights on one street than we had ever seen.

Valda Esau, 1958

I guess the thing that struck me immediately is these big beautiful resorts adjacent to the most desolate desert you can ever imagine.

Jim Seagrave, 1961

Coming out of that desert . . . the sun was starting to settle and you see the lights of the Stardust and I said, "Man, this is what it is like to die and wake up in heaven."

Harry Merenda, 1961

CONTENTS

PREFACE

How does a scholar who has spent over three decades researching and publishing articles and books on early American history turn to the history of Las Vegas? How does one pivot from a career focused upon investigating the mysteries of the Salem witch trials and the English colonization of Barbados to an analysis of the popularity of Sin City? Actually, the answer is quite simple: visiting Las Vegas, beginning in 1992 and returning every year for two decades. In 2009, David G. Schwartz, historian and columnist for *Las Vegas Weekly*, asked me what drew me to the city and its history. "The reason I like Las Vegas," I told him, "is because it's almost all the things that I am not. I'm rural America, I'm small-town America, I'm conservative in my personal finances, I'm not flamboyant, and Las Vegas is the opposite of all four of those."[1] In other words, this study is in part a personal quest to understand my attraction to Las Vegas, yet one that I believe will illuminate what has made the city such a powerful magnet for millions of tourists over the past century.

The quest is built on a simple assumption. People who had never been there assuredly encountered images and descriptions of the city in popular culture that made a trip to Las Vegas appealing. I examined 150 films, over 200 television programs, over 200 novels, nearly 1,500 newspaper articles, and over 200 magazine articles in addition to a large number of relevant secondary works seeking to discover the patterns of images of Las Vegas Americans encountered between 1905 and 2005.

The chapters that follow examine those patterns. Chapter 1, "'Bright Light City': The Introduction to Las Vegas," reveals how authors, journalists, and screenwriters shared with readers and viewers the remarkable lights, sounds, and action they would encounter should they travel to the southern Nevada resort city, no matter what decade they visited. Chapter 2, "Las Vegas: The Last Frontier Town," describes how most observers saw the city in the first half of the twentieth century: as a community that reflected much of the collective American view of the West, a place of prospectors and cowboys enjoying the vices associated with frontier towns. In print and in film, Las Vegas seemed to be one of the last bastions of rugged individualism, where one could experience all that the fabled frontier saloons had offered in the nineteenth-century West: liquor, women, and wide-open gambling. Chapter

3, "Bugsy Siegel and the Founding of Las Vegas," assesses the enduring legend of Benjamin Siegel and his role in the development of the resort city. Filmmakers, novelists, and journalists have contributed to a remarkable founding myth associated with Siegel, arguing that in 1946 he had a vision of a sophisticated resort city in the midst of a woebegone desert town of little consequence. That narrative credits him with pulling Las Vegas away from its tired frontier origins to a more cosmopolitan approach to building a resort city, similar to Miami and Palm Springs. Chapter 4, "Organized Crime in Las Vegas," presents a comprehensive account of how scores of journalists and muckrakers, as well as novelists and filmmakers, have described a city, from the time of Bugsy Siegel until the 1980s, largely built by members of some of the most powerful figures in organized crime—men who used the gambling city not only as a source of funds for their organizations, but also as a place to become legitimate and to live respectable lives. However, in the end, it is an account that explains how local, state, and federal officials broke their power as corporate America took over their properties. Chapter 5, "Images of Gambling in Las Vegas," deals with what almost everyone most associates with Las Vegas: the many games of chance. Observers have described gambling in Las Vegas in a multitude of ways, including the extraordinary dangers of becoming a compulsive gambler and the inexperienced tourist miraculously winning enormous jackpots; however, gambling is most often portrayed as a thrilling, edgy experience making the trip to Las Vegas well worth the money, even though the overwhelming majority of gamblers come away losers. Chapter 6, "The Entertainment Capital of the World," offers an extensive discussion of the favorite topic about Las Vegas in newspapers and magazines. From the 1940s, entertainment columnists have been effusive about the extraordinary entertainment options in Las Vegas, including great vocalists and comedians, elaborate production shows, and popular lounge acts. A handful of those entertainers came to define the Las Vegas style of entertainment and consistently attracted the attention of music critics and entertainment columnists alike, who filled the nation's press with appealing pieces on Liberace, Louis Prima, Keely Smith, Wayne Newton, Elvis Presley, and Frank Sinatra, the individuals who became the biggest stars in the pantheon of Las Vegas celebrities. Chapter 7, "'Beautiful Women Were as Commonplace in Las Vegas as Poker Chips': Images of Las Vegas Women in Popular Culture," deals with the limited ways that the women of Las Vegas have appeared in popular culture. Except for those seeking a quick marriage or divorce, most of the women in novels, films, television, and periodicals have been cocktail waitresses, prostitutes, strippers, or showgirls. Most are objects of men's attention, collectively creating an image of a city with multitudes of readily available women. Chapter 8, "'So Much Luxury in the Middle of the Desert': Images of Luxury and Amenities in Las Vegas," presents the many images of spectacular hotels, luxurious accommodations, excellent restaurants, and remarkable showrooms in post–World War II Las Vegas. Chapter 9, "'An Awful Place': The Negative Images of Las Vegas," deals with the elements of Las Vegas that attract the greatest criticism, most notably compulsive gambling, the types of people attracted to the city, and the ways that casinos manipulate those who enter their doors. Indeed, in many accounts, the city is not a fit place for respectable folks. Chapter 10, "Conclusion: The Ultimate Attraction of Las Vegas," discusses what most observers see as the ultimate appeal of Las Vegas: that it represents an escape from the mundane, everyday cares facing all people. It is a place to evade the normal and to experience uninhibited fun, at least for a few days. The brief "Afterword: The Intellectuals' Images of Las Vegas" reveals how the intellectual class has tended to view Las Vegas; predictably, it has been a dismissive assessment, although some seek to understand Las Vegas in the American context as either a mirror of national trends or a model for future American directions.

In nearly a decade of research, I have become indebted to many people who helped guide me on this quest. Most important have been the remarkable faculty and staff at Special Collections in the Lied Library at the University of Nevada, Las Vegas. Delores Brownlee, Su Kim Chung, Michael Frazier, Jonnie Kennedy, Kelly Luchs, director Peter Michel, Mary McCoy, Joyce Moore, Dave Schwartz, Tom Sommer, Kathy War, and Claytee White were always welcoming and helpful with my research queries. In eight years of research, I spent over one hundred days at Special Collections. In 2008, a research fellowship from the Center for Gaming Research at UNLV funded a month-long stay. The center is the best place to study all aspects of both contemporary and historical gaming. I have conducted research at dozens of manuscript repositories in the United States, England, and Barbados in my career and have never encountered a staff equal to the one at UNLV in knowledge and hospitality. It is a superb place to research the past.

Dave Schwartz not only listened to my ideas on the book, but he also frequently took me to an intriguing array of restaurants, from the famous to the obscure, for lunch. Wherever we went, I never failed to learn from Dave something new about the gambling city's past and contemporary challenges. Manuscripts librarian Su Kim Chung not only guided me to innumerable useful collections, she, along with her delightful parents, Al and Kelly, adopted me into their family. They made my many trips to Las Vegas a special treat. The entire staff at the Curtis Laws Wilson Library at the Missouri University of Science and Technology was exceptional in facilitating my research, particularly Mary Haug, Annette Howard, and Catherine Lindsey, who secured seemingly countless interlibrary loan books. Through their good research, students Ashley Grace, Amanda Kamps, Allyson Lutz, and Evan Mobley taught me much about Las Vegas. Several people consented to interviews, all of which helped me understand the context from which the many images of Las Vegas emerged: Harvey Diederich, Don English, Jamie Farr, Alan Feldman, Andrew J. Fenady, Oscar Goodman, Peter Graves, Michael Green, Brian Greenspun, Jan Jones, Don Payne, Millicent Rosen, Hal Rothman, Jim Seagrave, and Richard Taylor. Diana Ahmad, Su Kim Chung, and Dave Schwartz all read a portion of the manuscript, while Peter Michel, Doris Gragg, and Clair Willcox read it all. Their collective insights and suggestions truly improved this work. I particularly wish to acknowledge the contribution of Clair Willcox, who encouraged me early on to pursue this project and was consistently supportive. He is one of the most accomplished people I have encountered in the book-publishing business. I will not be able to repay the debt I owe to him. The book's referees offered invaluable advice for revisions, which I happily included. Fred Woodward and everyone else at the University Press of Kansas have been a terrific team. It was a pleasure working with them.

I also wish to thank the extraordinarily talented faculty members in my department for building an atmosphere of excellence in teaching and research. It has been an honor to chair this department for nearly seventeen years now, and I am working hard to keep up with them. Provost Kent Wray has been consistently supportive of my research and of me as department chair. He helps make Missouri S&T a great place to work.

Finally, and most important, my biggest debt is to my wonderful family. While I have always enjoyed exploring the history of Las Vegas and interacting with all the intriguing and helpful people I have met there, Doris, Julie, Curt, Buddy, Hopper, and Rascal are the real joy in my life.

Introduction

I begin this book about the famous city in southern Nevada fully aware of the caution offered by French philosopher Bruce Begout, who wrote, "Anyone planning to write about Las Vegas runs a serious risk of looking like the wet blanket who, in the midst of the festivities, cuts short the laughter and the dancing to make a speech that is bound to sound tediously in contrast with the party mood."[1] As Begout suggests, some find Las Vegas—the city of lights, gambling, beautiful women, mobsters, and spectacular entertainment—not a proper subject for serious consideration. Indeed, when I explain my research on the history of Las Vegas to colleagues, their typical response is a knowing nod and wink. Don English, the late gifted photographer of the Las Vegas News Bureau, explained to me a few years ago that the city promoters faced a similar challenge in trying to attract conventions to Las Vegas in the 1950s: "It used to be a laugh when somebody said they were having a convention in Las Vegas. They'd say, 'yeah, yeah, yeah, and you get a lot of work done.' And there was a stigma, you know, 'Sin City.'"[2] Yet a number of scholars have devoted much time and energy in a quest to understand the city, and the result is several excellent histories, all of which have enriched my understanding of Las Vegas. Eugene P. Moehring and Michael S. Green published a fine comprehensive work for the city's centennial. Moehring also has a monograph in which he describes Las Vegas as a typical Sunbelt resort city. David G. Schwartz has explained the significant development of the casino resorts in Las Vegas in the immediate post–World War II era as places where Americans, who otherwise opposed gambling in their neighborhoods, could enjoy that vice in a safe locale. John M. Findlay has argued that Las Vegas is best understood as an embodiment of the gambling cultures that have always accompanied America's frontiers. Hal Rothman has portrayed Las Vegas as the prototypical example of America's embrace of entertainment tourism.[3]

My own quest to understand Las Vegas began in 1992 during a visit to the fabled city. After several enjoyable trips, I became interested in the historical development of this extraordinarily popular place. Reading all the books and articles I could find on Las Vegas's past gave me an appreciation for the many factors that have contributed to the emergence of the largest urban area to develop in the twentieth century. Yet that research also led to one overarching unanswered question: What best explains the ever-greater popularity of Las Vegas to tourists? In 1930, before Nevada approved wide-open gambling, Las Vegas attracted 125,000 tourists. By 1941, the number had increased to 800,000. From there, the increases were astonishing: 9,000,000 in 1960, 11,900,000 in 1980, and 38,566,000 in 2005.[4] This book is my first of two in which I will offer answers to that query. In fashioning my explanation, I have worked from a fundamental assumption: It is critical to know what images of Las Vegas Americans encountered in the nation's popular culture that fueled their fascination with a city they had never visited. It is not difficult to find images of Las Vegas in words and photos, in print and on film, in fiction and nonfiction. There are hundreds of novels, movies, and television programs and thousands of newspaper and magazine articles that deal with Las Vegas in its first hundred years, 1905–2005. The challenge has been to gather all those portrayals and make sense of them, to find the themes and trends that developed over time, and to find the images that most attracted people to Las Vegas. Few scholars have taken this approach to the historical study of Las Vegas, and they have not looked at the range of materials that I utilize here.[5]

In the chapters that follow, the prevailing images clearly emerge as a kaleidoscope of impressions of lights, color, and sound; characters and characterizations; and praise and criticism—and, ultimately, amazement about the city that has attracted ever more people. However, there is another dimension that helps explain the success and popularity of Las Vegas. It is critical to understand how local journalists, civic leaders, hotel developers, and publicists crafted and distributed appealing images of the city. I will pursue that dimension in another book, but a brief description of that promotional effort here will help the reader appreciate what was involved in the emergence of the positive images of Las Vegas that I have included in this book.

From its earliest years, Las Vegas's civic leaders and businessmen have been excellent promoters. The Las Vegas chamber of commerce and its predecessor, the Las Vegas Promotion Society, worked diligently through the 1920s to push the potentials of agriculture, ranching, and manufacturing, as well as tourism. Once construction began on Boulder Dam in nearby Black Canyon in 1931, chamber of commerce leaders focused almost all their attention on tourism. For over a decade, they followed the example of other cities, promoting tourism by placing billboards and road signs throughout the Southwestern states, distributing thousands of promotional brochures and pamphlets, and sending civic leaders on speaking tours of major cities in the West. Utilizing these approaches, the chamber of commerce hoped to attract tourists by calling attention to the scenic wonders in the region, like Boulder Dam, Lake Mead, and nearby canyons such as Zion, Bryce, and the Grand Canyon. Other attractions they included in their promotions were the weather, the resort hotels with great entertainment, and annual events like the May frontier celebration, called Helldorado. In the immediate postwar years, as part of an aggressive, well-financed promotional effort known as the Live Wire Fund, the city secured the services of leading promotional firms like J. Walter Thompson and Steve Hannagan and Associates. These firms emphasized a practice begun earlier by the chamber of commerce: providing copy and photos to magazines and newspapers.[6] Hannagan established the Desert Sea News Bureau, later renamed the Las Vegas News Bureau, staffed with photographers and writers. This key office saturated the nation's media outlets with photos and stories about all the entertainers performing in Las Vegas, not to mention plenty of cheesecake—photos of attractive young women in swimsuits at the hotels—all in "an attempt," according to Joe Buck, one of the bureau's photographers, "to create the belief that if you came here you might be able to rub elbows with movie stars" and beautiful women.[7]

In the 1950s and 1960s, hotel publicists like Al Freeman, Harvey Diederich, Eugene Murphy, Herb McDonald, Dick Odessky, and Jim Seagrave, as successful publicists elsewhere have done, gained even more favorable coverage in the press by assiduously cultivating close relationships with entertainment and travel columnists. They provided not only good copy, but also complimentary rooms, meals, parties, and shows when the columnists visited Las Vegas. Relationships were so good that with a simple phone call, the publicists could have Walter Winchell, Earl Wilson, Leonard Lyons, Jim Bacon, or any number of the leading columnists "out here on the next plane" to cover a hotel opening or the debut of an entertainer in their hotel's showroom.[8] Because of these relationships, favorable press coverage was common. Two examples suffice to illustrate. When the Sands Hotel opened in December 1952, Al Freeman, the hotel's publicist, brought in over a hundred newspapermen to cover the event, and he provided rooms, meals, and even money for gambling. The outcome was golden for the Sands. Popular syndicated columnist Earl Wilson wrote, "Here in what has become the most amazing part of America, a new high in hospitality was attained when the new Sands Hotel, gambling spot, held its magniloquent opening." Another columnist was even more expansive: "No opening in history, could match the curtain-raising ceremonies that attended the launching of . . . the fabulous Sands Hotel. There were more celebrities, radio, television and wire service men and Broadway and Hollywood correspondents around than one-armed bandits."[9] Some entertainment columnists even offered a quid pro quo to publicists. Dixon Gayer of the *Daily News* in Garden Grove, California, seeking a deal on a room at the Sands Hotel, told Al Freeman, "I am [the] page one columnist and television columnist for the *Daily News* and believe you could get some page one mileage out of any effort you might be able to make to oblige."[10] Freeman gladly accepted the offer. By using such techniques, he and other publicists often got entertainment columnists to simply print articles verbatim that the publicists wanted in the nation's press.

The Las Vegas chamber of commerce and hotel publicists also worked diligently to shape the images of Las Vegas that Americans saw on the silver screen or on television. In 1940, Bob Griffith and Robert Kaltenborn, two members of the chamber of commerce, lobbied William LeBaron, the president of Paramount Studios, to make a musical comedy about Las Vegas. LeBaron ultimately agreed, and the result was *Las Vegas Nights*, which showcased the nightclub scene in Las Vegas with Tommy Dorsey's orchestra and emerging singing star Frank Sinatra. The 1941 film portrayed Las Vegas as "the friendliest little city in the world," and delighted town boosters saw it as a great publicity tool for the community.[11]

Hotel publicists likewise courted movie and television production companies, seeking films and programs that would portray their properties favorably. With movies like *Meet Me in Las Vegas* (1956), *Pepe* (1960), and *Ocean's Eleven* (1960), as well as television shows like Dave Garroway's *Wide, Wide World* (1955), the *Danny Thomas Show* (1957), *I Spy* (1966), and *Julia* (1970), Al Freeman gained much positive exposure for the Sands Hotel. He worked with the production companies to provide rooms and meals, and he worked with city officials to help them film along the Strip. The value Freeman saw in these efforts is evident in an internal memo he sent to all the hotel staff just before the filming of episodes of the television series *Julia*. "These three segments of 'Julia,'" he explained, "have a family type theme and should be good for the image of Las Vegas and especially the Sands."[12] In return for subsidizing some of the productions and permitting filming on their properties, hotel executives often demanded that they have a chance to review scripts to prevent the broadcast of negative images of their properties.

Chamber of commerce officials and hotel publicists strongly opposed projects they thought had the greatest potential to harm the city's image. In 1949, for example, Maxwell Kelch, the chairman of the chamber's publicity committee, refused to cooperate with producer Frank Seltzer, who was hoping to film a portion of *711 Ocean Drive* in Las Vegas. Seltzer's film is an exposé of organized crime's role in the national race wire service. Appalled by a script that featured a good bit of violence in the city and the implication that a national syndicate controlled not just the race wire but also the casinos, Kelch and chamber of commerce president Vern Willis refused to cooperate in any way with Seltzer. The local police would not provide escorts for film crews or clear the streets for filming. In the end, Seltzer had to build a set in Los Angeles to simulate a casino.[13] Twelve years later, the chamber of commerce threatened lawsuits to stop the production of two series, *Las Vegas Beat* and *Las Vegas Files*, because chamber of commerce leaders and most hotel publicists believed that the two series would have projected an image of Las Vegas tarnished by organized crime and extraordinary violence.[14] In 1970, NBC television approached Sands Hotel officials about filming an episode of the series *The Name of the Game* on their property. When he learned that the story line of the episode had "Las Vegas as the locale for a series of several derogatory scenes, including beatings, violence such as hotel doors being kicked in and finally an explosion in a hotel room," Al Freeman recommended to hotel management that they refuse, noting that the script included "several gangster-type characters."[15] The concern with scripts remained well into the twenty-first century. In 2006, Alan Feldman, senior vice president of public affairs for the MGM Mirage group, explained that he reviewed all scripts of productions shot at the company's hotels, pointing out to producers, "When you use our properties you play by our rules."[16]

Although it is clear the publicists, journalists, and the chamber of commerce carefully crafted many of the appealing images of Las Vegas, reality ultimately did not matter to the viewers and readers who encountered those images. Most reacted positively to the stories, photos, and films about Las Vegas and decided to visit a place that offered them an opportunity to leave the mundane behind and to enjoy a vacation city like no other. My hope is that you will see the following chapters as I intended them to be: an eclectic blend of stories, people, sights, and sounds that together make up the extraordinary appeal of Las Vegas—a place that by the early twenty-first century was luring nearly forty million tourists annually.

"Bright Light City"

The Introduction to Las Vegas

I've seen it a thousand times in pictures and on television and in movies.

Barbara Samuel, 2005

Then there is the sound, not only the sound of people, but the sound of things.

Chicago Tribune, 1961

The 1964 film *Viva Las Vegas* begins with an aerial view of several downtown casinos—Golden Nugget, Horseshoe, the Mint, Pioneer Club, Hotel Fremont, Silver Palace, and Lucky Casino—with their blazing neon signs in bright yellow, pink, and turquoise, as well as Vegas Vic, the forty-foot neon cowboy. Then the camera pans along the Strip, where the viewer sees the Stardust, Riviera, Sahara, Tally-ho, Desert Inn, and Tropicana; the final credits appear as the camera rests on the Flamingo with its neon champagne-glass tower.

With the colorful shots of popular hotels and casinos come the lyrics sung by Elvis Presley, the film's star and iconic Las Vegas figure, with "the now immortal percussion and twangy guitar sync" that have been endlessly used in the past five decades, "Bright light city gonna set my soul, gonna set my soul on fire."[1] This effective use of a montage of hotels and casinos, accompanied by music, had, by the release of *Viva Las Vegas,* become a standard, indeed obligatory, element in film and television portrayals of the resort city. It was incumbent on the motion picture or television director, the journalist, and the author to introduce the extraordinary city to those who had never been to Las Vegas. They emphasized that this was a tourist destination like no other, focusing on the kaleidoscope of lights, the cacophony of sounds, and the frenzied action in the casinos and nightclubs all occurring in the middle of a forbidding desert. *New York Times* journalist Gladwin Hill nicely captured the collective image with this vivid first impression: "The place roars," he wrote in 1953, "to a round-the-clock clink of silver dollars and rattle of dice in a setting of bright lights, liquor, music and dancing girls."[2]

The earliest accounts of Las Vegas in periodicals, novels, and films concentrated on downtown casinos along Fremont Street, near where the city began. The San Pedro, Los Angeles, and Salt Lake Railroad established Las Vegas in 1905 as a division point between Salt Lake City and Los Angeles. The locale had long been known as an oasis in the forbidding Mojave Desert because of its aquifers, fed by the snowmelt from nearby Mount Charleston. The railroad town, with its repair shops, slowly grew from a population of just under 1,000 in 1910 to over 2,300 ten years later. Fremont Street quickly became the center of commercial activity in the small downtown district. Along with several shops, the town's first substantial hotels were built along Fremont Street. Yet there was little prospect that the community would be much more than a small company town until President Calvin Coolidge signed legislation in December 1928 authorizing the construction of a dam in nearby Black Canyon to harness the Colorado River. Construction of the dam, which began in 1931, eventually brought over 5,000 workers to the area. Almost all the workers lived near the dam site in Boulder City, a government-built town that forbade gambling and the sale of alcoholic beverages even after the repeal of Prohibition. Las Vegas warmly welcomed the workers and their collective monthly wages of $750,000 to its saloons and gambling halls.[3]

Gambling has been legal during most of the state's history. Within a year of the founding of Las Vegas, according to a contemporary, saloons outnumbered all other types of businesses combined. The Arizona Club, the Gem, the Red Onion, the Turf, the Favorite, the Star—all offered, besides liquor, various games of chance: poker, blackjack, roulette, craps, faro, slot machines.[4] In 1909, reformers led by Governor Denver Dickerson and U.S. senator Francis Newlands persuaded state legislators to ban most forms of gambling. However, legislators in subsequent sessions relaxed the prohibition, permitting some "social" card games.[5] In early 1929, when it became evident that construction would proceed on the Boulder Dam project, several businessmen in Las Vegas, expecting a substantial "Saturday-night business" from the workers, quickly opened "card clubrooms" offering low-stakes card games like poker. In July, city commissioners issued licenses for twenty-three "gaming tables."[6]

The following year, Las Vegas realtor Thomas Carroll led an effort to elect state legislators who would repeal the restrictions on gambling in Nevada. He took out full-page advertisements proclaiming that legalized gambling would enable Reno and Las Vegas to become "famous as the Convention Cities of Nevada—the Playtown of the United States." Most businessmen in Las Vegas, as revealed in a November survey, supported "wide open gambling." They believed that legalized gambling would not only be profitable, but also that it would provide additional fees for both the state and local governments.[7] Shortly after state legislators approved an open gambling bill in March 1931, Las Vegas city commissioners quickly began issuing licenses for slot machines as well as for table games, wheel of fortune, and keno. The largest casinos in the 1930s, mostly along Fremont Street, were the Northern Club, Boulder Club, Las Vegas Club, Frontier Club, and the Apache Casino. Besides about three dozen slot machines, most offered a craps table, a couple of roulette wheels, poker and twenty-one tables, a wheel of fortune, and a room for keno.[8] These were the casinos that caught the attention of so many writers, journalists, and filmmakers over the next quarter century. Proprietors of most of these gambling establishments upgraded their exteriors in the 1930s with "plate glass window, chrome trim, and black Vitolite." The Apache Casino gained the reputation as the "plushest casino in town, with its own neon sign and terra-cotta facing."[9]

The various montages of downtown gambling halls, with their garish neon lights, in films and on television introduced viewers to these casinos.[10] Countless postcards that tourists visiting Las Vegas sent home reinforced the celluloid images with various nighttime shots of Fremont Street, its neon lights aglow.[11] By the early 1950s, the focus of the images was on the spectacular hundred-foot-high neon sign above the Golden Nugget gambling hall and the forty-foot neon sign called Vegas Vic, which stood atop the Pioneer Club. The image of Vic the cowboy had been used on chamber of commerce stationery and advertisements for Las Vegas, but he gained an iconic status as the neon symbol of the nation's gambling center. As Katharine Best and Katharine Hillyer wrote in their 1955 book *Las Vegas: Playtown U.S.A.*, the "monster animated cowboy" quickly had "become the Washington Monument, the Eiffel Tower, the Cleopatra's Needle of Las Vegas."[12] Journalists and authors struggled to find fitting adjectives to describe the neon kaleidoscope in downtown Las Vegas. Bright, brilliant, vivid, garish, and gaudy all seemed insufficient. The chamber of commerce provided an assist when it named the brightest two-block section of Fremont Street Glitter Gulch in 1947 and began using that label in press releases and advertising.[13]

Yet journalists found that moniker wanting as well. Like columnist Bob

Las Vegas lights in the 1930s with the Apache Hotel and Casino in the foreground and the Boulder Club just down the street. Source: UNLV Libraries, Special Collections.

Considine, they sought a "counterpart to Las Vegas in the average person's knowledge." To Considine, the most helpful comparison was to "a Western movie in Technicolor." Another journalist argued that seeing Fremont Street was like viewing "a rocket go off on the Fourth of July, crackling cheekily under the stars."[14] Most frequently, however, journalists tried to help their readers by comparing the lights of Fremont Street to those in other famous locales like Paris or Tokyo's Ginza district. The favorite comparison was to the lights of Broadway or Times Square. A column in a Zanesville, Ohio, newspaper, for example, claimed "Manhattan's 'Big Broadway' looks pretty puerile beside" the lights of Fremont Street. Similarly, a Long Beach, California, paper claimed "there are more bright lights in proportion than Broadway can flash, but these are more dazzling because they shine from the first instead of the 18th floor of a skyscraper."[15]

Novelists also found it essential to explain to readers the brilliant spectacle provided by Fremont Street. Richard Prather, in his 1951 mystery novel *Find This Woman,* described "what most people think of when Las Vegas is mentioned." Fremont Street "was a blaze of lights and color and neon."[16] Yet it fell to William Pearson, in his novel *Muses of Ruin,* to offer the most remarkable descriptive passage of Fremont Street. Hyperbole is too mild a word for his extraordinary rambling effort to help readers grasp the extraordinary sights:

Glitter Gulch: a neon collage of Roman candles, skyrockets, and shooting stars suspended at zenith like a mad surrealist's frenzied rendering of orgasmic transport. The three of us wait for the inevitable nacreous bursting, the coruscant earthward showering of fire opal and diamonds, the final coital shudder, but the wild embrace holds, cleaving space and time. Metallic reds and harsh yellows and electric blues clash like fighting cocks. Even the pedestrians, benthonic chameleons prowling the floor of this garishly iridescent sea, glow first green, then orange, then coral pink. At one in the morning the street emits the harsh, stabbing antimony of daylight leached through a migraine hangover.[17]

By the time Pearson published his novel in 1965, images of the Strip largely had supplanted those of Fremont Street both on film and in print. What quickly became known as the Las Vegas Strip in the 1940s was Highway 91, or the Los Angeles Highway, which ran southwest from downtown. Beginning in 1941, it became the locale of several casino resorts. Since 1918, town boosters had advocated the construction of a resort hotel in Las Vegas, a property that might attract folks who otherwise would vacation in places like Palm Springs, California.[18] A 1926 proposal, supported by city and county officials, the chamber of commerce, and the Union Pacific Railroad included plans for a 160-room hotel, a golf course, a riding academy, and a casino offering attractions similar to those in Monte Carlo.[19] A decade later, several Southern California businessmen announced plans to construct El Sonador, a $2.5 million hotel that would have a casino, spa, golf course, and race track.[20] Yet these efforts all failed to attract a sufficient number of investors. Even when Thomas Hull, the operator of El Rancho motels and luxurious hotels like the Hollywood Roosevelt in California, joined with wealthy San Diego investor Jack Barkley in 1938 to propose the construction of "one of the outstanding resorts of its kind on the North American continent" in Las Vegas, investors stayed away.[21] Finally, two years later, Hull found enough backers in Texas and Las Vegas to begin construction on the El Rancho Vegas just outside the city on the Los Angeles Highway. Designed by Los Angeles architect Wayne McAllister, this property, which opened in spring 1941, as historian David Schwartz has shown, "set the rough pattern for Strip casino resorts until the high rise era, with a central structure housing the casino, restaurants, and theater surrounded by motel wings."[22] Rather than the opulence of his Hollywood Roosevelt Hotel, Hull's El Rancho Vegas offered Spanish mission-style bungalows and a host of Western adornments, from wagon wheel chan-

The blazing neon of Fremont Street in the 1980s. Source: UNLV Libraries, Special Collections.

deliers to a dining room that resembled a corral. Its brochures promised a resort where "The Old West Lives Again."[23] El Rancho Vegas was the first of over two dozen major hotel-casinos constructed along the Los Angeles Highway over the next six decades. The highway soon became known as the Strip, a label bestowed on the boulevard by Guy McAfee, a former Los Angeles vice cop, owner of a nightclub along the famed Sunset Strip, and builder of the Golden Nugget in downtown Las Vegas.[24]

Like the El Rancho Vegas, the earliest properties along the Strip had a Western theme, most notably the Hotel Last Frontier, which proclaimed guests would enjoy the "Old West in Modern Splendor."[25] By the 1950s, however, developers pursued desert, Mediterranean, or modern themes, with the Desert Inn, Sahara, Sands, Dunes, Riviera, Royal Nevada, Hacienda, Tropicana, and Stardust. The opening of Caesars Palace in 1966 added a new dimension to the Strip properties with a themed fantasy resort where guests could experience an imagined trip to a luxurious, decadent ancient Rome. Three years later, Kirk Kerkorian opened the International, the world's largest casino resort, with over 1,500 rooms, a property that ushered in the era of the megaresort. Many of the vast resort hotels that followed the International adopted its "design of a Y-shaped triform hotel tower" developed by architect Martin Stern. In 1989, developer Steve Wynn triumphantly merged the themed resort and the Stern design in his Mirage with its South Seas theme. Over the next decade, the Strip exploded with a plethora of massive themed resorts: Excalibur; Luxor; MGM Grand; Treasure Island; Monte Carlo; New York, New York; Bellagio; Paris; Mandalay Bay; and the Venetian.[26]

Authors and journalists found describing the spectacle of the Strip at night to be as challenging as explaining the neon on Fremont Street. One columnist explained that the "multi-colored lights" viewed from 5,000 feet looked "like Tiffany's window through a telescope." Readers of a 1966 Look magazine article discovered that the galaxy of vivid colors along the Strip were so intense that the "electric signs hammer at the eyeballs and sear the brain." Three years later, Charles Champlin, in the Los Angeles Times, drew on alliteration in an attempt to explain the Strip's allure. It was, he wrote, over three miles of "urgent incandescence, one long, glowing shout, a blaze of blandishments to witness Berle, Benny, Barbara, babes, burlesque, even Bingo."[27] The multitudes of print descriptions catalog an array of dazzling colors. Some saw "white lights, yellow lights"; others saw "candy colors." Novelist Michael Ventura wrote about "the orange-red of the Rio, the ice blue of Caesars Palace, the gold of the Mirage," all "amid the pulsating shine of the Strip."[28]

Filmmakers found it easier to reveal the cascade of colors. Beginning with the 1951 film Painting the Clouds with Sunshine, most motion pictures about Las Vegas included a montage of Strip properties. One of the most effective was 1960's Ocean's Eleven. After a shot of downtown neon, there is an extended sequence featuring a long shot of the glowing neon marquees at the entrance of each of the properties Danny Ocean's gang will rob: the Flamingo, Sands, Desert Inn, Riviera, and Sahara. Incorporating such a montage permitted filmmakers, as in the 1997 Vegas Vacation, to show the arrival of a character or characters to the Strip. More often, the use of the montage was an effective way to provide a setting for the story line in the glittering city. Long, slow aerial shots at night over the Strip with the camera lingering above the hotel-casinos, as in *The Cooler,* are particularly impressive. As the camera proceeds north along the Strip, the viewer sees the blue and red colors of the Excalibur, the vivid green of the MGM Grand, the softly lit cupola of the Bellagio, the sparkling half-scale Eiffel Tower at the Paris, and then on to the glowing images of Caesars Palace, Treasure Island, the Stardust, Circus Circus, the Sahara, and the Stratosphere.

In contrast to such grand visions, a few filmmakers create scenes that offer more understated impressions of the Strip. In the 1988 film *Rain Man,* the character of Raymond, after a huge win at the blackjack table, stands at the window of a high-roller suite at Caesars Palace gazing at the neon below. The autistic savant says simply that it is "very sparkly, very twinkly."[29] Similarly, in the 1987 Las Vegas television series *Crime Story,* Captain Mike Torello, the program's lead character, looks over the Strip as the neon begins to shine and says, "There really is something beautiful about these lights, this place.[30] Regardless of the approach taken in film and print, the images of the Strip are of a magical place where a new arrival is bemused, tantalized, intrigued, or overwhelmed by the blinding electric signs—a place where "neon lights blaze, blind, beckon and dazzle."[31]

In most depictions of Las Vegas, a variety of sounds added to what Tom Wolfe called the city's "unique bombardment of the senses."[32] The noise associated with games of chance predominated. The rattle of the wheel of fortune, the click of the poker chips, the whir of the roulette wheel with its bouncing ivory ball, the clacking of the dice on the craps table, the shuffle of cards at blackjack and poker tables, the incessant clicking and ringing of slot machines, and, most important, the jingle of coins and the ringing of bells accompanying slot machine jackpots—all became an essential element in introducing the reader or viewer to Las Vegas casinos. The sounds of people added to the reverberating noise of the casino. The call of the croupier at the roulette wheel, the cry of the stickman at the craps table, players yelling for good rolls of the dice, an almost constant din of chatter at the table games, cheers for winning hands and groans at losses, and the frequent paging of famous people through the casino loudspeakers all contributed to the commotion. In their breezy 1955 book on Las Vegas, Katharine Best and Katharine Hillyer explained,

> It is not at all uncommon to hear "Paging Mr. Walt Disney, paging Mr. Walt Disney" echoing for miles around, or "Miss Sophie Tucker wanted on the telephone," or "Long distance for Miss Patti Page," or "Mr. Bob Hope, please, Mr. Bob Hope, telegram at the desk."[33]

Whether the pages were genuine or simple ploys to add to the excitement of the casino floor, they worked.

There would almost always be music as well: the piano player, jazz quartet, jazz band, or singer in the lounge, or the singing and dancing in the floor shows. Many films featured singers, including Frank Sinatra in *Las Vegas Nights,* Roy Rogers in *Heldorado,* Jane Russell in *Las Vegas Story,* Lena Horne and Frankie Laine in *Meet Me in Las Vegas,* Sammy Davis Jr. and Dean Martin in *Ocean's Eleven,* Elvis Presley and Ann-Margret in *Viva Las Vegas,* Louis Prima in *Rafferty and the Gold Dust Twins,* Wayne Newton in *Vegas Vacation,* and a host of guest stars on the television series *Las Vegas,* from Brooks and Dunn to Michael Bublé and John Legend. The music, excited chatter, jostling, joking, and general revelry invariably built into, as novelist Steve Fisher wrote, a "mounting babble" in the casinos.[34]

Novels, articles, and films regularly project an almost frenetic level of action in the casinos and along the streets of Las Vegas. Journalists in the 1930s found casinos "crowded day and night," "filled with patrons," even "packed to bursting."[35] These types of characterizations became standard in subsequent reporting—people jamming the table games two and three deep, filling the lounges and showrooms to overflowing, and packing the restaurants. All the elements created, as in the novel *Murder She Wrote: You Bet Your Life,* "a high energy hubbub."[36] Likewise, films presented a seemingly endless procession of people eager to join in the gambling at a fever pitch. For example, when the characters Diana and David Murphy arrive in Las Vegas in the 1993 film *Indecent Proposal,* the viewer sees first the Strip at night; then a lively lounge act with dancers and a saxophone soloist; happy, energized gamblers at slot machines; David winning a large slot jackpot; and three loud and happy female craps players, all amid a packed casino. Such scenes are common in film presentations, like *Las Vegas Nights* in 1941, as well as in television series, like *Las Vegas,* which featured such scenes in virtually every episode during its five-year run beginning in 2003.

This "slam of noise and light" had remarkable effects on first-time Las Vegas visitors, leaving many of them dazed, startled, disoriented, exhilarated, or simply overwhelmed.[37] Some journalists promised much for those who had never been. "The magic quality," of the lights, sounds, and actions of Las Vegas, according to a 1972 *Oakland Tribune* article, is that they "hold the visitor in a constant spell of enchantment." Or, as Herb Lyon in the *Chicago Daily Tribune* put it in 1953, "The excitement engendered is the most contagious known to man." In 1952, columnist Malcolm Epley predicted that a first-time visitor "is likely to go around in a daze amid scenes of undreamed color and

Packed Sands Casino in 1959. Source: UNLV Libraries, Special Collections.

glamor, the jingle of silver dollars filling his ears with the subtle suggestion that money is fabulously plentiful."[38] Jaw-dropping awe of the sights of both Fremont Street and the Strip is often featured in film depictions of people seeing Las Vegas for the first time. In the 1985 film *Las Vegas Weekend*, math whiz Percy Doolittle arrives in Las Vegas determined to use his system to win at blackjack. He drives down Fremont dumbstruck by the extraordinary display of neon. In *Vegas Vacation* twelve years later, there is a two-minute sequence showing the arrival of the Griswold family on the Strip. Driving past the "Welcome to Fabulous Las Vegas" sign at the south end of the Strip, they cruise past all the major hotels, wide-eyed and speechless at the spectacle of lights. Two English women in the 1998 film *Girls' Night* drive into Las Vegas and gaze open-mouthed at the neon-lit Strip, and when they walk into the Riviera casino and encounter the multitudes of jingling slot machines, one excitedly exclaims, "Now you're bloody talking."[39]

Yet Las Vegas also had an almost therapeutic effect on some people in fictional accounts. Although he loses every year he vacations at the Sands Hotel, a cowboy played by Dan Dailey in *Meet Me in Las Vegas* (1956) is made to feel right at home by everyone—the boys in valet parking, the cocktail waitresses, the blackjack dealers, the band in the lounge, the casino manager and owner Jake Freedman. In the novel *Mustang Sally*, an English professor named Packard Schmidt visits Las Vegas at the end of each semester: "But it's not just the games; it's the whole town, something I can feel in the back of my jaw every time I see a picture of the Strip on television, the way the town bathes itself in light, the way you can just walk into it and get lost and nobody will come chasing you with papers to grade." Upon walking into a casino, welcomed by the multitude of sounds, immediately his "fatigue lifts." His visits always have a long-lasting effect. "Everything goes better for a few weeks," and he feels "perked up and cleaned out, like a man who has just had a session of kidney dialysis."[40] Carolyn Thomas has a character, Linda, in her 1957 novel *The Cactus Shroud* driving into Las Vegas; "despite her weariness and the oppressive heat, Linda felt a lift of spirit."[41] Detective Shell Scott in *Find This Woman* calls the Desert Inn, and while on the phone, he "could sense the color and lights and gaiety" recalled from previous trips and "could almost hear the ivory ball rolling around the rims of the roulette wheels, and the whir of the slot machine. Just imagining it was so pleasant that the anger still with me faded a bit and I felt better."[42]

Whether it restored their mental health or gave them a unique thrill, those arriving in Las Vegas quickly realized that the magical city was a remarkable oasis in a most inhospitable desert. In the 1947 novel *The Honest Dealer,* Sam Fletcher and Sam Cragg approach Las Vegas from the west and encounter land "about as bleak as any they had seen, sand, a Joshua palm here and there, sand, tumbleweeds and more sand." Likewise, in the Erle Stanley Gardner (writing as A. A. Fair) mystery *Spill the Jackpot,* the plane carrying two detectives to Las Vegas "dipped down over the desert, skimmed low over a dazzling white surface spotted with clumps of sage and greasewood." Dick Pearce observed in a 1955 article in *Harper's* magazine that Las Vegas "is a very tiny green thumbtack stuck in a vast and scabrous desert floor."[43] The city of lights was a stark contrast to the barren, lifeless wasteland surrounding it, a contrast represented in dozens of films. Early movies like *Heldorado* in 1946 and *Sky Full of Moon* in 1952, as well as documentaries like *The Real Las Vegas* and *Las Vegas: An Unconventional History* produced decades later show viewers images of a cruel sun and unforgiving terrain—indeed, "a God-forsaken locale." In the 1991 film *Bugsy,* director Barry Levinson reveals the enormity of the Mojave Desert when showing the construction of the Flamingo Hotel. Levinson includes several scenes of the building and completion of the Flamingo, and the viewer gets a sense, from the camera slowly panning from left to right of the rising resort hotel and casino, of how vast the desert is; there is no other structure near the Flamingo property. When Siegel flies over the nearly complete fabulous structure, it is dwarfed by the desert. Yet close-up shots reveal beautiful green lawns, palm trees, and lush shrubbery,

Flamingo Hotel, ca. 1950, surrounded by the forbidding Mojave Desert. Source: UNLV Libraries, Special Collections.

a veritable oasis. It became a common approach to present to the viewer or reader a place within the barren surroundings with air-conditioned rooms, shimmering Olympic-size swimming pools, cool green lawns, fountains with sparkling water, plush resorts, and appealing, cool, dark casinos packed with action. In the 1999 film *The Runner,* for example, an aerial shot from a rapidly moving camera starts over the land to the northwest of Las Vegas, moves over nondescript suburban tract homes with little or no vegetation, then on to neighborhoods with lawns and trees; in the distance, one sees, almost like a mirage, the Strip. The sequence ends at a massive fictitious hotel (actually the Stardust) and into its casino, which is packed with eager gamblers. Similarly, *New York Times* journalist Gladwin Hill wrote in 1953, "The traveler approaching this surprising oasis in the mountain-ridged Nevada desert is confronted at dusk by a strange mirage that could pass for Broadway."[44]

Many journalists through the 1950s, acknowledging that they could not adequately convey the spectacle of this desert oasis to their readers, felt compelled to write that one had to visit the city to grasp its unique qualities. "Seeing isn't believing in Las Vegas," *Los Angeles Times* columnist Lee Shippey wrote in 1946. "Even when you see it you can't believe it," he continued. "A recent arrival from New York said, 'I wish I'd never before used the word fabulous.'"[45] Such sentiments became almost a mantra: "This place must be seen to be believed. Even then you wonder." "The first-time visitor to this desert playground is likely to let his jaw drop and not get it back in shape for a couple of days." "You have to see Las Vegas to believe it. Even then you occasionally pinch yourself, if you are a first-time visitor."[46] Novelists likewise felt obligated to argue that Las Vegas was an experience not to be missed. I. G. Broat, in *The Junketeers,* for example, has a character say, "Everyone should see it before he dies."[47]

In films, novels, newspaper and magazine articles, and on television, Las Vegas has a remarkable impact on the first-time visitors. It is breathtaking, stunning, exciting, and unexpected, unlike anything they had ever experienced. To be sure, actual visitors had a wide range of experiences, but their first impressions, their initial understanding of what they would encounter in the gambling center, drew on what they read and saw in popular culture. They anticipated a magical place, an escape from their reality, that promised lights, sound, and round-the-clock action, all in an amazing oasis in one of the world's most forbidding locales. For the first half century of the city's history, that escape was into a place that seemed to be the last frontier town.

Las Vegas

The Last Frontier Town

Talk about your boom towns [sic], Las Vegas has got one.
                                        Standard (Ogden, Utah), 1905

A frontier civilization where the cowboys and the prospectors still ride down from the hills for a few days' or a few weeks' fling at boisterous town life.
                                        New York Times, 1930

Every second or third man you meet has had about three drinks too many, and glad of it.
                                        New Republic, 1935

For three days modernity slinks out of sight while the cowboys and oldtimers [sic] put on their pageant of life in the last frontier town.
                                        New York Times, 1943

It's a robust pioneer Town, model 1951, with all the yahoo and yippee and red-eyed hallelujah of resurrected Tombstone and the Comstock and Custer's Last Stand.
                                        Richard S. Prather, 1951

Readers who opened the August 14, 1940, issue of *Look* magazine found an article entitled "Wild, Woolly and Wide-Open." The five-page piece, which included fifteen photos, carried the subtitle, "That's Las Vegas, Nevada, Where Men Are Men and Sin Is a Civic Virtue." The article revealed a community "posing as the last of the roaring frontier towns," a place with nineteen casinos and legal prostitution. The governing rule of the town was simple: "Do what you please, but mind your own business." The article's author even contended that the town fathers did not mind if one raced into the street to "shoot off a .38." Using photos of people arriving at bars on horseback; various games of chance, including the "most common sucker bait," slot machines; shills; and prostitutes, *Look* declared Las Vegas "the most sensationally cockeyed and self-consciously wicked place on earth."[1] Much of the story was an exaggeration, and civic leaders demanded a retraction of the characterization of their community. The president of the chamber of commerce even threatened a lawsuit.[2] Yet the feature article in *Look* reflected many of the images Americans read and saw about Las Vegas in the first half of the twentieth century. Newspaper and magazine articles, as well as films and novels, drew a picture of the desert community as one of the last frontier towns, a place populated by cowboys, prospectors, and prostitutes; a place with all the vices Americans associated with Wild West towns; a place that experienced periodic booms; a place where there were few rules; a place that represented one of the last bastions of rugged individualism.

The Old West and its associated mythology fascinated twentieth-century Americans. They embraced stories of selfless, honorable, chivalrous, and heroic cowboys caught up in struggles between good and evil, as symbols of the clash between civilization and wilderness. The nostalgic fantasy of a wide-open place of independence, freedom, opportunity, and boisterous excitement appealed to them in their increasingly urbanized and conformist lives.[3] There were many sources for these ideas about the West. Owen Wister's 1902 *The Virginian: A Horseman of the Plains,* Andy Adams's 1903 *Log of a Cowboy: A Narrative of the Old West Trail Days,* and Zane Grey's 1912 *Riders of the Purple Sage,* along with a number of cowboy autobiographies, helped define the mythological West. However, pulp magazines, the logical successors to the popular dime novel Westerns of the nineteenth century, played a larger role, flourishing between 1920 and 1950. Thousands of titles like *Action-Packed Westerns, Cowboy Stories, Real Western, Dime Western,* and *Ranch Romances* sold millions of copies each year. Max Brand, the most prolific of the pulp authors, not only published countless magazine articles, but also 150 western novels. Wild West shows, notably William F. "Buffalo Bill" Cody's with "King of the Cowboys" Buck Taylor, attracted large audiences from the 1870s through World War I featuring reenactments of events, real and imagined, in Western history. Cody created what one historian called "America's most bankable commercial entertainment."[4] Yet rodeos proved to be even more popular. By the mid-1930s, rodeos in Cheyenne, Wyoming; Pendleton,

Oregon; and Denver attracted over 100,000, and a three-week event in New York's Madison Square Garden drew almost a quarter of a million enthusiasts. By 1945, according to historian Kristine Fredriksson, "rodeo attendance was reported as second only to that of baseball."[5] Movies likely most influenced Americans' view of the West. Beginning with *The Great Train Robbery* in 1903, the western became one of the most enduring genres in film. There were more than 2,500 serials, B-movie westerns, and feature films between 1920 and 1950. There was a galaxy of stars like Buck Jones, William S. Hart, Ken Maynard, Tom Mix, Tim McCoy, Hoot Gibson, Gary Cooper, and John Wayne, who developed the image of the heroic cowboy as a symbol of righteous individualism vanquishing a host of villains. The West of popular culture was, for most Americans, a combination of images from film and print, as historian Robert Athearn has explained, "enhanced by brush strokes of their imaginations . . . that shaped for them an American utopia, occupied by an idealized people."[6]

Well into the fourth decade of the twentieth century, many commentators described Las Vegas and Nevada as anomalies in modern America. They acknowledged the population's hardy independent spirit. "The man whose tools of his profession are a hammer, a pick, and a pan, or a saddle, a bridle, and a horse," J. B. Griswold wrote in *American Magazine*, "is at heart a gambler, a happy-go-lucky individualist, hell-bent for quick and easy money, living his own life by his own laws and quite willing to let everybody else do the same."[7] Nonetheless, journalists frequently portrayed the town and the state as immoral, a male-dominated locale featuring the worst vices associated with imagined and real Wild West towns. Native Nevadan Anne Martin, who was a political activist and successful leader in the campaign that won women's suffrage in her state, wrote about this male culture in a 1922 article that was part of a series on states for *Nation* magazine. Martin argued that many in the country saw Nevada as "wild and wooly," a state that embraced gambling, drinking, prizefights, and easy divorce. It was a place where perhaps half of the men did not live in families. Rather, they were "cowboys, sheepherders, hay-hands, miners, and railwaymen" who lived in "bunk-houses or on the range." Absent families and permanent relationships, these men sought "social contacts" in the state's frontier towns like Las Vegas. There, they found a movie theater or a "gambling house with bootleg whiskey," or a "restricted district."[8] Other journalists offered similar characterizations of Las Vegas. It was, according to the *Chicago Daily Tribune,* "the last refuge of the American male from the matriarchate. Drop into a pool room—there sit men in hickory shirts and laced boots, playing cards, with money on the table."[9] Throughout the 1920s and 1930s, many journalists continued to describe Las Vegas as a wide-open frontier town.

Gambling provided the most attractive action. From its territorial days, Nevada and gambling were synonymous. In 1905, the *San Francisco Post* even argued, "In Nevada the church and the society are frankly subordinate to the gambling hall."[10] The earliest news dispatches from Las Vegas noted gambling establishments. The Las Vegas Land and Water Company, a subsidiary of the San Pedro, Los Angeles, & Salt Lake Railroad, conducted an auction for lots in the new community in May 1905.[11] The fledgling town attracted hundreds of new residents, almost all of whom lived in hastily constructed tents. There were also several stores and almost thirty "boose parlors" and gambling tents.[12] Over the next couple of years, newspaper accounts of Las Vegas invariably noted the importance of the "gambling house-saloon" with its "craps, roulette, and poker."[13] The Arizona Club, featuring beveled glass windows, mahogany columns, marble baseboards, a massive forty-foot mahogany bar, and "an elaborately designed back-bar of imported French plate glass of optic design," quickly developed a reputation as the town's premier gambling venue. In May 1907, the *Las Vegas Age* reported on delegations of Shriners stopping in Las Vegas en route to Los Angeles for a convention. Immediately upon arrival, they rushed to the Arizona Club, which quickly had become a gambling mecca. The club's reputation, which had "spread clear across the continent," drew female as well as male Shriners who "enjoyed their first experience at 'bucking the tiger,'" a reference to playing the game of faro.[14]

Before the state approved wide-open gambling twenty-four years later, visiting journalists found an easy acceptance of games of chance. As they walked into the shops along Fremont Street, they discovered gaming tables and slot machines ringing merrily behind curtain barriers. Virtually all in the community seemed to observe an unwritten code that sanctioned gambling regardless of state law. Duncan Aikman, who filed stories with both the *Baltimore Sun* and *New York Times* from Las Vegas in fall 1930, concluded from his observations that Nevada residents refused to acknowledge "that the old West ever died." As others had discovered, Aikman encountered an attitude that "men are men" and must "have their manly amusements" when they came to town. The gambling halls and nearly four dozen saloons were essential "in a frontier civilization where the cowboys and the prospectors still ride down from the hills for a few days' or a few weeks' fling at boisterous town life."[15]

Wooster Taylor, a journalist for the Hearst papers, visited Las Vegas shortly after the state government approved wide-open gambling in 1931. He found both men and women crowding into "a dozen gambling clubs." Downtown streets featured "an endless procession" of people. From the gaming halls came "the clink of money," and peering into them, one could see "stacks" of silver dollars "under the restless fingers of the croupier and dealer."[16] Zane Grey spent some time in Las Vegas in preparing his novel *Boulder Dam*. Although not published for three decades, his 1933 manuscript includes a vivid description of a casino, one that clearly appealed to cowboys. "Men stood ten deep" around the gaming tables in a "glaring hall . . . full of a blue haze of smoke, the sound of men's voices, the clink of silver coins and the rattle of roulette wheels."[17] The image of Las Vegas as a roaring frontier town with casinos galore persisted through the decade of the 1930s. Journalists enjoyed regaling readers with stories both true and apocryphal about how intense some Las Vegas gamblers became. For example, in 1939, a story made the rounds about a gambler who was "drawing to a possible straight when he collapsed and died of a heart attack." One of the men asked the proprietor to call a doctor, but the men went on playing. Eventually, "a doctor arrived, and there was a slight interruption while the table was moved so the body could be removed. Then the game continued."[18]

From its establishment, reporters also described Las Vegas as a wide-open town for booze. In 1905, there were more saloons than other types of businesses, and an account two years later claimed the citizens were noted for the "hilarious joy of getting drunk."[19] The Prohibition era drew the most press attention. Despite their support for a statewide initiative to prohibit the manufacture and sale of alcoholic beverages in 1918 and the state's ratification of the Eighteenth Amendment to the federal Constitution a year later, the legislature reversed the Prohibition initiative in 1923, and most Nevada voters in 1926 endorsed a resolution calling on the state legislature to oppose Prohibition.[20] In Las Vegas, residents acted as if the federal government had not imposed Prohibition. They maintained stills, and in January 1920, the local newspaper reported that the sale of whiskey had continued "steadily and systematically." Sam Gay, the Clark County sheriff, thought little of the federal restrictions and largely ignored violators.[21] These conditions inevitably led to a spate of newspaper articles describing dozens of roadhouses and speakeasies, free-flowing liquor, and bootleg rings operating under the eyes of forgiving law enforcement officers. "Las Vegas saloons are raided about once a month," an article in a Greeley, Colorado, newspaper explained, "their operators arrested, hauled before a magistrate, assessed a fine and allowed to operate without further molestation until the next month comes around."[22]

It fell to federal agents to enforce the law, which they did every few years, arresting eleven bootleggers in 1923, eight in 1926, and nineteen in 1929. In the latter case, they even arrested Mayor Fred Hesse, although he was later exonerated.[23] On May 18, 1931, came their most comprehensive sweep, one undoubtedly prompted by the national attention associated with the construction of nearby Boulder Dam. Led by Colonel George Seavers, fifty agents from San Francisco, Reno, and Los Angeles descended on Las Vegas. Armed with warrants and blocking all roads into town, "through the smartest, ramshackle liquor dens and the gayest night clubs of this desert city, the emergency force of officers . . . strode, clamping padlocks on doors, confiscating liquor and automobiles and jailing proprietors, white aproned bartenders and women entertainers." They arrested so many that the culprits had to be placed in a bull pen near the Brown Derby saloon. In all, ninety faced charges of illegal possession of alcohol, and the agents shut down twenty-five saloons, three stills, and five breweries in the biggest cleanup in the history of the American West, according to the *Oakland Tribune*.[24] Federal agents had used Ralph Kelly, the proprietor of a saloon named Liberty's Last Stand, as a front and collected vital information there by installing a Dictaphone. The following year, Kelly published his version of the federal sting in a book entitled *Liberty's Last Stand*. Kelly vividly described the many distilleries, roadhouses, and speakeasies, as well as corrupt Las Vegas officials unwilling to enforce the law. He also related a conversation with a federal agent named Kain who described the perception the nation had of the town. "There was much talk throughout the entire country," according to Kain, "about the liquor conditions in Las Vegas."[25]

Even after the repeal of the Eighteenth Amendment, journalists continued to be fascinated by the large number of saloons in Las Vegas and the evidence of excessive drinking. In a 1936 article, the *New York Times* claimed the city "offers the visitor any alcoholic concoction he may desire, at any time of day or night." A year earlier, Theo White, in an article in *Harper's* magazine, claimed, "The liquor is vile . . . but all drink and play furiously." The casinos, some "as large as small auditoriums," he reported, "are packed to bursting with sweating inebriates." Bruce Bliven, in the *New Republic*, was more frank. In describing the denizens frequenting downtown Las Vegas, Bliven contended that about a third of the men "you meet has had about three drinks too many, and glad of it."[26]

In her 1922 *Nation* article on Nevada, Anne Martin emphasized that the state's cowboys, miners, and rail workers eagerly went to town for more than gambling and "bootleg whiskey." They also investigated the "restricted district."[27] They were quite willing to spend their "hard-earned money" on prostitutes, and journalists discovered that Las Vegas did not disappoint them. From the town's founding, the women provided one more appealing element "of the old-time 'hell-roarin' camps."[28] Indeed, in the judgment of one observer, "prostitution must be recognized as a necessary part of Nevada's heritage as from the first men have far outnumbered women."[29] As one Nevadan explained in 1943, prostitutes served "functional needs in a male world." Because the state permitted prostitution, there was a "safety valve," a comfort for parents of daughters who could be "secure from women-starved men in from the desert."[30] Las Vegas restricted prostitution to Block 16 downtown, initially a "canvas tenderloin district." Several saloons like the Arcade, Double O, and Star housed prostitutes in rooms in the back, and by 1912, the Arizona Club, the classiest of Las Vegas saloons, also had prostitutes. By 1940, the block had a series of two-story structures that, to one observer, "preserved the architecture and customs of the old mining towns." The locals called Block 16 "the line" and the prostitutes there women "on the line."[31] In that infamous block, according to the *Sheboygan Press*, "Vegas has spread an old-fashioned table of typically frontier delights. A red-light district of a half-hundred girls flaunts vice more flagrantly than any Tia Juana, Truckee or Reno."[32] Las Vegas was hardly unique. In the early twentieth century, there were many red-light districts in the nation with legalized prostitution, and several of them had developed widespread reputations, such as "New Orleans's Storyville, San Francisco's Barbary Coast, Denver's Market Street Line, Baltimore's Block, Chicago's Levee, and New York's Bowery, Five Points, and Tenderloin."[33] Many of them flourished despite a concerted national antivice campaign in the first two decades of the century.[34] In Las Vegas, there were occasional investigations of prostitution. In 1912, for example, a grand jury reported that all saloons in town but two had prostitutes, and they had "white and black, all nationalities mixing indiscriminately." Yet little more happened other than an occasional arrest of proprietors without a proper license.[35]

Some reporters in the 1930s portrayed Las Vegas prostitutes as aggressive. They awaited those leaving the casinos and tugged at the potential client's coat, offering "a more intimate and active audience" or shouting "an endearing term" and beckoning men inside the brothels. Other accounts depicted them as "predatory women . . . cooly sitting in front of their establishments in tilted chairs along the cottonwood-shaded lanes of the notorious 'block.'" At night, along the poorly lit street, one might "catch fleeting glimpses of female figures lounging in negligees, in silk pajamas or in shorts."[36] Regardless of their approach in attracting business, the prostitutes were hard to miss. With "metallic-looking orange rouge," the prostitutes were given to wearing "raspberry-colored sailor pants, coral-tinted blouses and high-heeled slippers."[37] A former worker at Boulder Dam wrote a particularly vivid letter about the prostitutes' trade along Block 16 to *Nation* magazine in 1931. "There is," Victor Castle explained, "the unforgettable 'skidway,' where, for approximately a square block, the flotsam and jetsam are herded together for the purpose of satisfying the sex appetites" of the construction workers. Many of them, he predicted, would not remember their time there "as a triumph of engineering skill, but as the place where he contracted a venereal disease."[38] In his 1939 study of vice in America, Courtney Ryley Cooper argued that in Las Vegas, one could encounter "bold, bad Western bartenders" and "worn out hags 'on the row'" who "should be on view for every young-fool female who believes that there is an easy fortune in prostitution."[39]

Despite the risks, prostitution continued to thrive. In 1937, one of the local newspapers acknowledged that prostitution was the city's "number two tourist attraction."[40] In its 1940 article on Las Vegas, *Look* magazine noted both its legality and Block 16, where prostitutes performed a "modified strip tease" in front of the brothels. It even mentioned that a recent "fun" map of the city included "a picture of a girl standing under a red light."[41] In 1942, after deciding to locate an aerial gunnery school just northeast of Las Vegas, the federal government pressured the city to ban prostitution, following a long-established policy declaring prostitution "an off limits, undesirable by-product of military life." While the city shut down Block 16 and enforced its ordinance prohibiting the trade, prostitutes continued to flock to Las Vegas because of the increasing number of enlisted men.[42] Indeed, *Collier's* magazine reported in summer 1942, just two months after passage of the Prohibition ban, prostitutes could still be found "around the side-street bars, playing the juke boxes and keeping one eye on the door."[43]

The gambling, drinking, and prostitution were all symptomatic in many observers' eyes of a vibrant boomtown spirit in Las Vegas. Journalists compared it to the cattle towns of the Great Plains, other towns that developed at division points along transcontinental rail lines, and the communities that quickly developed near important mineral strikes. These nineteenth-century towns attracted hundreds, often thousands, of settlers and experienced feverish speculation in property, provided few public services, and furnished the obligatory saloons, brothels, and dance halls for their largely male populations. Visiting Las Vegas prompted journalists to liken it to Cheyenne, Wyoming; Dodge City, Kansas; Virginia City, Nevada; and Abilene, Texas.

Ironically, when William Clarke, copper baron and United States senator from Montana, decided to establish Las Vegas as a town in May 1905 as a

Two prostitutes in front of the Arizona Club in the early twentieth century. Source: UNLV Libraries, Special Collections.

good place to build repair shops and a layover for passengers for his San Pedro, Los Angeles, & Salt Lake railroad, he proclaimed, "It will not be a boom town, nor a wild west town, but will be built on a solid basis. All speculative tendencies will be discouraged."[44] Several newspaper dispatches in the town's first six months of existence revealed otherwise with reports of hundreds of tents and ramshackle wooden structures going up, licenses for almost three dozen saloons, high wages for skilled workers, expensive food and drink, and an "influx of men who think they see a chance to make money by investing in the desert town lots." A prospector from Ogden, Utah, after his return from Las Vegas in summer 1905, summed it up by telling his town's newspaper, "Talk about your town booms, Las Vegas has got one."[45] In December 1905, the *Los Angeles Examiner* explained that the town had "started with a wild and inexcusable boom," but it had recovered and was developing on a solid foundation, one that would permit many to make "fortunes." Located at a "division point" on a "transcontinental railroad," the town enjoyed an excellent climate, had "good indications for artesian water in large quantities," and had nearby "mineralized mountains."[46]

There would be fewer such articles in subsequent years as the community grew slowly. Nearby mines failed to produce reliable income, and the chamber of commerce, banking on the many artesian wells, vainly sought to promote the area's agricultural prospects. When Las Vegas rail workers joined in a 1922 national rail strike, the Union Pacific, which had absorbed the San Pedro, Los Angeles, & Salt Lake Railroad, shut down the repair shops, causing a loss of 300 jobs.[47] Prospects for growth were slender until President Calvin Coolidge signed the Boulder Canyon Project Act in December 1928, appropriating federal funds to construct a dam on the Colorado River just thirty miles from Las Vegas.

As news spread of the president's authorization for the funding of a massive dam project near Las Vegas, journalists across the country focused on the potential effects on the desert town. Breathless headlines once again proclaimed it the latest great boomtown, with all the promise and speculative risk that that entailed: "Las Vegas Goes Land Crazy as Dam Boom Hits," "Land Boom Caused in Desert Country," "The Boom at Boulder," and "Great Land Frauds at Boulder Dam."[48] As the nearest rail center to the dam construction site, Las Vegas would profit from the substantial movement of equipment, supplies, and workers. Indeed, there was much talk of a new Union Pacific terminal. Merchants would gain from the increased commerce, and because construction of the massive dam would surely attract tourists, the prospects for a large tourist hotel looked certain. Journalists described other prospects as "airy, fairy castles." Some dreamed of "great chemical and industrial plants" drawing on the cheap hydroelectric power the dam would provide and the hundreds of nearby copper, iron, silver, and gold mines, as well as the numerous deposits of borax, silica sands, gypsum, lime, salt, and magnesium. In short, one journalist noted, "optimism pervades the blistering desert air."[49]

Increased press coverage of the booming prospects for Las Vegas caused hundreds in some accounts, thousands in others, to descend upon the community in early 1929.[50] The *Saturday Evening Post* found a remarkable range of people crowding into Las Vegas: "miners, railroad men from the Union Pacific shops, old settlers, teamsters, real-estate men, tourists and their wives, and aviators."[51] There were no rooms to rent or homes to buy. As in the 1905 boom, new arrivals put up tents or constructed cabins from whatever material they could find. Las Vegas had its own Hooverville, with many living on the courthouse lawn. With all the people flocking in, some predicted that the community of fewer than 6,000 would rapidly grow to a metropolis of between 50,000 and 75,000 by the end of the decade of the 1930s. Journalists believed that Las Vegas, destined to be the nation's premier boomtown for the foreseeable future, not only would surpass Reno as the premier city of the Sagebrush state, but would also threaten "the supremacy of Salt Lake City as the most important city between the Rockies and the coast."[52]

But as with so many boomtowns in the West, there were problems in Las

Vegas in 1929. In a town gone land crazy, property prices skyrocketed, seemingly overnight, by 50 percent. In January, "autos filled with sellers and buyers kept whizzing around the town," and negotiations and deals went on all day, with men dashing "across the street to the abstract and title office with sheafs of paper in their hands." The real estate promoters, variously called "landsharks," "real estate sharks," "high pressure" promoters, and "a pack of get-rich-quick land swindlers," mainly from Southern California, used "unscrupulous advertising" in newspapers and on the radio to unload worthless lots "upon a gullible public."[53] Journalists predictably described the fevered speculation in the lexicon of the nineteenth century. It all rivaled "the colorful mining stampedes" of the past. Las Vegas had become the twentieth century's version of a "frontier city in the grip of a gold rush." The frenzied activity resembled the "hectic days of '49."[54]

Yet *Life*, the *Saturday Evening Post*, and *Collier's* magazines published articles in 1942 explaining that Las Vegas was experiencing, in the words of Richard English in *Collier's*, "a boom that makes the original Boulder Dam gold rush look like so much penny ante"; as *Life* magazine put it, "The big boom which the town enjoyed during the construction of Boulder Dam seems like high jinks at a church bingo compared to the preposterous prosperity of today."[55] As the nation moved closer to war with the Axis powers, Pat McCarran, Nevada's influential senior senator, persuaded the Roosevelt administration to locate a massive magnesium plant just outside Las Vegas, as well as a gunnery school northeast of the town and an army camp to guard Hoover Dam. This led to an influx of thousands of workers and military personnel almost overnight.[56] Unemployment virtually disappeared, weekly wages reached an average of $85, more than twice the national average, and again property values and rent skyrocketed. Las Vegas had never experienced such prosperity. The boom, however, inevitably created many problems. There simply was too little housing to accommodate the wave of new workers, who caused the city's population to double within a year. People lived in tent cities, trailer camps, makeshift houses, and old bus bodies; some even slept on the ground in bedrolls. Wesley Stout, in the *Saturday Evening Post*, explained that one could find the thousands of new residents living "in as picturesquely squalid discomfort as" pioneers in "a gold strike."[57]

The new people meant great business for the thirty-five licensed gambling halls in and around Las Vegas, all of them "roaring twenty-four hours a day."[58] While there was the new El Rancho Vegas and the just-opened Hotel Last Frontier hotel-casinos on Highway 91 in 1942, the hottest action was downtown along Fremont Street, where the "gambling palaces and bars" could not "handle the overflow crowd." At night, Las Vegas truly became "the last frontier," a place where "you can find faro, a fight or a frolic."[59] There was so much cheap booze available that over a quarter of the arrests in town were for "gross intoxication."[60]

Fully cognizant of the growing link in most Americans' minds between Las Vegas and the frontier, with its wide-open access to gambling, booze, and prostitution, along with its frequent booms, city leaders sought to take advantage of that connection every year with a celebration they called Helldorado. A traveling carnie barker named Clyde Zerby came up with the idea, and he persuaded the local Elks Club to sponsor it. He may have gotten the idea from a memoir of that title published by William Breakenridge in 1928, a book that detailed Breakenridge's time in the nineteenth-century West, or from Tombstone, Arizona's Helldorado Days, which began in 1929. Regardless of the inspiration, Zerby organized a three-day event with participants in Western garb, a Wild West show, a parade, and a girlie-girlie show to attract the Boulder Dam workers. In subsequent years, the event featured a Helldorado Village with hitching posts and wooden sidewalks, a rodeo, and a court to try men who failed to grow a beard. The city fathers believed it was an opportunity for tourists to enjoy "the experiences which can only be found in one of the pioneer cities of the old west."[61] The national press obliged Las Vegas leaders by covering the event every year, increasingly enamored by the ever-larger crowds eager to witness parades, fiddler contests, quarter horse races, beauty contests, and frontier relics like rodeos, buckboards, stagecoaches, buggies, people in Western costumes, men with whiskers, and a replica of a stockade town. "For three days," the New York Times reported in 1943, "modernity slinks out of sight while the cowboys and oldtimers put on their pageant of life in the last frontier town."[62]

Macy Lapham, a Western surveyor, happened to visit Las Vegas during the first Helldorado in 1935 and recalled it as a first-rate Wild West celebration involving the residents, who brought "out their carefully hoarded checkered and buckskin vests, flowing ties, low-crowned black hats of wide brim—such as worn by Wild Bill Hickok and other gunmen—and their derringers and pistols."[63] Helldorado's appearance in film and fiction gave Las Vegas even greater exposure. In 1946, Roy Rogers and Dale Evans, along with sidekick Gabby Hayes, starred in a movie called Heldorado (Republic Pictures dropped one "l" from the title to comply with Hollywood censors). A plot dealing with a syndicate's effort to use black market money at casinos develops amid the annual Helldorado celebration and includes several scenes of the rodeo, a jamboree, Helldorado Village, and a big parade at the end of the film. Virtually everyone in the film wears Western garb, and much of the action takes place at the Hotel Last Frontier. As Gabby Hayes's character proclaims, it is done to demonstrate that Las Vegas is a "rip-snortin' frontier town."[64]

Five years later, popular mystery author Richard Prather published *Find This Woman*. The cover promised a story of "murder, intrigue and enough beautiful dames to put the hell in the famed Las Vegas Helldorado." The case, involving a missing woman, leads Prather's detective, Shell Scott, to Las Vegas. The detective arrives on the first day of Helldorado. Prather described it in greater hyperbole than even the Las Vegas chamber of commerce could have mustered. His detective finds himself in "the wildest, shootingest, rooting-tootingest ruckus since the West was really wild." Scott experiences a twenty-four-hour party, with all its "drunken excitement," in a frontier town atmosphere:

> A whole town stands on its head and does a Western can-can complete with brass bands and parades, beauty contests and world-championship rodeos, cowboys and real Indians, and beards and babes and bottles. It's a robust pioneer town, model 1951, with all the yahoo and yippee and red-eyed hallelujah of resurrected Tombstone and the Comstock and Custer's Last Stand.[65]

By the time Prather published this exuberant description of Helldorado Days, journalists, novelists, and filmmakers had secured the image of Las Vegas as the last frontier town. It is a remarkable example of branding a destination community. Through the early 1950s, newspapers still frequently described the city as a frontier town or a Wild West town, a place where a visitor would encounter folks dressed in ten-gallon hats and Western neckties, and hear Vegas Vic, the forty-foot neon cowboy downtown, bellowing a greeting of "Howdy Podner."[66] Columnists loved drafting windy labels for the community. Drew Pearson called Las Vegas a "two-fisted Wild West town . . . now notorious as the last frontier." Hollywood columnist Bob Thomas claimed it was "the new Barbary Coast. This is where the wild west went when it couldn't go farther westward."[67] Novelists added only modestly to this image. Besides Richard Prather's, there were only a few mystery novels, like Richard Foster's *Blonde and Beautiful* and Carolyn Thomas's *The Cactus Shroud*, that noted the Western atmosphere of Las Vegas. Octavus Roy Cohen, in *A Bullet for My Love*, for example, described how "the Far West motif runs wild in Las Vegas: everybody wears cowboy clothes and hobbles around in high-heeled cowboy boots."[68] Yet few other novelists of the 1940s and 1950s were interested in drawing on the Western themes, opting instead for story lines dealing with organized crime.

There were nonfiction authors, however, who addressed the frontier fabric of life in Las Vegas. Richard Lillard, in his 1942 *Desert Challenge: An Interpretation of Nevada,* described Las Vegas as both "a frontier outpost, and a sophisticated cosmopolis."[69] Even though he found a community of neat neighborhoods with friendly and tolerant residents, many of whom belonged to fraternal organizations, Lillard saw those traits of "informality and congeniality" in the context of a "frontier liberality." Like other Nevada communities, Las Vegas did not "prohibit 'indulgences.'" Western vices remained. Booze was abundant, there were a dozen casinos, and prostitution was legal. There was also a good bit of "Western posing"—that is, the wearing of "cow[boy] boots, blue jeans, gay neckerchiefs, and Stetson hats" as the chamber of commerce actively promoted Las Vegas as "still a frontier town."[70]

Paul Ralli, local lawyer and town booster, published two accounts of life in Las Vegas in the 1940s and 1950s that confirmed Lillard's interpretation. Ralli arrived in his adopted hometown in 1933 and found a place where virtually everyone wore cowboy hats and everyone was friendly. Like the towns of the late nineteenth-century West, "there was a lack of formality in the air and absolute disregard for social distinction." In the best libertarian tradition, there were gambling and prostitution, as well as the kind of folks you would expect to meet in a Western town: natives "from nearby reservations; authentic cowboys and their Vine Street drugstore impersonators." It was all, Ralli contended, part of "the back-cloth of traditionally wide-open Western frontiers."[71]

In a nation of moviegoers, film likely had the greatest impact on people's perceptions of Las Vegas as the last frontier town. Before 1941, there had been a few movies shot in or near Las Vegas, including episodes for the 1915 and 1916 serials *The Hazards of Helen* and *The Girl in the Game, Pot of Gold* in 1929, *Speed Limited* in 1935, *Boulder Dam* in 1936, and *Frontier Town* in 1938. The latter film, starring Tex Ritter, actually included scenes from a Helldorado Days, but Las Vegas is not mentioned in the movie.[72] However, scenes in thirteen films between 1941 and 1956 reminded viewers that Las Vegas was the last frontier town.[73] In several of them, the men and women working the craps tables and the roulette wheels or performing in floor shows were in Western outfits, as were casino patrons. Three 1946 films, *Flight to Nowhere, Lady Luck,* and *Heldorado,* featured scenes at the Hotel Last Frontier, where all could enjoy the "Old West in Modern Splendor." In the 1950 movie *Dark*

City, Charlton Heston had a scene along Fremont Street, and one can see the neon sign for the Boulder Club flashing, "Enjoy the Old West." In the Dean Martin and Jerry Lewis film *My Friend Irma Goes West,* Martin's character performs in a fancy Western outfit in a floor show called "Western Square Dance."

Four of the films, *Las Vegas Nights, Heldorado, Sky Full of Moon,* and *Meet Me in Las Vegas,* most effectively portray Las Vegas as a frontier town, albeit a sanitized one. Singing cowboys, following the successful models of the musical westerns of Gene Autry, Tex Ritter, and Roy Rogers, open the movies.[74] In *Las Vegas Nights,* cowboys on horseback trot down Fremont Street singing "I Gotta Ride." In *Heldorado,* the Sons of the Pioneers are riding toward Las Vegas singing about the upcoming Helldorado Days, where people "live again the days of yesteryear." Later in the film, the singing group joins Roy Rogers in "My Saddle Pals and I." While Carleton Carpenter, as Harley Williams (Tumbleweed the Tonopah Kid), rides through a desert at the beginning of *Sky Full of Moon,* one hears the song "A Cowboy Had Ought to Be Single." Finally, the opening of *Meet Me in Las Vegas* features the Four Aces singing the film's theme song in cowboy shirts.

All four movies feature cowboys in lead roles. The mythic cowboy of film and fiction was a loner; although unable to settle down, he was a man of integrity and courage. Indeed, when faced with evil, whether gunslingers, marauding Native Americans, or grasping capitalists, the mythic cowboy became a heroic figure. Readers and moviegoers enjoyed the vicarious thrill of watching this champion for good not only vanquish the bad guys, but also win the heart of a virtuous woman. In some ways, the cowboy stars of these four films resembled the classic cowboy. None of them were married, and all were inherently good men. Only one, Harley Williams, was tempted to break the law. In *Sky Full of Moon,* Williams is a young cowboy in Las Vegas trying to get enough money to enter the Helldorado rodeo. When he cannot find a job, he tries to raise the entry fees playing slot machines, but he loses virtually all his money. When his girlfriend gives him a small drill that can make the machines pay out jackpots, Williams is tempted, but he ultimately rejects the device. There is romance in all of the films, with three of the cowboys getting the girl by the end of the movie.

However, these four characters largely do not fit the model of the mythic cowboy. Only one of them, Roy Rogers, had to confront evil. Rogers takes on an Eastern syndicate circulating black-market $1,000 bills in the casinos. Two of them own ranches, and Rogers is a Boulder Dam ranger. One is a transplanted Easterner who has been in Las Vegas only two years, and another has a college degree. They are handsome, charming, and gracious men, and three of them cannot avoid the lure of gambling. Bill Stevens in *Las Vegas Nights* and Chuck Rodwell in *Meet Me in Las Vegas* are superstitious gamblers; Stevens kisses a girl for luck and Rodwell holds a girl's hand for luck. Only Harley Williams exhibits the traits Americans would have most associated with cowboys. As the opening scenes and song reveal, he is a drifter with no time for a wife while he is rounding up cattle, working fence lines, and sharing a bunkhouse with several other cowboys. He yearns most, besides winning a rodeo event, to live in a small cabin, raising cattle far from any neighbors. Such a prospect does not appeal to the girl he befriends in Las Vegas, and it is clear at the end of the movie he will simply continue "driftin' through life" as a single cowhand.

In the town's earliest years, some civic leaders worried about the emerging image of Las Vegas as a wide-open community. In 1909, when the new Clark County impaneled its first grand jury, district court judge George S. Brown called on them to oppose the advocates of a "wide-open" town "where intoxication, gambling and prostitution are unrestrained" because such a community surely would experience greater crimes as a consequence.[75] For men like Brown, the reporting from Las Vegas over the next three decades was disappointing. The intrepid traveling journalist Basil Woon included a chapter on the town in his breezy 1933 book *Incredible Land: A Jaunty Baedeker to Hollywood and the Great Southwest*. To no one's surprise, Woon entitled the chapter "The Last Frontier: Las Vegas." Calling it a "raw frontier" town, Woon regaled the reader with anecdotes about his brief stay there. Although he called Las Vegas "one of my favorite cities," Woon noted a casino run by "Chicago gamblers," repeated violations of Prohibition, and a shoot-out "in a gambling club on the main street." The topper, assuredly apocryphal, involved an afternoon he spent in a saloon. Woon contended that "two cowboys rode their horses in, had them place their forefeet on the bar, and demanded whiskey for their mounts and themselves." He even quoted from one of the local papers to demonstrate that he was not exaggerating the Wild West elements of his account. Woon cited an editorial decrying the lawlessness evident just beyond the city limits: "There were and are now road-houses and questionable resorts where dope fiends and gangsters, thieves, thugs and murderers hang about and concoct their crimes."[76]

In his article in the *New Republic* a couple of years later, Bruce Bliven was more blunt. From his brief time in Las Vegas, Bliven concluded, as Judge

Brown feared twenty-six years earlier, "So far as anyone can discern from casual observation, the only occupations of Las Vegas, Nevada, are drinking, gambling, and prostitution. They must do something else there, but if so it is not discernible to the innocent tourist's eye."[77] Theo White agreed with Bliven. Downtown, at "every other door" one finds "a saloon, gambling house, or honky-tonk." Las Vegas was "but a twentieth-century manifestation of the Western towns of the last century," places where "licentiousness and wickedness" prevail and "inhibitions are not apt to be very deep."[78]

Although commentators were gentler with Las Vegas in the 1940s, it remained in their eyes a frontier town, or a modern facsimile. Even as more sophisticated resorts began to line the Strip, Las Vegas still evoked the "spirit of the Old West."[79] Town leaders vigorously promoted this notion. In its monthly report in April 1939, the chamber of commerce urged residents to wear Western clothing because the frontier theme indeed was attracting more tourists, and they "are disappointed when they arrive and do not find the cowboys, prospectors and general western atmosphere."[80] The town's "hawking of nostalgia," notably through its annual Helldorado Days, was part of a regional push to promote tourism.[81] By the 1940s, well over one hundred Western communities held Pioneer Day or Frontier Week celebrations. As in Las Vegas, residents grew beards, donned Western garb, and offered tourists rodeos and Western-themed parades. In 1946, Western historian and cultural critic Bernard De Voto lamented the development of these festivals. Because they were little more than tools of town boosters to promote tourism, De Voto explained that they were "fake" and "objectionable." The typical Frontier Week, he argued, "is conducted without reference to history, it is empty of idea and emotion, its data are anachronistic and preposterous."[82] Yet Americans eagerly embraced the imagined past that these festivals offered. Visiting a town's Western Days celebration offered twentieth-century people "a fantasy dreamscape," a momentary respite from modernity. It was an opportunity to "feel a kinship with the place and purpose of the West," a region, Americans wanted to believe, that still offered unfettered freedom, if only for a few days.[83]

While it was a twentieth-century city, Las Vegas enjoyed remarkable success in its association in popular culture with the frontier theme.[84] People who had never been to Las Vegas read about and saw movies about a desert community that resembled the fabled nineteenth-century West of high-spirited settlers, miners, and cowboys, strong individualists who enjoyed the many frontier vices amid repeated booms. From hundreds of newspapers, including the *Los Angeles Times, New York Times, Baltimore Sun, Washington Post,* and *Chicago Tribune,* as well as magazines as varied as *Life, Look, Collier's,* the *New Republic, Harper's,* and the *Saturday Evening Post* and films like *Las Vegas Nights, Heldorado,* and *Sky Full of Moon,* Americans came to believe that a journey to Las Vegas meant a trip to the last frontier town.

Bugsy Siegel and the Founding of Las Vegas

The father of Las Vegas, the late Benjamin "Bugsy" Siegel.
Tom Wolfe, 1965

He is to Las Vegas what Benjamin Franklin is to Philadelphia. Las Vegas was Benny Siegel's vision, his grand design. Had it not been for his dream, there might be nothing there at all.
Stephen Birmingham, 1984

The Flamingo . . . was entirely Ben Siegel's idea. In his desert rapture he dreamed up everything we mean when we say Las Vegas.
Michael Herr, 1987

Ben Siegel: Father of Las Vegas and the modern casino-hotel
James F. Smith, 1992

Las Vegas is his truest monument. He invented the place.
Pete Hamill, 1992

At 10:45 on the evening of June 20, 1947, a gunman rested a 30–30 carbine on the latticework of a trellis outside a Moorish-style mansion at 810 North Linden Drive in Beverly Hills, California. Benjamin "Bugsy" Siegel sat on a sofa just inside the French windows. Conveniently, the curtains had been drawn. Siegel, the handsome gangster who had just a few months before opened the hotel portion of his fabulous Flamingo Hotel-Casino in Las Vegas, was thumbing through a copy of the *Los Angeles Times* he had picked up upon leaving a restaurant, Jack's on the Beach. Just fifteen feet away from his target, the gunman squeezed the trigger, and nine rounds broke through the window. Two of the shots hit Siegel in the head, and one round knocked out his left eye. He died almost instantly. Ironically, the paper from Jack's had a small slip of paper inside that read, "Good night, sleep well."

Despite an intensive police investigation after Siegel's murder, the identity of his killer remains unknown. Some argue that Frankie Carbo, who had assisted Siegel in a 1939 hit, was the shooter, while others argue that Eddie Cannizzaro, a low-level operative for California gangster Jack Dragna, pulled the trigger. Most, however, have no idea, although there are frequent efforts to solve the Bugsy hit. One recent book, for example, argues that a World War II veteran named Bob McDonald murdered Siegel to eliminate a gambling debt he owed Jack Dragna.[1]

While the police scrambled to identify his killer, Siegel's gruesome murder captured the nation's attention. Hundreds of newspapers published a photo of his bullet-riddled and bloody body, slumped on the sofa in the Beverly Hills mansion. An article in *Time* magazine noted, "The tabloids of Manhattan, the sensational papers of Los Angeles and, to a lesser degree, papers all over the U.S. played it high, wide & handsome."[2] More important, Siegel's murder triggered a six-decade-long fascination with the mobster's path to his death, one that began in New York slums, led through Hollywood, and ultimately landed in Las Vegas, a place forever linked in popular culture with the slain gangster.

Most of the accounts of Siegel's life and his role in the development of Las Vegas are based on a dearth of reliable documentation. As Robert Lacey, biographer of Siegel's contemporary Meyer Lansky, pointed out, the challenge in writing about organized crime "is to separate the truth from the tissue of hearsay and folklore woven around it, and often this is quite impossible." Similarly, Otto Friedrich admitted in his account of Siegel's experience in Los Angeles, "Nobody knows with much precision what actually happens in the underworld."[3] One is left with assessments of Siegel, even those by some of his biographers, that have "few solid facts to get in the way," which is how *Time* magazine described the accounts of Siegel's murder in June 1947.[4]

Yet the collective result of the work of novelists, filmmakers, journalists, and biographers has been a remarkably cohesive life story, one that became a parody of the classic American rags-to-riches tale similar to many of the gangster films of the 1930s and 1940s. Many of those who comment on Siegel's importance to Las Vegas are given to a hyperbole that has helped secure the gangster's connection to the resort city's development. Author Pete Hamill, for example, claimed, "That garish skyline, those ten thousand blinking, popping, humming electric signs defying the night, defying time's passage, were imagined first by Ben Siegel."[5] Tom Wolfe saw Siegel's design ideas as truly revolutionary. Though an assassin's bullets took him while he was still young, "Siegel's aesthetic, psychological and cultural insights, like Cezanne's, Freud's and Max Weber's, could not die." Siegel's aesthetic, characterized by "incredible electric pastels," Wolfe argued, was a "Baroque Modern" form that made "Las Vegas one of the few architecturally unified cities of the world— the style was Late American Rich."[6]

In the process of attributing these transformational accomplishments to Siegel, observers have crafted a remarkable myth about the man. Although given to violent outbursts, he emerges as a figure who overcomes his origin in the poverty and despair of turn-of-the-century New York City slums, becomes a key player in a gang that dominated the city in the 1920s and 1930s, finds celebrity status in Hollywood, and, of course, invents Las Vegas. His wide-open and glamorous lifestyle, his connection to organized crime, his entrepreneurial bent, his independent, even rebellious character enabled the mythological Siegel to anticipate the flash, risk, glamour, luxury, and edgy entertainment of twenty-first-century Las Vegas. The remarkable interest in the connection between Siegel and other organized crime figures with the gambling city transformed the last frontier town into a city controlled by the mob.

Depictions of the life of Bugsy Siegel in print and on film mimic that of the classic movie gangster. Films of the early 1930s, notably *The Public Enemy, Little Caesar,* and *Scarface,* defined the gangster film genre. These movies portrayed gangsters as men, often second-generation immigrants, who rose from poor urban neighborhoods. They were ambitious, talented, and ruthless; they saw no future in following traditional paths to success in Depression-era America. Against the backdrop of gang wars, bootlegging, and the rackets, gangsters as portrayed by James Cagney, Edward G. Robinson, and Paul Muni gained wealth and status, but they inevitably met a violent end. As Robert Warshow, in his classic essay "The Gangster as Tragic Hero," explained the theme of these stories, "The typical gangster film presents a steady upward progress followed by a very precipitate fall."[7]

Siegel's parents, Max and Jennie Siegel, fled Russia because of the pogroms, the government-sanctioned attacks on Jewish settlements. The couple arrived in America in 1903 and settled in the Williamsburg neighborhood of Brooklyn. It was a densely populated working-class community with many first- and second-generation immigrants from Russia, Poland, Lithuania, and Italy.[8] The Siegels, while a respectable couple, could only afford

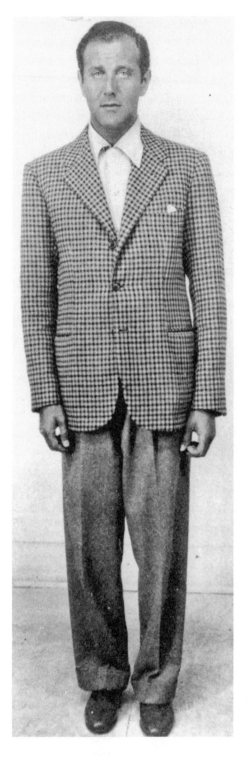

Bugsy Siegel, the organized crime figure long associated with the Flamingo Hotel. Source: UNLV Libraries, Special Collections.

accommodations in a slum, where they raised their five children: Ben, his three sisters, and a brother. Their home was little better than others in Williamsburg, where, according to Pete Hamill, "the tenements were filled with rats and roaches."[9] Home and family had less impact on the young Siegel than the tough streets he roamed as a youngster. He quit school at age eleven and joined a gang. Besides organizing craps games, Ben "set up a protection racket for the local street vendors."[10] In becoming "a night creature in a band of tough, ruthless, teen-age boys," he allied with teens that would later emerge as prominent players in organized crime.[11] The film *Mobsters* and the documentary *Don't Call Me Bugsy* have him joining up with Frank Costello, Lucky Luciano, and Meyer Lansky largely out of necessity. It was a question of survival. Life in Williamsburg and on the Lower East Side was a Darwinian struggle among tough street gangs.

In most accounts of his early life, this milieu was critical in shaping his character. Surviving the gang violence of his neighborhood required Siegel to become fearless. He "never hesitated when danger threatened," and he quickly concluded, as in the film *Lansky,* that to survive, one should "never fight fair." Siegel fought so savagely that, according to Meyer Lansky, "everybody said he was crazy as a bedbug"—hence the nickname he always hated.[12] Yet his contemporaries also saw this warrior of the streets as intelligent and charming. With his blue eyes and dark hair, the teenage Siegel "was tall and handsome, moving with a fluid grace, and displaying an openness that beguiled victims and friends."[13] Most filmmakers and authors note these traits—charm as well as ferocity—as evident throughout Siegel's short life.

In the various accounts of Siegel's rise to power, several organized crime luminaries appear: Joe Adonis, Dutch Schultz, Al Capone, and "Longie" Zwillman. But the focus usually is on Siegel's alliance with Lansky, Costello, and Luciano. Allegedly, Lucky claimed, "We was the best team that ever got put together. We knew our jobs better than any other guys on the street."[14] By the mid-1920s, they had a gang of approximately one hundred men, and they were making a fortune from protection rackets targeting pawnbrokers and money lenders, "insurance" for nightclub owners, burglary, holdups, fencing operations, gambling, and, most important, illegal liquor traffic.[15] Films like *Mobsters, Lansky,* and *Gangster Wars* and the A&E *Biography* episode about Bugsy Siegel, as well as innumerable print accounts, contend that the success of this alliance of young gangsters attracted the attention of some of the kingpins of organized crime like Arnold Rothstein, Joe "The Boss" Masseria, and Salvatore Maranzano. Rothstein, described as the "king of New York bootleggers," "the Man Uptown," the "gambling boss of New York," and "the Brain," was arguably the most influential underworld figure in the city during Prohibition.[16] Besides rum-running and gambling, Rothstein was a bank for many in the underworld. He financed drug operations and shady securities deals, bought judges, and even provided the funds to fix the 1919 World Series. Always on the alert for new talent, Rothstein became a mentor for young men like Lansky, Costello, and Luciano.[17]

In the mythological Siegel narrative, Rothstein's murder in 1928, apparently because of his gambling debts, led to open warfare in New York to control the bootlegging empire. Masseria and Maranzano were the main combatants. Lansky and Luciano, with the support of Siegel, skillfully manipulated the growing interest these bosses had in their organization. Yet they carefully plotted the elimination of both Masseria and Maranzano, and in several accounts Bugsy Siegel was on the hit squads that murdered the two men in 1931. Siegel's role in the dispatch of the Mustache Petes, as contemporaries called the old-guard Sicilian gangster bosses, was critical because their deaths led to a restructuring of organized crime. Most accounts have Maranzano conceiving the syndicate or national commission, including most of the leading families from New York and Chicago, but he did not live long enough to see its implementation. It fell to Luciano to lead in the development of a syndicate with regular national meetings and an enforcement arm known as Murder Incorporated, created to carry out authorized hits and end indiscriminate murders. Italians, first through Luciano and then Costello, with important Jewish allies like Lansky, led a syndicate characterized by policies reached through consensus and subordination of the individual to the group. By 1940, about a dozen men had emerged as the most influential in a system with no single, dominant boss, and one of them was Bugsy Siegel. Along with Albert Anastasia and Louis "Lepke" Buchalter, Siegel's most important role was as one of the three special assassins of Murder Incorporated, who eliminated those foolish enough to challenge the will of the syndicate.[18]

His participation in gang activity brought Siegel great riches and the means to develop a style some called gangster chic. He married Estelle Krakower in 1929, and the couple had two daughters, Millicent and Barbara. Siegel moved his young family into a Tudor-style home in the New York City suburb of Scarsdale.[19] Yet he also had an apartment at the Waldorf Astoria and vacationed at Al Capone's Florida vacation home as well as the spa hotels in Hot Springs, Arkansas. He, like Lansky, Costello, and Luciano, dressed elegantly and enjoyed the hot nightlife of New York City. "Exuding great sexual heat for the Broadway show girls," entertainment columnist Earl Wilson wrote, "Bugsy Siegel went swinging around the speakeasies—the 5 O'clock Club, the Napoleon Club, Zelli's, the Park Avenue, and the Stork Club."[20] Yet the suave and successful Siegel still exhibited the flaw identified by many in his earliest years. Several accounts of his life note his violent nature. This violence is depicted in popular culture accounts of his life: for example, when a young woman asks what he does for a living in the movie *Mobsters,* Siegel responds, "I kill people." Later in the film, in a confrontation with competing bootleggers, Siegel's gang disarms them and he warns if they continue in their challenge, "I will kill your mothers, fuck your sisters, and turn your brothers into eunuchs."[21]

The charming, successful, and dangerous Siegel left New York for California in the mid-1930s, and there are numerous explanations for his departure. In some accounts, Lansky dispatches him "to muscle in on the West Coast rackets."[22] In other accounts, Luciano made the decision to send Siegel "to attend to the Syndicate's expansion."[23] A third view is that Siegel made the decision to move. He had already made several trips in the early 1930s to Southern California to visit his brother and sister, who had moved there.[24] However, there is no consensus about his motives. Either he was escaping a possible murder indictment, pursuing investment opportunities, envisioning "new underworld opportunities," or hoping to become "a movie star."[25]

Whatever the reason, Siegel's move revealed two important traits of the now-mythological gangster: his entrepreneurial skills and his flair for glamour. He invested in real estate, a surplus metal firm, the Mocambo and Trocadero night clubs, and prostitution while handling the bulk of the heroin traffic from Mexico. More important, Siegel emerged as a critical figure in gambling in the state. Not only was he a partner in an illegal gambling operation at the Clover Club in Los Angeles, the Agua Caliente racetrack in Tijuana, and a dog racing track in Culver City, but he was also in Tony Cornero's popular gambling ship, the S.S. *Rex.*[26] Beyond all this, the syndicate leaders expected Siegel to gain control of the race wire service in the West. These national services, dominated by James Ragen's Continental Press Service, provided betting odds as well as changes in track conditions and race results. Drawing on the connections of local mobsters Jack Dragna and Mickey Cohen, Siegel soon had most of the race wire business in California, Arizona, and Nevada with the Trans-American wire service.[27]

Some estimates had him clearing over $25,000 a month, but Siegel was less interested in these ventures than in becoming a part of the Hollywood scene.[28] The Chicago Outfit was already deeply involved in the film industry, particularly through its control of the International Alliance of Theatrical Stage Employees. Willie Bioff and George Browne, Outfit minions who headed the union, were extorting money from motion picture producers to prevent threatened strikes.[29] Siegel saw how effective these shakedown efforts had become and organized the movie extras. He threatened producers and top film stars with walkouts if they did not pay him to keep the extras away from the picket line.[30] These many ventures, which would have been extraordinary challenges for the most sophisticated entrepreneurs of the era, according to the master narrative about Siegel, came easily to the largely uneducated gangster.

Beyond making money strong-arming the industry, Siegel loved everything about Hollywood: the glamour, the fantasy, the celebrity, the lavish parties, the attractive women, and the interest so many in Hollywood had in him. Longtime pal actor George Raft took Siegel to parties at the most fashionable nightclubs, introduced him to scores of celebrities and producers, and took him to the studios.[31] Countess Dorothy Di Frasso was equally important to Siegel's successful entrée into the film capital's society. Heir to a fortune her father made in leather goods, she had married Count Carlo Di Frasso, who conveniently stayed in Rome most of the time. This gave her the opportunity to have a number of affairs with men like actor Gary Cooper as well as Bugsy Siegel.[32] Di Frasso hosted numerous parties to showcase Siegel, and most of Hollywood welcomed him.

Siegel's experiences illustrate historian Kevin Starr's contention that actors and producers accepted gangsters because "Hollywood had already embraced the gangster as a mythic figure."[33] Screenwriter Charles Bennett later said, "Bugsy was so smooth, so charming, he was accepted in Beverly Hills society. People liked him. I liked him." He explained that Siegel was a "dashing, mysterious charmer," and for many in Hollywood "there was a certain glamour attached to a real mobster."[34] Young actors like Phil Silvers and Frank Sinatra "adored Bugsy Siegel." Silvers's wife, Jo-Carroll, explained the fascination: "Bugsy was handsome, charming, and very pleasant, but he also had an aura of danger about him that Frank would later cultivate."[35]

Most documentaries about Siegel include numerous photos of the handsome gangster during his Hollywood years.[36] To keep those good looks, according to one of his biographers, Siegel became a "fanatic on the subject of health and virility." He swam, worked out in a gym, and spent time in a steam room. "At bedtime . . . Siegel rubbed skin cream over his handsome face and donned an elastic chin strap to keep his profile from sagging."[37] He felt that it was essential to look the part of an important Hollywood figure. Journalists Ed Reid and Ovid Demaris, in *The Green Felt Jungle*, described the Siegel style: "He liked sharp clothes: broad snap-brimmed hats . . . pin-striped suits with high-waisted trousers and narrow pegged cuffs; rakishly tailored overcoats with fur-lined collars; hand-crafted shoes with pointed toes, and handmade silk shirts."[38]

Most accounts of Siegel's time in Hollywood reveal that the interest he had demonstrated in attractive young women while he was in New York had not diminished. Writers like Pete Hamill have Siegel, besides his affair with Dorothy Di Frasso, going out "with a series of starlets," including Wendy Barrie and Marie McDonald.[39] His daughter, Millicent, later contended that Barrie was "the love" of her father's life and that Jean Harlow "was supposedly my godmother."[40] Of course his most famous paramour was Virginia Hill. Although the film *Bugsy* has Siegel meeting her on a Hollywood film set, the two most likely became acquainted in New York when she was going out with gangster Joe Adonis. Reunited in Los Angeles in 1939, the two were often seen together—at Sunset Strip nightclubs, at the Santa Anita racetrack, at the Olympic Auditorium for boxing matches, and at movie studios where she was sometimes an extra. Because Siegel had moved his family to California, he and Hill had their liaisons at various places—at George Raft's house, at the Chateau Marmont Hotel, or Hill's home.[41] Theirs was a tempestuous relationship. They fought often, but the conflicts often resulted in sex. Indeed, Hill later claimed, after years of sleeping with several underworld figures, that with Siegel, "it was the best sex she ever had."[42]

Beyond being seen with beautiful women and wearing expensive suits, Siegel had to have residences that reflected his new status as a Hollywood sportsman. Initially, Siegel rented a mansion, but when he brought his wife, Esta, and their daughters to California, he had a more magnificent home constructed.[43] The thirty-five-room structure in Beverly Hills had "deep-pile, gray-toned carpeting," a bathroom with red marble, "silk and damask hangings," a lounge with "eighteen-foot divans," a dining room table that could accommodate thirty people, and a family room with slot machines; throughout the house were "objets d'art gathered from all over the world." Outside, there was an Olympic-size pool. The house and furnishings cost $150,000, and monthly maintenance costs reached $1,000. His neighbors were the Hollywood elite, including Claudette Colbert, Vincent Price, Bing Crosby, Alan Ladd, Humphrey Bogart, and Judy Garland. Siegel entertained stars like Cary Grant and Barbara Hutton, who came for dinner or poolside parties.[44]

Siegel suffered a temporary setback as a Hollywood figure when a Los Angeles County grand jury indicted him for the murder of Harry "Big Greenie" Greenberg in 1939. After Greenberg threatened to "sing to the cops" about Murder Incorporated, the syndicate authorized a hit. When it became known that Greenberg had journeyed to California, Siegel got the contract. He, along with Frankie Carbo, Allie Tannenbaum, and Siegel's brother-in-law, Whitey Krakower, killed Greenberg. Tannenbaum and Abe Reles, another member of Murder Incorporated, testified to a grand jury about Siegel's role, which led to the indictment.[45] Yet during his incarceration, Siegel lived in luxury. Another prisoner served as his valet, and Siegel ordered in gourmet meals and the best whiskey. He even had "tailor-made jail uniforms of soft denim, which were pressed for him daily." When rumors circulated that Siegel was gaining passes to leave jail, Jim Richardson, city editor of the *Los Angeles Examiner*, assigned photographers to cover the story. They discovered that "Siegel had been out no less than eighteen times on court orders to visit his attorney, his dentist, and a few favored drinking companions." He even enjoyed a meal with actress Wendy Barrie at a fashionable restaurant.[46] The Los Angeles County Superior Court judge dismissed the charges against Siegel when Abe Reles, a key source of evidence, fell to his death from a hotel room even though he was under police protection. While the widespread newspaper coverage of his arrest and incarceration made Siegel persona non grata for a time, he soon regained his celebrity status. In late 1941, columnist Paul Harrison described him as "a loose-lipped lug with slick hair and . . . he has sometimes been described as 'handsome' by local society reporters who for years have been identifying him as a 'wealthy Hollywood sportsman.'"[47]

In the mythological life of Bugsy Siegel, one stoked by his wide-ranging Hollywood connections, he had accomplished much while only in his thirties. This narrative of a self-made man, albeit one given to extraordinarily violent outbursts and one who found it easy to dispatch anyone who blocked his rush up the ladder of success, inevitably followed the story arc of the classic gangster picture. Gangster films are often morality tales, which must inevitably lead to the fall of the mobster. In Siegel's case, his decision to seek greater fortune and legitimacy in Las Vegas led to his demise. When the scene of his life story shifts to the gambling city, those who build his mythical life find it essential to make him a prophetic figure, one who sees a glorious future for a scarcely known desert town. There must be an element of tragedy and sadness for a man who sought to become legitimate through an extraordinary vision for a city that would become the gambling and entertainment center of the world.

That Las Vegas appears as an obscure place before Siegel pursues his dream of building a fabulous hotel-casino is central to this element of the Bugsy myth. This emerging sophisticate and prosperous entrepreneur, familiar with the nightclub scene in both New York and Los Angeles, cognizant of the widespread appeal of gambling, and aware of the appeal of celebrity, would have a vision of a new, elegant playground for adults in the desert. His hotel-casino would be a model for all that would follow. In Dean Jennings's biography of Siegel, *We Only Kill Each Other,* the author describes Las Vegas as "a sort of cowpoke town where gambling was just another Saturday night diversion for ranchers, toothless and bearded prospectors, workers from nearby Boulder Dam, or tourists." In his novel *Solomon's Palace,* Sam Ross essentially borrowed Jennings's description, adding, "Sometimes there would be more Paiute Indians wandering around the hot, dusty streets than white inhabitants." Max Allan Collins, in *Neon Mirage,* followed their lead: "Mixed in among the tourists, many of whom wore dude-ranch style Western clothes, were occasional real westerners: men with the weathered faces of the true rancher or ranch hand; an Indian woman with a baby cradled on her back; a toothless old prospector who made Gabby Hayes look like a Michigan Avenue playboy." *Las Vegas: An Unconventional History,* a documentary released in the city's centennial year, characterized Las Vegas as "a one-horse town. A train depot and a row of gaudy gambling joints."[48] These are only four of the many characterizations from authors, journalists, documentary filmmakers, and movie producers who presented a remarkably similar picture of Las Vegas before Bugsy Siegel's Flamingo Hotel-Casino.

The most influential version of early Las Vegas, however, is that depicted in the critically and commercially successful 1991 movie *Bugsy,* starring Warren Beatty as Siegel. In the movie, Siegel, Virginia Hill, and gangster Mickey Cohen drive from Los Angeles to Las Vegas to see how the mob's investments are faring in the small southern Nevada town. They drive down a dusty street with a few storefronts, dilapidated pickups along the curb, and some horses tied up out front. They enter a forlorn-looking casino. James Toback's script for the film offers a vivid description of the "glorified shack." There is "utter shabbiness: a couple of card tables, a few slot machines, a counter that passes for a bar, a tired bartender with five customers and two employees." Virginia Hill dismisses it as "a canker sore" that should be burned. Given these descriptions, it is beyond belief that anyone could have a vision of a future for this tired, undeveloped desert town in an obscure location.[49]

Yet the mythmakers have Bugsy seeing a remarkable future for Las Vegas as a luxurious playground of gambling and entertainment that would attract the wealthy and the middle class. In several accounts, he simply stares into the desert and envisions it. Sam Ross's *Solomon's Palace,* for example, has a Bugsy-like character named Joey Solomon standing along the Los Angeles highway, staring into the desolate desert: "It was hot. The land was baked, the creosote bushes dry and brittle. You could see the heat shimmering in the distance." As Solomon scanned the arid landscape, "he saw a mirage . . . a plush hotel, thickly carpeted, with an Olympic-size pool. A glittering, packed casino. A thousand rooms. Green fairways and Joshua trees. A diamond of a place. The Tiffany of casinos."[50] The most vivid version of Siegel's inspiration is in the film *Bugsy*. As portrayed by Warren Beatty, Siegel is driving away from Las Vegas with Mickey Cohen and Virginia Hill and pulls the car over after an argument with Hill. He walks off the highway into the desert. As he looks at the terrain, Siegel begins to nod knowingly, then races back to the car, exclaiming, "It came to me like a vision. Like a religious epiphany." As film critic Richard Schickel argues, Siegel "really does see this. It is all in his mind. He can see the Las Vegas of the future . . . in his mind before he's dug the first foundation for the Flamingo." James Toback agreed. "Bugsy," he contended, "was not just prescient. He was almost oracular."[51]

Siegel's alleged vision truly was grand. In the film *The Neon Empire*, a Bugsy-like character named Junior Moloff explains that he will build a place with the finest casino, hotel, and restaurants, as well as "the greatest comedians, singers, dancers, bands, you name it." Another Bugsy knockoff named Benji Danzig, in the novel *Chance Elson*, by W. T. Ballard, announces he will "build a big, fancy place, the best—restaurants, bars, floor shows, nice lawns, the biggest swimming pool in the world." Yank Karkov, a third variation on Bugsy, proclaims in Morris Renek's *Las Vegas Strip* that he will offer guests "the poshest rooms, the juiciest steaks, the biggest drinks for practically nothing. All they have to do is gamble."[52] Joey Solomon predicts "people would come from all over the world to see his place—Solomon's Palace. Rajahs, princes, dukes, and millionaires would come to gamble and cavort in the world's most luxurious resort."[53]

It fell to Warren Beatty's delivery of James Toback's version of Bugsy to give the character genuine insight. Toback's script has the leaders of the syndicate drop by Siegel's home in Scarsdale, New York, where they hear his pitch for the construction of a hotel-casino in Las Vegas. As Meyer Lansky, Frank Costello, Vito Genovese, Gus Greenbaum, Joe Adonis, and Moe Sedway listen intently, an excited Siegel proclaims that when he is finished explaining his vision, they will "understand for the first time the meaning of the word transcendent!" He tells these men, upon whom he will depend for funding, "I found the answer to the dreams of America." "Let me ask you," he continues, "what are people always having fantasies about? Sex, romance, money, adventure. I'm building a monument to all of them." Screenwriter Toback inserted these lines to illustrate his argument that Siegel saw "how gambling could seize the entire nation and a city could become a metaphor for it." "Now a theme park city," Las Vegas's mentality, in Toback's judgment, "basically has taken over every state and local government."[54]

Yet the evidence reveals that Las Vegas was not simply "a stupid patch of desert" before Siegel's alleged inspiring vision. Many journalists visited Las Vegas in the decade before the opening of the Flamingo in December 1946, and their characterizations of the gambling center are at odds with the dismissive descriptions critical to those who argue that Siegel was a transforming visionary. Newspapers and magazines as varied as the *New York Times,* the *Fresno* (Calif.) *Bee, Collier's,* the *Saturday Evening Post,* the *Modesto* (Calif.) *Bee,* the *Chicago Daily Tribune, Time,* the *Reno Evening Gazette,* the *Port Arthur* (Tex.) *News,* and the *Los Angeles Times* published articles about Las Vegas or printed syndicated columnists' views of the city between 1936 and 1946. A few examples illustrate how little the mythmakers relied on contemporary journalists' descriptions of Las Vegas in framing their portrayal of the city before and during World War II.

In 1939, *Los Angeles Times* columnist Chapin Hall wrote, "From a wide spot on the desert only a few years ago," Las Vegas "has taken on metropolitan airs, electric signs and the trappings of civilization."[55] Other journalists described the hotels and casinos in Las Vegas, primarily the El Rancho Vegas, Nevada Biltmore, and Hotel Last Frontier, as "attractive," "smart," "fashionable," "plush," and "swank."[56] A 1945 article in the *Chicago Daily Tribune* even proclaimed, "In the resort hotels of Las Vegas you will find a lavish and refined luxury hard to match anywhere." These "tony joints" and "snobbish places" had all the features one could want in a resort.[57] Richard English, in a 1942 article in *Collier's,* argued that Thomas Hull, owner of the El Rancho Vegas, intended "to do for the auto court what the late Florenz Ziegfeld did for American womanhood" by "featuring a handsome gambling casino, a tremendous swimming pool . . . and two nightly floor shows."[58] In the same year, journalist Wesley Stout found "innumerable bars and night clubs—one as swank as Hollywood's Mocambo. Add three new resort hotels with a Hollywood trade."[59] Even after the Flamingo opened, journalists were lumping it with the Hotel Last Frontier and El Rancho Vegas when describing the most luxurious accommodations in Las Vegas.[60]

Many of the patrons at these hotels and casinos did not resemble those described in the mythological sleepy backwater of Las Vegas. While journalists certainly found miners, cowboys, servicemen, ditch diggers, and other plain John Does, there also were many honeymooners, divorcées, movie stars, millionaires, and socialites. As early as 1937, visiting journalists were writing, "For every cowboy outfit seen around a roulette wheel there'll be a white tie and tails." In a 1942 photo essay, *Life* magazine included a well-dressed couple playing blackjack, two young women and a young man stylishly dressed and wearing sunglasses while playing roulette, and some of the glamor girls of Las Vegas.[61] In November 1945, *Life* featured "the first national fashion show ever held in Nevada" at the Hotel Last Frontier, a review focused on "Western fashion motifs—desert-color prints, lavishly embroidered riding shirts, Indian-fringed skirts, sleek play suits, and bare bathing suits."[62]

Las Vegas became an increasingly popular resort for celebrities. For some like Fred MacMurray, Nelson Eddy, Mary Martin, Judy Garland, Lana Turner, Tommy Dorsey, Dinah Shore, and Robert Montgomery, it was a convenient place to marry; for others like Martha Raye, Clark Gable, and Victor Mature, it was a good place for a quick divorce.[63] Hollywood columnist Erskine Johnson and others noted in 1946 that celebrities seemed to have turned Las Vegas into a resort colony of the film capital. Johnson wrote, "We thought we could escape Hollywood for a couple of days out here on the Nevada desert, but Hollywood and Vine, we soon learned, had moved 300 miles overnight. There were more movie stars than cactus bushes."[64]

It would be going too far to contend that the positive descriptions of Las Vegas before the opening of the Flamingo told the entire story about the desert community. After all, the city's chamber of commerce was skilled in cultivating visiting journalists, and those scribes may have been, on occasion, reciprocating for the complimentary rooms, meals, and entertainment. Indeed, there were occasional pieces that were not nearly as complimentary of the city's progress. In a 1940 article, *Look* magazine argued that Las Vegas was an "American Gomorrah." The magazine described not a fashionable resort city, but rather a place where one could "do what you please" as long as you minded your "own business."[65] Still, it is clear that Las Vegas was no "canker sore" awaiting salvation through a marvelous inspiration from Siegel. Indeed, there is slight evidence that Siegel had an expansive vision for the gambling town.

There are two uncorroborated conversations with Siegel that suggest a more modest ambition. Ovid Demaris, in *The Last Mafioso*, has Jimmy "The Weasel" Fratianno recollecting a less pretentious dream. Fratianno reported that Siegel told him that he hoped the Flamingo would begin a trend in Las Vegas, Reno, and Lake Tahoe of "vacation spots where people with a little money can have good rooms, good food, good shows, swimming pools, tennis, golf, and all the gambling they want."[66] In this version of Siegel's ambition, the amenities would simply be good, not spectacular. One may not trust the version of a story offered by a fellow nicknamed "The Weasel," but perhaps more reliable is a conversation reported by gambling expert John Scarne, who has Siegel describing a remarkably limited ambition. He allegedly told Scarne that when California attorney general Earl Warren had "closed gambling up tight as a drum" not only in California but also offshore, his "dream of a Monte Carlo in the ocean is killed." He began considering another "place like the ocean so that when people come to gamble they can't go anyplace else but have to stick with me." "I figured it this way, if people will take a trip out into the ocean to gamble, they'll go to a desert, too." Working on that assumption, he told Scarne, "One day I drive into Nevada looking for a nice desert spot and I picked this one because the price was right and it's on the main road to L.A."[67] There was no hyperbole in this explanation, just a matter-of-fact recounting of how he picked an inexpensive property at a good location. In its account of Siegel's murder, *Life* magazine argued that the hotel was not a major concern for the gangster. Because he devoted most of his attention to "dope, prostitution and the horse-racing racket," Siegel viewed the Flamingo as little more than a "personal sideline."[68]

The larger problem for the Siegel myth of an inspired decision to build the Flamingo lies in who actually had the idea for the resort hotel and casino. There is some evidence that the inspiration for the Flamingo came from Siegel's longtime friend and associate, Meyer Lansky. At least, that is the way Lansky recalled it. In *Meyer Lansky,* by Dennis Eisenberg, Uri Dan, and Eli Landau—a biography based largely on a series of interviews with Lansky—the syndicate leader contended that Siegel did not see the potential in Las Vegas because "he was too busy being a Hollywood playboy." Instead, it was Lansky who developed the expansive vision: "What I had in mind was to build the greatest, most luxurious hotel casino in the world and invite people from all over America—maybe the high rollers from all over the world—to come and spend money there."[69] Lansky certainly had experience in developing fine casinos like Piping Rock near Saratoga Springs, New York; the Colonial Inn near Miami Beach; and the Beverly Club just outside New Orleans. Besides gambling, "carpet joints like these offered dining, dancing, a floor show with a chorus line and big-name entertainers."[70] Davie Berman, another of Siegel's Las Vegas associates, was also hailed as the true visionary of Las Vegas at his funeral in 1957. His daughter, Susan, recalled their rabbi saying, "Davie Berman had a vision. He saw a boom town where others had just seen desert."[71]

A more persuasive argument can be made that Billy Wilkerson had the inspiration for the Flamingo. Founder and publisher of the *Hollywood Reporter,* Wilkerson had become a leading figure in the entertainment world of Southern California by the mid-1940s. Besides his influential trade paper, Wilkerson had owned, over time, a number of Sunset Strip restaurants including Ciro's, Café Trocadero, and LaRue, all of which attracted the celebrity crowd. Wilkerson was also a compulsive gambler. When his gambling losses in the first half of 1944 reached $750,000, he decided to follow the advice of movie producer Joe Schenk, who said Wilkerson should "build a casino. Own the house." After all, for a time in 1940, he had leased and managed the Arrowsprings Hotel in remote Lake Arrowhead, California, a property that offered gambling to its guests.[72]

According to George H. Kennedy Jr., Wilkerson's manager, his boss planned "a mammoth complex housing a casino, showroom, nightclub, bar–lounge, restaurant, café, hotel, indoor shops, and a health club with steam rooms and a gym." He would also have "a swimming pool, tennis, badminton, handball and squash courts" as well as a golf course and stables. His resort would be characterized by "beauty, grace and elegance." In short, Wilkerson "envisioned another Sunset Strip in the desert."[73] In 1945, through his attorney, Greg Bautzer, Wilkerson purchased thirty-three acres outside Las Vegas along the Los Angeles Highway, reached an agreement with experienced gamblers Moe Sedway and Gus Greenbaum to manage the casino, commissioned architects and designers, and secured some funding from the Bank of America and Howard Hughes. Although construction on his Flamingo hotel and casino project began in November 1945, Wilkerson was out of money within two months. At this point, according to the account of Wilkerson's son, Sedway informed Meyer Lansky about the project. Lansky then directed G. Harry Rothberg, a New York liquor distributor, to organize "a syndicate of investors to buy sixty-six percent of Wilkerson's Flamingo." On February 26, 1946, Wilkerson agreed to the sale with the understanding that he would, besides retaining one-third of the property, be the "operator and manager" of the club when it opened. In W. R. Wilkerson III's account, Siegel first became involved in the project in spring 1946, and only then because "Lansky pressured" him to represent the syndicate's interests.[74]

There is no doubt that Siegel quickly became intimately involved in the construction of the Flamingo, and he clashed frequently with Wilkerson. Because of their disagreements, the two agreed to partition the operation. Siegel became responsible for "the hotel portion while Wilkerson retained control of everything else." Wilkerson even secured a new architect (Richard Stadelman) and a new contractor (Del E. Webb) for Siegel. Eager to seize control of the entire project, Siegel established the Nevada Project Corporation of California on June 20. Over the following two months, he purchased all the land from Wilkerson in return for stock in the corporation, and he fired Wilkerson's architect and decorator.[75]

W. R. Wilkerson's account is not without problems. He explains that his father, facing a lawsuit from an ex-partner, "systematically destroyed all his documentation covering the period from 1930–1950."[76] Thus, the bulk of the material for his book comes from interviews from two people: his father's secretary and manager, George H. Kennedy Jr., and one of his lawyers, Greg Bautzer. Still, Wilkerson found enough material to underpin an account that makes it clear that Siegel came late to the Flamingo project and that, at best, he embellished another man's vision for the resort hotel and casino.

Yet there is evidence to confirm other elements of the Siegel myth. Most accounts portray Siegel as a charmer in Las Vegas before, during, and after the opening of the Flamingo, and, unlike other elements of the Siegel story, there is good evidence that he successfully cultivated the image of a generous and caring man with a good sense of humor, a person who sought to fit in. George H. Kennedy, Billy Wilkerson's manager, was struck by Siegel's "sentimentality." When Siegel learned that Kennedy's brother had died in his arms, Siegel offered Kennedy "the thickest roll of $100 bills" he had ever seen. Although he refused the money, Kennedy was deeply touched by "this display of sympathy and generosity."[77] Mort Saiger, who worked at the Hotel Last Frontier, where Siegel stayed during the construction of the Flamingo, took Siegel's daughters horseback riding. He recollected that Siegel was soft-spoken and generous, thanking him for taking care of his daughters and giving him $100, which in 1946 "was a month's wages."[78]

Las Vegas lawyer Paul Ralli wrote that Siegel "mingled" with residents and businessmen alike while in the community. He even "followed the Las Vegas custom of dressing informally in shirtsleeves." From Ralli's perspective, Siegel was "an affable, polished man," one "liked by most of the Las Vegas people who had known or met him."[79] John Cahlan, who was the managing editor of the Las Vegas Review-Journal in the 1940s, agreed, recalling that he met Siegel at a chamber of commerce meeting and often chatted with him at a downtown health club.[80] Indeed, Siegel played gin rummy with the locals and dropped in at the popular clubs and restaurants. The man so concerned with upscale living even dined at the Mexican restaurant in the Sal Sagev Hotel downtown, which had only a counter with eight stools, four booths, and one table. The proprietor, Marian Betran Decaro, was impressed that such an important man would come to her establishment several times, and she remembered him as a pleasant "nice looking young man."[81]

Even his encounter with an FBI agent in Las Vegas turned out well. Curtis Lynum, who was an FBI agent in Las Vegas in spring 1947, received a call from Siegel, who wanted to complain about some bad checks at the Flamingo. When Lynum dropped by Siegel's office, he "noticed a .38 caliber automatic on the ink blotter directly in front of Siegel." Lynum pulled his gun and aimed it at his host. Siegel asked, "What the hell are you doing?" Lynum replied, "This interview has to be on even terms—let *me* put your gun in your desk drawer, and I'll holster my gun, and we can proceed with the interview." Siegel chuckled in response and said, "Okay, have it your way." Later, one of Lynum's informants told him that Siegel related the story to his friends: "Imagine that young FBI agent pulling a gun on me." The informant also told him that "Siegel bore me no animosity and respected my 'guts.'"[82]

Once the Flamingo opened, Siegel truly captivated people. Performers particularly liked him. Jimmy Durante, his headliner on opening night, said, "I always got along swell with Ben."[83] Rose Marie, who opened with Durante, described Siegel as courteous, supportive, and protective of her. After her two weeks at the Flamingo, he told her, "You're all right. I like you and you do a great show. I hope to have you back here soon. Thanks for everything."[84] Liberace, who was under contract with the Hotel Last Frontier at the time, claimed Siegel "had a most convincing and ingratiating way about him."[85] Susan Berman, daughter of one of Siegel's partners, explained, "No one who met Ben Siegel ever forgot him. Charisma, power, call it what you will; he simply captivated others."[86]

The charisma noted by Berman is best explained by author Erskine Caldwell. A frequent visitor to Las Vegas, Caldwell dropped by the Flamingo shortly after it opened and was amazed at Siegel's ability to attract everyone's attention "merely by quietly appearing with his ever-present, half-smoked cigar clutched between two fingers of his left hand." The author of *Tobacco Road* vividly described Siegel's impact on the crowded casino:

> With his glowing personality, his handsome physique, and his expensively tailored dark-blue suit worn with a white-on-white monogrammed shirt and black silk necktie it was a magical combination that stated Bugsy's presence in unmistakable terms. Bartenders, cocktail girls, busboys, porters, and even hard-drinking barstool customers recognized Bugsy either with lingering glances of awe or with unconcealed signs of apprehension.[87]

The myth is enriched by the tragic end of Siegel. He emerges from the various accounts as an innovative, visionary man whom syndicate leaders did not trust. He was impulsive, unpredictable, and unwilling to abide by their efforts to restrain his expansive ideas about an ever-more expensive resort in the middle of a desert. Most important, he attracted the wrath of Lucky Luciano. Though Luciano had been deported from the United States, he remained a powerful figure in the syndicate. Indeed, as Richard Hammer noted in his *Illustrated History of Organized Crime,* in December 1946, "Luciano summoned all the major chieftains of the American underworld to Havana for the first full-scale convention of the Syndicate since the early Thirties." High on their agenda was Siegel's soon-to-open Flamingo. For days, they discussed their concerns about Bugsy and his project. He had gone way over budget on the hotel, and they believed he was skimming some of the construction money and having Virginia Hill place it in Swiss bank accounts. Ultimately, the leadership reached a consensus that Siegel was violating its rules. He had taken their money, defied their orders, and acted "as if he were in business for himself." Despite the growing success of the Flamingo in spring 1947, Siegel's death had been decided by a powerful organization unwilling to tolerate an independent agent.[88]

Rather than simply another dead mobster, Siegel became, over the subsequent decades, a heroic figure, one who had seen the future and, despite all the odds, had begun to see it come to pass. While many articles, books, essays, and films contributed to this myth, by far the one that attracted the most attention was the 1991 film *Bugsy.* Its release provided the critics an opportunity to discuss not just the character of the gangster, but also his role in the development of Las Vegas. The film angered a few critics. Joan E. Vadeboncoeur, in the *Syracuse Herald-Journal,* deplored the film because of the efforts of the screenwriter James Toback and director Barry Levinson "to turn a notorious killer into a romantic figure."[89] Most critics, however, were taken with Siegel's vision for Las Vegas. Calling Siegel "the man who dreamed up Las Vegas," Janet Maslin, in the *New York Times,* described him as "a visionary who saw the chance to create something very like himself only much, much bigger." Similarly, reviewing the film for the *Syracuse Post-Standard,* Doug Brode highlights the moment when Siegel "stares at an empty stretch of desert and vows to create an entertainment mecca for the country, a place where middle-Americans can go when, like Bugsy, they want to put aside their safe, solid lives for a moment and turn decadent."[90]

All these critics' assessments of the film's depiction of Siegel's vision are based largely on a fabrication. Screenwriter James Toback, with the assistance of a researcher, had examined "stacks of books, newspaper and magazine accounts, and video and film records of the period." However, what emerged after his script went through many drafts and after he "invented new lines, moments, and scenes daily during the three months of shooting" was a story that is only loosely based on Siegel's last years.[91] However, none of that matters in the development of a myth. The remembered past, not the documented past, is central in the creation of any enduring image, especially of a founding figure. How else does one explain the extraordinary lengths some observers, authors, and filmmakers have gone in softening the Siegel personality or in justifying his behavior? Even his biggest boosters and fans usually acknowledge that Siegel had not just a violent temper, but also a sociopathic personality. Still, they often quickly add that he was also an immensely charming fellow, or that he was a loving father, or that he was one of the great patriots of World War II.

Critic Roger Ebert pointed out that the film depicted Siegel "as a smooth, charming, even lovable guy, even though he was also a cold-hearted killer." Director Barry Levinson, when he later reflected on the production, contended that he did reveal Siegel's "ugly side." Still, he argued, "no one could have got where he did if he hadn't also been charming. Whatever he did in his private life, his public persona was—like, good God, he was a great guy, he was terrific."[92] *Bugsy* and several other accounts of the gangster successfully captured a critical aspect of Siegel's life. Contemporaries indeed saw Siegel as a charmer, and that evidence adds substance to the overall myth.

The doting father is evident at several moments in the film *Bugsy,* which opens with Siegel leaving his Scarsdale, New York, home after hugging his daughters, Barbara and Millicent. During a crucial moment in the film, as he is trying to persuade syndicate leaders to invest in his Flamingo project, Siegel is simultaneously baking a birthday cake for Millicent. When he tells his wife, Esta, that he wants a divorce, his greatest pain is watching his two children getting into a cab to leave him alone. A documentary entitled *Rogue's Gallery* includes a remarkable several minutes of a home movie filmed at his Holmby Hills mansion. In the backyard pool, Siegel is frolicking with his two daughters. "He was a good father," his daughter Millicent later recalled in another documentary. He was "very kind" to her, and she remained "very proud of him."[93]

Some accounts of Siegel's life include a claim that he took a curious trip to Italy with Dorothy Di Frasso, one that revealed him to be a great patriot with a desire to strike a blow against the Axis powers. Di Frasso had invested in an explosive device and sought to interest Italian dictator Benito Mussolini in buying it as he prepared his nation for war. When they arrived at Di Frasso's villa, she and Siegel learned that German leaders Joseph Goebbels and Hermann Goehring would join them. In several accounts, Siegel tells Di Frasso that he wants to kill them because of their treatment of Jews.[94] In the film *Bugsy*, James Toback changes Siegel's ambition. Three times in the film, Siegel explains that he wants to assassinate Mussolini. In a conversation with Meyer Lansky, Siegel explains, "Mussolini and Hitler have to be stopped. They're trying to knock off every Jew on earth. If I don't do something about it, who will? A bunch of Italians? I can stop Mussolini."

The Siegel myth has been truly compelling. As constructed by dozens of authors, journalists, and filmmakers, he lived not just a rags-to-riches story, one in which he invents America's adult playland, but also one in which he becomes a pioneer for organized crime figures' quest for legitimacy.[95] While he did not gain the latter, a few historians have conferred the former on Siegel. To be sure, most historians reject the notion that Siegel had an extraordinary vision for Las Vegas, but some historians, like John Findlay and Hal Rothman, have expressed respect not for Siegel the man, but for his efforts to create a fabulous resort hotel. "The most important thing about Siegel," according to the late Professor Rothman of the University of Nevada, Las Vegas, "is he raised the ante here. He had an idea, however bizarre, of what class was. As we become a resort destination, we actually owe him more and more."[96]

Several commentators have invoked the image of Bugsy's spirit as a way to appreciate his perceived role as the founder of modern Las Vegas. In 1955, journalist Bob Considine claimed that eight years after Siegel's death, "he's still very much alive along the 'strip' of Las Vegas today." The film *Neon Empire* closes with a montage of the modern Strip and a voice-over saying that the ghost of Junior Moloff, a Bugsy-like figure, "lives on. He did terrible things but he had a vision." Pete Hamill claims that when a "wind moans" through Las Vegas, "it blows steadily through the neon metropolis that lives because of Ben Siegel's fabulous dreams." Even Las Vegas journalist John L. Smith, who sought to debunk the myths surrounding Siegel's life, could not help contributing to it: "So wander through the new Las Vegas, and you will see Siegel's ghost in every glittering façade and exotic waterfall, each gourmet room and opulent suite. The city has become the class operation that had disturbed his maniacal dreams all those years ago."[97]

Developers like Tommy Hull, Robert Griffith, William Moore, Bob Brooks, and especially Billy Wilkerson, the man who developed the idea for a luxurious hotel-casino called the Flamingo, had also helped set the stage for the emergence of more glamorous properties like the Desert Inn and Sands hotels in the 1950s. But Hull, Griffith, Moore, Brooks, and Wilkerson did not die at the hands of an assassin. The grim demise of Siegel, his unmistakable

Bugsy Siegel's Flamingo in the late 1940s. Source: UNLV Libraries, Special Collections.

charisma, and the luxurious Las Vegas property associated with his name make an appealing story. Although the Flamingo Hilton destroyed the last vestige of his project in 1993 when it demolished his suite to construct a large swimming pool and garden area, it has retained a monument to Siegel on its grounds. The city, too, after years of trying to distance itself from his role in its creation, has embraced the Siegel legacy, featuring him in a mob museum.

Cities and nations have often traced their origins to an inspired hero. In popular culture, Las Vegas is no different. In novels and newspaper accounts, and as portrayed by actors as varied as Armand Assante, Brad Dexter, Warren Beatty, Ray Sharkey, Richard Grieco, Joe Penny, Alex Rocco, and Harvey Keitel, Bugsy Siegel remains the tragic visionary, the man who saw the future, the man who became the mythological father of Las Vegas.

Organized Crime in Las Vegas

The old Capone gang of Chicago and the Cleveland Mafia [. . .] took over Las Vegas last week-end.

Oakland Tribune, 1950

The Mafia controls all of Las Vegas.

Jack Lait and Lee Mortimer, 1952

Virgil W. Peterson, operating director of the Chicago crime commission, said today the old Capone gang controls or holds a major interest in a number of gambling casinos in both Reno and Las Vegas, Nev.

Chicago Daily Tribune, 1954

Las Vegas' fantastic gambling structure is controlled by hoodlums and racketeers.

Sid Meyers, 1958

Many major casinos are controlled by men who were bootleggers in the prohibition era. Some got their start as members of the gangs of the nineteen-twenties.

Wallace Turner, 1963

There is no question about it. The town belongs to the Mob.

Ed Reid and Ovid Demaris, 1963

*Las Vegas today, after more than 30 years of big time [sic] casino
gambling, is as infected by crime syndicate mobsters and crime syndicate rackets as any community in the United States.*

Chicago Tribune, 1979

*The old Las Vegas that was run by gangsters . . . is mostly a
romanticized fiction today.*

New York Times, 1991

SAM DONALDSON: *Well, we are told that the mob no longer controls
the town. Is the mob still here?*
MAYOR JAN JONES: *No.*

This Week with David Brinkley, 1994

For almost four decades after an assassin killed Bugsy Siegel in 1947, many
journalists focused on the connection between organized crime figures and
the development of Las Vegas. They brought before the reading public accounts of the investigations of hoodlums associated with Las Vegas, beginning with the Senate probe led by Estes Kefauver in the early 1950s and continued by Senator John McClellan's rackets committee. Robert F. Kennedy,
who served on McClellan's committee as chief counsel, launched a very visible
crusade against organized crime as attorney general. In the late 1950s and
early 1960s, the work of muckrakers like Sid Meyers, Ed Reid, Ovid Demaris,
and Wallace Turner told readers about the role of front men in casinos, the
corruption of government officials, and the huge illegal profits made in the
skim of casino income. In the late 1960s, journalists became enamored with
the entry of Howard Hughes into the casino business, often arguing that the
eccentric billionaire was eliminating the mob. In the following decade, journalists focused on the exploits of representatives of the Chicago and Kansas
City mobs in Las Vegas, notably Allen Glick, Frank "Lefty" Rosenthal, and
Anthony Spilotro. Finally, the nation's media highlighted the extraordinary
success of federal investigators in destroying the mob's influence in Las Vegas.
By the end of the twentieth century, journalists were writing about the demise
of organized crime in the gambling center. From the 1940s, novels, movies,
and television programs offered a narrative about gangsters in Las Vegas that
closely paralleled that provided in the press. Postwar Americans thus had no
problems linking the development of Las Vegas with the underworld.

Bugsy Siegel was not the first underworld figure who sought his fortune
in Las Vegas. When the state legislature began to debate a wide-open gam-

bling bill in 1931, the press covered several public meetings in Reno where citizens discussed the wisdom of the proposed legislation. Beyond concerns that legalized gambling would harm the working class and undermine the moral fiber of the citizenry, opponents argued the bill "would be an invitation for racketeers and gangsters to start operations" in Nevada.[1] The *Los Angeles Times* likewise questioned the bill. Gambling houses, the paper editorialized, would "attract a horde of the usual hangers-on, sharpers, touts, blacklegs, thieves and desperate adventurers." The "big gaming-house promoters" would not be locals; rather they would be men "from the purlieus of many cities outside the confines of Nevada itself."[2] Indeed, rumors abounded that "outside interests" had spent large sums in Las Vegas in the campaign leading up to the critical legislative session. Specifically, the rumors pointed toward one figure in Los Angeles: Guy McAfee.[3] Widely known in the city of angels as a "powerful gambling boss," McAfee became an important figure in Las Vegas for over two decades.[4] He was, as the opponents of the wide-open gambling bill predicted, one of several illegal gamblers and racketeers who came to Las Vegas in the 1930s and early 1940s. Although not closely tied with organized crime syndicates in the East, McAfee nonetheless was heavily involved in illegal activities in Los Angeles, as were other émigrés to Las Vegas like Tony Cornero and Milton "Farmer" Page. Their backgrounds in vice and their links with crime syndicates in Southern California contributed to the developing perception that the growth of Las Vegas was closely associated with figures from organized crime.

Although fired from the police force in 1917 for operating illegal games in a precinct house, Guy McAfee nonetheless was rehired to head the Los Angeles police department vice squad until he was caught alerting suspects of impending raids by whistling "Listen to the Mockingbird" on the telephone. He then simply sought wealth through the crimes he had been hired to eliminate, opening a casino in 1920. By 1928, McAfee owned the *Johanna Smith*, a gambling ship anchored off Long Beach, with Albert Marco, whom one historian described as "the caliph of the local prostitution industry," and fellow gambling boss Farmer Page. McAfee also ran a casino called the Clover Club on the Sunset Strip. By 1931, McAfee had emerged as a leader of the city's underworld in part by paying off city officials for protection. Indeed, a local magazine called *The Critic of Critics* dubbed McAfee the Capone of Los Angeles and published a cartoon called "The Octopus" showing McAfee's tentacles involved in illegal liquor, gambling, political corruption, and Las Vegas.[5] The tall, angular McAfee, sometimes called Slats or Stringbean, intrigued journalists, who found him to be good copy and labeled him variously as a "gambling dictator," the "Los Angeles gambling king," the city's "alleged underworld overlord," a "gambling baron," the "Grey Wolf" of the syndicate, and a "prince of percentage."[6] By the late 1930s, McAfee was one of a very few men in the city heading up "well organized syndicates" controlling "an estimated six hundred brothels, three hundred gambling houses . . . [and] twenty-three thousand slot machines."[7] Although mildly interested in Las Vegas in 1931, McAfee actually paid little attention to the possibilities in southern Nevada through much of the 1930s because vice in Los Angeles under corrupt mayor Frank Shaw was so lucrative. At the end of the decade, *Collier's* and *Look* magazines claimed that he had become a millionaire with a mansion and a yacht.[8] However, in 1938, reformer Fletcher Bowron won the mayor's office and began a campaign against prostitution and gambling, which prompted McAfee to apply for gambling licenses in Las Vegas. On Fremont Street, he opened the Frontier Club and then purchased a small club called the Pair-O-Dice, renaming it the 91 Club because it was located on Highway 91, which was outside town leading to Los Angeles. Describing McAfee as "the overlord of the gaming tables" in their community, the *Los Angeles Times* reported his move in June 1939.[9] McAfee prospered in Las Vegas, making enough by 1946 to open the million-dollar Golden Nugget on Fremont Street as its co-owner.

Tony Cornero was another California underworld figure who sought to profit from the legalization of gambling in Las Vegas. By 1931, Cornero had become a legendary bootlegger along the California coast. An Italian immigrant, Cornero grew up in San Francisco. He committed a robbery at age sixteen and went to reform school. Upon his release, Cornero drove a taxi for a time before moving to Southern California, where he quickly became involved in shipping illegal booze. At first Cornero hijacked bootleggers' cargoes, but he soon became a successful bootlegger himself, shipping as much as 7,000 cases at a time from Canada and Mexico in freighters and off-loading them to powerboats for delivery. In the mid-1920s, Cornero was making hundreds of thousands of dollars.[10] Stories about Tony and his brothers, Frank and Louis, appeared often in newspapers in the West in the 1920s—tales of daring bootlegging exploits, imported gunmen to battle hijackers, murders and attempted murders, competition with other bootleggers like Farmer Page, arrests, and escapes. As with Guy McAfee, journalists could not resist giving Cornero impressive titles: "czar of rumland," "the Southern California rum baron," "king of the liquor runners," "chieftain of international liquor smugglers and former gangster," and the "Admiral of the Rolling Bones."[11] Federal officials likewise saw him as a key player in the booze traffic. One Prohibition agent dubbed the Cornero brothers "the prime movers" in the illegal trade. There was even a rumor that Al Capone helped finance Cornero's ventures.[12]

Police arrested Cornero, who complained about having to pay as much as $100,000 for police protection, ten times in the 1920s on charges ranging from bootlegging to murder. However, judges usually dropped the charges for lack of sufficient evidence. When policemen arrested him in 1927, "a bribe loosened their grasp," and Cornero escaped to Canada. From there he made his way to Europe, where he purchased a ship and 100,000 gallons of booze. Instead of sailing through the Panama Canal and on to California, the German crew turned the ship in to federal officials in New Orleans, anticipating a reward. Cornero then surrendered, and after a conviction on rum-running charges, he served two years in prison.[13] Although Tony was still incarcerated in 1931, his brothers, Frank and Louis, went to Las Vegas, anticipating passage of a wide-open gambling law. They built the Meadows, the most luxurious nightclub and casino in the area, just beyond the city limits. According to historian Frank Wright, the Corneros also mistakenly thought that city leaders were going to close down the red-light district along Block 16, and they would be able to control prostitution in Las Vegas. After city leaders failed to shut down prostitution in Las Vegas and a fire destroyed part of the hotel portion of the property, the Corneros sold out and left Las Vegas.[14]

By 1938, Tony Cornero was operating a fleet of four gambling ships just off the Southern California coast. His prize possession was the S.S. *Rex,* an old fishing barge he refurbished at a cost of a quarter of a million dollars. The two-deck vessel had a bingo parlor, three hundred slot machines, and an array of roulette wheels and craps tables. In 1939, Cornero spent almost $70,000 advertising his vessels in Los Angeles newspapers, with some ads claiming "All the thrills of Biarritz, Riviera, Monte Carlo, Cannes—surpassed." He attracted as many as 3,000 patrons a day on the S.S. *Rex*—people who gambled as much as $400,000 a night. California attorney general Earl Warren finally shut down Cornero's operation in a public duel that lasted several days. The legal clash provided great fodder for journalists all across the country; they regaled readers with stories about the "battle of Santa Monica bay."[15] Cornero returned to Las Vegas in 1944, leasing the casino in the Apache Hotel downtown and naming it the Rex, after his ship. As in the early 1930s, Cornero lasted only a short time in Las Vegas, but he ultimately returned in the 1950s. He had begun the construction of his dream resort casino, the Stardust, but he died of a heart attack in 1955 while gambling at the Desert Inn Casino.[16]

Other Californians involved in illegal gambling followed McAfee and

Cornero's path to Las Vegas in the 1930s and early 1940s: J. Kell Houssels, who actually arrived in 1930 (Las Vegas Club), Marion Hicks and John Grayson (El Cortez), Tutor Scherer, Chuck Addison, Bill Kurland, and Farmer Page (Pioneer Club), and Wilbur Clark (Monte Carlo Club). Many of these men had been part of the syndicate described by George Creel in *Collier's* magazine in 1939 that "ran vice and crime as an organized business," one that "used part of its huge annual 'take' to corrupt officials and control the police department."[17] Rumors that businessmen in the city were little more than "tools of Los Angeles gambling interests" plagued Las Vegas officials in the late 1930s.[18]

Yet the California gambling bosses were scarcely known outside Southern California and southern Nevada, and their exploits did not capture the nation's attention as Bugsy Siegel did, particularly in the aftermath of his bloody demise. For over a year, there were dozens of articles about Siegel's murder. Most involved speculation about the motives for the slaying: Had he been involved in a narcotics ring? Was he in trouble over forcing people to subscribe to his wire service? Had his creditors grown tired of his failure to make the Flamingo successful? Did Siegel threaten to go to the authorities and inform on the business enterprises of the syndicate? No persuasive answers emerged, but the stories kept the link between Las Vegas and the brutalities of the mob in front of the reading public. For example, popular columnist Westbrook Pegler wrote, "'Bugsy' Siegel, murdered in a revival of the quaint old machine-gun process of the Capone era, had become one of the most formidable criminals of the new underworld of Hollywood, New York, Miami and the grand circuit of summer and winter gambling resorts."[19] In the mid-1950s, Long Beach, California, journalist James Phelan reported that city leaders were still trying to eliminate the Siegel connection: "Bugsy's blood spattered across Las Vegas' reputation and Las Vegas, like Lady Macbeth, has been scrubbing at the stain ever since."[20]

This was not a propitious development for Las Vegas because postwar Americans grew increasingly concerned about the threats posed by organized crime, particularly its link to gambling. The FBI contributed to this fear of a crime wave by reporting in 1946, 1947, and 1948 that crime rates were increasing; the bureau's director, J. Edgar Hoover, argued that the evidence indicated that the old gangs were redeveloping. In 1949, articles in *Collier's, Newsweek, Time,* and the *New York Times* identified New York's Frank Costello as the leader of a revived nationwide underworld network. Indeed, Costello was on the cover of the November 28 issue of *Time,* an issue that explained, "Millions of newspaper readers considered him a kind of master criminal, shadowy as a ghost and cunning as Satan, who ruled a vast, mysterious and malevolent underworld and laughed lazily at the law."[21] Civic leaders in Las Vegas cringed when the nation's newspapers reported, "Big-time racketeers, operating nation-wide syndicates from Cleveland and Chicago, were reported moving on California today from a newly established Las Vegas base."[22]

Several cities, such as St. Louis, Dallas, and Gary, Indiana, responded to the challenge by establishing crime commissions. Other cities revived crime commissions originally created in the 1920s. The most influential was in Chicago and directed by Virgil Peterson. With a law degree from Northwestern, Peterson had first served twelve years in the FBI and had participated in the capture of several notable criminals, including Baby Face Nelson and John Dillinger. When he took over the Chicago crime commission, he employed several former FBI agents. Peterson even had a contact in the old Al Capone gang who provided important information. Much in demand as a consultant and speaker, Peterson also published several influential articles and books, besides editing the *Journal of Criminal Law and Criminology* in his twenty-eight years heading the commission. As historian David Schwartz has shown, Peterson's work led him to conclude that organized crime was "dominated by 'the Syndicate,' the organization originally built by Al Capone and, by the late 1940s, effectively administered by Tony Accardo and Jake Guzik." Peterson further argued that gambling was a critical source of revenue for the underworld, and he linked Las Vegas casinos to the syndicate. "Elements of the mob of the late Al Capone," he said in 1954, "have taken over at least partial control of a number of gambling houses in Las Vegas."[23] Peterson was one of a growing number of voices, notably in large cities, calling on the federal government to take action against this rapidly growing challenge for law enforcement.[24] In response, Attorney General J. Howard McGrath convened a conference on organized crime in Washington in 1950, which was attended by local, state, and national law enforcement authorities.[25]

In January 1950, Tennessee senator Estes Kefauver introduced a resolution calling for an inquiry into "organized interstate gambling," and the next month, with the endorsement of President Harry Truman, his fellow senators authorized a broadened mandate to investigate all interstate crime.[26] They also tapped Kefauver to chair the special committee on organized crime in interstate commerce. The seventeen-month investigation included testimony from eight hundred witnesses in fourteen cities and culminated in a report with 11,000 pages of data. One of the key witnesses was Virgil Peterson. His lengthy testimony in July prepped the committee for its trip to Las Vegas in

November. *Chicago Daily News* reporter Edwin A. Lahey explained that committee members "expect to find that the soul of a racketeer is not necessarily ennobled when a state legalizes gambling." Lahey pointed out that Peterson "suggest[ed] that some wrong brothers have infiltrated the ranks of the public spirited and civic minded citizens who make up the legalized gambling profession in Nevada." Morris Rosen, for example, "who showed up in Las Vegas from New York shortly after the assassination of Benjamin (Bugsy) Siegel in 1947 and acted as though he were the heir to Siegel's interest in the Flamingo Hotel and gambling casino," according to Peterson, "was believed to be a representative of the Frank Costello group in New York." Peterson also advised that Moe Sedway, one of Siegel's partners, was still involved with the Flamingo. Moreover, Peterson testified that "Moe Davis [Dalitz], Morris Kleinman, Sam Tucker and . . . Thomas Jefferson McGinty" of the Cleveland syndicate provided most of the financing for the Desert Inn hotel and casino. Finally, he pointed out that a "big gambling racketeer" from Dallas named Benny Binion was also in Las Vegas, perhaps teaming up with Jack Dragna, "the alien gangster of Los Angeles."[27]

On November 15, Kefauver, his colleagues Charles Tobey and Alexander Wiley, and their staff gathered in the federal building in downtown Las Vegas, where they questioned six witnesses. Newspaper coverage was substantial, and readers across the land learned that committee members were shocked and outraged over what they learned about the connections between state officials and the casinos and the dependence of some owners on outside criminal organizations for funding. Lieutenant Governor Clifford Jones acknowledged that he earned over $20,000 a year from his percentage of ownership in the Thunderbird Hotel, the Golden Nugget, and the Pioneer Club. In addition, Jones's law partner, Louis Weiner, was the lawyer for Bugsy Siegel's estate. William Moore, a member of the state tax commission that regulated gambling, made over $70,000 from his percentage of ownership in the Hotel Last Frontier. Wilbur Clark's Desert Inn was financed largely by men from the Cleveland gambling syndicate.[28]

Although they did not do so during their Las Vegas stop, committee members did permit television cameras during their hearings in several other cities like New Orleans, St. Louis, Detroit, and Los Angeles. When they reached New York City in March 1951, Kefauver authorized the televising of over forty hours of the proceedings, not just in New York, but also in twenty other cities in the East and Midwest. The hearings became, in the words of *New York Times* television critic Jack Gould, "a social phenomenon virtually without parallel in the community's life." But it was not just New Yorkers who became engrossed with the proceedings; it seemed almost all who had a television tuned in. As Lee Bernstein has shown, "At a time when fewer than 8 million television sets were in use in the United States," there were at least seventeen million viewers of the hearings. Bars and restaurants were packed, and some movie theaters offered free broadcasts. More people watched the hearings than tuned in to the 1951 World Series. It was compelling to view some of the leading figures of organized crime like Frank Costello.[29] Pulitzer Prize–winning journalist David Halberstam later described the "innately explosive drama" that attracted so many:

> There, live and in black and white, were the bad guys on one side, looking very much like hoods, showing by the way they spoke and in other ways they never quite realized that they were part of the underworld; on the other side were Kefauver and his chief counsel, Rudolph Halley, the good guys, asking the questions any good citizen would about crime. Estes Kefauver came off as a sort of Southern Jimmy Stewart, the lone citizen-politician who gets tired of the abuse of government and goes off on his own to do something about it.[30]

The hearings, particularly those in New York, generated a flood of media coverage: a CBS radio documentary series entitled *A Nation's Nightmare;* a newsreel entitled *The Kefauver Crime Committee,* shown in movie houses across the nation; and feature articles in countless newspapers and in several popular magazines like *Time, Newsweek, Life, Harper's,* and *Collier's. Billboard,* for example, hailed the New York hearings as the "greatest TV show television has ever aired," and *Life* magazine proclaimed, "Never before had the attention of the nation been riveted so completely on a single matter."[31] *Time* magazine received over 100,000 letters about the investigation, most of them endorsing Kefauver's efforts. Indeed, the committee's efforts prompted overwhelming support; well over 90 percent of the letters to the committee were positive. In the process, Estes Kefauver, who traveled over 50,000 miles and chaired over ninety days of hearings, became an overnight national celebrity.[32] Not only was he on the cover of *Time* magazine, but he also appeared on the popular quiz show *What's My Line.* He provided the introduction to two feature films on organized crime, gave several speeches, and granted countless interviews. Kefauver published a four-part series in the *Saturday Evening Post* and a best-selling book about the investigations entitled *Crime in America,* which newspapers across the country published in a twenty-part series. Polls of newspaper correspondents and political scientists ranked him as the second most effective senator, and his hearings earned Kefauver an Emmy "for bringing the workings of our government into the homes of the American people."[33]

Beyond clearly advancing his own presidential aspirations, Kefauver's celebrity also demonstrated widespread support for his crusade against organized crime, one that repeatedly linked the gambling business in Las Vegas with the underworld. Whether readers consulted the committee's report, Kefauver's articles and book, or articles about Kefauver and his committee's work, they found an unflattering picture of Las Vegas. Arguing along lines similar to those of Virgil Peterson, Kefauver contended that there were two national syndicates—"the Costello-dominated 'Combination' on the East Coast and the Capone Syndicate in Chicago." The influence of these syndicates extended "across state boundaries to every important crime center in the country," including Las Vegas. There "hoodlums from the East and West Coasts have invaded the legalized gambling setup." Reno and Las Vegas had become, in Kefauver's judgment, "headquarters for some of the nation's worst mobsters." He noted not only that the late notorious Bugsy Siegel had been "undoubtedly the gambling boss of Las Vegas," but also that "ex-convict and long-time racketeer" Moe Sedway was still there, along with Texas "hoodlum" Benny Binion and Cleveland bootleggers and gamblers Sam Tucker, Thomas J. McGinty, Moe Dalitz, and Morris Kleinman. Nevada had too cozy a relationship between government officials and the gambling industry. While the state tax commission had since 1949 sought "to keep out persons known to have criminal records or strong affiliations with out-of-State gambling syndicates," it had failed "to eliminate the undesirable persons who had been operating in the State before that time."[34] Committee members thus concluded that in Nevada, "too many of the men running gambling operations . . . are either members of existing out-of-State gambling syndicates or have had histories of close association with underworld characters who operate those syndicates." In short, Kefauver concluded, "both morally and financially, legalized gambling in Nevada is a failure."[35]

The work of the Kefauver committee had unintended consequences. The senator sought to cripple the gambling industry with a federal tax of 10 percent on wagering, but Pat McCarran, the powerful senior senator from Nevada, helped kill the tax bill. Ironically, instead of curtailing the gambling industry in Nevada, the Kefauver committee drove dozens of gamblers to Las Vegas through its exposure of illegal gambling in many other states. In the face of the publicity surrounding the Kefauver committee investigations, local and state authorities cracked down on illegal gambling, driving dozens of gambling operators to Las Vegas—men whom journalists enjoyed covering over the next few decades.[36]

A decade after Kefauver's investigations, another powerful Washington figure focused his attention on Las Vegas—an examination that attracted great interest. In a November 1961 issue of the *Saturday Evening Post,* Peter Wyden reported that Attorney General Robert Kennedy had "ordered the first co-ordinated Federal investigation into Las Vegas and the forces that make it run." Wyden explained that Washington officials were "curious about rumors that 'interest holders,' camouflaged behind licensed operators, call the shots in some casinos, and that untaxed millions disappear 'off the top' of the gambling take in the ultra-private counting rooms."[37] Kennedy had developed a keen interest in organized crime while serving as chief counsel for the Senate permanent subcommittee on investigations (more popularly known as the Senate rackets committee) headed by John McClellan. Kennedy devoted over two and a half years leading the investigation, which focused on the ties between the powerful International Brotherhood of Teamsters and organized crime. With a staff of over one hundred, Kennedy participated in hundreds of days of hearings involving over 1,500 witnesses and over twenty thousand pages of evidence.[38] Senator McClellan agreed with the Peterson–Kefauver interpretation of a largely monolithic criminal organization in the United States. There was, he concluded, a "close-knit, clandestine, criminal syndicate" that drew on "narcotics, vice, and gambling" to finance its far-flung activities.[39] Kennedy similarly saw his work for the committee as a profound education in the power of organized crime. In 1960, Kennedy published *The Enemy Within,* in which he argued that "the gangsters of today work in a highly organized fashion and are far more powerful now than at any time in the history of the country." Because organized criminals had so successfully corrupted businesses, unions, and governments, only a concerted national effort to stop them could prevent gangsters from destroying the nation.[40]

When his brother appointed him to the post of attorney general, Kennedy had an opportunity to attack organized crime. In his testimony before the Senate judiciary committee, Kennedy stated his intention to "pursue" organized criminals "to the full vigor of the Department of Justice."[41] This self-proclaimed crime buster had embraced the view of Virgil Peterson, Estes Kefauver, and John McClellan that organized crime figures were using Las Vegas casinos to help bankroll their national operations, and he was eager to shut them down. Ronald Goldfarb, one of the lawyers in the organized crime and racketeering section of Kennedy's justice department, explained that they wanted "to penetrate the mob's huge financial bonanza—the Las

Vegas casinos. If gambling was the multibillion-dollar bank for organized crime, Las Vegas must have been its federal reserve."[42] Thus, in the summer of 1961, according to Nevada governor Grant Sawyer, the justice department asked Roger Foley, the state's attorney general, to "deputize sixty-five federal agents" as part of "a federal strike force that was being put together to invade every major casino in Reno and Las Vegas." "Bobby Kennedy," in Sawyer's judgment, "wanted to show the people of the United States that he was the guy to clean up all sin and corruption, and Nevada was a great place to start." Only Sawyer's quick trip to Washington, with Foley in tow, to meet not just with the attorney general, who Sawyer claimed treated him with disdain, but also with President John Kennedy, headed off the raid.[43]

Yet in August, a Reno, Nevada, newspaper learned that federal officials were preparing a report on Nevada gambling for Attorney General Kennedy, a man "who in the past has looked down his nose at legalized gambling with the air of a properly indignant Bostonian encountering an uncovered garbage can."[44] By early November, newspapers across the land anticipated the report mentioned in the *Saturday Evening Post*. The *Los Angeles Times* specifically noted that the investigation was focusing on "the backgrounds of the operators of the gambling casinos" and whether or not Las Vegas was "being used as a meeting place for heads of organized crime."[45] As had happened in early summer, Nevada officials—Senator Howard Cannon and Governor Sawyer—called on Kennedy to explain his intentions, which forced the attorney general to reassure them that Las Vegas was only one of twenty-five cities in a comprehensive investigation; Las Vegas was not the sole "target of the nationwide probe into U.S. criminal syndicates."[46]

Although Kefauver's and Kennedy's investigations did not shut down gambling in Las Vegas, reports of the federal efforts helped energize a number of muckraking journalists who found the mix of gambling and mob bosses an irresistible topic to explore. Three books published between 1958 and 1965 were particularly important in shaping the popular understanding of the connection between organized crime and Las Vegas. In 1958, Sid Meyers published *The Great Las Vegas Fraud*. Five years later, Ed Reid, who was a reporter for the *Las Vegas Sun*, and Ovid Demaris published *The Green Felt Jungle*, and in 1965, Wallace Turner released *Gamblers' Money*, a book based on a series of articles published in the *New York Times*. These men not only developed the major terms and themes of the conversation about the role of the underworld in southern Nevada, but also the righteous tone that dominated the coverage in the press. They told readers that mobsters from cities like New York City, Chicago, Detroit, St. Louis, and Kansas City controlled

Las Vegas. Moreover, these hoodlums were part of the syndicate identified by Peterson, Kefauver, McClellan, and Kennedy, which used front men with no criminal records to gain licenses to run their casinos. These muckrakers also named the gangsters involved, as well as their successful efforts to skim the profits of the casinos and dispatch it via couriers to major hoodlum centers in the East. Finally, they explained how organized crime figures drew on the massive pension fund of the Teamsters union to fund not only casinos, but also other, more legitimate enterprises in Las Vegas.

Meyers's *The Great Las Vegas Fraud* is an unqualified condemnation of the men who ran the gambling halls. "The Vegas casino operators," he argued, were not just "interlopers," they were the worst kind of parasites. "They are not members of the community, and do not have their homes or raise their families here. They have swooped down upon Las Vegas like a bunch of hungry vultures—and have accomplished nothing either for the city or its inhabitants." These gangsters quickly crafted a powerful machine, one "affiliated with the syndicate" and supported by the "unscrupulous politicians" and "unprincipled businessmen" of Las Vegas.[47] Skimming a large chunk of the profits before making their official count of the winnings in their casinos, these "hoodlums and racketeers" found men with clean records to obtain their gaming licenses to front their fraudulent operations. Although he clearly overstated the case, Meyers described an unprecedented spectacle of urban crime. "The Capone empire in Chicago, the Pendergast machine in Kansas City, and the Tammany machinations," he wrote, "were mere bagatelles compared to legalized gambling in Las Vegas."[48]

Wallace Turner published a series of hard-hitting articles in the *New York Times* in November 1963 on the underworld's influence in Las Vegas, material then organized into his 1965 book *Gamblers' Money*. He shared Meyers's moral indignation and likewise described the skim, which he called black money. Turner drew on "highly qualified official sources" to estimate that the take from the skim had reached $2 million a month. He explained that the casino bosses dispatched the money weekly to men in the East. The couriers, Turner argued, delivered the cash to men "high in the councils of organized crime in the United States."[49] He also described the various fronts for the casinos—men who made it possible for the old bootleggers, the gangsters from the 1920s, and the men who ran illegal casinos in the Midwest to become legitimate. That is one significant departure in Turner's work. Whereas Meyers saw the casino bosses as mere parasites, Turner described them as shrewd businessmen who saw the value of courting public favor in Las Vegas. They engaged in "public-pacifying good works," giving money to support churches and various civic and charitable causes, all in a successful effort to "ingratiate themselves with all the leading office holders and molders of public opinion." More important, they made themselves indispensable by making 40 percent of the jobs in Las Vegas "dependent on the gambling operations."[50] Turner also detailed the cozy relationship between the Teamsters union and Las Vegas. Under the leadership of Jimmy Hoffa, the Teamsters made substantial loans from its Central States Pension Fund to men in Las Vegas, notably Moe Dalitz, who headed "the Desert Inn crowd." Dalitz, whom Virgil Peterson and Estes Kefauver had identified as an old bootlegger and operator of illegal gaming back in the Midwest, used the money not just to expand casino operations, but also to purchase housing developments and a golf course, as well as to construct the Sunrise Hospital.[51] This was the most pernicious development, in Turner's view. Casino bosses like Dalitz were taking their ill-gotten gains and expanding into legitimate businesses in Las Vegas and beyond, "where their lack of ethics and their heavy cash support have constituted a new force in the economy."[52]

The Green Felt Jungle, by Ed Reid and Ovid Demaris, was the most powerful and influential of the Las Vegas exposés. Published in late 1963, the book reached the *New York Times* best-seller list in February 1964 and remained among the top ten nonfiction titles for six months, reaching as high as number six. Advertisements claimed it was "the first book that goes behind the headlines to explode the truth about hoodlum-owned Las Vegas." The book earned good reviews and even became the focus of an episode of David Susskind's nationally televised program *Open End.*[53] Like Meyers and Turner, the authors did not mince words. "There is no question about it," Reid and Demaris argued; Las Vegas "belongs to the mob," and they named the mobsters they believed involved: Moe Dalitz, Marshall Caifano, Tony Cornero, Jake "The Barber" Factor, Tony Accardo, Sam Giancana, Frank Costello, Phil Kastel, Joe Adonis, Joseph "Doc" Stacher, and Frank Sinatra, the entertainer they believed to be most closely associated with the mob.[54] To Reid and Demaris, these men were hoodlums protected by "a goon squad of psychopaths whose greatest pleasure in life is the torture of their fellow human beings."[55] They also discussed Benny Binion at great length, a man with a record of "theft, carrying concealed weapons, and two murder raps" in Texas. Although they displayed no regard for the other men they discussed, Binion was beyond the pale, a man of no consequence on the Strip. He was relegated to the old downtown "sawdust" joints. "Even in a den of thieves and murderers," they wrote, "Binion lacked class. He was a barbarian as well as an illiterate. Instead of silk suits and Italian loafers, Binion preferred cowboy boots and ten-gallon

Moe Dalitz (left) with two unidentified men in 1980. Dalitz was one of the most notable organized crime figures involved in the development of Las Vegas Strip hotels. Source: UNLV Libraries, Special Collections.

hats. He was loud, coarse, and a pompous bore."[56] As had Meyers and Turner, Reid and Demaris discussed the respectable front men in Las Vegas, taking particular aim at Wilbur Clark of the Desert Inn, whom they regarded as "a well-dressed puppet to the gambling fraternity." They also discussed the critical link between the Teamsters and the casino bosses.[57] In the end, they agreed with Sid Meyers's characterization of the men who ruled the gambling industry in Las Vegas, their sordid ways, and the threat they posed. "Make no mistake about it," they wrote, "this is war, war against parasites and sycophants who feed and grow strong on human weaknesses."[58]

Although critical, these were not the only voices shaping readers' perceptions of the city's ties to organized crime. In the 1950s and early 1960s, dozens upon dozens of journalists in newspaper and magazine articles hammered away at the sins of the underworld in Las Vegas. Several newspapers published a series of articles on the city. In 1955 alone, Seymour Korman had a six-part series in the *Chicago Daily Tribune,* Jim Phelan published a four-part series in the Long Beach, California, *Independent Press-Telegram,* and Bob

Considine produced a seven-part series syndicated across the land, which he consolidated into a feature article entitled "Las Vegas Exposed" in *PIC* magazine. All of these series dealt at least in part with organized crime in Las Vegas.[59] Major magazines also published exposes. For example, Dan Fowler published a piece in *Look* magazine in 1954 called "What Price Gambling in Nevada?" Five years later, *Reader's Digest* published "Las Vegas: The Underworld's Secret Jackpot," and in 1960 came Fred J. Cook's "Treasure Chest of the Underworld: Gambling, Inc." in *Nation* magazine.

In all these pieces, the authors, while adding little new information, seemed to be competing for the most colorful descriptions of the underworld's control of Las Vegas. Dan Fowler claimed that "gangsters [were] jamming Nevada like flies in a sugar bowl." There were so many hoodlum-run casinos, and the competition for customers so fierce, that "Nevada," Fowler claimed, "in fact, may have set the stage for the bloodiest gang war since prohibition days." Obviously familiar with the arguments of Virgil Peterson and the Kefauver committee, Fowler argued that "a loose organization known as the Syndicate" dominated the casino bosses. This powerful group, at least in Fowler's estimation, was almost omniscient about all things gambling in the city. It was "personified around Las Vegas by its Board of Elders—those well-dressed, gray-haired old gentlemen you see wherever you go, saying little but observing everything."[60] Lester Velie contended that legalized gambling in Nevada was "pouring a vast underground river of gold into the underworlds of our big cities" and that "big-name gangsters are entrenched in the palatial gambling casinos in Las Vegas."[61] Investigative reporter Fred Cook's conclusion about Las Vegas's sellout to organized crime and the impact of that betrayal on the nation was the most damning:

> Nevada by legalizing gambling has given the powers of the American underworld a haven. The tremendous investment of the underworld in the legal gambling casinos of Nevada is detailed on too many records to be disputed. This investment, this interest, means simply that legal gambling in Nevada is bankrolling the underworld with millions of dollars annually—perhaps with more millions than the average person can readily conceive as a result of the "off-the-top" racket. The net result has been to make "fun-loving" Las Vegas virtually the capital of American crime.[62]

Some reporters uncovered stories that permitted them to go beyond hyperbole and reveal both the corruption of some Nevada authorities and the links between organized crime and Las Vegas gambling operations. In 1954, Hank Greenspun, the publisher of the *Las Vegas Sun,* facing a libel suit over his paper's reporting on corruption in the Clark County sheriff's office, hired an undercover investigator named Pierre Lafitte to expose corrupt local politicians. Posing as Louis Tabet, a supposed gangland figure whose rap sheet included charges of bootlegging, manslaughter, and murder, Lafitte taped conversations not only with Sheriff Glen Jones, but also with Lieutenant Governor Cliff Jones and Jones's lawyer, Louis Wiener. The latter two assured Lafitte that despite his criminal background, they could help him obtain a gambling license. Moreover, Wiener claimed that the members of the state tax commission knew that Meyer and Jake Lansky were investors in the Thunderbird Hotel and Casino, and that Joseph "Doc" Stacher, an eastern crime boss, was behind the Sands Hotel. Papers across the country carried the story, which led to Jones's resignation as a Democratic National Committee member, and which confirmed for many the Lanskys' investment in the Thunderbird.[63] On May 2, 1957, a gunman shot Frank Costello, one of the nation's leading underworld figures, in the head as he entered his Central Park West apartment in New York City. As doctors treated him for what turned out to be a superficial wound, police officers were going through Costello's clothes and found a curious slip of paper. It included a reference to "casino wins" of $651,284, which turned out to be the same figure for the take at the recently opened Tropicana Hotel in Las Vegas for the period April 3 to April 26. Although Theodore Schimberg, president of the Tropicana, "categorically denied that Frank Costello ever had, or now has, any interest whatsoever in Hotel Tropicana," a clear link between Costello and the hotel emerged when the police traced the handwriting on the note to one of the assistant cashiers at the Tropicana.[64] Such a story seemed to confirm journalists' predictions about potential gang warfare. That potential must have become much more evident to readers on the news the following year of the murder of Gus Greenbaum in Phoenix, Arizona. Both Greenbaum and his wife had their throats slit in their home. News accounts pointed out that Greenbaum was one of the owners of the Riviera Hotel and Casino in Las Vegas and had been owner of the Flamingo after the murder of Bugsy Siegel. Although police investigations could not track down his killer, most speculated that the gangland slaying was related to his connection to the gambling industry.[65]

There were also criticisms of state and local efforts at regulating gambling in these accounts. One reporter claimed that "state officials privately concede that the gambling laws have more holes than an imported Swiss cheese." Particularly damning were quotes from current and former regulators. In

1955, Harley E. Harmon, a former member of the Clark County commission, which was the licensing board, noted the problem front men posed for officials. Claiming that the licensees were only fronts for hoodlums, Harmon asserted, "If we turn down one front man, the hoodlums just send another to apply." Similarly, Roger D. Foley, a former district attorney, concluded, "With some of the people we have licensed, we might as well bring in Al Capone. He wouldn't be any worse than what we have."[66]

Not all the news about Las Vegas and organized crime was negative. Indeed, some journalists developed a competing narrative about the role of organized crime in Las Vegas. Several lauded the efforts of Nevada officials to keep the underworld away from gambling. City, county, and state authorities fully understood that they needed to take decisive actions to convey to the nation that they had established control of the gambling industry. Until 1945, cities and counties had issued licenses and had oversight responsibilities. Applicants for licenses had to do little more than prove that they were U.S. citizens. To improve the collection of the state tax on gambling, the Nevada legislature passed a law requiring a state license, and it also placed the state tax commission in charge of gambling. In the wave of negative national publicity after the murder of Bugsy Siegel, state officials scrambled to create the impression that they were cleaning up gambling. First, Alan Bible, the state's attorney general, informed the tax commission that it had broad powers to investigate "the antecedents, habits and characteristics of the individual applying for" a license, and that it could deny a license to a person for "just cause, unsavory reputation, or other reasons of public interest." Second, the legislature passed an additional law in 1949 which incorporated Bible's opinion and provided more funding for staff to carry out the investigations. Subsequent legislation in 1955 and 1959 led to the creation of a two-tiered system of control, with an appointed gaming commission that served as an oversight body having ultimate authority in approving, modifying, or rejecting licenses, and an appointed professional gaming control board to investigate each applicant for a license and to enforce gaming laws and regulations. Finally, during the Grant Sawyer administration, Nevada created a list of excluded persons, or a black book, which prohibited some people with substantial criminal records from entering hotel-casinos.[67]

Some visiting journalists praised local and state officials for doing all they could to block mobsters from gaining gambling licenses. All license applicants had to be fingerprinted and had be cleared by an FBI background check. Indeed, all employees of casinos down to the cocktail waitresses had to be fingerprinted. State officials barred anyone convicted of committing a felony, other than illegal gambling in another state, from gaining a license. Further, a licensee could not be involved in illegal gambling in another state after gaining approval in Nevada. Robbins Cahill, the executive secretary for the tax commission, came in for particular praise as an "active crusader for clean gambling."[68] The Las Vegas police and Clark County not only required all ex-felons to register when they moved to Las Vegas, but also maintained a record of "hoodlums and crooks all over the country." The *Los Angeles Times* noted that when Chicago gangland boss Tony Accardo arrived in Las Vegas in January 1953, the police chief told him to leave town.[69] As William Sinnott, the acting chairman of the gaming control board, explained in 1959, "We diligently scrutinize each individual who comes in here for a license." When board members hear rumors of mob infiltration, "we move quickly under the breadth of the law to run these rumors down. Invariably, there is absolutely no proof." Indeed, Sinnott noted that Frank Costello, Phil Kastel, and Meyer Lansky "were all either directly or indirectly here for a while—and they left."[70] In 1962, a journalist quoted Nevada gaming control board chairman Edward A. Olsen as claiming "that of the more than 700 persons whom federal investigators suspect of being engaged in illicit gambling operations in the nation, only six are holding legal gambling licenses in Nevada."[71] In his examination of this collective effort, Kenneth Rudeen concluded in *Sports Illustrated,* "In sum, Las Vegas seems to be scrubbed reasonably clean."[72]

However, an avalanche of newspaper and magazine articles on the skim in 1966 and 1967 smashed the notion that Nevada regulators had eliminated organized crime's hold on gambling. Journalists revealed not only that the skim—the practice of taking money from casino winnings before doing an official count of the coins and cash collected for tax purposes—was ubiquitous in the casinos, but also that the money found its way into the hands of organized crime leaders around the country via couriers dispatched from Las Vegas. Readers had encountered occasional reports about the skim in newspaper and magazine articles in the late 1950s and early 1960s, as well as in the muckraking works of Meyers, Turner, Reid, and Demaris, but the full extent of the practice was not evident until 1966. In June of that year, there were revelations about FBI wiretaps in Las Vegas casinos dating from 1961.[73] The agency had eavesdropped on conversations in casino executives' offices to determine the dimensions of the tax scam. *Chicago Sun-Times* crime reporter Sandy Smith, drawing on documents leaked to him by the justice department, fueled the story with an exposé of the skim. According to Smith, the skim from the Desert Inn, Stardust, Flamingo, Sands, Fremont, and Horseshoe casinos amounted to at least $6 million a year—money that couriers dispatched to "crime syndicate gangsters around the country." To protect this lucrative scam, some of the skim money went to politicians. "The gifts," Smith explained, "were labeled political contributions but were considered as payoffs by the gangsters and the casino frontmen."[74] The *New York Times, Washington Post, Los Angeles Times, Wall Street Journal, Chicago Tribune,* and hundreds of newspapers in smaller markets, as well as popular magazines like *Look, Holiday,* and *Life,* followed Smith's lead and kept the story alive for over a year. NBC News also weighed in with an *American White Paper* on organized crime in America, a documentary that included the assertion that federal officials had known about skimming in Las Vegas casinos for years.[75] The almost daily articles in the nation's press became a withering indictment of state and local officials' inability and disinterest in eliminating organized crime from the gambling industry.

State officials responded to the charges in late summer 1966. Governor Grant Sawyer ordered the state's gaming commission to conduct a closed-door investigation of skimming charges and hidden ownership of casinos. Commissioners called dozens of witnesses, including Edward Olsen, chairman of the state gaming control board, journalist Sandy Smith, casino executives, slot machine supervisors, and casino cashiers.[76] As the commissioners listened to the testimony, Governor Sawyer launched a counterattack against the federal government, charging that it was engaged in an "undeclared war" on the gambling industry in his state, and he called on the justice department to give to Nevada authorities whatever evidence it had on skimming. Later in the fall, he charged that the FBI was acting like Nazis in their eavesdropping campaign against Nevada casinos. This charge led to a public exchange of letters between the bureau's director, J. Edgar Hoover, and the governor. Hoover charged, "The gambling industry of your state occupies a position of major importance in the scheme of organized crime and racketeering. Funds illegally skimmed from certain Nevada casinos have been used for a multitude of nefarious purposes." Sawyer countered that the FBI director's letter constituted "a frank admission that the Federal agency which you head has violated the laws of Nevada relative to the right of privacy of the people of this state." Sawyer was referring to the state's ban on the use of either telephone wiretaps or electronic eavesdropping devices.[77]

At the conclusion of the Nevada gaming commission hearings in Las Vegas and Carson City, the *Las Vegas Sun,* in a huge page-one headline, proclaimed, "State 'Skim' Probers Fire Back—Most Casinos 'Clean.'"[78] Governor Sawyer sent a copy of the commission's report to both President Lyndon Johnson and Attorney General Nicholas Katzenbach. The commissioners offered three clear conclusions: there was no evidence that "substantial amounts" of money were being skimmed, there was "no evidence of concealed ownership," and "there was no evidence that money was transported from any gambling casino to out-of-state persons who were not licensed owners of that casino." Moreover, the commissioners contended not only that Katzenbach's justice department had refused to cooperate in their investigation, but also that it had continued the harassment of Nevada citizens begun under the Robert F. Kennedy–led justice department.[79] Despite this resounding defense of the state's regulatory record, the gaming commission did recommend that the state legislature approve legislation that would tighten both counting and accounting procedures in casinos.[80]

The skim story nonetheless had remarkable traction. In November 1966, a federal grand jury summoned casino bosses, the auditor for the gaming control board, pit bosses, cashiers, and security personnel from the casinos to investigate the skim. Even Frank Sinatra was called. The inquiry produced enough evidence for the justice department to indict former owners of the Fremont Hotel and the owners of the Riviera Hotel on conspiracy charges to evade federal taxes—in other words, they charged them with skimming.[81] Even a breezy article on Las Vegas in *Holiday* magazine in spring 1967 noted "the skim probe had Las Vegas mighty uneasy."[82] The culmination of all the attention on the skim came in a two-part piece on organized crime in *Life* magazine by the same Sandy Smith who triggered the journalistic frenzy. Smith repeated most of the charges he made in his *Chicago Sun-Times* series but emphasized that among their many sources of income, "the true bonanza the Mob has struck in legitimate business is 'skimming.'" He also noted that Meyer Lansky had always overseen the skim. Indeed, Smith argued that "when the skim was running smoothly, the bagmen shuttled between Las Vegas and Miami with satchels of cash," where Lansky determined its distribution.[83]

After the *Life* magazine stories, most newspaper and magazines lost interest in the skim for nearly a decade. Instead, the lead story about Las Vegas for most journalists was Howard Hughes. The reclusive Hughes, who had parlayed an inheritance and his business acumen into a fabulous fortune, had developed a reputation as a daring aviator, movie mogul, and playboy as his Hughes Aircraft, Hughes Tool Company, and controlling share in TWA produced a personal bankroll of about $2 billion. Increasingly eccentric and addicted to painkillers because of injuries suffered in plane accidents, Hughes decided to move from California to Las Vegas in 1966. From the early 1940s, Hughes had enjoyed visiting Las Vegas. As one of his biographers, Michael Drosnin, explained:

He liked the all-night ambiance, he liked the showgirls, he liked the whole tone and feel of the place. In the early 1950s, before he went into seclusion, he used to fly in regularly for a night or a few days or a few weeks, catch the shows, perhaps pick up a showgirl, dispatching one of his lackeys to arrange the assignation, always ordering him to first get a signed release. He rarely gambled, just occasionally dropped a nickel in a slot machine, but he cruised the casinos and was a familiar figure at ringside in the showrooms, and he kept coming back.[84]

As the head of RKO pictures, Hughes had made *The Las Vegas Story* with Jane Russell, Victor Mature, and Vincent Price at the Flamingo "to represent all that is glamorous and exciting about Las Vegas."[85] Hughes had even leased a small house near the Desert Inn where he lived in 1953 and 1954 as he contemplated moving his enterprises to Las Vegas. However, he did not make the move until November 27, 1966, in an effort to avoid heavy California taxes after the sale of his TWA stock for $546,549,171. He booked the entire top floor of the Desert Inn Hotel. However, when the owners wanted him to come out to welcome high-rolling gamblers, Hughes directed Robert Maheu, his top aide, to negotiate the purchase of the hotel. After taking control of the Desert Inn in March 1967, Hughes went on a spending spree buying the Sands, Castaways, Silver Slipper, Frontier, and Landmark hotel-casinos. Attorney General Ramsey Clark stopped his purchase of the Stardust because that property would have given Hughes a near monopoly of lodging in Las Vegas.

Many hailed Hughes as the man who would purge the mob from the gambling center. Local spokesmen, like Gaylord Prather, the president of the chamber of commerce, trumpeted a new era for Las Vegas: "If Hughes is in, our image has to look better." In January 1968, syndicated columnist Bob Considine, who had been away from Las Vegas for five years, humorously claimed to be shocked by the absence of mobsters: "I've been here for six hours and have yet to see a broken nose, a cauliflower ear or hear a 'dese' or even a 'dem.' Where did the Old Guard go? Back to Detroit? Cleveland? Miami?"[86] Yet the euphoria was only momentary; journalists quickly realized that the mob remained.

Indeed, between 1975 and 1986, Las Vegas faced another barrage of accounts not just about skimming, but also about hidden ownership of some casinos and tainted loans from the Teamsters union's central states, Southeast, and Southwest pension fund. The nation's press produced many detailed accounts of Chicago mobsters' control of the Stardust and Fremont hotels and the influence that the Kansas City mob had in the Tropicana Hotel. Three men became the focus of the Chicago connection to Las Vegas. Allen Glick, a successful real estate developer from San Diego who had purchased the Hacienda Hotel through his Argent Corporation in 1971, obtained a loan from the Teamsters' pension fund three years later to purchase the Stardust and Fremont hotels. Frank "Lefty" Rosenthal, a successful sports handicapper, became the inside man for the Chicago mob at the Stardust. Rosenthal, not Glick, ran the casino despite having seemingly harmless titles like food and beverage manager and entertainment director. Anthony Spilotro, the outside man, emerged, as the *Chicago Tribune* described it, as the "reputed watchdog for the underworld's money in Las Vegas."[87] The diminutive Spilotro—he was only five feet, five inches tall—was a violent enforcer who had developed a reputation in his Chicago days for burglary, bookmaking, and debt collection. He was also implicated in a number of murders. Representing the interests of Chicago crime bosses, Spilotro, under the name of Anthony Stuart, opened a gift shop in the Circus Circus Hotel shortly after his arrival in Las Vegas in 1971; he also quickly started a burglary ring.

The multifaceted story of crime, gangsters, skimming, and shady funding of casinos surfaced in several newspapers and magazines in 1975 and 1976. An article in the *New York Times* revealed that the Teamsters' pension fund had loaned $150 million to Glick, a thirty-two-year-old man with "little business experience," to purchase Las Vegas casinos "from which several million dollars has been stolen through 'skim-offs.'" Moreover, "law-enforcement officers have identified Mr. Glick as an associate of organized-crime figures."[88] There were some stories about Glick's spectacular rise, his lavish lifestyle, one featuring "a California estate, swimming pool, tennis court and foreign cars," and his emergence as one of the wealthiest men in Las Vegas—indeed, the most powerful casino owner after the death of Howard Hughes.[89] Most of the articles, however, dealt with the unsavory elements of Glick's ascension to influence in Las Vegas. Major newspapers reported that the Nevada gaming control board determined in summer 1976 that over $7 million had been skimmed from slot machines in his properties, and in the fall that Glick had taken questionable personal advances from his company.[90] Most troubling were the stories about Glick's association with organized crime figures, notably Lefty Rosenthal, who had become executive director of operations for the Argent casinos soon after Glick obtained his loans from the Teamsters' pension fund. The Nevada gaming commission refused to issue Rosenthal a gambling license in January 1976 for a number of reasons: a 1963 "convic-

Gangster Tony Spilotro (left) and his lawyer and future Las Vegas mayor, Oscar Goodman, in 1980. Source: UNLV Libraries, Special Collections.

tion for attempting to bribe a New York University basketball player" to shave points in a game, several arrests in Miami and Las Vegas on various charges, and his association with "known criminals."[91]

Complicating Glick's relationship with authorities in Las Vegas was Rosenthal's association with Tony Spilotro. The gaming commission had learned from the Illinois investigating crime commission that Spilotro was "one of the syndicate's most dangerous gunmen and a specialist on the invasion of legitimate businesses by the mob." While Rosenthal acknowledged that he had known Spilotro from their days in Chicago, he contended to the gaming commission that he had not had any contact with the gangster while managing the Stardust. The commission members, however, had reports that Rosenthal had frequently seen Spilotro. Pete Echeverria, chairman of the gaming commission, concluded that Rosenthal was "one of the most scurrilous" individuals to ever seek a license. "Granting a license to him," Echeverria argued, "would be a mockery of everything we've tried to uphold in Nevada gaming."[92]

Glick consistently maintained that the stories were nothing more than the product of a "malicious press" seeking to destroy him when, in fact, he explained in late 1975, "I have never been convicted or guilty of a crime greater

Frank "Lefty" Rosenthal, gangster who became executive director of operations for Argent casinos in the 1970s. Source: UNLV Libraries, Special Collections.

than a traffic violation. The truth is that Allen R. Glick has never nor will ever be associated with anything other than what is lawful."[93] The facade of probity that Glick tried to maintain quickly collapsed in 1978. On June 19 and 23, over a hundred FBI agents, armed with dozens of warrants, searched Glick's office and his apartment as well as his secretary's apartment. They were interested not only in Glick's Teamsters loans, his connections with Lefty Rosenthal and Tony Spilotro, and skimming at his casinos, but also whether he was paying a Las Vegas police officer for information on the department's investigation of his criminal activity. Additionally, the agents were interested in Glick's possible involvement in the 1975 murder of Tamara Rand, a former San Diego business associate. Just before her death, Rand allegedly was ready to talk to authorities about Glick's illegal finances. These story lines were irresistible, and journalists followed the tangled webs of intrigue and chicanery for almost a decade. Readers of the *New York Times, Washington Post,*

Wall Street Journal, Chicago Tribune, Los Angeles Times, and *Time* magazine, among dozens of other periodicals, discovered a narrative that reinforced all the stereotypes about Las Vegas and organized crime. They saw the power of the Chicago mob, a foolish front man, extraordinary examples of skimming, threats of violence, and corrupt politicians.

Glick indeed served as a front man for the mob, a role that put him in an ever-more dangerous position. When he sought to purchase the Recrion Corporation, which owned the Stardust and Fremont hotels, Glick approached officials of the Teamsters pension fund for a loan. Milwaukee crime boss Frank Balistrieri intervened on his behalf with the fund's board of trustees. However, the loan for Glick's Argent Corporation to cover the purchase of the two hotels came at a price. Glick had to agree that Balistrieri's two sons would have an option to buy half of his corporation for only $25,000. As Balistrieri explained, Glick "had an obligation arising from assistance . . . in obtaining a pension fund commitment."[94] A month after Glick obtained the loan, Balistrieri told him to elevate Rosenthal to the post of advisor on gambling and promotions. Rosenthal quickly began exercising managerial authority, firing staff members and replacing them with his friends. When Glick told Rosenthal to stop meddling in all aspects of casino management, he learned not only that he had lost control of his properties, but also that he faced threats to himself and his family. Rosenthal told him, "I was told not to tolerate any nonsense from you because you are not my boss. If you don't do what you're told, you will never leave this corporation alive."[95]

The two clashed until March 1975, when Rosenthal ordered Glick to fly to Kansas City, where he met Nick Civella, the city's most powerful underworld figure. Civella and his brother, Carl, were in Nevada's "First List of Excluded Persons," a black book that listed underworld figures not permitted in the state's casinos. According to Glick, Civella told him that he "should cling to every word he said because 'You don't know me, but if it was my choice, you would never leave this room alive. If you listen, you may.'"[96] Civella told Glick that he owed the mob a $1.2 million commission for the Teamsters loan, and if he did not pay, he was a dead man. Moreover, Civella ordered Glick to permit Rosenthal to manage the Stardust, where the latter was running a successful skim, one focused on the slot machines. In the count room, the staff adjusted the scales used to weigh the coins. According to federal estimates, this technique had led to a skim that had become the largest theft in Las Vegas history. In April 1978, Carl "Tuffy" DeLuna, one of Nick Civella's lieutenants, went to Las Vegas to meet with Glick. In the office of lawyer Oscar Goodman, who had represented Glick's Argent Company, according to Glick, DeLuna issued a chilling warning. The mobster told Glick that his partners were "sick of having to deal" with him and the negative publicity surrounding the federal government's investigation into skimming, and he informed Glick that he would have to sell the properties; otherwise, DeLuna would have Glick's sons murdered.[97] Facing this ominous threat and pressure from the Nevada gaming commission, Glick sold his Las Vegas properties to Allan Sachs in 1979 after paying a $700,000 fine for not stopping the skimming on his properties.[98]

While Glick escaped with his life, Frank "Lefty" Rosenthal barely survived. In October 1982, Rosenthal suffered serious burns in a car bombing in the parking lot of a Las Vegas restaurant. City detectives had warned him that the Chicago bosses had targeted him because he was "holding back . . . part of the mob's share of his earnings."[99] Spilotro did not fare so well. In 1986, while he was awaiting trial in Las Vegas on racketeering and conspiracy charges, Spilotro and his brother, Michael, who were in Chicago at the time, were beaten to death and buried in an Indiana cornfield.[100]

Besides the exploits of Glick, Rosenthal, and Spilotro, in 1979 the nation's readers learned about Carl Civella's control of the fabled Tropicana hotel and casino "through the hotel's show producer, ex-convict Joseph V. Agosto." Indeed, a five-year federal investigation into the intersection of the Chicago and Kansas City mobs' involvement in Las Vegas led to indictments of nearly two dozen men for their roles in skimming and control of the Stardust, Tropicana, and Fremont hotel-casinos. When all the trials concluded in 1986, twenty stood convicted, and their sentences ranged from three to thirty years. The roster included some of the most powerful mobsters in America: Chicago crime boss Joseph Aiuppa and his underboss, Jackie Cerone; Milwaukee crime boss Frank Balistrieri; and Carl Civella and Carl DeLuna of Kansas City. Nick Civella died before going to trial, and Joseph Agosto died before sentencing.[101]

The investigation that led to these convictions produced an avalanche of newspaper and magazine articles, pieces that enthralled readers with accounts based on hundreds of conversations among leading underworld figures in Las Vegas, Chicago, and Kansas City, picked up through court-ordered electronic eavesdropping. The stories included detailed discussions on how to most effectively skim money from casinos; the continuing links between the Teamsters and organized crime; efforts on the part of the Kansas City mob to buy out the Las Vegas interests of the Chicago mob; Detroit mobsters' control of the Aladdin Hotel; reputed efforts to blackmail Nevada governor Robert List because of his stays at Las Vegas hotels; and boasts from mobster Joe Agosto that he controlled Harry Reid, the chair of the Nevada gaming commission. Not all of the stories were accurate. For example, a Nevada gaming control board investigation exonerated Harry Reid. Still, many of the accounts had credibility because of the wealth of information that federal and Nevada state authorities uncovered through phone taps, electronic recordings, raids on count rooms in casinos, information provided by insiders, and the extraordinarily detailed records of the skim maintained by Carl DeLuna.[102]

As the powerful press narrative about the mob's influence in Las Vegas developed from the 1940s through the 1980s, a plethora of novels, movies, television programs, and documentaries in the five decades after World War II describing crime bosses, syndicates, fronts, and the skim contributed to a parallel fiction and film narrative. A particularly effective depiction of this narrative occurs during the January 16, 1987, episode of the television series *Crime Story*. A coalition of crime families, led by an aging Manny Weisbord, decides to seize control of Las Vegas. During a 1963 meeting in Chicago, a character named Max Goldman explains, "We don't care about running hotels. They got to operate straight up and down. Hookers in the bar are freelance. We throw out the slugs. Our main action in each joint is the casino operation where we operate a cash skim. Other than that, we keep our act as clean as possible so that we don't attract any unnecessary city, state, or federal heat to ourselves." He is followed by Ray Luca, the character who will, for a time, gain control of Las Vegas, "With this new 707 jet airplane Vegas is going to boom. O'Hare is the airport hub of this country and most of the gamblers fly right out of here. You might say Vegas is just an extension of Chicago." The mob's legal counsel, Steve Kordo, describes their ultimate dream: "We have a ten-year plan. If we handle Las Vegas correctly, we can legitimize our entire operation by 1973. We are choosing directors as clean as a baby's bottom to run the domestic corporations, and we are setting up our offshore holdings in such a complex way it will take five federal administrations to unravel it. By 1983, your children will be living in Malibu. Their only connection to what we do here today will be their stock portfolios with companies on the New York board." After some cajoling by Weisbord, the Chicago mob agrees to the plan and kicks in $10 million to help them purchase properties in Las Vegas. After the meeting, the dissenters are killed, sealing the decision to use Las Vegas as a way to legitimacy for the major crime families.[103] All the key elements of the narrative are in this scene: major crime families deferring to a boss who speaks with authority for the syndicate, plans to use Las Vegas as a way to gain legal status for their lucrative business, and the easy use of violence to assure compliance.

Movies about Las Vegas as early as *Dark City* in 1950 and *Las Vegas Story* two years later often dealt with crime's connection with the city, but they usually featured individuals or small-time hoods. For example, *Guns, Girls, and Gangsters* (1959) and *They Came to Rob Las Vegas* (1969) are about attempted robberies of armored cars carrying a casino's cash, and *3000 Miles to Graceland* (2001) is about the robbery of the Riviera Hotel. Likewise on television was an episode of *The Racket Squad* (1951) that dealt with check kiting, and there were several stories of robbery, murder, and fraud in Las Vegas in *State Trooper* (1956–1959), a series about crime all across Nevada, and in an episode of the detective series *The Lone Wolf* (1955). Most often, however, viewers of movies or television encountered the insidious influence of organized crime in Las Vegas.

The 1946 Roy Rogers and Dale Evans film *Heldorado* dealt with a syndicate's black market scheme to buy fake bills at a discount and use them in the casinos of Las Vegas, notably the Hotel Last Frontier, where much of the movie was filmed. Four years later, Edmund O'Brien futilely challenged a "national syndicate's" control of a race book operation in *711 Ocean Drive*. There was a horse-racing syndicate in Barbara Stanwick's *The Lady Gambles* (1949) and a powerful gambling syndicate in Joan Crawford's *The Damned Don't Cry* (1950). In the comedy film *My Friend Irma Goes West* (1950), the Corrigan Gang opens a Las Vegas casino called the Quicksand Club. Even the whimsical 1960 heist movie *Ocean's Eleven* had Cesar Romero playing Duke Santos, a man with considerable underworld connections (in Terre Haute, Indiana; Detroit; and Palm Beach), and there is one scene where the bosses of the Flamingo, Sands, Sahara, Desert Inn, and Riviera discuss their plight after Danny Ocean's gang has robbed them on New Year's eve. They were worried about the "partners we have to answer to" in a way that left little doubt that they were discussing mob partners.[104] Vengeful East Coast mobsters hunt down and kill Hank McCain, who was working with a West Coast mobster named Charlie Adamo, to rob the safe of their Royal Hotel and Casino in the 1970 film *Machine Gun McCain*. The Prizzi family owns three Las Vegas casinos in the 1985 film *Prizzi's Honor*, and Jack Nicholson enforces their will as their hit man. When Shelly Kaplow, portrayed by Alec Baldwin, challenges the mob's efforts to transform his Shangri-La casino into a family-friendly place, they ultimately take him out in the 2003 film *The Cooler*.

Television likewise contributed to the impression of a gangster-dominated city. In a 1957 episode of *State Trooper* entitled "Cash Out," a suspect in a robbery in Las Vegas was in the Chicago rackets. The *Mike Hammer* series had a 1958 episode about Las Vegas called "Hot Hands, Cold Dice" in which one character had a connection to "a big gambling syndicate in the East." Rod Serling included a high-rolling gangster in "The Prime Mover," a 1961 episode of *The Twilight Zone* series. The mob makes an occasional appearance in *Vega$*, a series that ran from 1978 to 1981. In 1983, the *A-Team* encountered a powerful mob boss in an episode titled "The Rabbit Who Ate Las Vegas." Characters with organized crime connections also appeared in *The Strip* (1999–2000), *The Pretender* (2000), *CSI: Crime Scene Investigation* (2000–2012), and *Las Vegas* (2003–2008).

Novelists and screenwriters incorporated some actual mobsters into their accounts. In his 1958 novel *Chance Elson,* W. T. Ballard made a passing reference to the gambling "men who came in from California" like Guy McAfee, Farmer Page, and Tony Cornero.[105] James Ellroy populated his noir novels *American Tabloid* (1995) and *The Cold Six Thousand* (2001) with mobsters Sam Giancana, Carlos Marcello, Santos Trafficante, Johnny Rosselli, and Moe Dalitz, men who had Las Vegas connections. Meyer Lansky appeared frequently in Clark Howard's sprawling novel about Nevada entitled *Quick Silver* (1988). Sam Giancana also figured prominently in two HBO films, *Sugar Time* (1995) and *The Rat Pack* (1998). The former film explores his relationship with frequent Las Vegas performer Phyllis McGuire, and the latter dealt with his relationship with Frank Sinatra and the Rat Pack. The two films depict a violent, coarse hood who represented the Chicago outfit's interest in Las Vegas, his complicity in a CIA plot to assassinate Fidel Castro, and his willingness to help the presidential aspirations of John F. Kennedy by funneling money into the West Virginia primary and getting out the Chicago vote that was critical in Kennedy's win over Richard Nixon.

Bugsy Siegel, however, proved to be the favored mobster for authors and screenwriters as well as producers of Las Vegas documentaries. Between 1948 and 2005, there were thirteen novels, thirteen movies or television programs, and six documentaries featuring Siegel or men whose lives closely emulated his, men known variously as Mr. Didrick, Nick Prenta, Larry Mason, Martin Heidel, Benji Danzig, Joey Solomon, Yank Karkov, Junior Molov, Moe Greene, and Jacob King. Depictions of Siegel and Siegel-like characters fell into a predictable pattern. From the New York slums, Siegel became involved in gang activity from his childhood. He parlayed his success in bootlegging, protection, prostitution, bookmaking, and narcotics into a life of luxury living in the Waldorf Astoria, the exclusive New York City suburb of Scarsdale, and a mansion in Beverly Hills. Siegel emerges from the pages of novels and from the screen as a stylish, handsome, charming, soft-spoken ladies' man. He exuded a Hollywood flair and was popular with celebrities in the movie industry as well as the nightclub scene. This polite, generous, and affable gentleman, however, was easily angered. A tough, often vicious fighter, Siegel was a feared hit man, a key figure in Murder Incorporated, and was responsible for at least a dozen murders. He had been loyal, dependable soldier for the syndicate until inspired to build the fabulous Flamingo hotel and casino in Las Vegas. In a quest for legitimacy, Siegel betrayed his underworld bosses through his extravagance and died a martyr to his vision.[106]

As attractive and useful as the Siegel mythology has been to those crafting the city's connection to the mob, authors and screenwriters have created dozens of fictional gangsters who played crucial roles in the development of Las Vegas. These gangsters were most often Italian or Sicilian: Rick Menotti, Tommy Fracatti, Manny Perino, Cianni Christian, Vincent Petrocelli, Domenico Clericuzio, Nick "Fingers" Bonnatto, and Paul Mantilini are just a few examples. Regardless of their ethnicity, most were older, ugly, violent men. Al Sirago was an aging, fat, repulsive man given to beating, stabbing, or shooting anyone who gets in his way. Sam Talmadge looked "like a bilious green toad." Sam Makowsky was "paunchy" and "balding." Al Marta was "a stocky, powerful man with a sallow, fleshy face. He was almost exactly half bald."[107] Many were not very bright. In *Diamonds Are Forever,* author Ian Fleming, for example, has special agent James Bond dismissing the underworld figures in Las Vegas. "There's nothing so extraordinary about American gangsters," he explains. Indeed, "they're not Americans. Mostly a lot of Italian bums with monogrammed shirts who spend the day eating spaghetti and meat-balls and squirting scent over themselves." Novelist William Cox concurred. In *Murder in Vegas,* Cox has a character concluding, "The myth that all the rulers of the underworld organization are brilliant has been disproved a thousand times." "Very few of them have more than a high school background to begin with and are too busy stealing ever to learn anything after they are launched."[108] Yet not all were completely repellant figures. Tommy Fracatti "was like a photograph, a handsome man just over forty, faultlessly attired even when preparing for bed." Paul Mantilini was a handsome man with a "tanned, lined, rumpled, and smiling" face. While "the left side of it was cold and watchful, the cheek hard, the eye almost dead-looking; the right side, the side he showed us now, was bright and alive, alert and intelligent, almost friendly."[109] Don Michael Corleone in *Godfather II* likewise is a handsome, immaculately attired organized crime figure in Las Vegas.

Regardless of intellect or appearance, these fictional characters were almost always made men from the major crime centers like New York, Chicago, Detroit, Cleveland, and Miami. Al Marta, in John D. McDonald's *Only Girl in the Game* (1960), "had what is called a heavy record. Twenty-six arrests, three convictions." Morris Weiner "and his family," in Charles Fleming's *The Ivory Coast* (2002), "had worked around the edges of the law, running everything from numbers to gambling to girls." Manny Perino "had been in the same line of work all his adult life, starting out as a lowly soldier for the Organization on the East Coast. Using his innocuous appearance and a shrewd brain, he had worked his way up until he was now second in command to Tony Rinaldi in the Vegas operation."[110] Some were powerful men like Rick Menotti, "who succeeded Bugsy Siegel as the contact man for the Crime Syndicate in the West"; or Sam Makowsky, "former consul of an eastern murder syndicate"; or Vincent Margolia, a "big Mafia" man whose "father probably was responsible for starting the Mob in America"; or Steve Adriano, who "owned the Sahara-Sands" and "at least six other of the tourist traps." Indeed, "Las Vegas was mostly Steve Adriano."[111]

These fictional accounts drew heavily on the fundamental building blocks of journalists' story lines. Skims, fronts, and syndicates became predictable elements. Arthur Moore and Clayton Matthews stated it bluntly in their 1974 novel *Las Vegas:* "All Vegas spots skim."[112] Descriptions of count room skullduggery, secretive couriers with suitcases, claims of "pure profit," and happy hidden investors in Kansas City, Cleveland, Detroit, Chicago, New York, and Miami were all part of the a perfect scam. As aging mobster Tony Parisi explained about the old days in Gerald Petievich's 1988 novel *Shakedown,* "When we owned the casinos we didn't have to worry about collecting a little taste here and there. The countroom people, the casino managers, the pit bosses . . . we was all one big happy family. The biggest problem was finding somebody to drive the skim money back East every week."[113] Most of the fictitious hotel-casinos had a front man. Many, like Steve Walters in Jack Waer's *Murder in Las Vegas,* were Las Vegas residents with a clean record because "a local Vegas boy always makes a good front for a boss who lives elsewhere." Others were like Abe Berger in Ovid Demaris's *Candyleg,* who was "a former Cleveland beerlord in the old prohibition days and later a dope pusher" who "had miraculously blossomed out as the most popular impresario on the Vegas Strip." To state officials and his guests, he owned the fictitious Arabian Hotel, but to the real underworld owners, Berger "was strictly a stooge."[114] In many fictional accounts, the National Council, or the Combination, or the "St. Louis syndicate," or "Chicago and Miami syndicates," or "Murder, Incorporated, the Hudson Dusters, offshoots of the old Capone mob, the Milwaukee Mooncalves, the Mafia or Syndicate" controlled the Las Vegas casinos.[115]

The fictional versions of the mob–Las Vegas nexus and the wave of accounts in newspapers, magazines, and muckraking books thus were mutually reinforcing. Readers and viewers may not remember all or most of the names of the crime figures, but there was an unmistakable message in the thousands of accounts. The mob controlled Las Vegas at least through the 1980s, a conclusion reinforced by a host of documentaries about the city, presentations that offer an almost omniscient voice about the mob and Las Vegas, lending a clear sense of authority to the narrative. These one- to four-hour sagas all affirm the importance of the mob to the city's development. In 1996, the History Channel aired *The Real Las Vegas,* a comprehensive look at the neon oasis. In describing the rapid growth of Strip properties in the 1950s, it contended, "Most were financed by individuals from the various Eastern mob syndicates." That same year, an A&E production, *Vegas and the Mob,* frankly concluded, "The truth is, the mob built Las Vegas." A 2002 documentary titled *Las Vegas: The Money and the Power,* an adaptation of a book of the same name, argued, "For most of its modern history, Las Vegas has been dominated by an intimate circle of syndicate cronies who skimmed casinos, laundered money, and funneled the cash to bosses in cities across America." Two years later, a multipart documentary titled *La Cosa Nostra: The Mafia, An Expose,* quoted George Knapp, a veteran local investigative reporter, who explained that during "the heyday of the mob, the early to mid-'50s and into the mid-'60s, virtually every hotel on the Strip was owned by the mob, run by the mob." Finally, the 2005 PBS production *Las Vegas: An Unconventional History,* a program aired during the city's centennial, concluded, "In 1960, Las Vegas enjoyed a national reputation as America's unofficial mobster metropolis. No other place in America boasted such a rogue's gallery of city fathers."[116] Other documentaries offered similar interpretations of the link between Las Vegas and organized crime.

Other than the various film and fiction accounts of Bugsy Siegel, Mario Puzo and Martin Scorsese likely have had the most impact in conveying to the reading and viewing public the intimate connection between powerful organized crime families and the development of Las Vegas. Besides his novels *The Godfather* and *The Last Don,* Puzo cowrote the screenplays for the *Godfather* trilogy of films. Millions have read the novels and seen the movies and the television miniseries based on *The Last Don.* In *The Godfather,* the powerful Corleone family has been financing three hotels in Las Vegas in the 1950s. In a critical scene in the film, Michael Corleone explains that the family "is thinking of giving up all its interests in the olive oil business—settling out here." He is in Las Vegas to persuade Moe Greene, a man they have heavily financed, to sell to them his hotel-casino. When his brother, Fredo, contends that Moe will not sell, Michael responds with the classic line, "Well, I'll make him an offer he can't refuse." At the beginning of *Godfather II,* the Corleone family has gained control of two Las Vegas hotels and is about to take over the Tropicalla. This was all part of an effort of the dons of the Corleone family to become legitimate businessmen.[117]

While assuredly not unique, Puzo's story line reflects his fundamental belief about the importance of Las Vegas to organized crime families. In his 1976 book *Inside Las Vegas,* Puzo argued:

> Remember that many of the gambling entrepreneurs who started
> Vegas had violated their social contract. Because they broke the laws
> against gambling (and maybe a few others). As owners of illegal
> gambling operations they were outsiders in the worlds they lived in.
> But Vegas gave them their legal world. They could function finally as
> members of the social order. They could renew their social contract. It
> is no accident that they brought their families, that they settled in, that
> they became part of the community. For the first time in their lives
> they fulfilled their part in the contract that every human being must
> have with the society he lives in. Must, if he is to live what is called
> a normal life. Under the influence of these men Las Vegas became
> a more structured, lawful society despite the influx of gambling
> degenerates from all over the world. Schools sprang up. Universities
> expanded. Tourism exploded.[118]

This argument was also the foundation for his sprawling 1996 novel and 1998 miniseries *The Last Don.*[119] An aging Dominico Clericuzio, head of the nation's most powerful crime family, seeks to make the family more legitimate by moving into legal gambling in Las Vegas. After vanquishing a rival family, he takes their interest in the fabulous Xanadu Hotel in Las Vegas, leaving Alfred Gronevelt as the front for the operation. First his nephew and then grandnephew serve as the *bruglione,* or baron, for the family's interests in Las Vegas. Puzo's Las Vegas is a place of showgirls, casino bosses, murder, high rollers, gambling junkets, and huge gambling debts—a place where the family skillfully manipulates the hordes of players in their casino into losing fortunes that swell the Clericuzio coffers.

Although Mario Puzo had no direct contact with organized crime figures when he crafted his stories, director Martin Scorsese explained that he grew up "around many of these men, and most of them were very nice. They treated me and my family well, and they were attractive. I knew they were tough, and some were tougher than others." There is no mistaking the director's effort to create a sympathetic story about gangsters. "Very often," he explained, "the people I portray can't help but be in that way of life. They're bad and they're doing bad things. And we condemn those aspects of them. But they're also human beings." Indeed, in his films Scorsese wants "to push audiences' emotional empathy with certain types of characters who are normally considered villains."[120] In his successful and critically acclaimed 1995 film *Casino*, based on Nicholas Pileggi's book of the same name, Scorsese crafted a story that depicted Las Vegas as a place of redemption for underworld characters. The city represented the last opportunity for "street guys"; it offered them a "morality carwash," a chance to become legitimate businessmen. *Casino* is a tale of the skimming of the Stardust and the mob's control of the Teamsters' union. Character Andy Stone, the head of the union's pension fund, representing Allen Dorfman, acting on the mob's instructions, puts up the money for front man Philip Green, representing Allen Glick, to purchase the Tangiers Hotel Casino, which represents the Stardust, Fremont, Frontier, and Marina hotel-casinos. The film featured Ace Rothstein, representing Lefty Rosenthal, who "doubled the drop" of the Tangiers, a man who comped local and state politicians, managed the skim, had gambling cheats beaten, and failed to obtain a gaming license. When he becomes expendable, the mob tries to kill him with a car bomb. Nicky Santoro, representing Tony Spilotro, emerges as the protector and collector for the mob. His excesses, including too many murders, lead to his demise.[121] Reviewers almost universally judged the film to be an accurate depiction of the Las Vegas of the 1970s. Janet Maslin of the *New York Times* was typical in her praise: "It outlines the intricacies of casino cheating; the complex financial structure linking casino profits to mob bosses in Kansas City; the greased-palm etiquette ruling all Las Vegas, from it politicians to its valet parkers; the Federal investigation that had Ace and Nicky dodging surveillance planes, wiretaps and lip-readers, and even the blinding peculiarities of local fashion and interior décor."[122] Ultimately, the film argues that gangsters, through their greed, their overreaching, their too-easy resort to violence, lost their last, best chance at legitimacy and were overwhelmed by corporate America. The film ends with the implosion of their hotels, replaced by megaresorts that resemble Disneyland. The narrator concludes, "The town will never be the same."

This cinematic version of the mob's demise released in 1995 meshed with the dozens of documented investigations and arrests in the 1980s and led newspapers and periodicals, like *Time* magazine, to conclude that organized crime's hold on Las Vegas gambling truly was on the wane:

So the Mob controls several Las Vegas casinos. So the gangsters bought the gambling palaces with huge loans from Teamster pension funds, using front men to disguise the Mafia connection. So the crooks reaped vast untaxed profits by skimming millions in cash off the top of the gambling take. So? Hasn't all that been widely known for at least 20 years? It has. But proving it is something else. After years of only sporadic success, the FBI and the Justice Department finally may be shaking the Mob's grip on Las Vegas.[123]

This became the new narrative about organized crime and Las Vegas in the nation's media. "Though in the popular imagination Las Vegas is still associated with the Mafia," according to journalist Trip Gabriel in 1991, "it's been years since an organized-crime figure was hauled in on casino-related charges."[124] Those hoodlums not arrested had been pushed aside by corporate entities, according to the general story line. The Hilton Hotels and MGM quite simply had more money than organized crime figures. As Mayor Jan Jones explained on ABC's *This Week with David Brinkley* in 1994, "If you look at gaming corporations, they're some of the largest publicly traded companies in the country. This corporate America runs Las Vegas today."[125]

Despite an occasional muckraking article or book like Sally Denton and Roger Morris's *The Money and the Power* that reminded readers of the city's past link with organized crime, by the early twenty-first century, most readers of the print media found little evidence of the mob. In fact, some historians, in retrospect, became quite critical of the thousands of indictments printed in the post–World War II era about the hoodlum influence on the city. Las Vegas historian Michael Green has argued that "books and articles invariably oversimplified the mob's role in Las Vegas to make everyone involved look like cut-throat killers. They were the villains in a morality play that they hadn't written and couldn't change."[126] Wilbur Shepperson went further. "That organized crime actually existed and made substantial inroads into Nevada gambling cannot be denied," he has argued, "but that reality had little bearing on the intensity of the imagery used to describe it." Sharply critical of those writing about Las Vegas in the postwar period, Shepperson contended, "the narrative which unfolded in them . . . was so florid, so permeated with fraud, violence and corruption that their mood of malevolence carried them beyond the realm of objective reporting and entered the real of sensationalizing myth."[127]

The most ironic twist of the redemption of Las Vegas from the clutches of hoodlums was the successful run by Oscar Goodman, the mob's most effective lawyer in the 1970s and 1980s, for mayor of the city in 1999. Goodman's candidacy gained nationwide attention. *Time* magazine, for example, in its article about his campaign, noted, "He calls his swanky law office 'the house the Mob built.' Its walls are decorated with newspaper stories about acquittals he won for alleged organized crime figures."[128] Besides being a fascinating story for the nation's press, Goodman's candidacy challenged residents not only to ponder the meaning of having the mouthpiece of the mob running their community, but also their level of comfort in having their city perpetually linked in the popular mind with organized crime.

In virtually all the news accounts, journalists reminded readers that Goodman had represented men like Meyer Lansky, Tony Spilotro, Lefty Rosenthal, and Anthony Civella. Many also noted his portrayal of himself as a mob lawyer in the 1995 movie *Casino* as well as his appearance on *60 Minutes* in 1986 and in a British documentary called *Mob Law: A Portrait of Oscar Goodman* twelve years later. Journalists also found fascinating the great divide in Las Vegas over the prospects of having such a civic leader. A March 9, 1999, editorial in the *Las Vegas Review-Journal,* the city's largest-circulation paper, gained particular attention. Publisher Sherman Frederick called for "Anybody but Oscar." Because he had represented "some of the most notorious Mafia and criminal syndicate figures of the late 20th century," Frederick argued, "Oscar Goodman is the wrong man for mayor of Las Vegas." He would be "a PR catastrophe." Pat Shalmy, the president of the city's chamber of commerce, agreed, pointing out that "many people are concerned about what kind of image it would project to have a mayor who has represented the people Oscar's represented." Terry Lanni, the CEO of the massive MGM Grand hotel complex, joined in the chorus of condemnation, contending that Goodman was "too emblematic of the 'old' Las Vegas."[129] The city establishment's fundamental concern was the impact all this would have on tourism for a city that had spent so much money and effort in the 1990s selling itself as a place that was divorced from its notorious past—a place where tourists could safely bring their families.

On the other hand, journalists found a great deal of support not just for Goodman, but also for the proposition that Las Vegas should not shed its historic association with the underworld. A *Los Angeles Times* reporter found businessmen who believed Goodman's election would actually improve tourism. Small businessman Howard Bock, for example, argued that a Goodman victory would "redouble people's interest in coming here, because of the myth of the mob and Bugsy Siegel." Indeed, a poll of voters revealed that almost two-thirds believed Goodman's association with organized crime figures would "not hurt the city's image."[130] The voters evidently had accepted the Oscar Goodman maxim as explained by Connie Bruck in the *New Yorker:* "He preached a kind of communal self-acceptance: Las Vegas should not feel embarrassed about their Mob heritage but should embrace it, since it fascinates the world." As Goodman bluntly said, tourists coming to Las Vegas "don't want to see Mickey Mouse—they want to see Bugsy Siegel." The best measure of the power of Goodman's argument can be found in the election results. The man who represented the mob for so long captured 64 percent of the votes in 1999 and won two subsequent elections with even larger percentages of the votes.[131]

Once in office, Goodman capitalized on his background in promoting the city. In 2008, he reflected on his role in the ever-greater popularity of Las Vegas. He argued that his visible representation of "all the reputed mobsters here and elsewhere" contributed to the "mystique" of the city.[132] Don Payne, the longtime manager of the Las Vegas news bureau, agreed, pointing out in 2005 that he would like to have had "the money to hire some guy with a bent nose and a bulge" under his jacket and a "striped suit to stand at the airport because the aura of rubbing elbows with a Mafia person . . . was part of the mystique of Las Vegas."[133] By 2012, Las Vegas had truly embraced this underworld mystique noted by Goodman and Payne, as visitors could visit a city-financed Mob Museum downtown or the Mob Attraction Las Vegas at the Tropicana Hotel. These developments suggest the best way to understand how the city has come to terms with its mob past. Few would advocate a return to mob control of hotels (although some would prefer it to corporate ownership), but for many, the historical association of Las Vegas with organized crime gives the city an unmistakable promotional edge over other resort communities.

Images of Gambling in Las Vegas

Outside of fishing and an occasional movie gambling is the universal entertainment.

Los Angeles Times, 1939

Present-day Vegas gambling is the most honest that has ever existed. It is the best place for a gambler to get an even break.

Mario Puzo, 1976

She learned that losers in Vegas weren't beaten as much as they were pulverized. The mills of the casinos grind slow, but they grind relentlessly.

Ron Abell, 1985

I experienced the old familiar gambler's rush, a surge of adrenaline that cleared my mind and focused my concentration.

Brian Rouff, 2001

In 1976, celebrated novelist and screenwriter Mario Puzo published *Inside Las Vegas*, a paean to the world's best-known city of gamblers. Puzo acknowledged that he had "the reputation of being a degenerate gambler" and that gambling had done "a lot of harm" over time to many people. Yet he explained that his book represented an attempt to describe the benefits of gambling, arguing that it "makes life bearable for so many people and why even though you wind up a 'loser' in the long run, the short run 'wins' can make it worthwhile for all but the degenerate gambler." Known best for his acclaimed novel *The Godfather*, which depicts an organized crime family's effort to control much of Las Vegas gaming, Puzo sought to explain what he saw as the universal appeal of gambling. Arguing that the "urge to gamble has enthralled mankind through recorded time," Puzo claimed it "must fill some kind of human need." "Everyone regrets his loss of childhood," he wrote, "because then the world was pure and new. That is why so many people gamble. I think it is a desire to be happy in an innocent way." In childhood, one enjoyed "irresponsible happiness. And that's what gambling is to some degree." Puzo drew on his own experiences to explain the lure of gambling. "I got more pure happiness," he explained, "winning twenty grand at the casino crap table than when I received a check for many times that amount as the result of honest hard work on my book." He had given up high-stakes gambling—indeed, Puzo acknowledged that he had lost his love for gambling, but he might eventually "settle in Las Vegas" in his old age, for only there can one experience the essence of gambling. The magical lure might return, but even if it did not, Puzo anticipated a magical afterlife, a heaven not with "haloed angels riding snow-white clouds," but rather an exalted Las Vegas with "a vaulting red-walled casino with bright lights" and "horned devils as dealers. Let there be a Pit Boss in the Sky who will give me unlimited credit. And if there is a merciful God in our Universe he will decree that the Player have for *all* eternity, an Edge against the House."[1]

In the 1960 movie *Pepe*, the featured character portrayed by Mexican actor Cantinflas travels to Las Vegas to help a friend who is trying to finance a film. Pepe, an innocent farmhand, decides to try gambling to raise the money. Although he has only about three dollars in his piggy bank and his lucky bull's ear, Pepe begins his quest playing slot machines, blackjack, and roulette. He does not even know where to insert the money into a slot machine or how to pull the machine's handle. Fortunately, a character played by actor Cesar Romero is there to assist him, and Pepe wins $8,000 on the first pull. He then wins a few dollars in a game of cards with Jimmy Durante before finding Dean Martin for a quick game of blackjack, which he also wins while the chips he left on the roulette table keep winning. After a most remarkable run of success, Pepe, who had never gambled, has won over $250,000 from Durante, Martin, and Frank Sinatra.[2] In just a few hours, the unsophisticated Pepe has taken a small fortune from the smartest of the famed Rat Pack.

Irving Shulman published a novel in 1951 called *The Big Brokers*. In this sprawling story about organized crime's role in Las Vegas, Shulman included a scathing portrait of gamblers. First, the reader encounters "old women with deeply lined faces and stiff fingers" who "sat at the roulette tables and clutched old-fashioned purses in their laps as they played systems." Elderly, lonely, forlorn women desperate for a jackpot became a fixture in negative depictions of gamblers, particularly older women at slot machines. Yet there was more. Shulman described a host of exhausted and feckless gamblers: "Clustered at the tables, fatigued from the long hours of the day and night behind them, the players stood in the first hours after midnight on their complaining feet; seated on their protesting haunches, pushing their flagging bodies and forcing their bloodshot eyes to function, the gamblers made their last promised bets, but they had made this sad final promise hours before, and they were still in the casino." Shulman concluded with an indictment of all gamblers, people who simply did not understand that they were suckers. "If the players came out ahead it was only for a little time," he wrote, "for loss was as certain as death; neither could be avoided." Even when they won, they did not have the common sense to quit. "Never had he seen so much money being brought in willingly to be given away." Indeed, "for every winner there were ten losers."[3]

These conflicting images and depictions of gambling illustrate the ways most journalists, authors, and filmmakers have chosen to depict the gaming experience in Las Vegas. By turns, it appears as a benign, remarkably rewarding, even therapeutic activity, then as an irrational destructive behavior pattern. The absence of a consistent portrayal of gambling in Las Vegas gives the individual who has never been in the gambling center an ambiguous sense of the experience. Should they go, the experience, like the outcome of all gambling games, is unclear. The uncertainty adds to the edgy appeal of gambling in Las Vegas.

As more journalists visited Las Vegas in the late 1930s, they increasingly portrayed gambling, unlike their counterparts earlier in the decade, as an accepted, well-regulated, and honest leisure time activity. "Outside of fishing and an occasional movie," *Los Angeles Times* columnist Chapin Hall wrote, "gambling is the universal entertainment." He found that residents "drop in for a round of keno or to risk a two-bit piece on the erratic meanderings of the little ball, as nonchalantly as and with much the same idea that we, in our 'reformed' city, stop at the corner store for an ice cream soda."[4] Mildred Seydell, a columnist for the *Atlanta Georgian,* who had covered the Scopes trial and had interviewed Italian dictator Benito Mussolini, visited Las Vegas in early 1938.[5] Seydell explained that she had always considered a "gambling den" as a place of "iniquity," and to her, a gambler "was a man with a villainous face" and "black moustache long enough to twist." Yet when she dropped by "one of the most renowned" gambling halls in Las Vegas, Seydell discovered female keno players sitting at a table "exactly like those in the gathering of one of our missionary societies—kindly-faced women with no make-up, motherly-looking women, many with graying hair." There were also people enjoying roulette and poker in a remarkable atmosphere. "There was no one drinking or misbehavior; everyone was dignified, quietly—except for the calling of the numbers—enjoying themselves." Seydell concluded that "gambling in Las Vegas is considered no more wicked than a game of bridge in Georgia." Indeed, "In Las Vegas grandma instead of calling grandpa to meet her at the movies is likely to say, 'See you at 3:30 at the gambling joint.'"[6] Truly, according to several journalists, a visitor to Las Vegas could expect to find slot machines almost everywhere: "in the 5-and-10-cent stores, in the markets, groceries, oil stations, drive-ins and newsstands."[7] There was a sense of a genuinely orderly, unthreatening atmosphere to visiting journalist Hubbard Keavy in 1941. It appeared family friendly. Children could not play the games, but they could "accompany their elders into the halls of chance." The dealers at the table games, "unlike their brethren in the illegal emporiums of chance," were consistently courteous and "always agree with the customer."[8]

Those with moral qualms about gambling in Las Vegas need not worry. "There is a widespread notion among people who consider themselves nongamblers," *New York Times* journalist Gladwin Hill wrote in 1957, "that gambling is an aberration, a vice in the category of taking dope, indulged in by a minority of social deviates." Yet Las Vegas provided an opportunity where even the "nice" people could "indulge that secret flare for gambling with perfect impunity."[9] Although clergymen generally railed against gaming, some religious figures declined to condemn gambling when visiting Las Vegas. In 1931, popular Southern California evangelist Minnie "Ma" Kennedy, mother of the even more widely known crusader Aimee Semple McPherson, traveled to Las Vegas. With a police escort, "sirens screaming," Kennedy arrived at the Boulder Club and used a gambling table as her pulpit. In front of about 500 gamblers, Kennedy delivered "religion to the raw men of the desert." Yet in her short address, Kennedy offered a "message of love and hope" rather than a criticism of gambling.[10] Over four decades later, Reverend Billy Graham brought his crusade to Las Vegas. The popular evangelist characterized Las Vegas as "a nice place to visit" and certainly surprised many by telling reporters, "Probably the greatest center of gambling in the United States is Wall Street. I would not condemn Wall Street, and I did not come here to condemn gambling." Although he noted that he would not play a slot machine, for that might set a bad example, Graham explained that the Bible did not specifically address gambling, and hence it may not be a sin. From his pulpit at the convention center, Graham declared, much like Ma Kennedy in 1931, that he had come to Las Vegas to "preach the gospel of salvation," not "to condemn" the community.[11] Gambling even gained an endorsement in some academic circles. In 1976, *Time* magazine cited the work of Felicia Campbell, a professor of English at the University of Nevada at Las Vegas, whose Ph.D. dissertation was on gambling. Campbell argued that gambling could be a positive, even therapeutic, activity for most adults, whether they were professionals, elderly, or working class. "Even though the final result is often negative," Campbell argued, "it's a positive impulse. The peak experience is almost more important than winning. When he grabs the dice, the blue-collar worker is in control of his destiny."[12]

Besides the patina of legitimacy such statements provided for gambling in Las Vegas, many commentators in the 1930s and 1940s noted that the city regulated the games of chance, thus ensuring their honesty. Before evidence of the influence of organized crime in Las Vegas, journalists like Chapin Hall argued that the gambling halls were legitimate entertainment venues. Indeed, Hall explained that the men who ran the casinos and gambling clubs were "mostly, longtime residents." Because of that, gamblers could expect games "on the level" and "transactions conducted on as orderly a basis as those occurring in any mercantile store."[13] In his article in *Collier's* in 1942, Richard English agreed. He wrote that the casino proprietors were "some of Las Vegas' most respected citizens." For example, the man running the Jackpot was state legislator Jerry Thompson, and the "the owner of the Boulder Club" was a man "in his seventies whom no one would ever dream of calling anything but 'Mister.'"[14] Several who followed Hall and English emphasized that gambling in Las Vegas was "on the up-and-up," "honest," and "entirely on the square." As novelist Frank Gruber explained, "the percentages are enough for the house," or as the *Chicago Daily Tribune* put it more definitively, the honesty of the games "is guaranteed by the ever alert state inspectors and by the games proprietors themselves, who wouldn't take a chance of jeopardizing their tremendous investments."[15] To be sure, when the *Tribune* made such a bold assertion, there was increasing evidence of organized crime's influence in Las Vegas, but journalist and author of several "Inside" books on various global locales John Gunther addressed that apparent contradiction in 1956. "The hotels may be full of shady money," Gunther wrote, "but the games are straight."[16] Mario Puzo, whose enthusiasm for Las Vegas exceeded that of the chamber of commerce, wrote that his review of gambling history persuaded him "that present-day Vegas gambling is the most honest that has ever existed. It is the best place for a gambler to get an even break."[17]

National polls reflected this growing acceptance of gambling. A Gallup Poll revealed that 53 percent of Americans gambled in 1937, mostly in church lotteries. That figure remained fairly constant until the 1970s, when the National Gambling Commission found a new plateau: "Nearly two-thirds of the American people make wagers of one kind or another."[18] Although most Americans continued to oppose casino gambling in their state well into the 1970s, polls from the 1950s revealed that a majority no longer considered it immoral. Typical was a 1990 *Minneapolis Star-Tribune* poll, which found that nearly 60 percent agreed that "gambling is just another form of entertainment, no better or no worse than going to a movie or any other entertainment that costs money."[19] Drawing on the evidence from these polls, Wade Goodwin, on National Public Radio in 1999, concluded that most Americans "look upon the gaming industry as a mostly benign pastime, that people should be able to spend their time and money as they choose."[20]

To many observers, another measure of the acceptance of gambling in Las Vegas was the egalitarian quality of the crowds in the casinos and gambling clubs, whose doors were "open to every passerby."[21] Frank Gruber, in his 1939 novel *The French Key*, describes a casino with Boulder Dam workers, ranchers, people "in evening dress from Hollywood," and a "desert rat or two," and playing blackjack was "a middle-aged woman who would have been more at home in an Iowa Tuesday Ladies' Bridge" club.[22] The Works Projects Administration 1940 guide to Nevada noted that casinos attracted "Hollywood celebrities, miners, prospectors, divorcees, corporation presidents, cowboys, and little old maids bent on seeing life at last."[23] Erle Stanley Gardner, writing as A. A. Fair, included "professional gamblers, panhandlers, touts, and some of the higher-class girls from the red-light district" along with tourists in the casinos of his novel *Spill the Jackpot*. A journalist in 1941 wrote that one is likely to find "a be-diamonded divorcee, a greasy, sweaty truck driver, a Japanese just in from a nearby mine, and a Mexican woman in black mantilla," all at the same table.[24] This democratic element of Las Vegas gambling, the opening of casino doors "to all classes and both sexes," was clear to virtually all observers in the 1930s and early 1940s.[25]

While most journalists and novelists continued to portray gamblers in this egalitarian trend, the fashionable mixing with the humble, the merchant prince standing alongside the cowboy, most movies in the 1940s and 1950s depicted a more elegant crowd.[26] *Las Vegas Nights, Flying Blind, Moon over Las Vegas, Flight to Nowhere, Lady Luck, The Invisible Wall, My Dear Secretary,*

Egalitarian male gambling crowd at the Northern Club in 1935. Source: UNLV Libraries, Special Collections.

Once More My Darling, The Lady Gambles, Las Vegas Story, Las Vegas Shakedown, and *The Girl Rush* all feature patrons mostly well dressed, often men in tuxedos and ladies in evening gowns. The peak of elegance came with the release of *Ocean's Eleven* in 1960, when the gamblers at the Sands, Flamingo, Desert Inn, Riviera, and Sahara were dressed for a fashionable New Year's Eve celebration.[27] Some television images also contributed to this theme of exclusivity. A 1951 episode of the series *Racket Squad* took place in Las Vegas, where the narrator explained that the resort city was a pretentious place: "None of that wild and wooly stuff here. It's a nice spot for those who can afford plush living." The two different casino scenes in the program feature only wealthy patrons.[28] Similarly, an episode of the 1954 comedy series *Topper* depicted only wealthy gamblers, as did a 1960 episode of *The Twilight Zone*.[29] These images of a clientele of high rollers diminished over time in film and on television. Increasingly, the image of Las Vegas casinos returned to the more democratic atmosphere described in 1930s and early 1940s newspapers and magazines. Most television programs about Las Vegas after 1960 included the casually dressed as well as the well dressed in casinos. Episodes of programs as various as *I Spy, The A-Team, Remington Steele, CSI: Crime Scene Investigation,* and *Las Vegas* included middle-class as well as high-roller gamblers.[30]

Fashionably dressed roulette players, Sands Casino, ca. 1960. Note that all the players here are not only elegantly dressed, but they are all women. Source: UNLV Libraries, Special Collections.

There were always exceptions, as in the 1964 episode of the series *Arrest and Trial* entitled "A Role of the Dice," which featured very wealthy, well-dressed men and women, many of the latter in mink coats, gambling at the Dunes.[31] Still, the sense of exclusivity portrayed in the 1950s was gone. Likewise, most filmmakers portrayed visitors to Las Vegas casinos as mainstream Americans. Viewing films like *Viva Las Vegas, Diamonds Are Forever, Rafferty and the Gold Dust Twins, The Electric Horseman, Going in Style, The Vegas Casino War, Rain Man, Honeymoon in Vegas, Casino, Vegas Vacation, Ocean's Eleven,* and *The Cooler,* one saw the gamut of the poorest to the most fashionable, old and young, men and women, black and white.[32] The message from television and films from 1960 was clear. Las Vegas gambling was for everyone.

Accentuating that tantalizing point was the proclivity for tourists in movies and television to win jackpots. As with the 1960 film *Pepe,* arrivals in Las Vegas win jackpots so often that the viewer has an expectation that anyone can win, from the novice to the expert. Indeed, gambling in Las Vegas represents one of the few times in life when a neophyte has a chance to trump an expert. Some of the biggest laughs come from ludicrous situations in which characters who know absolutely nothing about gambling win very large jackpots. In the 1956 film *Hollywood or Bust,* the main character, played by comic Jerry Lewis, who has not gambled, develops a tingle in his fingers and a twitch in his right eye. His arm starts jerking, and he heads to a slot machine with a quarter, proclaiming, "I got it!" On the first play on the machine, Lewis hits a jackpot, then moves to the craps table. Although he does not understand the game, Lewis simply feels it, and despite not even knowing where he must toss the dice, wins over $9,000 on a 30–1 roll of the dice.[33] Rusty Griswold's character, in the 1997 movie *Vegas Vacation,* has an even more incredible run of luck. Too young to gamble, he purchases a fake identification card and becomes Nick Pappagiorgio. He wins a car on his first play on a slot machine and then wins big at craps even though, like Jerry Lewis, he is clueless about the game. Because of his big win, the management at the Mirage Hotel comps Rusty a gorgeous suite. He later wins three more cars, all on his first play on a slot machine.[34]

Spectacular wins almost always happen for sympathetic characters. In both the musical comedies *Las Vegas Nights* and *Meet Me in Las Vegas,* there is an essentially good man who happens to like to gamble, but he is not particularly good at it. Bill Stevens in *Las Vegas Nights* kisses a girl for good luck, and then the two of them proceed to hit all the casinos in Las Vegas, winning at whatever game they play. Similarly, in *Meet Me in Las Vegas,* Chuck Rodwell, who loses all his money at the Sands Hotel every year, seeks to hold a woman's hand as a way finally to win. When he holds the hand of dancer Marie Corvier, he wins at casinos up and down the Strip.[35] *Las Vegas Shakedown* included a story line about Mr. and Mrs. Ernest Raff, an elderly banker and his wife from Northpoint, Nebraska, a straightlaced small town. Raff has lived a model life as a community leader, and he and his wife have given a small fortune to charity and set up trust funds for their children and grandchildren. He simply thought it would "be a great kick to be reckless once in my life." Even though he has never gambled, Raff simply studied the players at the craps table and took notes, drew on his facility in mathematics, and won consistently. Before he started rolling the dice, one of the veteran players mumbles, "Never saw an amateur yet that ever won." Yet because of his background, it is a given that this sympathetic character will win. Indeed, Raff wins $15,000 at craps.[36]

Jeff Bridges portrays a peaceful alien in the 1984 film *Starman.* To return to his home planet, he must reach Winslow, Arizona, to be picked up by his mother ship. He and Jenny Hayden, who has befriended him, reach Las Vegas but have almost no money. Making matters worse, federal officials are pursuing the alien, eager to dissect the security risk. Hayden has only 30 cents, but the alien takes the quarter, places it in a slot machine, and when it does not win anything, he simply touches the machine to get a small jackpot. He takes that money, proceeds to a dollar machine, and immediately wins $500,000, enabling them to buy a car and make it to the rendezvous point in time.[37] Jackie and Dawn, two English friends, fly to Las Vegas after Dawn learns that she has a terminal cancer in *Girls' Night*. Immediately upon their arrival at the Riviera Hotel, Dawn puts a dollar in a large slot machine, pulls the handle, and hits a jackpot of $1,000 on the first pull amid the banging sounds of the gigantic machine.[38]

One of the most popular of these examples of unexpected players winning big money came in the 1988 film *Rain Man*. Raymond Babbitt, portrayed by Dustin Hoffman, is an autistic savant, and his brother, portrayed by Tom Cruise, uses Raymond's extraordinary talent for memorizing to count cards in blackjack. Playing at Caesars Palace, Raymond wins $86,000 even though the security men say "no one in the world can count into a six-deck shoe." "Ah, the satisfaction," *New York Times* movie reviewer Walter Goodman wrote, "in watching Mr. Hoffman predict the cards that will be coming up in blackjack and Mr. Cruise raising his bets accordingly and shoveling in the chips. They are outfoxing the fixers. If one of the injunctions of entertainment is to satisfy the imagination's cravings, that scene from 'Rain Man' is the real unreal thing and a casino the natural unnatural setting."[39]

In 1979, George Burns, Art Carney, and Lee Strasberg portrayed three retired friends living in a small apartment on Long Island. The three men in *Going in Style* struggle with loss, loneliness, and regrets over mistaken opportunities in their lives, as well as small Social Security checks. They spend their days sitting on a park bench, bored and feeling obsolete. As the character, Joe, portrayed by George Burns, puts it, "I'm sick of this shit." They decide to rob a bank for the money, but also to break up the boredom. The heist is successful, but Willie, the character portrayed by Lee Strasberg, dies from a heart attack. Joe and Al, portrayed by Art Carney, after giving most of the money to Al's nephew, fly to Las Vegas to try their luck at the tables. Joe remembered how to play craps from his days in World War I, but Al has never played. He doesn't even know what to do with the dice. Still, the two of them win over $73,000 in just two sessions at the craps table. Director Martin Brest portrays them as laudable characters even though they robbed a bank. After all, no one got hurt, the bank had insurance, and they end up giving virtually all the money away to family. Indeed, after their big win, the two men, rather than having a spectacular feast and going to a show, have a simple meal of jelly and cream cheese sandwiches and then head to the airport to return home. As with Ernest Raff in *Las Vegas Shakedown,* they simply got to be reckless once in their lives.[40]

The hope of hitting a jackpot assuredly was one of the enticements of Las Vegas gambling, but journalists, authors, and filmmakers offered a plethora of other enticements. One thing is clear: a roll of the dice, a pull of the slot machine handle, a spin of the wheel, or a flip of the cards at blackjack were lures almost none could resist. John Gunther, when researching his article for the *Washington Post,* found that among 1955 visitors to Las Vegas, 85 percent gambled even though 65 percent of that group "had never gambled before except for a friendly game of bridge or poker."[41] For some of those folks, gambling represented a tantalizing walk on the wild side, particularly "the timid kind from Dubuque and Kalamazoo, to whom a fast whirl at roulette is just a teeny bit wicked."[42] Lucius Beebe, magazine writer, railroad historian, and publisher of Nevada's *Territorial Enterprise,* argued that the fascination with Las Vegas gambling was part of "the national dream of something for nothing," and Katharine Best and Katharine Hillyer believed it was the hope of "making a killing" that provided the draw.[43]

The challenge of beating the house odds, or a heightened sense of anticipation of a good outcome, or the excitement of the play, or a feeling of relaxation, or, most simply, the fun of it all prompted many to gamble in Las Vegas. "Why, then, do myriads of people flock to the casinos?" John Gunther asked in 1956. They believe "they can beat the game. And some do."[44] Some took it quite seriously; it became a war for them. As novelist Arlo Sederberg contended, the casino was "their battleground, their test."[45] In "A Role of the Dice," an episode of the television series *Arrest and Trial,* a character named Ronald Blake, portrayed by Nick Adams, explains it simply to his girlfriend: "You know what the biggest thrill in the world is?" he asked her. "To beat the odds." The victory over the house was "pure religion."[46] Detective Harry Bosch, in Michael Connelly's *Trunk Music,* contended that he had no interest in gambling, but the gamblers he knew had explained that "it wasn't the winning and losing, it was the anticipation. Whether it was the next card, the fall of the dice or the number the little ball stopped on, it was those few seconds of waiting and hoping and wishing that charged them."[47]

The sheer excitement of the games, the gambler's rush, most often explained the appeal of Las Vegas gambling. In the novel *Shooter's Point,* author Gary Phillips has his character, Martha Chainey, concluding that Las Vegas and the gambling it offered were "the best drug there was. It consumed all your money, but the rush was instantaneous, and it occasionally kicked back a little."[48] Tourists arriving in Las Vegas in a 2001 documentary explained the lure similarly: "I love to gamble because it gives you a high. It's like a runner's high."[49] Brian Rouff, in his novel *Dice Angel*, has a character explain the effect of sitting down at a blackjack table and watching the dealer delivering the cards: "I experienced the old familiar gambler's rush, a surge of adrenaline that cleared my mind and focused my concentration."[50]

Authors and journalists offered a multitude of other explanations for people scrambling to play the machine and table games as soon as they arrived in Las Vegas. Irish author Sean O'Faolain, in *Holiday* magazine, suggested, "Gambling, like love, is a passion that grows by what it feeds on." Novelist Robert Nathan has a character who says, "A man gambles because of a feeling he has inside. It's a sociable feeling; when you win you feel like a success. Nobody is alone in the world when he is gambling."[51] For others, it was a welcome change from the ordinary. In the movie *Meet Me in Las Vegas,* Chuck Rodwell explains, "I like gambling. It is hard to explain. There are rules and there are so many rules about everything. It leaves out all the surprises."[52] Gary Phillips, in *High Hand,* argued it was a welcome relief from an often dismal life: "It got you out of the house and was a diversion from that sucker job you had to go to to feed your ungrateful kids every day till they laid you out in your best duds, arms folded over your chest."[53] Gambling was, in essence, a temporary escape from routine, regulated, predictable, and unrewarding lives.

Some of the descriptions and images of Las Vegas gambling, however, smack of keen elitism, dismissive of the behavior, intelligence, morality, and even the dress of the gambler. These negative views portray the gamblers in Sin City as sad, poorly educated fools. Thomas A. Nixon and his wife, of Greeley, Colorado, visited Las Vegas in 1932. On their return home, the local newspaper published a front-page account of their trip. The Nixons dropped by some of the "gambling saloons" and were particularly taken by a keno game where they saw over 100 players. They noted that "most of the patrons at the gaming tables could ill afford to play."[54] In his mystery novel *Void Moon,* Michael Connelly has his character, Cassie Black, walk into a fictitious hotel-casino named the Cleopatra. Once past the casino entry, Black sees a wall with photos of the winning slot machine players. "Cassie noticed that many of the winners posed in front of their winning machines were smiling in a way that suggested they were hiding missing teeth. She wondered how many of the winners used the money to see a dentist and how many dumped it right back into the machines."[55]

To the critics of Las Vegas gamblers, they were not only poor, but also stupid. For some novelists, the slot players drew their censure. In *The Per-fect Play,* Louise Wener has a character check into the Luxor Hotel; she then promptly gets lost in the casino on her way from the registration desk to the elevators. The character is struck by "the shrill notes of two thousand clang-ing slots." More arresting, however, is the spectacle of all the pathetic, almost infantile people playing the machines:

> Gangs of people are plugged into them like saline drips—buckets of quarters bleeding into the machines. Some of them play in groups; crossing themselves before they press the button, and holding hands while they wait for the wheels to stop. Some of them are still and silent like they've been hypnotized, and others are chattering all the time. They sigh and growl and curse when they lose, and shriek like hyperactive children when they win.[56]

Other novelists focused on foolish roulette players. John Goodger's *Druper-man Tapes* has a cynical roulette dealer characterizing the people who come to his wheel. "Even after a decade behind the wheel," the dealer "still mar-veled at the incredible stupidity of roulette players. Long-term, none of them had a prayer of winning; their only hope was to get lucky fast and get out." Some of the players, not understanding the house advantage or the random outcomes of the spinning of the wheel, tried to come up with systems to predict wins. "For the dealer," Goodger wrote, "the most galling aspect of the whole charade was having to humor his players—to congratulate them on their wins, to sympathize with them on their losses, to gravely nod his head while they spewed their moronic theories."[57]

One of the most common refrains was the charge that people were simply throwing their money away. To critics like Julian Halevy in *Nation* maga-zine, "the sight of thousands of people shedding their financial inhibitions and traditional respect for money is somewhat startling."[58] Indeed, they were suckers. Four examples illustrate. In his novel *A Short Bier,* Frank Kane has his character, Johnny Liddell, drop into the fictitious Desert Oasis casino, which "was filled with chattering tourists hoping loudly that they wouldn't lose more than they could afford." As Liddell walked through the crowd, he smiled condescendingly, wondering "if the hicks knew how high the stakes really were." In Ron Abell's *Tap City,* Shayna Levinson goes to a dealers' school, where she quickly learned a valuable lesson. Not only were all the games "strictly for suckers," but she also comes to understand "how merci-less the house percentage really was. She learned that losers in Vegas weren't beaten as much as they were pulverized. The mills of the casinos grind slow, but they grind relentlessly." Gerald Petievich, in his novel *Shakedown,* has mob boss Tony Parisi sit down to watch gamblers: "He gazed down the enormous, high-ceilinged, plushly carpeted room full of losers, turkeys, cornball Okies, dumb farmers, cripples, tourists, and working stiffs from L.A. who were getting a charge out of pissing away their bucks."[59] Or, as Robert De Niro, as casino manager Ace Rothstein, emphatically explained in *Casino,* "The end of all the bright lights, of all the champagne, and all the broads, and all the booze. It's all been arranged just for us to get your money. That's the truth about Las Vegas. We're the only winners."[60]

Ian Fleming, who created the famed sophisticated agent James Bond, visited Las Vegas in the mid-1950s and poured his contempt for the place and the people drawn to it into his novel *Diamonds Are Forever.* Fleming has Bond concluding "that Las Vegas seemed to have invented a new school of functional architecture, 'The Gilded Mousetrap School' he thought it might be called, whose main purpose was to channel the customer-mouse into the central gambling trap whether he wanted the cheese or not." To reach the restaurants or shows, one had to pass "between the banks of slot machines and gambling tables." "It was," Fleming contended, "an inelegant trap, obvious and vulgar, and the noise of the machines had a horrible mechanical ugliness which beat at the brain."[61] The cruelest exposition was that of sports columnist Red Smith, who in 1960 was unmerciful: "What flabbergasts the visitor, and would even daze Phineas T. Barnum, is the incredible abundance of suckers, the limitless, inexhaustible flow of raw material that pours through Nevada's gigantic cream separators twenty-four hours a day."[62]

To most critics, the greatest indictment of Las Vegas gambling was the impact it had on the behavior of the players. Some sought answers in the social sciences. In a ten-part series on Las Vegas in 1963 for the *Denver Post,* Bob Whearley related a conversation between a patron at the Desert Inn and one of the hotel's executives. The woman asked, "What psychological motivations compel people to throw away their money when they know perfectly well the odds are against them?" Whearley sought to provide an answer for his readers. "Weighty tomes," he told his readers, "have been written about the psychology of gamblers and gambling." He chose only to draw on the work of cultural anthropologist Charlotte Olmstead, whom Whearley claimed "attaches a phallic symbolism to the lever of a slot machine." Moreover, with roulette, "Miss Olmstead observes, 'the fact that the ball always finds a slot may have a particular appeal to the socially isolated player with a poor sense of identity.'"[63] Novelist William Pearson also weighed in on the question.

"Gambling," he contended, "attracts those who are psychologically unable to cope with uncertainty. They turn to gambling because winning or losing is an instantaneous event. They prefer the immediate, even if the immediate is failure, to delay or ambiguity in an outcome."[64]

In some accounts, gambling turns out to be a joyless experience for most. "The sound of the casinos," Norma Lee Browning wrote in the *Chicago Daily Tribune* in 1962, "is a muted, funeral clatter. The faces that swarm above the gambling tables have an unsmiling life-or-death look." Novelists, too, noted this grim pursuit of gambling success. "Most of the people who played the machines," popular talk show host and prolific author Steve Allen wrote in his mystery *Murder in Vegas*, "seemed to win and lose without any apparent change of expression, as though they had taken a bus to Vegas from the land of the living dead, to which they would return once the weekend was over." Ovid Demaris, in *Candyleg*, likewise found that watching people gamble looked "like a mass wake."[65] In his mystery *Ringers*, Tim Underwood vividly described the remarkably rapid transformation of tourists after twelve hours of gambling: "Last night they had felt youthful, on the verge of adventure. Now they were older, on the brink of defeat. The cocoon of the casino made the metamorphosis regressive, turning from a colorful, soaring butterfly to a more basic creature groveling along the ground."[66] Critic Al Alvarez, in his widely read 1983 study of poker in Las Vegas, offered a depressing picture of the desperate people along Fremont Street downtown:

> Old women in lime green or banana yellow or Florida orange pants suits, clutching Dixie cups of small change in one hand, the lever of one of one of Vegas's fifty thousand slot machines in the other; old men with plastic teeth and sky blue plastic suits shooting craps for a dollar, playing fifty-cent blackjack and three-dollar-limit stud poker; wrecks in wheelchairs or with walking frames, the humped, the bent, the skeleton thin, and the obese, cashing in their Social Security checks, disability allowances, and pensions, waiting out their time in the hope of a miracle jackpot to transform their last pinched days.[67]

Novelist Michael Ventura offered the grimmest assessment of the impact of gambling on people, particularly those that played the slot machines for hours on end:

> the slots were the tombstones, and at nearly every one sat an old
> ghost in cheap rags, moving mechanically, inserting coins, pulling

the handle or hitting the button, each with the same expression, an expression that was no expression at all, each gray wrinkled face a flag of disappointment, each nickel spent for a dream that didn't matter to them anymore.[68]

Occasionally, writers, rather than praising or condemning gambling, look for a larger meaning to its popularity in Las Vegas. They find something profound about themselves in the arena of a gambling casino. "Vegas lives," cultural critic Dave Hickey wrote, "in those fluttery moments of faint but rising hope, in the possibility of wonder, in the swell of desire while the dice are still bouncing, just before the card flips face-up. And win or lose, you always have that instant of genuine *justifiable* hope. It is always there."[69] Poet Diane Wakoski offers a variation on that theme. "I don't know if I can ever explain to non-gamblers the beauty I see in Las Vegas or why gambling attracts me as much as art, serious books, music or film," she wrote in a 1995 book of poems entitled *The Emerald City of Las Vegas*. In this introspective passage, she searches for the real draw of the experience and in so doing captures the ambiguity inherent in the games of risk:

> I do know that I am intrigued by the image of democracy that I see
> in gambling, where everyone has an equal chance to win and only
> a mysterious thing called "luck" seems to take away that equality. I
> continue to try to explain to everyone that I am calmed and reassured
> by gambling, being someone who seldom wins. I need to convince
> myself that in my life I haven't failed because I was stupid or because
> I was a bad person; I have failed because I played the game and lost.
> Thus, unlike most people, I gamble as much to have the experience
> of losing—though I certainly don't like losing—as to have the
> pleasure of winning. When I lose, I feel as if my life wasn't all some
> large, terrible set of mistakes that I made. That what happened to
> me was simply the luck of the draw. Is this a way of renouncing
> responsibility?[70]

Wakoski's remarks identify what some commentators and visitors find most intriguing about gambling in Las Vegas. They are not entirely sure why it draws them and so many others, and that is part of the allure. To be sure, most Americans have long understood that should they venture a visit to Las Vegas, they would find "gambling galore."[71] Those who gained their knowledge about gambling in Sin City from film, television, novels, or newspapers and magazines would have found a fairly consistent argument for going. The Las Vegas gambling experience would be open to virtually all; if you had cash, you were welcome. They could rest assured that no one needed to feel guilty in going to Las Vegas because in doing so, they would simply be acting on an inherent human passion for games of chance. Moreover, a few prospective visitors likely assumed that they would be one of the lucky ones for whom a big jackpot would be awaiting upon their arrival. Stories of suckers being fleeced by the casinos may have given them some pause, but most of the images of gambling in Las Vegas in popular culture would have offered them a tantalizing prospect. Joining in the games of chance, visitors would find excitement, perhaps even the intoxicating gambler's rush, but more important, they would find a temporary release from everyday cares. Ultimately, though, the message from film and the printed page is quite simple. One can see it most clearly in an insightful article by longtime Las Vegas watcher Gladwin Hill in the *New York Times*. In summer 1957, Hill decided to walk through the casinos and "buttonhole people at random" and ask a straightforward question: "Why do you gamble?" He reported that the "almost unvarying response" to his question was "for the fun of it." Therein lay the fundamental appeal. Visitors hoped they would win, but for most, it was the excitement of the moment, the challenge of the game, and the joy of the play.[72]

The Entertainment
Capital of the World

*Las Vegas is close to Hollywood and is heavily patronized by men and
women who earn tremendous salaries in the movies, in radio and in
the night clubs.*

Charleston Gazette, 1947

*Las Vegas resorts offer the most lavish night club entertainment at the
highest prices ever paid performers.*

Chicago Daily Tribune, 1955

The live entertainment capital of the world.

Los Angeles Times, 1965

*Every top name in the business can be seen in Las Vegas sometime or
other throughout the year.*

Oakland Tribune, 1972

Gambling will always tantalize the Las Vegas tourist, but in the years after
World War II, the possibilities of enjoying some of the world's finest entertainers became an ever-greater lure. Newspapers, magazines, television specials, and novels about Las Vegas invariably dealt with the entertainment
scene along the Las Vegas Strip. A newspaper article in 1954 was typical in
reporting, "Las Vegas is being ballyhooed today as 'the world's entertainment capital' as well as the No. 1 gambling spot of the U.S.A."[1] The nature
of entertainment changed over the decades. Initially, headliners, usually a
popular singer or top comedian, ruled, but there were too few of them to
fill all the showrooms. Over time, lounge acts, production shows, Broadway

plays, magicians, and impressionists became part of the entertainment mix. Among the thousands of acts that have performed in Las Vegas, a few stand out, both because of their remarkable popularity and their contributions to the image of the city as the nation's premier entertainment center. Regardless of wherever else they performed, Liberace, Louis Prima, Keely Smith, Wayne Newton, Elvis Presley, and Frank Sinatra are most identified with Las Vegas, a city where visitors expect the entertainers to be in turns flashy, loud, cool, and memorable performers who provide the audience with a remarkable escape. These six performers, between 1944 and the turn of the twenty-first century, best defined a Las Vegas style of entertainment often emulated elsewhere. They brought glamour, glitz, high spirits, great energy, often extravagant costumes, and, most important, an uncommon rapport with their adoring audiences.

When they opened the Meadows in May 1931, Frank and Louis Cornero promised to offer fine entertainment in their cabaret just outside Las Vegas on the Boulder Highway. They retained Jack Laughlin, a seasoned producer of Broadway hits like *No, No, Nanette,* to produce the *Meadows Revue.* On opening night, according to the *Las Vegas Review-Journal,* "Jack Liddell and his band, known as the 'Meadow Larks,' began its music and from then on until nearly dawn the casino was a riot of jazz." Over 5,000 locals and Southern Californians attended the stylish black-tie affair.[2] The Corneros hoped to attract the Los Angeles party crowd with exciting nightclub entertainment and booked performers like the Gumm Sisters, including nine-year-old Frances Ethel, later known to the world as Judy Garland. Though not as elegant as the Meadows, several other nightclubs opened, "with show girls from Los Angeles," in anticipation of business from the construction workers at Boulder Dam.[3] However, a Labor Day fire gutted the hotel portion of the Meadows, and the Corneros sold out in 1932. With their departure, there were few other efforts in the 1930s to promote entertainment as a lure for tourists, although some newspapers continued to report that there was an active nightlife, featuring jazz bands, to accompany the wide-open gambling available in Las Vegas.[4]

The 1930s and 1940s were the heyday of swanky nightlife in America. Estimates suggested that there were over 60,000 nightclubs across the country, with over 1,200 in New York City alone.[5] The Chez Paree in Chicago, the 500 Club in Atlantic City, the Riviera in Fort Lee, New Jersey, the Bal Tabarin in San Francisco, and Ciro's, Mocambo, the Trocadero, the Clover Club, and the Florentine Gardens in Los Angeles all gained national attention, but the true center of nightclub action was in New York City. Amid rowdy and fly-by-night clubs, there were several high-class resorts like the Stork Club, El Morocco, Colony 21, Casa Manana, the Diamond Horseshoe, Cotton Club, Rainbow Room, Casino de Paree, French Casino, International Casino, the Latin Quarter, and the Copacabana. Some catered to an exclusive clientele, but the trend was to appeal to a broad middle-class audience. The successful clubs dropped their cover charges and offered inexpensive meals and alcohol with plenty of entertainment. Most featured a supper show followed by late-night and early morning encores. Typically, there were crooners and torch singers supported by comics, specialty acts, and beautiful chorus lines. The top swing orchestras—led by Paul Whiteman, Guy Lombardo, Benny Goodman, and Xavier Cugat—played the nightclubs, as did headliners like Joe E. Lewis, Jimmy Durante, Jack Benny, Martha Raye, Frank Sinatra, Betty Hutton, Rudy Valle, Helen Morgan, Milton Berle, Louis Armstrong, the Ritz Brothers, and Louis Prima.[6] They appealed to a public eager for escape and edgy entertainment; as *Life* magazine more simply explained, they existed "on human beings' propensity for crowding into small, noisy rooms and enjoying one another's more or less alcoholic company."[7]

With the opening of the El Rancho Vegas in April 1941, Las Vegas finally had an opportunity to tap the lucrative nightclub business. Its Round-Up Room, with a ceiling of log trusses, wagon wheel chandeliers, and leather drapes, accommodated about 300. Garwood Van, the original bandleader, recalled that the initial production show featured veteran vaudeville actor, comedian, and cabaret singer Frank Fay, along with "Ernie Rayburn and the 'El Rancho Starlets.'"[8] However, owner Tommy Hull either did not have the money to afford headliners for the Round-Up Room or chose not to invest in them. Instead, patrons who regularly filled the room saw veterans of the national nightclub circuit rather than the big-money acts.[9] For example, in November 1942, the El Rancho featured Fifi D'Orsay, "famed comedienne of radio, screen and stage," along with "Rod Rogers, clever impressionist and new master of ceremonies," fresh "from a successful engagement in New York and the El Morocco Club." The Dells, "eccentric comedy dance stars," completed the show bill. Three months later, the comedy dance team of Burton and Kaye, "feature attractions at the Roxy and Radio City theaters in New York City," headlined a show with master of ceremonies Jeffrie Gill, who recently had performed at the Cocoanut Grove in Los Angeles. The show also included dancer Patricia Jackson and the "lilting songs of Martha Demeter," who had just performed "with the Folies Bergere in New York and San Francisco."[10]

In 1942, R. E. Griffith and William Moore opened the Hotel Last Fron-

The iconic "Welcome to Fabulous Las Vegas" sign, which was erected at the south end of the Las Vegas Strip in 1959. Source: UNLV Libraries, Special Collections.

Postcard from Boulder Club on Fremont Street in the 1930s emphasizing that Las Vegas is "Still a Frontier Town." Source: UNLV Libraries, Special Collections.

A 1939 chamber of commerce brochure promoting Las Vegas as a frontier town. Source: Las Vegas Chamber of Commerce.

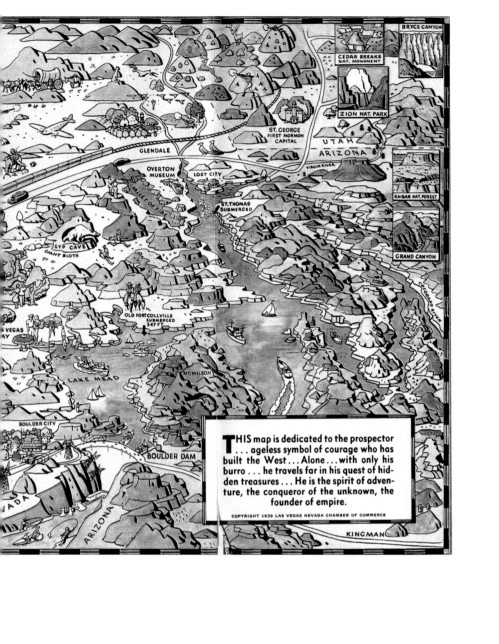

THIS map is dedicated to the prospector ... ageless symbol of courage who has built the West ... Alone ... with only his burro ... he travels far in his quest of hidden treasures ... He is the spirit of adventure, the conqueror of the unknown, the founder of empire.

Brochures hawking the frontier appeal of the El Rancho Vegas and Hotel Last Frontier in the 1940s. Source: UNLV Libraries, Special Collections.

1945 LAS VEGAS 1945
HELLDORADO
SOUVENIR ANNUAL

Sponsored by Las Vegas Chapter Nine International Footprinters Ass'n.
Price $1.00

Cover for the 1945 Helldorado program. Source: UNLV Libraries, Special Collections.

The Stardust Hotel shortly after its opening in 1958. Promoters claimed it had the largest neon sign in the world. Source: UNLV Libraries, Special Collections.

Cover for menu at the Hotel Last Frontier's Ramona Room in the 1940s. Source: UNLV Libraries, Special Collections.

Sketch of the luxurious Clover Room at the Riviera Hotel in 1955. Source: UNLV Libraries, Special Collections.

Sands Hotel in the late 1950s featuring the city's premier entertainer, Frank Sinatra. Source: UNLV Libraries, Special Collections.

El Rancho Vegas in the early 1940s. It was the first of the western-themed hotels. Source: UNLV Libraries, Special Collections.

Flamingo Hotel lobby in the early 1950s illustrating the move from western-themed hotels to those with luxury. Source: UNLV Libraries, Special Collections.

Cover of the 1963 Sands Times celebrating the eleventh anniversary of the hotel and featuring some of its galaxy of headliners: Danny Thomas, Frank Sinatra, Dean Martin, Jerry Lewis, Sammy Davis Jr., Red Skelton, Joey Bishop, Paul Anka, Edie Gorme, Steve Lawrence, Lena Horne, Carol Burnett, Corbett Monica, Nat King Cole, Steve Rossi, Marty Allen, and Vic Damone. Source: UNLV Libraries, Special Collections.

COME
AS YOU
ARE

DO
DIS

Red Skelton

Star of the Red Skelton Hour (CBS-TV, 8:00 p.m. Tuesdays) relaxes in one of the opulent new Penthouse Suites at the Sands

COMPLETE CONVENTION FACILITIES *including Private Meeting and Dining Rooms.* **NOW BOOKING FUTURE RESERVATIONS**: *Call your Local Travel Agent or our Nearest Office:* ■ *Chicago/CEntral 6-3317* ■ *Dallas/RIverside 2-6959* ■ *Houston/CApitol 8-6292* ■ *Las Vegas/735-9111* ■ *Los Angeles/BRadshaw 2-8611* ■ *New York/PLaza 7-4454* ■ *Pittsburgh/391-4028* ■ *San Francisco/EXbrook 7-2287* ■ *Toronto/EMpire 3-6728* ■ *Washington, D.C./347-2644 or Teletype direct 702-248-7069*

THE *Sands* LAS VEGAS, NEVADA

The Sands Hotel used Red Skelton's popular character "Freddie the Freeloader" to promote its "Come as You Are" theme in 1963. Source: UNLV Libraries, Special Collections.

The DUNES HOTEL & COUNTRY CLUB presents . . .

Casino de Paris

DIRECT FROM PARIS

ALL NEW
1966 EDITION

CAST OF 100

DUNES

HOTEL AND COUNTRY CLUB

Las Vegas, Nevada

The Dunes Hotel relied heavily on showgirl production shows, here promoting the 1966 edition of its Casino de Paris show. Source: UNLV Libraries, Special Collections.

Caesars Palace in 1986 with towers added to the original 1966 structure. Source: UNLV Libraries, Special Collections.

The Flamingo Hilton in 1986. The Hilton Hotels chain purchased the Flamingo in 1971 and added the tower. Source: UNLV Libraries, Special Collections.

The lights of Fremont Street in the 1980s. Source: UNLV Libraries, Special Collections.

An explosion of lights along the Las Vegas Strip in the 1980s. Source: UNLV Libraries, Special Collections.

The Tropicana Hotel, which opened in 1957 with its famed Tulip Fountain, was considered at the time as the "Tiffany of the Strip." Source: UNLV Libraries, Special Collections.

As with the Strip properties, the downtown casinos like the Pioneer Club with the iconic Vegas Vic used ever more neon in the 1970s. Source: UNLV Libraries, Special Collections.

The MGM Grand Las Vegas opened in 1992 with a Wizard of Oz theme, complete with a Yellow Brick Road, Dorothy, and Toto. The property has since been dethemed, but it is world recognized for its size and grandeur. Source: MGM Resorts International.

The iconic Bellagio, here in the early 2000s, opened in 1998, and the Bellagio fountains soon became known as the world's favorite free tourist attraction. Bellagio added a second tower, called the Spa Tower, in 2003. Source: MGM Resorts International.

tier just south of the El Rancho Vegas on Highway 91. The Ramona Room, which could accommodate 600 guests, was the showroom. Film comedian and vaudevillian Bert Wheeler, who had starred in *Las Vegas Nights* the previous year, was the headliner on opening night, backed by Gus Martell and his 5th Avenue Orchestra.[11] Initially, the budget for the floor shows was only $1,000 per week, but it gradually increased. The owners ended up spending about $100,000 on talent in their first year, guided by producer Maxine Lewis, who had "no definite show policy." She simply booked "anything which . . . will please the public." That included Irene Vermillion and her Swing Harp Quartette, the Yacht Club Boys, and Lester Cole and his six Debutantes. The biggest star was Jimmy Wakely, a country-and-western singer who had performed on Gene Autry's *Melody Ranch* radio show and had appeared in several B westerns.[12] Despite the absence of big names, the hotel placed an advertisement in *Billboard's 1943 Music Year Book,* boldly proclaiming that the Ramona Room had become "second only to the old Cocoanut Grove, the Trocadero, Radio City's Famous Rainbow Room, Ciro's, and other internationally known entertainment rooms."[13]

Although there were no major headliners performing in Las Vegas in the early 1940s, the nation learned from many publications that celebrities vacationed in Las Vegas. For example, a fall 1942 article in the *Saturday Evening Post* noted that the El Rancho Vegas was hosting "an eloping Lana Turner posing for news photographers with her newest groom, . . . Ilka Chase yawning at the floor show, . . . Sec. Lieut. Burgess Meredith, in a beautifully cut doeskin uniform, idling at the roulette wheel . . . [and] John Steinbeck effacing himself in a corner."[14] Four years later, a reporter proclaimed, "Las Vegas is your town . . . if you're the type who swallows your gum in the presence of Hollywood luminaries."[15] Indeed, journalists frequently described Las Vegas as a playground for celebrities. Moreover, some, like Irene Dunne, Loretta Young, and Norma Talmadge, purchased property nearby. There were even rumors that stars like Bing Crosby and Frank Sinatra were planning to develop resorts. For many years, readers of the nation's press were led to believe that should they vacation in Las Vegas, "the man or woman beside you at the roulette wheel may be a movie director, a star or a producer."[16] One journalist claimed, "We had the pleasure of placing a bet along with Red Skelton at the roulette table."[17] Another reported tourists "playing Twenty-one at a table with Vic Damone," and four women sitting next to Joey Bishop.[18]

In 1944, the Hotel Last Frontier began to attract some of the notable celebrities to play in the Ramona Room, including popular crooner and songwriter Gene Austin; Buster Crabbe, who had starred as Tarzan, Flash Gordon, and Buck Rogers among his dozens of films; the jazz and pop vocal group the Delta Rhythm Boys; and Walter Liberace.[19] By early 1945, *Billboard* proclaimed that the Last Frontier was a "big-bracket operation" after signing nightclub stars Sophie Tucker and Harry Richman. Tucker had been a popular vaudeville performer for many years, known for her jazz songs, ballads, and an earthy style. Richman, a songwriter and performer on Broadway and in movies, whose theme was the Irving Berlin tune "Puttin' on the Ritz," was still a big star in 1945.[20] Their performances represented a critical breakthrough for Las Vegas. Ever more impresarios were willing to pay premium wages for name entertainers because, as Al Fischler explained in *Billboard*, hotel owners had quickly come to realize the value of using entertainment as an "attraction to gaming rooms." They offered $3,000 to $5,000 a week for the likes of Tucker, Richman, ventriloquist Paul Winchell, Liberace, jazz singer Arthur Lee Simpkins, and fan dancer Sally Rand. Compared to other cities, Fischler pointed out, "shows are not always first-rate production efforts." Nonetheless, there were ever more nightclubs, including the Nevada Biltmore and the El Cortez, and "a score of smaller clubs which offer musical combos and sporadically some acts."[21]

Fictional depictions of Las Vegas reinforced the descriptions of the elegant nightlife found in the press. In his 1939 novel, *The French Key*, Frank Gruber describes a casino with "two large rooms on the main floor. In one a Hawaiian orchestra played haunting music. The lights were dim and a few couples dance slowly on the little dance floor."[22] In the 1941 film *Las Vegas Nights*, director Ralph Murphy portrays a large fictitious Nevada Club that featured stylishly dressed guests and the popular Tommy Dorsey orchestra accompanying rising pop star Frank Sinatra singing the number one hit, "I'll Never Smile Again."[23] Three years later, *Moon over Las Vegas* depicts a floor show featuring a crooner, an orchestra, a dance team, a headliner singing the title song to the film, and guests in elegant attire.[24]

The opening of the Flamingo in December 1946 triggered a rush to embrace big-name entertainers in Las Vegas. The story spread that Bugsy Siegel had offered as much as $25,000 a week to attract headliners to the Flamingo showroom.[25] Siegel brought Jimmy Durante, one of the most popular comedians on the nightclub circuit, to Las Vegas for his December 26 opening, backed by the famed bandleader Xavier Cugat and popular singer Rose Marie, and promised to bring Frank Sinatra, Lena Horne, and the Andrews Sisters to his showroom.[26] Although he was unable to sign Sinatra, Siegel did bring Lena Horne to the Flamingo in January 1947; the Andrews Sisters, along with comics Abbott and Costello, in March; and famed comedian

Joe E. Lewis in May. Siegel's bold move prompted the competing properties to lure in big-name headliners as well. To compete with the Flamingo's opening-night lineup, the El Rancho Vegas brought in the Ritz Brothers, one of the nation's leading comedy teams, and promising singer Peggy Lee. This sudden emergence of headliner talent in Las Vegas led entertainment columnist Bob Thomas to write, "Perhaps good, live entertainment in the West is making its last stand where it got its start—in the gambling saloons of the frontier."[27] Throughout the late 1940s and early 1950s, readers of newspapers, magazines, and novels encountered echoes of Thomas's characterization. Visitors to Las Vegas would find "top-billed floor shows," the "nation's finest orchestras," the "world's foremost entertainers," "some of the best night club entertainment," a place where "big names are a dime a dozen." Las Vegas had quickly become the "Broadway in the sagebrush."[28] Octavus Roy Cohen put it most succinctly in his novel *A Bullet for My Love:* "The leading hotels in that town all put on shows which are out of this world. They pay top money for their acts and their orchestras. You won't get better night club entertainment anywhere in America."[29]

In early 1947, Bugsy Siegel hired Maxine Lewis to book shows for the Flamingo—shows to meet the heightened expectations of tourists. A record of her bookings between 1948 and 1951 reveals much about the kind of entertainment offered in the showroom and the rising cost of the talent. Lewis usually put together a new show every two weeks with a standard nightclub lineup of a headliner singer or comedian, an orchestra, a dance line (the June Taylor Dancers, the Flamingo Girls, the George Moro Line, among others), and a second singer. Over these four years, Lewis was willing to pay a few headliners like crooner Vaughn Monroe, bandleaders Spike Jones and Harry James, the comedy team of Olsen and Johnson, singer and comic Danny Thomas, and the Andrews Sisters between $10,000 and $12,500 a week. Several others, like Lena Horne, Tony Martin, and Frankie Laine, made at least $7,000 a week.[30]

By 1951, there were two more hotel casinos on the Strip—the Thunderbird and the Desert Inn. With five Strip properties, entertainment directors like Lewis scrambled to find enough headliners for their showrooms. Because, like the Flamingo, they changed shows every two weeks, if not sooner, each hotel needed at least twenty-six headliners every year. Yet there were not 130 star attractions available.[31] With every new property, the challenge became worse. Between October 1952 and July 1958, eight new properties—Sahara, Sands, Royal Nevada, Riviera, Dunes, Hacienda, Tropicana, and Stardust—opened on the Strip.

Entertainment directors first turned to Hollywood for a solution. In 1953, the rapidly growing popularity of television had driven down attendance at movie theaters, and the release of films dropped dramatically. The "mad economy spree" of the studios "derailed the cinema gravy train," leaving several stars eager for work. Las Vegas entertainment directors quickly signed them up. In 1953 alone, movie stars Dorothy Lamour, Van Johnson, Jane Powell, Betty Hutton, Howard Keel, Ray Bolger, Anna Maria Alberghetti, and Tallulah Bankhead appeared in Las Vegas. As entertainment columnist Erskine Johnson proclaimed in April 1953, "So it is Movie Stars—In Person every night along the Great White Way in Nevada."[32] The arrival of so much talent in Las Vegas attracted the attention of major magazines and newspapers. In 1953, the *Wall Street Journal, New York Times, Los Angeles Times, Variety, Saturday Evening Post, Life, Look,* and *Time,* among dozens of periodicals, published articles that noted the explosion of celebrities appearing in the showrooms. Gladwin Hill, in the *New York Times,* claimed that Las Vegas tourists had "a wider choice of top-banana talent than the average New Yorker," and syndicated entertainment columnist James Bacon proclaimed Las Vegas "the new night life capital of the U.S." A booking agent for William Morris went further, telling the *Saturday Evening Post,* "Show-business wise, there's never been anything like it."[33] Journalists continued to dub Las Vegas the entertainment capital for many years, seldom resisting hyperbole. In 1962, Mort Cathro, *Oakland Tribune* travel writer, asserted that Las Vegas "outdoes the Great White Way, Hollywood, London, Paris, San Francisco and all the other great show towns put together in the array of talent it displays around the clock, around the calendar."[34] Similarly, Caskie Stinnett, in *Holiday* magazine, argued, "Las Vegas has become the undisputed heart of the entertainment world."[35]

Just as remarkable to readers as the glittering array of celebrities performing on Las Vegas stages was the extraordinary bargain for tourists who got to see them. As Dick Pearce wrote in *Harpers* magazine in 1955, those who dropped in on Las Vegas showrooms could see the great "movie stars, singers, funnymen, and Broadway folk" for the simple "price of a bottle of beer."[36] Or, as journalist John Gunther posed the question, "Where else can people have an hour or so of Liberace or Frank Sinatra, to say nothing of Tallulah Bankhead or Lena Horne, for a $2 minimum?"[37]

Novels, movies, and television contributed to this growing sense that Las Vegas had become the entertainment center of the nation. Elliot Paul even has a character in *The Black and the Red* proclaim, "The world leadership of Las Vegas in the entertainment field has come to stay for many generations."[38]

Promotional photo of Milton Berle, Red Skelton, Gale Storm, Spike Jones, Anna Marie Alberghetti, Vic Damone, and Herb Shriner. These celebrities all appeared in Las Vegas in September 1953. Source: UNLV Libraries, Special Collections.

Among the several films dealing with Las Vegas in the 1950s, four richly illustrate the lively entertainment offered in casino showrooms. Dean Martin sings in a Las Vegas nightclub in *My Friend Irma Goes West* (1950), while Virginia Mayo and Dennis Morgan in *Painting the Clouds with Sunshine* (1951) and Rosalind Russell and Fernando Lamas in *The Girl Rush* (1955) were featured in lively and colorful production numbers. Most impressive, however was the 1956 film, *Meet Me in Las Vegas*. Starring Cyd Charisse, Dan Dailey, and Agnes Moorehead, the lavishly choreographed musical comedy reflected the cornucopia—great singers, remarkable dance numbers, and a panoply of celebrities—that the larger hotel-casinos offered to tourists. Lena Horne, Frankie Laine, and Sammy Davis Jr. all sang in the film. Cyd Charisse, as a world-acclaimed prima ballerina, was featured in a number of stylish dances, including a lengthy version of "Frankie and Johnny" with up-and-coming dancer George Shakiris (he also danced in *The Girl Rush*). The extraordinary teaser, however, was the number and variety of cameos in the film. Actor Peter Lorre and singers Tony Martin, Vic Damone, Debbie Reynolds, and Frank

Sinatra all had their moment as people who just happened to be at the Sands Hotel and Casino, confirming the impression developed in the press about the high probability of running into celebrities if you went to Las Vegas.

Television reinforced this sense of familiarity with stars and the rich array of talent on display in Las Vegas. Two episodes of the *Danny Thomas Show* in 1957 featured Thomas, along with Peter Lind Hayes and Mary Healy, performing at the Sands Hotel. Nat King Cole and Ed Sullivan brought their variety shows to Las Vegas, and in November 1957, NBC telecast a holiday show in Las Vegas starring Vic Damone, the Will Mastin Trio with Sammy Davis Jr., Ann Sothern, and Tony Randall. In 1955, Dave Garroway's Sunday NBC program *Wide, Wide World* included a segment from the Sands Hotel in Las Vegas. Besides showing the famous Copa Girls, the segment included shots of Frank Sinatra and Sammy Davis Jr. In his narration, Garraway called the Sands "the playground of the stars. You may not meet them face to face in Hollywood, but you will at the Sands."[39] The biggest splash for Las Vegas on television in the 1950s came on the popular *Milton Berle Show*. On February 21, 1956, the evening of the premiere of the movie *Meet Me in Las Vegas,* the show was telecast live from the Sands Hotel. Berle had on his program the movie's stars, Dan Dailey and Cyd Charisse, as well as Peggy Lee, Jimmy Durante, Eddie Cantor, and the singing group the Four Aces.[40] Radio also informed a national audience about the entertainment bonanza in Las Vegas. NBC's *Monitor* weekend program and Mitch Miller covered the entertainment news about Las Vegas, and for three mornings in September 1955, *Breakfast with Dorothy and Dick,* New York City's highest-rated morning talk show, broadcast from the Sands Hotel. Columnist Dorothy Kilgallen and her producer husband, Richard Kolmar, chatted with their listeners about the shows they saw at the various hotels.[41]

However, Hollywood could not provide a sufficient number of headliners, so entertainment directors increasingly turned to television stars to fill the showrooms. Indeed, some entertainment directors preferred television celebrities. One hotel executive explained to entertainment columnist Bob Thomas that he wanted "attractions that can draw a mass audience, and that means television names." By 1960, nearly 90 percent of American homes had at least one television, and they became familiar with stars like Red Skelton, Milton Berle, Dennis Day, George Burns, Ed Sullivan, Tony Martin, Victor Borge, Nat King Cole, Edie Gorme, and Jack Carter. When tourists came to Las Vegas, they wanted to see the routines that these celebrities performed on television.[42]

Even with the infusion of dozens of television celebrities, entertainment directors like Maxine Lewis struggled to find talent. She met frequently with talent agents, auditioned acts in Los Angeles, New York, San Francisco, and Chicago, and placed ads in the trade papers in a quest to find new acts.[43] However, she and the other entertainment directors quickly learned that their audiences wanted to see name stars in the showrooms, not new talent. Some entertainment directors brought in unconventional stars as headliners. Stan Irwin, entertainment director at the Sahara, signed opera singers Helen Traubel and Lauritz Melchior, flamenco dancer Jose Greco, and actress Eleanor Parker to headline.[44] Pierre Cossette, a booking agent for the Musical Corporation of America, created headliners: he persuaded aging screen vamp Mae West to perform at the Sahara and Ronald Reagan, a struggling actor in B movies and host of television's *G.E. True Theater,* to perform at the Hotel Last Frontier the following year.[45] In 1955, the Desert Inn signed playwright, actor, director, and cabaret singer Noel Coward to perform for a month in the Painted Desert Room. Newer properties like the short-lived Royal Nevada tried to make virtue of this approach. Eddie Rio, the booking agent for the hotel, signed entertainers who had not performed in Las Vegas, hoping that their novelty value would be appealing to audiences. In 1955, the Riviera paid famed actress Joan Crawford $10,000 simply to be a hostess for their grand opening.

Some of these experiments were a disaster. Wally Cox, who played a popular television character named Mr. Peepers, and movie stars Jeff Chandler and Orson Welles bombed.[46] Mario Lanza, opera and popular singer and star of the 1951 film *The Great Caruso,* was the greatest disaster. The New Frontier Hotel signed him to open its Venus Room in April 1955. However, opening night jitters, combined with the consumption of alcohol and barbiturates, caused Lanza to flee Las Vegas without singing a note.[47]

The furious quest for headliners prompted an unprecedented bidding war for the top headliners. In 1953, with Betty Hutton reportedly earning $25,000 a week, Red Skelton $32,500, and Milton Berle $35,000, the *Oakland Tribune* called it the "lushest price war in U.S. entertainment history."[48] The Flamingo signed vocalist Kay Starr to a five-year contract guaranteeing her $20,000 a week for eight weeks each year. The Riviera drove salaries to new heights by paying Liberace $50,000 as its opening act in 1955. One report had the hotels collectively spending $20 million on talent in 1955, twice as much as the previous year.[49] Stories surrounding celebrities and their ever-higher paychecks were common for decades. In 1969, the Flamingo paid pop singer Tom Jones $70,000 a week, but Tony Bennett quickly eclipsed that figure the following year with $100,000 a week. By 1980, Frank Sinatra was making $300,000 and country singer Dolly Parton $350,000 a week. Celine Dion captured the all-time high paycheck in 2003 with $100 million for a three-year run at Caesars Palace.[50]

Faced with too few headliners and escalating salaries for the ones they could book, entertainment directors sought other ways to attract customers. Signing the Mary Kaye Trio in 1953, the Hotel Last Frontier developed the lounge act as a less costly alternative. Lounge acts performed as many as four or five shows each night in small rooms that were often near bars. When Bill Miller, entertainment director at the Sahara, signed Louis Prima and Keely Smith to perform in the Casbar Lounge, he triggered a remarkably successful five-year run for the "hottest jazz man in the country." Strip hotels quickly added lounge performers like the Treniers, Artie Shaw, Freddy Bell and the Bellboys, Red Norvo, Wayne Newton, Cab Calloway, Mel Tormé, Sonny King, Shecky Greene, and Don Rickles.[51] Some entertainment directors opted for Broadway plays. From the late 1950s to the late 1960s, *A Funny Thing Happened on the Way to the Forum; Flower Drum Song; Bye, Bye, Birdie; Anything Goes; Fiddler on the Roof; Guys and Dolls; Sweet Charity; South Pacific; Funny Girl;* and *The Odd Couple* all appeared in Strip showrooms, although most were shortened to no more than ninety minutes so that those in attendance could get back to the casino to gamble.[52]

Topless production shows were yet another alternative to the high-priced headliner show. In 1957, Major Riddle, one of the co-owners of the financially strapped Dunes Hotel, brought in Harold Minsky's *Minsky Goes to Paris* show, and it was an immediate hit. The Dunes' success prompted Frank Sennes, entertainment director at the new Stardust Hotel to bring a French-style revue, the *Lido de Paris,* to Las Vegas in 1958. Beldon Katleman at the El Rancho Vegas quickly followed suit. Although some of the established successful hotels, notably the Sands and Sahara, opposed the move, and religious and political leaders decried the shift to topless shows, they quickly became a standard part of the entertainment offering in Las Vegas. As the *Chicago Tribune* reported in 1965, "More and more Strip hotels are abandoning big-name entertainment in their main rooms in favor of production shows."[53] It was true that the production shows dominated the entertainment picture in Las Vegas for many years. The *Folies Bergere* at the Tropicana, *Hallelujah Hollywood* at the MGM Grand, *Jubilee* at Bally's, the *Casino de Paris* at the Dunes, the *Lido de Paris* at the Stardust, *Thoroughly Modern Minsky* at the Thunderbird, *Hello America* and *Pizzazz* at the Desert Inn, and *Splash* at the Riviera became the quintessential Las Vegas shows for several decades, with statuesque women in elaborate, beautiful costumes. Whether topless or not, the feather-and-fishnet productions attracted droves of tourists.[54]

In 1990, Siegfried Fischbacher and Roy Horn opened a new kind of production show at the Mirage Hotel. Veterans of the Strip, the two magicians had performed at the Tropicana, Stardust, and MGM Grand before getting their own show, called *Beyond Belief*, which ran from 1980 to 1988 at the Frontier. In their Mirage show, Siegfried and Roy performed in a theater that cost $60 million. In their thirteen years at the Mirage (their run tragically ended when one of their white tigers mauled Roy), they performed over 5,700 shows in the 1,500-seat theater. The millions who came saw a show filled with illusion, big cats, and spectacular special effects. In his 1999 book *24/7: Living It Up and Doubling Down in the New Las Vegas,* Andres Martinez wrote, "The show is an exhausting, overwhelming assault on the senses, with statuesque dancers, fire-spitting steel monsters, the two aging German magicians, and some of the most majestic animals you've ever seen."[55] Richard Corliss in *Time* magazine described it as a show that "changed the town." Siegfried and Roy offered "an astounding farrago of illusion and sorcery, acrobats and armies of knights, [and] vanishing tigers and elephants." The two performers changed fans' expectations for magic shows with "a larger stage, grander effects, a cast of many dozens . . . plus the stars, mixing authority with intimacy, and their gorgeous props, the white tigers."[56] The illusionists' Mirage show got substantial exposure in the 1997 comedy film *Vegas Vacation* by incorporating Chevy Chase's character into their act. They also appeared in the animated series *Father of the Pride,* which aired in the 2004–2005 television season.

While Siegfried and Roy transformed the magic show, Cirque du Soleil truly redefined the production show for Las Vegas. Founded by Guy Laliberte in Quebec, Cirque du Soleil (Circus of the Sun) is a company whose global shows combine elements of street entertainers and a circus. Beginning with *Mystere* at Treasure Island in 1993, Cirque du Soleil had four permanent shows in Las Vegas by 2005: *Mystere, O* at the Bellagio, *Zumanity* at New York, New York, and *Ka* at the MGM Grand. Expensive to stage, the shows cost from $18 million to $170 million and featured extraordinary acrobats, colorful costumes, impressive soundtracks, intricate choreography, and athletic feats by large casts. As Peter Bart wrote in *Variety,* they are "extravagantly theatrical and metaphysically confusing." Although "no one can define precisely what it's all about, or what it's telling us . . . it works."[57] Though they commanded high ticket prices, the shows have all been remarkably successful at attracting sellout crowds. *O*, for example, regularly made over $100 million annually. There have been other similar spectacular, sophisticated, special effects–driven shows like *EFX* at the MGM Grand and *La Reve* at the Wynn.

Yet headliners have remained popular, and entertainment directors have never stopped scrambling to find name entertainers who can also attract a gambling crowd. Max Walkoff, publicity director at the Desert Inn in 1969, claimed that there were scarcely "a dozen name stars in the country that are sure to fill the house."[58] Eleven years later, columnist Dick Kleiner, after interviewing Burton Cohen, president of the Desert Inn, learned that the fundamental problem for the city's entertainment directors was that "there just aren't enough really big names any more that mean anything at the Las Vegas box office."[59] Because of this quest for appealing entertainment—acts that will not only attract crowds, but also customers willing to gamble—Las Vegas has offered a remarkable variety of entertainment options. Pop singers, stalwart standards crooners, and country singers have been an almost constant part of the entertainment picture. Eddie Fisher, Patti Page, Connie Francis, Judy Garland, Johnny Mathis, Billy Eckstine, Robert Goulet, Harry Belafonte, Julie London, Nat King Cole, Paul Anka, Ella Fitzgerald, Vic Damone, Bobby Darin, Lena Horne, Little Richard, Perry Como, Pearl Bailey, Barbara Streisand, Liza Minnelli, Johnny Cash, Dolly Parton, Tom Jones, Kenny Rogers, Engelbert Humperdinck, Gladys Knight, Bette Midler, Cher, and Elton John are a representative sample of the famed singers who appeared as headliners in Las Vegas through 2005. Stand-up comics and performers with a comedy routine likewise remained a big attraction for tourists. Joe E. Lewis, Jack Benny, Jerry Lewis, Danny Thomas, Milton Berle, George Burns, Red Skelton, Jack Carter, Alan King, George Goble, the Smothers Brothers, Bill Cosby, Johnny Carson, Dan Rowan and Dick Martin, Phil Silvers, Bob Newhart, Carol Burnett, Danny Kaye, David Brenner, Imogene Coca and Sid Caesar, Shecky Greene, Buddy Hackett, Don Rickles, Redd Foxx, Jackie Mason, Woody Allen, George Carlin, Totie Fields, Jay Leno, Jerry Seinfeld, and Carrot Top all were featured from the mid-1950s through the early twenty-first century. Amid the singers, production shows, and comics, a variety of other acts played Las Vegas. Magicians were increasingly popular, notably Doug Henning, Lance Burton, David Copperfield, and Penn and Teller.[60] Indeed, in 1996, Mark Wilson, president of the Academy of Magical Arts, proclaimed, "Las Vegas is the world capital of magic."[61] Impressionists often appeared, and some, like Danny Gans in 2000, even became headliners.

Many of the performers in Las Vegas appeared after their careers had peaked. Some journalists noted that the older nostalgia crowd appreciated the opportunity to see the survivors of the big band era, like those led by Benny Goodman, Harry James, and Russ Morgan, or veteran acts from the 1940s, like the Ritz Brothers comedy team, in the mid- to late 1960s.[62] Some charitably characterized Las Vegas from the late 1960s to the early 1980s as "a sort of working Hall of Fame for a good many of yesterday's stars."[63] Others were more harsh. Tom Wolfe claimed, in his 1964 visit, "Much of the entertainment in Las Vegas . . . will recall for an aging man what was glamorous twenty-five years ago when he had neither the money nor the freedom of spirit to indulge himself in it."[64] In the film *Destiny Turns on the Radio,* a record producer dismissively says, "Nobody, but nobody comes to Vegas looking for fresh talent. This is where careers go to die."[65]

Early in the twenty-first century, a new entertainer emerged who dramatically changed the entertainment landscape in Las Vegas. Between 2003 and 2005, Canadian vocalist Celine Dion played to an almost always filled 4,100-seat Colosseum at Caesars Palace, bringing in more than $240 million in revenue for the hotel. Dion's nearly five-year contract, which rewarded her with over $30 million a year to perform forty weeks (five shows a week), dramatically brought back the headliner show to the Las Vegas Strip. After years dominated by production shows, magicians, and impressionists, Dion's *New Day,* at the new massive $95 million performance hall, created a remarkable demand for tickets. Before she opened on March 25, 2003, Caesars had already sold over 250,000 tickets. As *Newsweek* proclaimed, Las Vegas had secured the talents of the "top-selling female pop star in recording history." Dion had already sold over 150 million albums at just age thirty-four.[66] The show on the 120-foot stage, included, besides Dion, almost fifty dancers, "a blow-the-door-off sound system . . . and the largest indoor light-emitting diode screen in the world." Designed by Franco Dragone, "the former Cirque du Soleil guru," the show had lights, acrobatics, and rapidly changing scenes.[67] Commercially, the new show was a remarkably successful merging of the sophisticated production show with a celebrated headliner. It became a new model for Las Vegas entertainment: "the headliner with a creative show that cannot tour."[68] In other words, the fans would have to come to Las Vegas to see the knockout act. Dion's success led to similar long-term contracts for well-established stars, notably Elton John and Barry Manilow.

While all of these performers contributed to a distinctive style of entertainment that visitors expected when coming to Las Vegas, a handful of celebrities truly defined the city's entertainment allure. Walter Liberace first appeared in Las Vegas in the Ramona Room of the Hotel Last Frontier in November 1944. Forty-two years later, he made his last appearance at Caesars Palace only a few months before his death. In his several hundred performances during those four decades, Liberace (he dropped his first name by 1946) created an image for the press and television that not only defined him but also in part defined the appeal of Las Vegas in the post–World War II era. Born in 1919, Liberace grew up in Milwaukee.[69] A child prodigy, he quickly emerged as an extraordinary talent, playing a Liszt concerto with the Chicago Symphony at age twenty. After playing community concerts in the upper Midwest, Liberace went to New York in the early 1940s, where he worked as a rehearsal pianist and an accompanist while performing in a few nightclubs. He then went on the supper club circuit, playing in cities like Minneapolis, Detroit, St. Louis, Boston, Cleveland, Toronto, and Montreal. He began sending out postcards to entertainment directors around the country asking, "Have you heard of Liberace?"[70] Maxine Lewis at the Hotel Last Frontier responded and offered the twenty-five-year-old pianist a six-week run in the Ramona Room. He was an immediate hit, and the Last Frontier brought him back twenty-four times over the next decade. He later performed at the Riviera, Sahara, Hilton, Caesars Palace, and MGM Grand.

Liberace, while most closely associated with Las Vegas, was remarkably popular across the United States and internationally. He played to record audiences in many venues: the Empire Room at the Palmer House in Chicago; Ciro's nightclub in Los Angeles; Madison Square Garden, Radio City Music Hall, and Carnegie Hall in New York; and the Palladium, the Royal Albert Hall, and the Café de Paris cabaret in London. He began appearing on radio and releasing records in the late 1940s. He was even involved in a national ad campaign selling Blatz beer.[71] His successful syndicated television program in the early 1950s prompted a flood of fan mail for the emerging matinee idol. By the mid-1950s, he was selling hundreds of thousands of albums. In 1953, *Life* magazine claimed that Liberace "at 33 is the biggest solo attraction in U.S. concert halls, a TV star, one of the biggest sellers of record albums."[72] The leading variety television shows of the 1950s, those of Ed Sullivan, Red Skelton, and Milton Berle, invited him on frequently. He also appeared on Edward R. Murrow's popular *Person to Person* program. In the 1960s and 1970s, *Tonight Show* hosts Jack Paar and Johnny Carson had almost an open invitation for him to appear. He even was a guest host for Carson. In the 1980s, he appeared both on the David Letterman show and *Saturday Night Live.*

Over his career, Liberace developed an ever-more flamboyant performance style, one that earned him the sobriquet of Mr. Showmanship. Although he began as a concert pianist playing to highbrow audiences appearing in a conservative suit, he decided to broaden his appeal to a wider audience. In the 1940s, Liberace began offering concerts that included show tunes, folk songs, and some boogie-woogie in addition to what he came to call *Reader's Digest* versions of classical pieces focusing on the late Romantic composers. He began to ad lib with his audiences and included self-deprecating humor. In 1945, he placed a candelabrum on his piano as a prop and added flair to his playing through exaggerated hand movements. At a performance at the Hollywood Bowl in 1952, Liberace, worried that he would simply blend in with all the black tuxedos of the orchestra, performed in white tails, the first of his many costume variations. From that point, he felt obligated to appear in ever-more outrageous costumes.

As the opening act at the Riviera hotel in 1955, Liberace wore a Christian Dior–designed white tuxedo and then changed into a tuxedo with over a million sequins. He had his designers using velour, brocades, and furs. Because Las Vegas had what he called an "ever-better-onward-and-upward attitude," Liberace felt obligated always to top his previous outfits on stage.[73] Among the hundreds of outfits, he appeared in a $300,000 blue fox cape, a patriotic pantsuit, and a diamond-studded ermine coat. He also opted for spectacular entrances. Typically, it was an extraordinary automobile. For example, in a performance at the Las Vegas Hilton, he arrived in a Phantom V Landau Rolls-Royce, and in 1984 at the Radio City Music Hall he made his appearance "in a custom-made Rolls covered with tiny silver mirrors."[74] At other times, he flew onto the stage suspended in a harness. For a performance in Reno, Nevada, Liberace came onto the stage riding "on an elephant named Bertha."[75] Regardless of the approach, he delighted in spectacular entrances.

Music critics thought little of Liberace's performances. They lambasted him for simplifying and condensing the classics and ridiculed his style. One critic called him the "evangelist of kitsch," and another concluded that he was "a kitsch pianist with a scullery maid's idea of a regal wardrobe," a "synonym for glorious excess."[76] Yet none of the critics could deny that "his public loves him."[77] While his fans adored him in New York, London, Chicago, and Milwaukee—wherever he played—his greatest fan base was in Las Vegas. There, his boundless enthusiasm, joy, panache, sly winks, jokes, costumes, staging, and dazzling musicianship all combined to make him a record-setting hit. The hotels richly rewarded him. He was making $25,000 a week at the Hotel Last Frontier in 1954 after starting for $750. When he switched to the Riviera the next year, the hotel paid him $50,000 per week. In 1971, he set a new standard when he appeared at the Hilton for $300,000, and in 1985 Caesars Palace paid him $400,000. As *Time* critic Richard Corliss noted late in Liberace's career, "He gave the audiences what they never knew they wanted: a polyester blend of classics and crass, Van Cliburn and Van Halen. Oh, yes—and their

Liberace in predictably outlandish performance attire. Source: UNLV Libraries, Special Collections.

money's worth of high dazzle."[78] Moreover, Liberace came to symbolize for many people what Las Vegas entertainment would be like should they choose the city as their tourist destination. There would be beads and rhinestones, flash, glamour, exuberance; in essence, there would be uninhibited indulgence. As Liberace put it in 1976, "I think the most wonderful thing about Vegas is that it's actually a place where you can enjoy yourself no matter what you like to do."[79]

Five months before Liberace performed as the opening act for the new

Riviera Hotel in April 1955, Louis Prima and Keely Smith opened at the Casbar Lounge at the Sahara. Their seven-year run, first as a lounge act and then as headliners, at the Desert Inn profoundly transformed the Las Vegas entertainment scene. While Liberace was attracting sellout crowds with glitter and excess, Prima and Smith offered a raucous night of fun in a style that the town had never before seen.

Born in 1910 in New Orleans, Prima grew up with jazz, even becoming a band leader at age thirteen.[80] At age fourteen, Prima took up the trumpet, the instrument that defined his professional playing days. He began playing professionally in the 1920s, developing a reputation as a fine Dixieland trumpeter and so impressed Guy Lombardo, leader of the Royal Canadians, that the latter encouraged him to take his considerable talent to New York. After a bit of a struggle, Prima formed a group, hit the nightclub circuit, released some successful records, made a few movies, and composed "Sing, Sing, Sing," which became the signature tune for Benny Goodman and his band. Yet by the early 1950s, Prima's career was in decline. Fortunately, he had hired a marvelous vocalist in 1948 named Keely Smith, whom he married in 1953. Desperate for work (Smith later explained they were playing in dumps), Prima called a friend in Las Vegas named Bill Miller. Miller, the entertainment director at the Sahara Hotel, had owned the successful Riviera nightclub in Fort Lee, New Jersey, for many years. Although he had no room for them in his headliner schedule, Miller offered to let them play the lounge. Prima had played Las Vegas as a headliner at the El Rancho Vegas, and playing the lounge was tantamount to a demotion. As Prima biographer Tom Clavin explained, "The stigma was that you played the lounge because you weren't enough of a headliner to attract an audience to fill the main showroom." It "was a venue for those on the way down, not the way up."[81] However, Prima and Smith were so successful that their initial two-week run, which began on November 24, 1954, turned into a five-year stay at the Sahara.

Prima and Smith changed not only the perspective people had on lounge entertainment, but also on the kind of music that Las Vegas offered. Their performances consistently drew raves from critics locally and nationally. The *Las Vegas Review-Journal,* for example, reported that "Prima's extended stay in the Casbar Lounge" was "the high point of Las Vegas' musical entertainment."[82] Over the next six years, the national press showed little restraint in describing the Prima–Smith triumph. Entertainment columnists Dorothy Kilgallen and Erskine Johnson said they were "rocking the town" and that Louis was the "hottest jazz man in the country." The *San Mateo* (Calif.) *Times* claimed they reigned "supreme in Las Vegas," and *Oakland Tribune* colum-

Louis Prima, the musician who, with Keely Smith, transformed the lounge act into a Las Vegas institution. Source: UNLV Libraries, Special Collections.

nist Russ Wilson dubbed them "today's hottest music-variety act in the mad world of the nation's nightclubs." When they were guests on her show in 1959, singer Dinah Shore proclaimed they were "the greatest nightclub act in the country. They're knockin' 'em dead at the Sahara in Las Vegas."[83]

The Prima–Smith sound and style is what captured the critics' attention. Las Vegas crowds had never seen such a show. The Sahara lounge in late 1954 had a very small stage and could accommodate only about 150 people. Keely Smith recalled "a low ceiling, poor ventilation, one spotlight, one micro-

Singer Keely Smith was, with Louis Prima, the most successful of Las Vegas lounge acts.
Source: UNLV Libraries, Special Collections.

phone, an upright piano—no room for a baby grand. And there was a service bar right in front of us!"[84] Yet in that small, crowded space, Prima and Smith quickly developed an ever-larger loyal following for their five forty-five-minute shows between midnight and dawn six nights a week. Initially, Smith explained, it was "cabdrivers, hookers, waitresses" who filled the seats.[85] The word spread, and high rollers and celebrities like Frank Sinatra, Dean Martin, Red Skelton, Debbie Reynolds, Spencer Tracy, Gary Cooper, and Sammy Davis Jr. were soon dropping in. Las Vegas audiences had enjoyed crooners and jazz performers for years but had experienced nothing like Prima. As he explained to entertainment columnist Erskine Johnson, "It's hot jazz, swing, progressive jazz, Dixie and rock 'n' roll all rolled into one. Man, it's just me."[86] Prima delivered that sound with a unique style he developed in New York, where he jumped and danced about the stage while blaring tunes on his trumpet. Soon after his opening at the Sahara, Prima brought in Sam Butera, a popular saxophone player from New Orleans, who assembled a backup group called the Witnesses. Butera worked with Prima on arrangements to showcase this new grinding music. "Butera and the Witnesses," one jazz critic noted, "supplying a wild, relentless, driving beat that punched through the lounge's smoke and chatter and left crowds in awe. There was nothing like it."[87] There were few dissenters to the adulation heaped on the pioneering lounge show. However, a 1959 article in *Time* magazine judged the show, with Prima's "off-color phrases and gyrations," to be vulgar.[88]

Keely Smith offered an intriguing counterpoint to the antics of Prima, Butera, and the Witnesses. Feigning disinterest, even boredom, Keely was the foil to her hyperactive husband, a routine that audiences loved. As the *Chicago Tribune* explained, she "just stands there while husband Louis Prima cavorts and doodles his way through a song. Everyone in the house usually breaks up as Louis performs—everyone except Keely of course. . . . Then Keely steps out and in that smoky voice of hers sings everything back into place again."[89] Veteran entertainment columnist James Bacon wrote, "Her seeming boredom with all hell breaking loose around her made for unexpected comedy relief."[90]

Whenever they were performing, everyone wanted to see them. Fans began lining up long before their midnight show. *Time* reported, "The space between lounge and gambling room piles up ten deep with waiting fans," and they would wait around until the fourth or fifth show of the early morning hours to see them—and this was after the Sahara enlarged the Casbar Lounge.[91] Prima and Smith took their chaotic, rollicking act frequently to television in the late 1950s. Besides appearing on Dinah Shore's show, they appeared on shows with Ed Sullivan, Milton Berle, Frank Sinatra, and Dean Martin. They released six best-selling albums with Capital Records between 1956 and 1959, focused on their reputation as the wildest act in Vegas. When they switched to Dot Records, they released eight more albums in just two years. As Prima biographer Garry Boulard explained, "Prima rightly looked at recordings as the best and most convenient means of exporting the Casbar thrills."[92] When not performing in Las Vegas, the duo took the wildest show on the road, performing to sellout crowds at the Copacabana in New York, the Chez Paree in Chicago, and the Mocambo in Hollywood. In 1958, they even appeared in two movies, *Senior Prom* and *Hey Boy! Hey Girl!*, a move that gave them another opportunity to showcase their Las Vegas act to a national audience. Keely Smith also starred in a feature with Robert Mitchum titled *Thunder Road.* In 1958 they released "That Old Black Magic" and won the Grammy for best performance by a vocal group or chorus.

In 1959, after a remarkable run at the Casbar Lounge, Prima and Smith signed a five-year contract as headliners at the Desert Inn. Wilbur Clark paid them $3 million to perform twelve weeks a year. However, their remarkable success collapsed with their divorce in 1961. They both continued to perform, often in Las Vegas, but neither could continue their success as solo artists. Louis, in particular, became passé in the face of the changing music scene led by the British invasion. His career did revive for a time when he provided the voice for a character in Walt Disney's 1967 animated feature *The Jungle Book.* Eight years later, he underwent surgery for a brain tumor and lingered in a coma for three years before dying in 1978.

Prima and Smith gave Las Vegas a truly edgy show. It was energetic, exuberant, and loud, with great vocals by Smith and dancing, jumping, shuffling, and jiving by Prima, all the while blaring on his trumpet, backed by the grinding saxophone style of Sam Butera. Perhaps the best characterization of their breakthrough show, and why it had such an impact on audiences, comes from a successful contemporary lounge performer. Don Rickles, who frequently performed between the Prima–Smith shows in the lounge, explained, "With singer Keely Smith looking sultry and seductive, with his backup band Sam Butera and the Witnesses blowing their brains out, Louis rocked and rolled every night of the week. He sang, he joked, he carried on with songs like 'Just a Gigolo' and 'Oh Marie' until the audience was exhausted. . . . Every night I asked myself: How can I follow that guy?"[93]

In less than a decade, Wayne Newton became the guy who was hard to follow. In the 1960s and for decades after, Newton became the entertainment icon of Las Vegas for many fans. In 1982, journalist Ron Rosenbaum, working for *Esquire,* shadowed Newton for two weeks, researching a feature article that remains the most revealing piece written about the singer's appeal to fans. "If you know Las Vegas," Rosenbaum wrote, "you know Wayne Newton is more than the Midnight Idol, more than Mr. Excitement in Vegas; he's the center of a veritable *cult* in the town."[94] Although he included biographical tidbits about Newton, the importance of Rosenbaum's article lies in his description of the singer's performance style and his appeal to his audiences. "From the very opening minutes of his act Wayne begins playing on the expectation of something special happening, the dream that tonight some magic suspension of the rules is in the offing—the ultimate unpurchasable Vegas experience." Backed by an orchestra, he sings "a couple of up-tempo opening numbers," and, after suggesting he might perform for three hours, Newton is "back to singing up a storm—a saloon-music medley, a soul-gospel medley, a Waylon-and-Willie-C&W medley" all amidst the "whoops and hollers" of the sold-out audience. When he gets them to quiet down, Newton "turns to the audience, and, with husky-voiced sincerity, tells them, 'You know, sometimes we get an audience that's so special we just throw away all our plans, take a right turn, and keep on going.' Or, he flatters the audience, 'You know, I don't often do this next song; it requires a special kind of group, a special kind of mood. So let's do it.'" He then launches into the lover's lament, "MacArthur Park . . . with emotion-choked narrative sections, dry-ice fog machines pumping away like mad, and . . . a gleaming Mylar glitter curtain that is meant to simulate rain dropping down dramatically."[95]

"Having established the illusion that there's something extremely special going on tonight, some magical show-biz chemistry between himself and his audience," Newton begins energetically playing a variety of the instruments on stage, from banjo to electric fiddle. After introducing the members of the orchestra, he ends the show. "Everyone leaves The Show," Rosenbaum explained, "feeling totally satisfied, thinking how hip the whole evening was" when "Wayne drove himself past his own limits."[96]

In Rosenbaum's judgment, Newton was one of the creators of Vegas soul. With songs like "Lady," "Feelings," and "MacArthur Park," he had transformed Las Vegas from Sin City into "syrup city, soppy city, woozy, sentimental city." The baby boomers in his audiences had grown up with Newton and had traveled to Las Vegas for "nostalgia: to help them make it through the night, to cry a tear for the good times they've lost. You can see it if you sit in the Bagdad Showroom during Wayne's act, the youngish middle-aged couples leaning together, smiling through the tears, dreamily melting into the sea of sentiment washing over them, knowing they'll 'never have that recipe again.'"[97]

A native of Roanoke, Virginia, Newton, along with his brother, Jerry, started performing in Las Vegas as a teenager in 1959 at the lounge in the downtown Fremont Hotel, six shows, six nights a week.[98] After appearing on the Jackie Gleason television program and at the Copacabana lounge, releasing a hit single called "Danke Schoen," and touring for nearly three years as an opening act for comic legend Jack Benny, Newton first opened as a Las Vegas headliner at the Flamingo in 1964. He was a consistent hit in Las Ve-

Wayne Newton, "Mr. Las Vegas," performing in the late 1970s. Source: UNLV Libraries, Special Collections.

gas. Journalists noted that marquees in the 1960s and 1970s called him "MR EXCITEMENT" or the "Midnight Idol." Over time, he gained the title of "Mr. Las Vegas," "America's Number-One Nightclub Act," "an institution," the man "who epitomizes Sin City."[99]

Over time, Newton developed a remarkably appealing style. As a 1976 *Newsweek* article explained, in the beginning, Newton was "a pudgy, baby-faced, adenoidal tenor," but he evolved into a svelte 175-pound "silky baritone." Or, as Rosenbaum described his voice by the early 1980s, "Imagine a husky, laid-back, low-key, good-ol'-boy, southern-frat-rat, beer-brawl drawl and you get an idea of how impeccably macho Wayne Newton sounds now."[100] Over time, his voice weakened. In his autobiography, Newton admitted that by the early 1960s, his thirty-six shows a week in the Fremont lounge had taken their toll. He began learning new musical instruments to play in his shows because his "voice couldn't take it anymore."[101] Performing more than forty weeks a year for decades did not help. In the 1990s, a reviewer of a Newton performance in Chicago referred to his "creaky vocals," and a reviewer of a Los Angeles concert concluded that his "once golden voice has gone to gravel." In 2002, travel writer John Denier, in the *Washington Post,* agreed: "Wayne's voice is in shambles." Yet there was more to Newton than just his voice; there was the Newton style. His attire evolved over time. In the mid-1960s, it was a black tie and tuxedo, but a decade later, it was sequined cowboy suits. By 1979, he took the stage "resplendent, a vision in scarlet, his tails open in front to show off a turquoise-and-silver belt buckle." In the 1980s, he was adorned in "a white cowboy suit, white chiffon scarf, and mammoth silver-and-turquoise belt buckle." By the early twentieth century, Newton had returned to the black tuxedo.[102]

Yet to focus on the voice and outfit is to miss the essence of his shows. Newton awed the audiences with his mastery of musical instruments—drums, violin, banjo, trumpet, guitar. Sometimes he played eight, sometimes nine, sometimes eleven—whatever was on the stage. As one journalist explained, "It almost seems as if he *is* the band."[103] The individual tunes changed over time, but his repertoire remained a mix of pop, country, easy listening, and Elvis medleys mixed in with his hits "Danke Schoen," "Daddy, Don't You Walk So Fast," and "Red Roses for a Blue Lady"—"saccharine favorites," *Time* magazine called them.[104] In between the songs and the instrumental pieces, Newton developed a popular patter with his audiences. Some of it was self-deprecating and some of it biographical, but mainly he worked diligently to build a rapport with his fans. Grinning, winking, and dancing, Newton, one journalist wrote, worked "harder than a man changing a tire in the rain."[105] As Robert Kerwin explained in the *Chicago Tribune* in 1978, "He constantly moves from one side of the stage to the other, winning first this group here, then that group there, building rapport, establishing family ties."[106] Over time, he began going down into the audience during the show. For "ten minutes or so," John Denier observed in the *Washington Post*, "he clambers up and down the aisles and jumps from table to table, shaking hands and kissing."[107] He also engaged in the "patented Wayne Newton push-me–pull-you routine, praising and scolding the crowd toward frenzy." He prompted ever-greater applause with promises of an ever-longer performance. When Newton got the ovations he wanted, he typically told the audience, "You know there's a lot of unhappy pit bosses out there in the casino, because you people aren't out there gambling! They don't want me to keep singing! They want you out there! And I say . . . I say the hell with them!"[108]

The audiences always rewarded him with multiple ovations, not just at the end of the performance but frequently during the show. "Unashamed, unembarrassed. Spontaneously, when Wayne finishes a rouser, the audience is on its feet uninhibitedly roaring, shaking friendly fists at Wayne's stage."[109]

When journalists interviewed them, fans explained Newton was the only Las Vegas headliner they saw, and many said they had gone frequently to his shows. "Newton's rapport with the audience," Robert Windeler concluded, "is unfailing."[110] Although his most ardent fans were women, he attracted many couples as well. Most journalists concluded that the audiences were "predominantly middle-aged and Middle American."[111] Fans of what Ron Rosenbaum called M.O.R. (middle-of-the-road music), Newton's audiences of the 1970s, for example, would also have been fans of singers like Neil Diamond, Barry Manilow, and Kenny Rogers.[112]

Besides his genuine enthusiasm on stage ("He doesn't tire, he doesn't fake; he wins us, and we want him to win"), Newton led readers of articles about him to expect a spectacular show from a performer truly committed to his audience. In 1978, he said, "I love to perform. I love to know an audience. I like to feel those vibrations—you know, it's like ESP." A year later, he explained, "The performer's first responsibility is to his audience, way over his responsibility to the club and its policies." In 1999, he said he tried to "give the audiences what they wanted to hear. I'm not one of the performers that walks out onstage, looks at his watch, and says, 'Be thankful that I'm here.'"[113] So journalist Robert Kerwin asked in 1978, "What's the attraction?" It was both simple and magical. "You get a great night: music, pace, friendliness, family warmth: you get your emotions touched, you laugh, you feel, you're part of something big and exciting."[114]

To the most ardent fans, Newton was a deity. The 1997 film *Vegas Vacation* offered a humorous parody of some fans' adulation and of Newton as a ladies' man. On vacation in Las Vegas with her family, Ellen Griswold sees Wayne Newton walking through the Mirage Hotel and is awestruck while he is smitten on seeing her. He sends an evening gown to her room as well as four complimentary front-row tickets to his show. The Griswold family attends his performance at the MGM Grand. While waiting in line for the doors to open, Ellen coos, "Wayne Newton just happens to be one of America's greatest entertainers." Her daughter adds, "You don't know the effect he has on women." During the show, Newton sings directly to Ellen and even sits beside her while singing a tune, prompting Ellen's son, Rusty, to observe, "Holy crap, Wayne Newton is hitting on mom!" Later in the evening, he has a drink with Ellen, and in a quiet moment with her husband, Clark, Newton explains, "I love women. I observe them. I cherish them. Don't let that one get out of your sight." The following day, Ellen takes a cab to his home, Casa de Shenandoah, where she and Newton go horseback riding and have a great meal while an artist paints them. He even gives her a lock of his hair and explains, "I wish I could spend the rest of my life with you." Eventually, Clark Griswold comes to Newton's home to rescue his wife.[115]

In his long career in Las Vegas, Wayne Newton broke all performance records. No one has come close to his number of performances—over 25,000 by 1994 at the Fremont, Flamingo, Sands, Frontier, Desert Inn, and Aladdin. Averaging 20,000 people a week at his shows, he had appeared before six million people by 1976, twelve million by 1990, and fifteen million by 1992. Starting at $280 a week when he and his brother worked at the Fremont in 1959, Newton was making $40,000 a week in 1967 and $400,000 a week in 1978. He had, by one journalist's analysis, become the "highest-paid cabaret entertainer ever" by 1979. Two decades later, he signed a ten-year contract with the Stardust Hotel that included an agreement to rename its showroom the Wayne Newton Theater. He was even part owner, for a couple of years, of the Aladdin Hotel and Casino. Though most identified as a Las Vegas headliner, Newton also toured regularly, appearing at venues as various as the Empire Room in Chicago, Harrah's in Reno, Branson, Missouri, the Astrodome in Houston, state fairs, and before over 200,000 on the mall in Washington, D.C. He also took his act to England, Australia, and Mexico. He released over 150 records, appeared in more than a dozen films, and made numerous appearances on television programs.[116]

The press also noted Newton's career low points. He filed for bankruptcy 1992, and NBC aired stories claiming that he used mob money to finance his purchase of the Aladdin, which led to a defamation suit against the network that Newton won. And there have always been critics of his shows. Nancy Spiller explained in *USA Weekend,* "The more 'culturally correct' baby boomers . . . snigger at his dyed pompadour and refuse to take seriously his treacly tunes and his tepid jokes. To them, Wayne Newton is the High Priest of Kitsch."[117] Even friendly critics note his "smarmy, up-close-and-personal charm" and "campy humor and over-the-top effects." Of a Newton Chicago performance, critic Howard Reich, who actually admired the performer, wrote, "Like some Vegas lounge act run amok, Newton's show unearths every cornball song and prehistoric joke in the book, and then some." There was little more than "pulpy show tunes, pseudo-Western ballads, ancient pop anthems, third-rate vaudeville patter." He concluded, "Some of this material is so dated and flimsy that it probably would have been booted off the old 'Ed Sullivan Show.'"[118] Regardless of their complaints about his shows, even Newton's harshest critics acknowledge he represents something essential about Las Vegas. This charismatic performer, indeed consummate entertainer, "down to the neon-dazzle of his jewelry" symbolized "a certain accessible, nickel-and-dime opulence."[119] Ultimately, it was Newton's remarkable connection to his audiences, the fifteen million fans who attended his Las Vegas shows, that explains his attraction. "If show business," critic Howard Reich wrote, "is about the romance that flows between a performer and his fans, if entertainment is about the way one man or woman makes an audience forget the passage of time, then Newton clearly ranks among the best in the business."[120]

On April 24, 1956, Les DeVor, entertainment columnist for the *Las Vegas Review Journal*, reported that Elvis Presley, "unanimously acclaimed by critics as the most important singing find since Johnnie Ray," had opened the night before at the New Frontier Hotel. Signing the young man who had enjoyed such a "sensational rise to fame" had to be considered "a Las Vegas entertainment scoop."[121] Presley truly was riding an extraordinary wave of success. Born in Tupelo, Mississippi, in 1935, he released his first hit, "That's All Right, Mama," for Sun Records in 1954. He began recording for RCA in early 1956, and that spring, "Heartbreak Hotel" became his first number one hit. Over the next two years, he would have nine more. In January 1956, he made his national television debut on Tommy and Jimmy Dorsey's *Stage Show*. After seven programs, he appeared on the April 3 *Milton Berle Show*. Aboard the U.S.S. *Hancock* in San Diego harbor, Berle enthusiastically introduced Presley as "America's new singing sensation." To the delight of the sailors on board, he sang both "Heartbreak Hotel" and his newest release, "Blue Suede Shoes." He then had a screen test with producer Hal Wallis that led to a contract with Paramount studios.[122]

Presley, drawing on the rhythm and blues, gospel, and country music he heard growing up in Tupelo and Memphis, contributed much to the rise of rock and roll music, a genre enthusiastically embraced by millions of teens who loved the driving, rhythmic sound so different from their parents' ballads. Presley's performance style was just as important as his songs, a style nicely captured by *Time* magazine in May 1956:

> In a pivoting stance, his hips swing sensuously from side to side and his entire body takes on a frantic quiver, as if he had swallowed a jackhammer. Full-cut hair tousles over his forehead, and sideburns frame his petulant, full-lipped face. His style is partly hillbilly, partly socking rock 'n' roll. His loud baritone goes raw and whining in the high notes, but down low it is rich and round. As he throws himself

into one of his specialties . . . his throat seems full of desperate aspirates . . . or hiccupping glottis strokes, and his diction is poor. But his movements suggest, in a word, sex.[123]

The New Frontier welcomed the acclaimed rocker with a twenty-four-foot-high photo of Presley out front, even though on the marquee he had third billing as "an added attraction." Drawing on the city's embrace of the nearby atomic testing site—atomic cocktails, atomic hairdos, an Atomic Café and Atomic Motel, even a movie called the *Atomic Kid*—the hotel labeled Presley the "Atomic Powered Singer." Despite the great anticipation, Presley's two-week run of two shows a night did not measure up to the advance hype. The headliner was saxophonist Freddy Martin and his orchestra. Martin, noted for a "sweet and mellow" sound, emphasizing popular versions of classical themes, offered a program of big band selections and a salute to the popular Broadway hit *Oklahoma*. There were accolades in the local press for "Martin's musical pleasantries" and the "uninhibited comedy style" of Shecky Greene, who did "a bang-up job of providing fun."[124]

The largely middle-aged crowd who had gathered to enjoy Martin's mellow dance band was not prepared for Elvis. Martin's orchestra played an arrangement of Bill Haley's anthem of rock and roll music "Rock Around the Clock" as the curtain went up for Elvis and his three-man backup group.[125] Presley never truly connected with the audiences in his twenty-eight twelve-minute performances of "Heartbreak Hotel," "Long Tall Sally," "Blue Suede Shoes," and "Money Honey." At best, he got polite applause, but little enthusiasm. Indeed, some in the audience, like Las Vegas resident Thelma Coblentz, were "shocked at his performance," concluding that it was simply "vulgar."[126] The local reviews were mixed. Bill Willard, in the *Las Vegas Sun*, argued that Elvis failed "to hit the promised mark." He concluded that Presley's "musical sound . . . is uncouth, matching to a great extent the lyric content of his nonsensical songs." While he may be a "whiz" to teenagers, "for the average Vegas spender or show-goer" Elvis was "a bore."[127] Les Devor, in the *Review-Journal*, explained, "The contrast between Presley and the melodic tunes of the Martin band is readily distinguishable." The former's music was "loud and insistent." Once he delivered his opening number, "the highly stylized delivery became repetitious, and the similarity of his numbers was apparent."[128] However, Ralph Pearl at the *Las Vegas Sun* enjoyed the performance of "the Shake and Shiver Kid." Although all the shaking made it appear to Pearl like Elvis was "suffering from itchy underwear and hot shoes," he understood the appeal of the "hysterical rock and roll rhythm." Pearl believed that Presley could challenge the popularity of Louis Prima's lounge act, but acknowledged that a "lad . . . hotter than a cauldron of boiling oil" would be better served appealing to the teen crowd.[129] Indeed, Elvis gave a matinee concert to raise money for the local baseball federation. A huge crowd of teens, charged only a dollar each, tried to crowd into the Venus Room. A Memphis journalist, covering Elvis's run at the New Frontier, described the predictable chaos: "They pushed and shoved to get into the 1000-seat room, and several hundred thwarted youngsters buzzed like angry hornets outside. After the show, bedlam! A laughing, shouting, idolatrous mob swarmed him."[130]

The national press was also watching Presley's performance. The *Chicago Daily Tribune* noted his Las Vegas show and included photos of him on stage and of teenagers applauding with gusto.[131] *Time* magazine contended that the "more adult audiences" of a Las Vegas hotel were nearly as enthusiastic for Elvis as "some fully grown female listeners matched the star squirm for squirm."[132] *Newsweek* deemed him a failure, frankly concluding that Presley was "like a jug of corn liquor at a champagne party."[133] The *Los Angeles Times* joined the negative chorus: "Elvis Presley didn't stampede the Venus Room of the New Frontier." Although the audience applauded Presley's appearance on stage, he could not keep their support. "Presley's rock and roll, rhythm and blues style, replete with wiggling of knees, failed to knock out the opening nighters here, as he has done with younger audiences elsewhere."[134]

The most intriguing response to Elvis's Las Vegas debut came from the king of crooners, Bing Crosby. He attended one of the young singer's shows in the Venus Room and came away impressed. In a 1957 interview, Crosby acknowledged that he was not a fan of Presley's sideburns and his greasy ducktail, but he predicted that Elvis would "be a star in other fields than rock and roll. He has an appealing personality and he's a good-looking kid." Further, he is a good singer: "He sings in tune and he's got good rhythm. He hasn't developed enough voice to handle a ballad yet, but that will come in time if he keeps on yelling and screaming enough to develop strength in his diaphragm and lungs."[135]

During his last performance, Elvis responded to the mixed reviews and generally tepid audience reactions to his singing. After singing "Heartbreak Hotel," Presley paused to chat with the audience, saying, "It's really been a pleasure being in Las Vegas." He then hurriedly corrected an acknowledgment of his struggles: "We've had a pretty hard time—stay . . . ah, had a pretty good time while we were here."[136] Yet Elvis enjoyed his two weeks in Las Vegas. He met some of the headliners like Liberace, Johnnie Ray, and Ray Bolger. When Liberace dropped in on a show, he and his brother, George, went backstage to meet Elvis, and the three of them were caught on camera clowning around, singing "Blue Suede Shoes," with Liberace grabbing a guitar and hamming it up.[137] Of all the other shows, Elvis was particularly taken by the lounge act of Freddie Bell and the Bellboys, who performed a rhythm and blues tune called "Hound Dog" that had been recorded by Big Mama Thornton three years earlier. Elvis not only eventually added it to his act for the *Milton Berle Show* in June, but he also made a hit recording of "Nothing but a Hound Dog." During the days, he went to movies, hung around the pool flirting with cocktail waitresses, and, with his backup group, Scotty Moore, Bill Black, and D. J. Fontana, spent hours riding dodgem cars at an amusement park. The casinos were of little interest to him on this trip. He neither gambled nor drank.[138] When he returned to Memphis, Elvis told a local journalist, "Man I really like Las Vegas. I'm going back there the first chance I get."[139]

Elvis indeed returned to Las Vegas; it became his favorite getaway city. After his two-year hitch in the army, he went often, usually staying at the Sahara. Unlike his 1956 visit, Elvis gambled, losing $10,000 in 1960; he also went to the shows and picked up women.[140] On July 15, 1963, however, he was there to begin filming what became for many the film anthem for the city, *Viva Las Vegas*. Elvis had made fourteen films since his appearance at the New Frontier. Presley films were little more than vehicles to enhance his celebrity. Production values tended to be low, scripts were simplistic, and most of the songs were forgettable. Critics generally did not like them, but they were consistently popular with audiences because the charismatic singer was in them. Hal Wallis, who produced several of the films, said, "A Presley picture is the only sure thing in Hollywood." As with his other films, critics largely panned *Viva Las Vegas*. *Variety* proclaimed, "The production is a pretty trite and heavyhanded affair, puny in story development and distortedly preoccupied with anatomical oomph." *Time* magazine noted its "wholesome, mindless spontaneity," and the *New York Times* called it "about as pleasant and important as a banana split."[141]

What sets *Viva Las Vegas*, the highest-grossing of Elvis's movies, apart from most of his other celluloid efforts is the presence of Ann-Margret, "one of the most alluring girls to reach the screen in many a moon."[142] Dancing with "a stem-to-stem fury that makes Presley's pelvic r.p.m.s seem powered by a flashlight battery," Ann-Margaret rattled "the rafters in several rhythm numbers."[143] She and Elvis sang several duets, including a climactic face-off in a talent contest, and the two of them are on screen together for most of the picture. While they were making the movie, there were rumors in the press about a passionate affair. Whether true or not, there was an unmistakable

Ann-Margret and Elvis Presley in a dance sequence from the iconic 1964 film Viva Las
Vegas. *Source: UNLV Libraries, Special Collections.*

chemistry between the costars. *Variety* noted their "sizzling combination,"
which, despite a weak story, carried "*Viva Las Vegas* over the top."[144]

Just as important as Ann-Margret's presence was the locale of the film.
The hotels, late-night action, showgirls, and casinos are the backdrop to the
movie's slight plot involving Elvis's character's, race car driver Lucky Jack-

son's, attempt to enter the Las Vegas Grand Prix. A reviewer in the *Los Angeles Times* acknowledged that the film was a "musical poster advertising the Nevada gambling center's glittering lures." Howard Thompson, in the *New York Times,* also noted "the stunningly picturesque background of the famed desert resort."[145] The lasting memory of the film, however, is the theme music. Elvis sings "Viva Las Vegas," composed by Doc Pomus and Mort Shuman, three times during the movie: while the opening credits are rolling, during a talent contest, and over the ending credits. The tune became and remains the signature song for the city.

Over the next four years, Elvis made a series of mediocre films and recorded several albums, few of which featured rock tunes. Taken seriously by few, he had been reduced, according to Richard Goldstein in the *New York Times,* to "singing gauzy ballads that slip across your lap like napkins."[146] However, he appeared on an NBC special, *Singer Presents Elvis,* on December 3, 1968. In an all-leather black outfit, Elvis performed before an intimate audience singing his early hits. With over 40 percent of viewers tuned in, it was the highest-rated program of the year and represented Elvis's comeback. The success of the program led his manager, Colonel Tom Parker, to engineer Elvis's return to live performances by negotiating a four-week deal at the new International Hotel in Las Vegas.[147]

Backed by two quartets and a thirty-five-piece orchestra, Elvis appeared before an invitation-only crowd on July 31, 1969. He had recently released "In the Ghetto," his biggest single in years, and was about to release an even bigger hit tune, "Suspicious Minds." Hollywood stars like Cary Grant, Angie Dickinson, and Donald O'Connor; Vegas stars like Wayne Newton, Sammy Davis Jr., and Totie Fields; and a large press contingent saw a svelte Presley take the stage in a "dark blue variation on a karate suit, tastefully tapered and belled," and the audience exploded in an ovation.[148] The King had returned. He sang his 1950s hits like "Heartbreak Hotel," Blue Suede Shoes," "Love Me Tender," and "Jailhouse Rock," as well as "Suspicious Minds." As one of his biographers noted, "As he sang, he grooved with the band, fell to his knees, slid across the stage; at points, he even performed spontaneous somersaults and flips."[149] The response was extraordinary. Thunderous applause, cries of "Bravo" and "More, more!," and frequent ovations followed virtually all the songs. He also skillfully played to the crowd: "Between the songs he wiped his brow with handkerchiefs from his audience. Leaning over, he accepted embraces from clutching arms."[150]

The critics were virtually unanimous in their praise of the King's return to the stage. Local entertainment columnist Ralph Pearl was one of the rare dissenters who "found the glamorous rock and roll movie hero really cashing in on his reputation and not truly earning the enormous standing ovation at the close of his one hour song session." Pearl said that, with a couple of exceptions, "there was a pounding, ear aching sameness to many of Presley's songs."[151] For the other critics, he had been remarkable. The reviewer in *Time* magazine, for example, wrote that Presley took the audience back to "the innocent '50s." He "stepped onstage in front of a gold lame curtain at Las Vegas' new International Hotel, coordinated his pelvic girdle and his phallic guitar, closed his eyes, tossed his head and sent a solar wind of nostalgia over" the audience. Richard Goldstein agreed: "It felt like getting hit in the face with a bucket of melted ice. He looked so timeless up there, so constant." For Goldstein, and by implication for the audience, "he was still the boy who makes little girls weep. Still the man of the people, even though the people had moved to the suburbs. And still the jailhouse rocker."[152]

In his four-week run at the International, Elvis shattered all attendance records, attracting over 101,000 audience members, and the hotel signed him to a multiyear contract. For seven years, Elvis was the biggest attraction in Las Vegas, drawing over two million people to 837 consecutive sellout performances. Critics wrote that Elvis was "simply, the most dynamic performer in the entertainment business." In an otherwise negative review of a Presley performance in 1972, Robert Hilburn still concluded, "If there was one show I'd recommend someone seeing in Las Vegas, it would have to be Presley's show. He's a legend and everyone should see him."[153]

Even though his later performances were pale imitations of that electrifying night in July 1969, Elvis Presley emerged as a true Las Vegas icon. A 1970 documentary titled *Elvis: That's the Way It Is* focused on his performances at the International. It was the first of many documentaries, movies, television specials, and miniseries about Presley and his link to Las Vegas. Moreover, there was a proliferation of Elvis slot machines, wedding chapels featuring Elvis, thousands of Elvis impersonators including those at tribute shows on the Strip, as well as a life-size statue of him at the Hilton Hotel (the Hilton chain purchased the International Hotel) and a city street bearing his name.[154] There were even "Flying Elvi" featured in the 1992 movie *Honeymoon in Vegas*. Early twentieth-first-century Las Vegas mayor Oscar Goodman, whenever he made promotional trips for the city, made sure to take along a couple of showgirls and an Elvis impersonator because he had become the entertainer the world beyond Las Vegas most readily identified with the city.

On May 12, 1960, after the completion of his two-year hitch in the army,

Elvis made his first television appearance on the *Frank Sinatra Timex Show*. The program brought together for the only time in a joint appearance the two performers who had the most enduring impact on Las Vegas entertainment. The reviewers noted that Elvis, sporting a "luxurious pompadour" but minus his signature sideburns, appeared "healthy" after his army service. He sang a couple of new releases, "Fame and Fortune" and "Stuck on You," and then joined Sinatra for a duet. It was an awkward moment as Elvis sang a Sinatra hit, "Witchcraft" with, one of his biographers concluded, "elegance and humility," but Frank muddled through Elvis's hit, "Love Me Tender."[155] This should have been a powerful pairing of great singing stars. In fact, the show attracted the largest audience for a television special in five years, and *Life* magazine characterized it as "a bright funny show." However, most critics were not nearly as kind. The review in *Time* glumly concluded that the show was largely "gaudy, pretentious and dull—one of the worst TV shows in memory."[156]

There was more than one irony surrounding the lackluster program. Three years earlier, when Elvis was topping the charts and performing to sellout audiences, Sinatra, in an obvious jab at Elvis, called rock and roll musicians "cretinous goons." Elvis shot back: Sinatra "has a right to his opinion but I can't see him knocking my music for no good reason."[157] Yet Sinatra clearly understood the remarkable appeal Presley would bring to his ABC special. He not only offered the rock star $125,000 for his appearance, but Sinatra also retreated a bit from his earlier harsh statement about Elvis's music. He told reporters, "After all, the kid's been away for two years and I get the feeling he really believes in what he's doing."[158] In 1960, Sinatra was at the peak of his influence in the entertainment world. "Frank," Tom Allen wrote in the *Chicago Daily Tribune*, "is so big now—in movies, records, music publishing houses, night clubs, and financial holdings—that his power in show business is virtually limitless."[159] Yet he had not been as successful on television; this program to welcome back Elvis finally gave him the ratings success that matched his accomplishments in other media.[160]

Sinatra taped the program at the Fontainebleau Hotel in Miami on March 26, only days after completing the filming of his playful heist film, *Ocean's Eleven*. The film, starring Sinatra, Dean Martin, Sammy Davis Jr., Joey Bishop, and Peter Lawford, involved a New Year's Eve theft from the vaults of the Flamingo, Desert Inn, Sands, Sahara, and Riviera hotels in Las Vegas. When filming in Las Vegas between January 20 and February 16, the five, dubbed the Rat Pack, appeared in the Copa Room of the Sands Hotel. The press coverage of their performances and their filming of the movie created a genuine phenomenon, one anchored on the personality of Frank Sinatra. Jack Entratter, entertainment director of the Sands, characterized the Rat Pack's performance the Summit, a take on a proposed meeting of American, Soviet, French, and British leaders. Sands publicist Al Freeman placed advertisements for the shows sure to entice crowds into the Copa Room:

> It's a guessing game, and you'll be a winner at the show-of-shows any night . . . every night! Yes, there's magic in the Sands air. Frank Sinatra, Sammy Davis, Jr., Dean Martin, and Peter Lawford! A galaxy of great stars . . . one–two–three—or all four on stage at once! It's a Jack Entratter special, and it *is* special, even for the Sands. That's Jan. 20–Feb. 16 in the fabulous Sands Copa Room, America's No. 1 Nightclub![161]

The opening night show was a humorous mix of song, dance, heckling, and mischief. Sinatra began with several songs, enduring gentle heckling from the others from backstage. Joey Bishop then presented a monologue. Peter Lawford and Sammy Davis Jr. followed with some dance numbers. Dean Martin wobbled onstage singing a number of ballads affecting the role of the happy drunk. As he stumbled through his numbers, Lawford and Bishop strolled across the stage in their shorts, and all the others in the wings "heckled and threw lines at him." They ended by singing "several confused choruses of 'Together' before being joined by their boss, the large Jacques Entratter." As they left, Bishop jumped on Entratter's back. The opening night set the tone for the remainder of the programs: five friends sharing in "assorted shenanigans" to the delight of sellout audiences every night.[162]

Beyond the stars on the stage, the Rat Pack shows attracted a galaxy of celebrities who dropped by for the shows. On opening night, the audience included "heavyweight champ Ingemar Johansson, Dinah Shore, Cyd Charisse, Lucille Ball, Zsa Zsa Gabor, Peter Lorre," and "the Fabian of the Roaring Twenties, George Jessel, America's Toastmaster General."[163] Ralph Pearl, veteran Las Vegas entertainment columnist, later recalled, "Of the more than ten thousand shows I've seen in Las Vegas, there's no question" that the Rat Pack opening was "the most exciting night in a showroom during those twenty years." Moreover, the Rat Pack engagement, he argued, "was the most profitable three-weeker for the Sands casino in the history of that hotel."[164] The Hollywood crowd and high-roller gamblers all sought access to the Copa Room. The young men parking cars got great tips because the Rat Pack brought in "a real money crowd." Comedian Buddy Lester remembered,

The Rat Pack—Peter Lawford, Frank Sinatra, Dean Martin, Sammy Davis Jr., and Joey Bishop—performing at the Sands Hotel. Source: UNLV Libraries, Special Collections.

"It was nothing for a guy to slip the maitre d' a hundred for a table."[165] Contemporary estimates claimed that the Sands turned away between 18,000 and 30,000 people from the Copa Room in those three weeks. Just as important, entertainment columnist Hedda Hopper reported "press and photographers winging in from all over the country" to cover the excitement.[166] One of them, Cecil Smith, concluded, "It may be the night-club act to end them all."[167]

While the shows attracted the Hollywood elite from Bob Hope to Kirk Douglas, the biggest star to drop by was Sinatra's friend, Senator John F. Kennedy of Massachusetts. Campaigning in the West for the Democratic nomination for president, Kennedy observed some of the filming of *Ocean's Eleven* and attended a Rat Pack show on January 29.[168] Sinatra introduced Kennedy as the "hottest personality in the political field," and the senator, according to the local press, "basked in the spotlight directed to his table by Sinatra's introduction and graciously accepted a warm ovation from the capacity audience on hand for show."[169] Joey Bishop directed his monologue to the senator: "If you get in, Frank has to be ambassador to Italy and Sammy to Israel, I don't want too much for myself—just don't let me get drafted again." Bishop then introduced Sinatra and Martin: "Frank Sinatra and Dean Martin are going to come out and tell you about some of the good work the Mafia is doing."[170]

When *Ocean's Eleven* premiered in Las Vegas in August, more than fifty newspaper, television, and radio journalists covered the event. The evening began with a cocktail party for the stars, journalists, and invited VIPs at the

Sands, followed by a dinner show featuring the Rat Pack. It ended with the film's world premiere at the downtown Fremont Theatre. Jack Paar had special footage shot for later broadcast on his late-night show, and newsreels were made "at the request of television news editors around the country for showing in their respective areas."[171] Although the critics were, at best, lukewarm about *Ocean's Eleven,* it offered a dazzling view of Las Vegas. It "looks flashy in color," Bosley Crowther wrote in the *New York Times,* "as naturally it would, and there's plenty of atmospheric detail, such as gaming tables, girls and 'one-arm bandits.'"[172]

Sinatra, the city's largest draw, and his Rat Pack pals had a six-year run at the Sands. In April 1966, they still packed the Copa Room, and "hundreds of people were turned away." As John Scott explained in the *Los Angeles Times,* "To attend these rare multi-star appearances . . . has become a status symbol in this city of croupiers and celebrities. If you're a member of the 'in' group, you're in the showroom; otherwise forget it."[173]

Sinatra's route to Las Vegas in the 1960s included a number of ups and downs. Born into modest circumstances in Hoboken, New Jersey, in 1915, he developed an interest in music as a child. In his teen years, he began singing in all kinds of bars, clubs, and lounges, as well as on local radio stations.[174] Following the lead of the great crooners of his era, Sinatra focused on the songs of Cole Porter, Irving Berlin, Jerome Kern, and Lorenz Hart. In 1935, as part of Hoboken Four, Sinatra won a contest on Major Bowes's radio show, the *Original Amateur Hour,* which led to a nationwide tour for the group. After years of scrambling for radio time on local stations and singing at any club that would let him perform, his biggest break came while he was singing at a roadhouse called the Rustic Cabin near Englewood, New Jersey. It was there that trumpeter Harry James saw Sinatra in 1939 and hired the young vocalist to tour and record with his band. He joined the more successful Tommy Dorsey band the following year, and his career took off. In 1941, he and the Dorsey band released his first number one hit, "I'll Never Smile Again." His rapidly growing popularity led Sinatra to embark on a solo career in 1942.

Sinatra quickly became America's top-selling artist and the idol for millions of adoring young women, the bobby-soxers. The reviews of his singing were consistently positive. "The young man with the gaunt face and frail-looking frame," a critic wrote in the *New York Times,* "is an expert hand at dispensing a popular ballad. He has a warm voice that is carefully controlled and a resonant tone." *Time* magazine called him a "crooner extraordinary."[175] He not only released a series of hit records on the Columbia label, but also starred in a number of movies, including *Higher and Higher,* in which he essentially played himself, *Anchors Aweigh* with Gene Kelly, and *The House I Live In,* a short film on intolerance, which earned an Oscar. Sinatra was on a series of radio programs as well: *Your Hit Parade, The Frank Sinatra Show,* and *Songs by Sinatra,* all the while playing major nightclubs all across the country. In 1948, a journalist calculated that he had made $11 million in six years.[176]

Sinatra's remarkable success, however, turned to ashes by the early 1950s. His record sales began to decline in 1947, and Columbia Records eventually released him. His live performances garnered few positive reviews. Indeed, a critic wrote of one of his performances at New York's famed Copacabana in 1950, "The music that used to hypnotize the bobbysoxers . . . is gone from the throat. Vocally, there isn't quite the same old black magic."[177] Indeed, he literally lost his voice one night performing at the Copa. He had trouble attracting audiences. At the Chez Paree in Chicago, he drew only 150 people in a 1,200-seat room. Sinatra was in a series of forgettable films like *The Miracle of the Bells,* which led MGM to drop him, as did MCA as his agent. He had no greater success on radio or television. *Variety* concluded that his television show in 1950 was characterized by "bad pacing, bad scripting, bad tempo, poor camera work and an overall jerky presentation."[178] Beyond being heavily in debt to the IRS, Sinatra also engaged in a public affair with Ava Gardner that led to a separation and eventual divorce from his first wife, Nancy. It all led a trade journal in 1950 to ask the question almost all in the entertainment industry were wondering: "Is Sinatra finished?"[179]

Arguably, one could date his comeback, in part, to his performance at the Desert Inn in September 1951. Sinatra had a history with Las Vegas. While the filming took place in Hollywood, he appeared in *Las Vegas Nights* in 1941 with the Tommy Dorsey Band and the Pied Pipers. He found the gambling center a great getaway in the 1940s, and many thought he would build a resort casino there. It is not clear how he got the Desert Inn booking, but Sinatra got a positive review in the *Las Vegas Sun,* which proclaimed, "The guy is one of the greatest showmen seen these parts."[180] He did not fill the place, but when Sinatra returned the following year, he packed the Painted Desert Room, and Jack Cortez, local booster and publisher of a chatty entertainment weekly *Fabulous Las Vegas* gave his performances an over-the-top review. Cortez wrote, "Frank has a natural flair for comedy and is acquiring a great sense of timing for it. With these things, his undisputed ability in the art of phrasing, and an air of humbleness, he will remain at the top for many, many years to come."[181]

In 1953, Sinatra signed to perform at the new Sands Hotel in the Copa

Room, which would become "His Room" for fourteen years. When he appeared for a week beginning on October 19, Sinatra was basking in the glory of the critics' praise for his work as Angelo Maggio in the movie *From Here to Eternity* and enjoying his six-month relationship with Capitol, a new record company, and a new arranger named Nelson Riddle. His partnership with Capitol led to more than a dozen successful albums, beginning in early 1954 with *In the Wee Small Hours of the Morning*. As the money required to sign headliners had begun to skyrocket, the owners of the Sands wanted to nail down a long-term relationship with the suddenly again-popular vocalist. As Doc Stacher, one of the gangster owners of the Sands, later explained, "The object was to get him to perform there because there's no bigger draw in Las Vegas. When Frankie was performing, the hotel really filled up."[182] They granted him a 2 percent interest in the hotel, a share that eventually grew to 9 percent, and the Nevada tax commission approved his license.

Sinatra's years at the Sands, staying in the presidential suite with his own swimming pool and playing with unlimited gambling credit, were magical for him and his fans. He was on top of the entertainment world, and his fans always filled the Copa Room to see him. In his 1961 book *Sinatra and the Rat Pack,* freelance writer Richard Gehman explained Sinatra's meteoric return to prominence: "Once considered washed up, Sinatra staged an astonishing comeback and stands today, in the vernacular of show business, as the greatest of them all in every field into which he thrusts his talents—recordings, radio and nightclubs, television and films." Gehman argued, "There simply is nobody in the world like him." His impact on Las Vegas was clear to all who saw him there. Movie director Billy Wilder explained, "Wherever Frank is, there is a certain electricity permeating the air. It's like Mack the Knife is in town and the action is starting." According to movie producer Jerry Wald, Sinatra performances at the Sands were a magnet for celebrities: "His audiences are always full of performers, and they're all looking at him with great excitement."[183]

To be sure, the fans wanted to hear the great vocalist, the top popular singer of the post–World War II era. His songs evolved from "romantic idealism" in the 1940s, to loss and loneliness in the 1950s, to a tone of "mellow nostalgia" in the 1960s, and his voice became "stronger, surer, more relaxed."[184] Yet there were other elements that contributed to the Sinatra charisma. Some newspapers described his loyalty to friends, extraordinary generosity, staunch opposition to intolerance, and devotion to his three children. Most, however, focused on his "charm and sharp edges."[185] Notably, they wrote about Sinatra's powerful independent streak. "I'm going to do as I please," he told *Time* magazine in 1955. "I don't need anybody in the world. I did it all myself."[186] A decade later, Gay Talese, in a lengthy *Esquire* essay, saw that as the defining element in Sinatra's persona. "He seemed," Talese argued, "now to be also the embodiment of the fully emancipated male, perhaps the only one in America, the man who can do anything he wants, anything, can do it because he has money, the energy, and no apparent guilt."[187] In other words, he smoked, drank excessively, chased women—many women—and stayed up all night while performing or filming a movie.

Sinatra exhibited this machismo most impressively by associating with figures from organized crime in incidents that drew much press attention. For example, in early 1947, he took a trip to Havana, Cuba, and stories circulated about him hobnobbing with leading mobsters like Lucky Luciano at the Hotel National.[188] In 1963, the Nevada gaming control board revoked his gambling license because he "had associated with hoodlums." Specifically, he had permitted Chicago gangster Sam Giancana to stay at his Cal-Neva resort in violation of Nevada's black book ban on certain organized criminals being in the state's casinos.[189] Even though he was no longer part owner of the Sands, a federal grand jury nonetheless subpoenaed Sinatra to appear in 1967 in its investigation of organized crime's skimming from Las Vegas casinos.[190] Political cartoonist Garry Trudeau even did a strip on Sinatra as a friend of gangsters in 1985.[191] Sinatra certainly was not the only celebrity to associate with organized crime figures—indeed, performing in Las Vegas in the 1950s and 1960s necessarily meant working in a mob-owned property. Yet he was a favored performer among crime figures. In 1977, for example, *Time* magazine published an article on a gathering of top mob bosses in New York and noted that many like Jimmy "The Weasel" Fratianno and Tony Spilotro attended a Sinatra concert in Tarrytown, New York.[192] Sinatra not only acknowledged his association with men from organized crime, in the view of some in the 1950s, but he also looked "like the popular conception of a gangster" and dressed like them as well, "with a glaring, George Raft kind of snazziness—rich, dark shirts and white figured ties, with ring and cuff links that almost always match."[193] Though not involved in organized crime, Sinatra enjoyed being on the periphery, playing the role of the tough guy.

His explosive temper also caught the attention of journalists, particularly when it led to fisticuffs. On several occasions, Sinatra punched those who angered or offended him. In 1947, for example, he slugged columnist Lee Mortimer because the latter, according to Sinatra, had said, "There goes that dago" as the singer was walking into a restaurant in Hollywood. Beyond the ethnic slur, Sinatra was angry at the journalist: "He's needled me for two years. He's referred to my bobby-soxer fans as morons. They're not morons. They're just kids."[194] In 1966, Sinatra got into a fight at a Beverly Hills lounge that left the other man hospitalized.[195] There were other incidents involving intrusive photographers, but the most significant of his battles led to his departure from his long-term relationship with the Sands Hotel. In 1967, a drunk Sinatra, who had driven a golf cart through a window, demanded that Sands vice president Carl Cohen extend his gambling credit. When Cohen refused, an outraged Sinatra challenged him, and Cohen punched the singer in the mouth, knocking out the caps of two teeth.[196]

It was a combination of these traits—the great vocalist, the mike in one hand and a cigarette or a tumbler of Jack Daniels in the other; the tough guy afraid of no challenge; the risk taker willing to associate with underworld figures; the famed lover of dozens of women—that appealed to the Las Vegas crowds, with or without his Rat Pack. He was the great singer who took no crap from anyone and didn't give a damn what people thought about what he did. After his debacle with Carl Cohen, he left the Sands and took his talents and formidable image to Caesars Palace, where he appeared to huge audiences from 1968 to 1983. His appearances were such big events that the management did not even need to put his name on the marquee; they simply posted, "He's Here." From 1984 to 1994, when he made his last Las Vegas appearance, Sinatra performed at the Golden Nugget, Riviera, Desert Inn, Bally's, and the MGM Grand.

The lasting memories for most, however, were his days at the Sands, particularly when performing with Dean Martin, Sammy Davis Jr., Joey Bishop, and Peter Lawford. One journalist in 1960 contended that the Rat Pack displayed "a wild iconoclasm that millions envy secretly or even unconsciously—which makes them, in the public eye, the innest in-group in the world."[197] According to Mike Weatherford, they epitomized Las Vegas cool with "the casual swagger, the flick of a cigarette, the snappy patter."[198] But not everyone approved. Some saw the Rat Pack as misogynist juvenile drunks. Yet Sinatra and his cohorts appealed to post–World War II men seeking to shed their cares for an evening or a few days in Las Vegas. As Richard Lacayo argued in 1998, middle-class men of the 1950s and 1960s "wanted to cut loose, the way Sinatra wore his tie—undone, a sign of his narrow escape from a workaday world."[199] For others, Sinatra and the Rat Pack represented something culturally significant. While in the spotlight in Las Vegas, they demonstrated the nation's multiethnic possibilities. Max Rudin contended they redefined America's sense of class, one no longer determined by WASP Americans: "One black, one Jew, two Italians, and one feckless Hollywoodized Brit, three

Frank Sinatra, the biggest entertainment star in Las Vegas history, in 1967. Source: UNLV Libraries, Special Collections.

of them second-generation immigrants, four raised during the Depression in ethnic city neighborhoods."[200]

In the end, Sinatra's significance for Las Vegas came not from his 2,000 recorded songs or his sixty movie appearances; it was his work on the stage, particularly at the Sands' Copa Room. That is where he developed the Sinatra brand; that is where the Rat Pack became the iconic group for the city, creating for visitors an expectation of a certain style of show one linked intimately with the desert setting. Presley, Newton, Prima, Smith, Liberace, and the hundreds of other headliners and production shows gave Las Vegas an unbeatable aura as the entertainment capital of the nation. They tantalized prospective visitors with the prospect of shows with glamour, glitz, elaborate staging, great costuming, and high energy. This Las Vegas style of entertainment, a style that drew on the best of nightclub and cabaret talent, offered performances that added immeasurably to the allure of Las Vegas. And among them all, it was Sinatra who emerged as the premier performer in the entertainment capital of the nation. His shows attracted crowds like no other. As Don Payne, the longtime manager of the Las Vegas News Bureau, pointed out in 2005, a great performer like "Liberace would fill a hotel," but "Sinatra filled the town."[201]

"Beautiful Women Were as Commonplace in Las Vegas as Poker Chips"

Images of Las Vegas Women in Popular Culture

Amid the plush, neon-lit casinos and fabulous hotels, Boulder Dam, sage brush and cactus, there is an abundance of women, all kinds of women; buxom hausfraus, bulging in blue jeans, cocktail waitresses who can be talked into working after hours, strip-tease girls and out-and-out harlots who cruise about in Cadillac convertibles.

Pose Magazine, 1955

When people were asked in a poll what they thought of first when they heard Las Vegas, they answered: sex.

Forbes, 1973

Las Vegas has more beautiful women than any town its size in the world. It may have as many beautiful women as any city in the world no matter what its size. The reason is quite simple and only super-ficially cynical: MONEY *and beautiful women zing together like two magnets. Especially in Vegas.*

Mario Puzo, 1976

Las Vegas, perhaps more than any other American city, has objecti-fied women. The majority of Las Vegas production shows continue to feature topless showgirls and erotic dance even though audiences are mostly couples. Lounge servers and keno runners are almost exclu-sively women, invariably attired in revealing outfits.

Bob Sehlinger, 1994

Amid the images of a frontier town, a haven for gangsters, a Mecca for gamblers, and the center of a rich tableaux of entertainment, women were always a critical element in the appeal of Las Vegas, so much a man's town. The beautiful, blushing brides, the jaded wives seeking a quick divorce, the glamour girls offering free drinks, the prostitutes, the strippers, and the fabulous showgirls represented some of the many faces of women in Las Vegas on film and in print. The "gorgeous chunks of flesh floating around" the casinos offered a strong "hint of sexuality," what Wallace Turner in the New York Times called "a vision of Las Vegas that casino owners hope is burning in the minds of people across the continent."[1] The journalists, authors, and filmmakers crafting these images of women in Las Vegas had a profound impact on the perceptions of Americans. As romance novelist Stephanie James argued, "In the minds of the vast majority of the male population, the illusion of Las Vegas was woven not only with the promise of gambling but with the promise of easily available women."[2]

Happy, beautiful brides in Las Vegas frequently graced the pages of the nation's magazines and newspapers and appeared in films as they exchanged vows in the helter-skelter quick-marriage capital of the world. Because there was no blood test or waiting period for marriage, Nevada became a magnet for the romantically inclined who did not want to delay their nuptials. In 1939, the small town of just over 8,400 had 5,434 marriages. Within two years, the number had reached 21,308, a figure that doubled in just over a decade and continued to grow rapidly. By 1982, there were 57,702 weddings.[3] Popular magazines of the 1940s delighted in regaling readers with stories about the extraordinary efforts Las Vegans made to attract couples and to simplify access to wedded bliss. For those driving into Las Vegas, one encountered a big billboard explaining, "For Wedding Information Go Direct to Court House." Indeed, one reporter noted, "Your eyes pop, as you drive into Las Vegas, at the number and boldness of the signs proclaiming easy and quick marriage." In a 1940 article in Look magazine, readers learned that "the good parson Sloan, Baptist, who sleeps with his boots handy" is ready to respond "to a marriage call like a fireman," and the following year, the Reno Evening Gazette reported that even when the courthouse was closed, "any one of the many wedding chapels has only to telephone the night or Sunday marriage license clerk at her home. She keeps blank forms in her handbag and, so friendly is Las Vegas, the deputy will hop into her car and bring you the license."[4] The New York Times reported that a wedding could even be as simple as stepping off the train. In 1940, the city opened a "new ultra-modern air-conditioned Union Pacific passenger station that will house a marriage license bureau in the waiting room to accommodate elopers."⁵ For those too impatient to drive or take a train to Las Vegas, a *Collier's* article in 1941 noted, "All over California and in Utah and Arizona, airlines advertise 'Honeymoon Fliers' with the slogan: 'Only one and three-quarter hours to Paradise.'"⁶ A couple of movies reinforced this impression. *Flying Blind* (1941) was about Honeymoon Airlines, a firm that transported couples to Las Vegas for quick marriages, and *Flight to Nowhere* (1946) has a pilot explaining to a friend, "Do you realize that in the last 24 hours I've flown four couples up to Las Vegas to get married?"⁷ One local tour company made weddings in Las Vegas as simple as possible, offering to take care of all the arrangements for only $46.50 per couple. Besides a wedding at the rustic Little Church of the West, the fee included "organ music, license fee, minister, marriage fee, corsage, witnesses, and tour of the city." A more bare-bones service could be had for much less. You could be married in "less than an hour after you arrive, day or night." All one needed was "the gal and the ring and $12."⁸

These images from the 1940s largely set the pattern for what became the essential elements in a Vegas wedding: dozens of kitschy wedding chapels with Elvis impersonators giving away the bride or singing, marriage licenses easier to obtain "than stamps in a postage vending machine," weddings that could be had in "a flat minute and a half," and the perfect place for a wedding and honeymoon "amid the glitter of the Strip."⁹ Several movies depicted Las Vegas as the ideal locale for an impulsive couple: *Lady Luck* (1946), *Once More My Darling* (1949), *Viva Las Vegas* (1964), *Honeymoon in Vegas* (1992), and *Fools Rush In* (1997). The almost constant string of celebrity marriages contributed an element of glamour to the Las Vegas wedding scene. From the 1950s through the early twenty-first century, Americans read about the Las Vegas nuptials of entertainment stars like Rita Hayworth and Dick Haymes, Paul Newman and Joanne Woodward, Cary Grant and Dyan Cannon, Frank Sinatra and Mia Farrow, and Elvis Presley and Priscilla Anne Beaulieu.

Not all of the weddings depicted in films and reported in the press turned out well. For example, in 2004, the nation followed the bewildering fifty-five-hour-long marriage of pop singer Britney Spears, featuring a bizarre wedding in which she marched down the aisle of a wedding chapel at 5:30 A.M. in torn jeans and a baseball cap.¹⁰ A 1999 episode of the popular television series *Friends* had the characters Ross and Rachel going to Las Vegas and doing what some newspaper articles reported frequently happened to real-life couples: after a long drinking binge, they got married and then quickly had the marriage annulled. Most depictions of Las Vegas weddings, however, offered a positive image of women. They typically were happy brides participating in a themed wedding, perhaps even a drive-through ceremony, serenaded by Elvis, enjoying a moment of impetuous exuberance. "It's kind of a cool thing," one couple said in a documentary, "to say you got married in Vegas. It makes your whole life seem a little bit racier, a little cooler."[11]

However, the Las Vegas divorcée was also a frequent image encountered by readers and viewers. In August 1911, readers of the *New York Times* learned that tiny Las Vegas, Nevada, had "designs on Reno's reputation and prestige as a divorce market." The paper reported that there was talk about town that a divorce lawyer had plans to build a large hotel in hopes of making Las Vegas "especially attractive for a divorce colony."[12] Nevada had the nation's shortest residency requirement (six months), and Reno had emerged as the divorce capital. According to the *Times,* "There are more than two hundred Eastern divorce-seekers in this city all the time."[13] Las Vegas made little progress even when the state legislature shortened the waiting period to six weeks in 1931 in response to some states that had reduced their residency requirements. Reno's business skyrocketed, with its judges granting nearly six times as many divorces as those in Las Vegas. Promotional efforts by the city to make Las Vegas "the foremost divorce colony" failed, and "the national press remained stubbornly uninterested" through most of the 1930s.[14]

That all changed in 1939, when Ria Gable, wife of Hollywood star Clark Gable, who was busy finishing the filming of *Gone with the Wind,* came to Las Vegas to establish residency for a divorce. Ria became a familiar face around town, boating on Lake Mead, riding horses in the desert, skiing on Mt. Charleston, and gambling at the Apache Hotel. The *Las Vegas Evening Review-Journal* published a feature story on Ria's experiences, and the chamber of commerce sent the story to newspapers across the country to get national attention. It worked remarkably well, as dozens of papers "used the story as a Sunday feature" with the headline "Gable Divorce Booms Las Vegas."[15] Ria was helpful in this promotional campaign. Upon her arrival, she told reporters, "I like Las Vegas much better than Reno. Clark and I came through here frequently on his hunting trips to Utah." She permitted photographers to take numerous pictures, and she entertained Hollywood luminaries like George Raft, as well as Clara Bow and Rex Bell, who lived on a ranch near Searchlight, Nevada.[16] Tourists began dropping by in hopes of seeing Ria. Beyond the speculation that her husband was going to marry actress Carole Lombard after the divorce, there were also romantic rumors about Ria. A columnist from an Ogden, Utah, paper heard that "Mrs. Gable may beat her husband to getting married again. There's some big wealthy financier interested in her and I happen to know he telephones her from Los Angeles every night!"[17]

The folks in Las Vegas expected that the Gable divorce would produce big results for the town's divorce business. "We're going to wipe Reno right off the map as far as this marrying and divorcing business goes," a drugstore clerk claimed to a reporter.[18] In 1940, *Look* magazine described an almost immediate impact. Ria Gable "uttered a few kind words for the little town," and Las Vegas "has been capitalizing on it ever since." Because the town could offer "all the easy divorce terms that can be had in Reno, plus a wider variety of horseplay and a friendlier atmosphere, the town booms again."[19] Readers of the article discovered that Las Vegas "courtroom procedure frees a woman in an average of four minutes, seven seconds, after which it is customary to buy the judge a drink."[20] There were also some news stories and novels that made Las Vegas an appealing locale to women thinking about divorce. Reporters suggested that it was relatively inexpensive. One could get by in 1941 on as little as $200 for a six-week stay. Five years later, a columnist reported that one could stay "at one of the swank hotels for around $20 a day for six weeks or sweat it out in a $1.50-a-night hotel."[21] Beyond that, it was "a nice place to relax," as a character in Richard Prather's 1951 novel *Find This Woman* explained. One could enjoy the life of the casinos or become part of that "special breed of women" who "idly played cards or lounged around a pool until the six weeks' residence period was over."[22] To be sure, there were accounts that highlighted the challenges of enduring the residency requirement. Many had to look for temporary jobs, sometimes as "change girls and shills" in casinos, or they found themselves reduced to pawning their possessions. A few became compulsive gamblers or became "easy prey for sharp-eyed pimps."[23] As a character who became a prostitute in the 1965 novel *Muses of Ruin* explained, "Came for the cure. Then I decided to work my way through Vegas, and couldn't kick the habit."[24]

On balance, however, women across the nation concluded that Las Vegas would be the best locale for a divorce, and they came in ever-greater numbers. In 1931, the first year with the new six-week residency requirement, there was only a divorce about every other day, but a decade later, there were three a day. At the end of the war, the number reached eight per day, and by 1948, there were twenty-five divorces granted on most days in Las Vegas.[25] As the numbers rapidly increased, women waiting for a divorce became stock characters in the novels of the 1940s and 1950s—women who had come to Las Vegas for what was known as the six-week salvation, the six-week stint, or simply the cure.[26]

In some accounts, the environment of Las Vegas, the libertarian mores of the place with its wide-open gambling and drinking and all-night entertainment, changed the women. They not only ended their marriages, but they also found it too difficult to resist the lax moral code that prevailed in Las Vegas. Erle Stanley Gardner (writing as A. A. Fair) illustrated this view in his novel *Spill the Jackpot,* where he argued that lonely women, far from home and counting the days until they met the residency requirement, became women on the make. One of his characters explains:

> Y'understand Las Vegas is different from other places. Girls come here to get a divorce. They have to wait to establish a residence. It ain't a long time, when you just think of it as so much time out of a year, but when you stay here, it gets pretty long. The girls get lonesome, and if a good-looking guy gives 'em the eye, they figure what the hell. They ain't got nothing else to do, and they fall. Back in their home town, they'd give him the icy stare, but out here, they want something to break the monotony and they're just getting a divorce so they figure it's sorta in between drinks, and a little cheating don't count.[27]

Alice Denham, in her short story "The Deal," agreed that waiting for the cure in Las Vegas changed women. In her tale, an artist named Linda was in a casino when "she glanced at the divorcees at the bar scouting out a man for the night, acting like they thought their husbands had. Those that didn't start caring again sometimes stayed and made good money."[28] The most cynical interpretation came in a 1955 issue of the men's pulp magazine *Pose,* which claimed that there are "thousands of divorce-seekers who have settled down to sweat out the six-week 'residence.'" After "the dull routine of keeping house for the wrong man," Las Vegas provided these women the ultimate escape of pleasure. "Surrounding them is an army of sun-tanned men, a sea of alcoholic anesthesia, a boatload of moral abandonment. Few of them will be bored." While these women may have been "downhearted" upon arrival, "they will soon forget their troubles in the lush night-life which rules Las Vegas" with "a horde of fast-talk-gigolos" at their disposal. "Why do women go wild in Las Vegas?" According to *Pose,* in part, it is due to "female frailties," but also "because this desert-sprung phenomenon of unbounded hedonism overwhelms every trace of restraint in their newfound freedom. When the six-week sinerama is ended, they drift homeward, some filled with a longing for the husband they have forsaken, others brimming with a desire to renew the orgy of pleasure they lived in Las Vegas."[29]

These bleak, misogynistic characterizations of divorcées in Las Vegas were typical of hard-boiled detective fiction and the pulp magazines of the postwar era. The women in this popular genre were beautiful, lusty, treacherous sexual predators—the classic femmes fatales leading the hero into danger. A 1957 short story about Las Vegas neatly fit this model. A detective named Jerrold, investigating a counterfeit money scheme, is attracted to the beautiful Iris Dumont, who lures him into a house. She "turned and pressed close to him, her gray eyes luminous, her fragrance rising in heady waves." As they embraced, "the night was filled with shimmering rapture, and time ceased to exist." Yet she had led him to Stratton Shenfield, the man heading the counterfeit ring. "Jerrold knew in that instant that he was a dead man. Iris Dumont had betrayed him beyond a doubt."[30]

In most of the postwar narratives, Las Vegas women were essentially portrayed as gorgeous targets for admiring men: "From a strictly biological angle she looked like dynamite. Dynamite scantily clad." "She had jet-black hair combed back tight against a well-shaped head, and her figure was something that no normal male would care to forget." "From across the room the girl had a finger-snapping kind of class. Her simple red dress proved that she didn't need a build-up anywhere. She was legit 36–24–36." "She was small and dark and good looking enough, and she had a body which made her an adjunct to the establishment." "She was one hell of a nice-looking woman, this Mrs. Tanner, a delightfully-stacked sweetheart somewhere in her late twenties. She had tucked herself into a low-cut, clinging, blue-crepe dress and, going on visible evidence, I was willing to make book at five-to-one that the curves were all her own."[31]

The lurid and sensational pulp magazines marketed to World War II veterans continually built the image of a Las Vegas filled with attractive women who could be found in beautiful gowns, swimsuits, or nearly nude. Men's magazines and their feature articles, accompanied by racy photos, told a familiar tale—that there were beautiful and available women in Las Vegas: *Hit!* ("Flamingo Girls at Work and Play"), *Topper* ("Inside the Dressing Rooms at Vegas!"), *Male* ("Women Who Hunt for Sex in Las Vegas"), *Modern Man* ("Backstage at Vegas"), *Adam* ("Lures of Las Vegas"), *Sheer* ("Las Vegas Showgirl Edition"), *After Hours* ("Girls & Gambling in Las Vegas"), *She* ("Sex in Las Vegas"), and *Inside Story* ("What Elvis Presley Learned about Sex in Las Vegas"). In 1955, *Brief* magazine offered photos of eighteen attractive Las Vegas dancers and strippers.[32] Three years later, *Real Men* published an article with ten pinups of showgirls. "When these talented showgirls make the rounds of the Vegas night spots, even the dice tables empty in a hurry." A caption on one photo proclaimed, "Girls, choruses and choruses of them!

Enough beauty to set men's imaginations afire round the entire world!" Every night, "this bevy of beauties has set the town on its ear!"[33]

Postwar mainstream magazines like *Life, Business Week, Newsweek,* and the *Saturday Evening Post;* Sunday news magazines like *Parade;* major newspapers like the *Chicago Daily Tribune,* the *Los Angeles Times,* and the *New York Times* all published articles about Las Vegas that included photos of scantily clad women at hotel swimming pools, dancers in the shows, and gambling in the casinos. Movies like *Moon over Las Vegas, The Lady Gambles, Las Vegas Story, Painting the Clouds with Sunshine, The Girl Rush, Las Vegas Shakedown, Meet Me in Las Vegas,* and *Hollywood or Bust* also portrayed Las Vegas as a resort city adorned with beautiful women. Indeed, this became an expected pattern of cinematic images for the resort city over the next several decades, with a plethora of attractive actresses like Ann-Margret in *Viva Las Vegas,* Elizabeth Taylor in *The Only Game in Town,* Natalie Wood and Dyan Cannon in *Bob and Carol and Ted and Alice,* Jill St. John in *Diamonds Are Forever,* Jane Fonda in *The Electric Horseman,* Annette Bening in *Bugsy,* Sarah Jessica Parker in *Honeymoon in Vegas,* Demi Moore in *Indecent Proposal,* Sharon Stone in *Casino,* and Julia Roberts in *Ocean's Eleven.* The television series *Vega$, Crime Story,* and *CSI* all featured gorgeous women as regulars and guests, but the show *Las Vegas* placed a premium on beautiful and available women. In the first three episodes of the show's premiere season in 2003–2004, viewers saw, besides a beautiful casino host, pit boss, and entertainment director, a woman having sex in an elevator, hookers, dancers in a strip club, women by the pool in skimpy bikinis, and "French maids" provided for a visiting U.S. senator.

Women are seldom independent or successful in the popular culture about Las Vegas. Hope Lange did portray the owner of Caesars Palace in the television movie *Pleasure Palace,* and Lara Flynn Boyle momentarily was the owner of the fictitious Montecito Resort and Casino in the television series *Las Vegas,* but Lange's character had to be saved by a male professional gambler, and Boyle's character died in a freak accident.[34] Instead, women appear most often as possessions, objects of men's attention, or hustlers.[35] Ovid Demaris was not unusual in the way he described character Irene Biddick in his novel *Candyleg.* "She was," he wrote, "just a piece. That's all she had ever been. A quick and easy piece."[36] In *The Golden Greed,* Brad Curtis included a character named Al Braden as the majority owner of a hotel-casino. To Braden, character Nancy Maurer "was a tool, useful at certain moments." Maurer "was a tramp. Oh, not an ordinary one but a very special one. She dangled on the end of strings Al held, and she moved when he jerked those strings. She was polished to perfection, and she had a definite commercial value to him. She would sleep with anybody Al Braden designated."[37] Similarly, in the novel *Las Vegas*, Nona Adrian was a pit girl, and "it was part of her job to cater to the highrollers, and sometimes that meant hitting the sack with them."[38]

Men as predators is óne of the constant themes in these novels. In Steve Fisher's *No House Limit*, a man offers a showgirl $500 to sleep with him. Needing the money, she goes to his room, where he simply hands her the money. She told a friend, "He just wanted to see if I'd show up." "Don't you understand," she explains, "he wanted the mental satisfaction of making a prostitute out of me."[39] In Alice Denham's Las Vegas short story "The Deal," a famed poker shark offers a young woman named Linda $1,000 to sleep with him. Linda knows this is common; indeed, "the cocktail waitress who lived in the one-room hovel next to Linda's had lost her job by refusing five hundred from an important customer." At first, Linda refuses, declaring, "Everything's not for sale." However, she concludes that she can never make such good money as an artist, and she agrees to sleep with the man. Afterward, she escapes to the bathroom, throws up, starts to cry, and takes a shower to wash off the shame.[40]

Although most typically found in the detective fiction of the 1950s, this story line returned in two movies released four decades later. In both cases, a wealthy man offers a great deal of money to sleep with a beautiful woman. Tommy Korman offers $65,000 to sleep with Betsy Nolan, the fiancée of Jack Singer in *Honeymoon in Vegas* (1992), and John Gage offers $1 million to sleep with Diana Murphy, the wife of David Murphy, in *Indecent Proposal* (1993). Although Diana Murphy tells Gage, "You can't buy people," and both women eventually return to their true loves, they temporarily succumb to temptation; the city, at least momentarily, has upset their moral compass. "Women have always been objectified in the Las Vegas image of fun," M. Gottdiener, Claudia C. Collins, and David R. Dickens have pointed out, but in the case of these two films, women are "no different than a stack of poker chips to be won or lost."[41]

Yet several women in the fiction and films about Las Vegas became the predators. Readers of fiction through the 1970s found women in Las Vegas casinos described as "parasites," "tramps," "molls of mobsters," "discontented housewives," "cocktail lounge tarts," and "women's lib members flaunting sexual freedom as a religion."[42] These women on the make were hustling to make a quick buck, find a wealthy husband, or both. They loitered around the casinos looking for the best target, watching "the size of wallets as they are pulled out time and again to buy another drink or another stack of chips."[43]

Hustlers were the sharpest of the predatory women. According to novelist Emily Elliot, "Chip hustling is the most common hustling you'll see out here. A girl wants to have a good time and make a little money too. So she spends the evening flirting and gambling with some guy who is convinced that she's bringing him luck and she drops money into her purse all night long."[44] Similarly, Norman Herries described this phenomenon in his 1956 novel *My Private Hangman*. He has a male character gambling in a casino as "a compactly knit redhead with décolleté dress and fancy ideas pressed invitingly into my right arm." The gambler "knew she was trying to build me up to the point where she would be able to relieve me of some part of the bankroll I was rapidly accumulating."[45] Viewers who saw Ginger, portrayed by Sharon Stone, in the 1995 film *Casino* encountered a woman described by the narrator as "one of the best known, most respected hustlers in town. Smart hustlers like her could keep a guy awake for two or three days before sending him home broke to the little woman and his bank examiners."[46] Showgirls were also on the hunt. In some novels, showgirls, after their performances, accompany "doctors, lawyers, and business executives out for a fantasy experience," hoping to cash in.[47] Readers are left with the impression that there are scores of women in Las Vegas eager to "latch on to 'spare change' after working hours."[48]

Those who read about and saw films and documentaries about Las Vegas certainly came to understand how pervasive prostitution seemed to be in the city. In 1970, Harvey Hardy wrote about being in Las Vegas over six decades earlier and picking up on "rumors about some place in the back of Block Sixteen where there was dancing and many beautiful ladies just waiting to bestow their affection (for a consideration of course)." Many Americans like Hardy associated Las Vegas with prostitution from its beginnings.[49] Visiting journalists invariably noted the fabled block. For example, Gordon Gassaway, a travel columnist for the *Los Angeles Times* in 1918, reported on his encounter with an aggressive prostitute there named Daisy as he walked about the town. "In my wanderings," he explained, "I came to a strange and restricted district and decided to take myself away from there at once, escaping from a buxom lass of doubtful color and antecedents at great peril to my coat tails."[50] Block 16 remained the center of a thriving business for more than thirty years. Relying largely on rail travelers for business, nearly fifty prostitutes worked in Las Vegas in the 1920s, a number that grew more than sixfold during the construction of Boulder Dam in the early 1930s.[51] The city had to shut down its red-light district after the U.S. Army established a gunnery school just outside Las Vegas during World War II. After the war, community leaders extended their efforts to eliminate prostitution in the county. Yet some notable brothels, like Roxie's Four Mile Motel, remained in business just outside the city limits, and there were still street hustlers and taxi drivers involved in promoting prostitution in the town.[52] Authorities finally shut down Roxie's after its operators were found guilty in 1954 of violating the Mann Act because they had brought prostitutes to their "20-girl bawdy house" from California.[53]

Prostitution remained a thriving business even though the state of Nevada eventually prohibited brothels in Clark County. For example, in 1960, Hank Greenspun, crusading editor of the *Las Vegas Sun*, complained about the call girls frequenting Las Vegas hotel lounges. He claimed, "For every girl picked up by the sheriff's department, I can point out 10 that got away."[54] In their 1963 muckraking book on Las Vegas, Ed Reid and Ovid Demaris noted that the police arrested 135 prostitutes on the Strip in 1961, but that number did not truly reflect the dimensions of the problem. Indeed, the authors proclaimed that the city was "one huge whorehouse."[55] The reported number of prostitutes working the city grew dramatically over time. In 1977, the *Los Angeles Times* claimed that the police had "dossiers on about 7,000 prostitutes," and four years later, *U.S. News and World Report* told readers that "there are 10,000 prostitutes active in the city."[56] These kinds of news stories, whether accurate or not, created an impression that prostitutes were everywhere tourists would go, whether along the Strip or downtown. As novelist Carole Nelson Douglas put it in 1990, "Hookers were as ubiquitous a Las Vegas commodity as casino chips."[57]

There were many sources for this multitude of prostitutes. Besides the hundreds of regulars, there were many sweating out a divorce, and some of the latter joined ranks with the former. But there were many other types of women who joined in the flesh trade. Casey Shawhan and James Bassett, in the *Oakland Tribune* in 1953, quoted local sources who asserted, "Vegas is loaded with private secretaries on a spree, wives who have shed their husbands for a weekend, scores of chorus girls with plenty of time between shows." In addition, "high-priced Hollywood girls carefully check Vegas for important night club openings."[58] Most commentators focused on the "weekend warriors" or "moonlighters"—the housewives, secretaries, waitresses, and schoolteachers who flew into Las Vegas from Los Angeles, San Francisco, Denver, Dallas, and Phoenix.[59] In his 1976 book on Las Vegas, famed author Mario Puzo described how some young women became a "Weekend Call Girl." "They may be secretaries, manicurists, dental technicians, etc. Maybe it started when they went to Vegas for a weekend of fun and shows with a boyfriend or even a girlfriend. The Vegas gambling executives, Pit Bosses and Shift Bosses, have an eagle eye for such girls. They 'chat them up,' 'put them into a show' (that is give them a free meal and seat to a show), and then give the girls their business cards and tell them to call whenever they're in town and need something. On a later solo trip the girls will usually be fixed up for a date with a hotshot gambler."[60]

Readers learned that there were various ways men could secure the prostitutes' services besides in a bar or lounge. Many of the women simply walked the Strip, along Fremont Street downtown, or the side streets; others, the drive-in hookers, prowled the casino and hotel parking lots in their cars. Men hoping to exercise a little more discretion asked taxi drivers or bellmen and pit bosses at the hotels and casinos. In 1963, Richard Taylor and Patricia Howell, in *Las Vegas, City of Sin?*, told their discriminating readers that "strong, unconfirmed rumors persist that several of the larger hotels have between 15 and 20 girls at their beck and call around the clock. These girls are the upper level, or social registers, of their profession."[61] For the uninitiated, one travel book for Las Vegas even offered guidance by having a local working girl explain the best way to find a prostitute. "Unless he's very shy," she advised, "he should go to into any bar in a casino, and pick out the best looking girl there. Talk to her, tell her where you're from, what you're doing here, who you work for, how much you make, and what your credit line is." The woman might "say she's a showgirl, or whatever. Take her gambling and give her money as a gift. If it's a working girl, she'll make clear the terms of the contract—$50 and up, to a maximum of around $1,000."[62]

By the 1970s, there was a new way to procure temporary companionship. Escort services proliferated in Las Vegas, and they advertised in entertainment weeklies and in the yellow pages.[63] Indeed, by the early twenty-first century, there were several hundred listings in the telephone directory leaving little to the imagination: "I want to please you," "Whatever you Desire," "We Have an Escort for Every Need," or "The Perfect Way to Climax Your Stay in Las Vegas."[64] Viewers of NBC's *Dateline* program in 2003 learned about the city's new marketing slogan—"What happens here, stays here"—and the meaning of that compelling line. Viewers followed a man with a hidden camera going to two casinos on the Strip and watched as several different women approached him, asking, "Are you looking for any company?" The episode illustrated one man's contention that being picked up by an escort in Las Vegas "is as easy as buying a gallon of milk at a grocery store."[65]

Because so much of the material on prostitutes in print, on television, and in films made it appear simple to secure the services of prostitutes in Las Vegas, some travel guides urged tourists to be careful. In 1981, Hank Kovell, author of *Poor Man's Guide to Las Vegas* and a Las Vegas publicist, explained how often prostitutes rolled their tricks. A metro vice cop told Kovell that over 60 percent of prostitutes were thieves. Indeed, they investigated about eighty rolls a month, with the average theft being about $2,000. Kovell pointed out that at a recent convention in Las Vegas, "nearly 300 prostitutes were arrested during the first three days of the show, but not before several of them had taken their clients for money and jewelry." Kovell's "strong advice" to visitors to his city was simply to abstain.[66] Another guidebook author explained that soliciting prostitutes was a misdemeanor crime in Clark County, and that about fifty men a month were arrested for solicitation. Joyce Wiswell thus warned the would-be traveler to Las Vegas, "Beware: That alluring hooker may actually be an undercover cop whose only interest in handcuffs is slapping them on your wrists."[67]

Novelists, journalists, and filmmakers characterized Las Vegas prostitutes in a variety of ways: a faded fashion model at a bar picking up any trick who comes along, a young woman traveling to Las Vegas hoping to become a hooker, call girls who service only high rollers, a cocktail waitress who is available to special guests, showgirls willing to entertain important businessmen, and a prostitute as serial killer.[68] A handful of the fictional accounts of Las Vegas prostitutes delved into the kinds of women who became and remained prostitutes. Some authors, like novelist W. T. Ballard, are disparaging, indeed cynical. In his *The Seven Sisters,* Ballard has a character saying, "I'm not sentimental about these girls. Most of them are of low mentality, arrested juveniles whose wits can't compete in the conventional pattern of life." Alice Templeton, one of the prostitutes in the novel, explains, "I'm a whore. Because I like men, and I'm too lazy to do anything else, or maybe I just haven't got enough sense."[69] Carrie Reasoner, a prostitute in Marilyn Lynch's novel *Casino,* is a working-class wife who becomes a compulsive poker player and hopes to win big so that her family can escape a poor neighborhood in north Los Angeles. "All she needed was one good trip to Las Vegas to win the down payment of twelve hundred dollars, plus a few thousand more for new furniture. She would get the twins bicycles and maybe they could have a pool, too." Reasoner complicated her gambling addiction by turning to prostitution. She loved being in Las Vegas: "No neighbors to frown, no husband to chide her, no kids screaming for attention." Typically, when "in Vegas she picked up men who could not complicate her life back home. Carrie did not consider it to be hooking. It was just a way of having fun when her own money ran out."[70]

Other treatments are more sympathetic, but they nonetheless paint a portrait of women struggling with frustrating, lonely, often meaningless lives. In his short story "Stop, Rewind, and Play," John Irsfeld describes a prostitute named Lilla who lives alone in an apartment off the Strip. She works six nights a week, and on her day off, Lilla dreams "about the future." After winning a cassette recorder in a drawing at Binion's Horseshoe Casino, Lilla decides to dictate her life story: "a high school romance, the Vietnam war, her fiancé a prisoner and then dead." Yet she chastises herself for her wasted life, tearfully acknowledging that she is "just another hooker." Lilla tapes a different, false version of her life and leaves it in the hotel room where she made the recording. Then she prepares for another night of work in a job that has destroyed her identity.[71] In the John O'Brien novel *Leaving Las Vegas* and the film of the same name, one encounters a Las Vegas prostitute named Sera. What she makes at night working the streets and bars, Sera gambles during the day. Controlled by a brutal pimp, Sera also is physically abused by several of her tricks. When she meets a man named Ben, who is determined to drink himself to death, "her life has become somewhat pointless." Although she believes that she actually helps some people in her business, "Sera tries not to look too deeply at things anymore, for fear that they may not hold up to scrutiny." Like Lilla, she lives alone and is "thirsty beyond even her own reckoning for companionship." Ben, near the end, notes "the basic loneliness of her humanity," and she cares for him in a hopeless effort to remain emotionally connected to another person until his dying moment in an extraordinary example of unconditional love.[72]

Strippers and exotic dancers were also a familiar image in popular culture's treatment of Las Vegas women. Indeed, *Las Vegas Review-Journal* entertainment columnist Mike Weatherford explained, "Burlesque revues were part of the entertainment menu from the Strip's beginnings, though at first the gals wore pasties or dropped their tops at the end of a song, just as the spotlight blacked out."[73] Occasionally, early journalists referred to the "naughty" shows. Hollywood gossip columnist Jimmy Fidler, for example, noted in 1946 that famed fan dancer Sally Rand was performing in Las Vegas "in the 'altogether.'" Six years later, news wire services reported that stripper Lili St. Cyr had been fined for being a public nuisance in a previous year's performance. An embarrassed and outraged Roger D. Foley, the district attorney, had attended her show at the El Rancho Vegas and watched her "disrobe except for a towel and climb into a bathtub on the hotel stage."[74] By the mid-1950s, strippers were performing all across Las Vegas. Hotels tantalized visitors with large ads in the local newspapers promoting performers like "Tina, Hollywood Cover

Girl," "Ginger Briston, The Red Head—Toast of the Coast," and "Thunder, the Most Talked About Girl in Show Business Today."[75] The nation's leading strippers, including Tere Sheehan, the "Girl in the Champagne Glass," and Candy Barr, played Las Vegas.[76] Barr, who performed to big crowds at the El Rancho Vegas, certainly caught the eye of local entertainment columnist Ralph Pearl in a 1958 appearance. He described her as "a human mixmaster who sets up a series of shakes and shimmeys" while disrobing. He wondered how she "doesn't throw her hips into left field with all that gyrating."[77] Tempest Storm, America's "burlesque queen," made her premiere in Las Vegas in 1957, and once again, Ralph Pearl was there to report on the exploits of the "orange haired, generously bosomed" dancer. Pearl told his readers, "Tempest rocks and rolls, bumps and grinds with a furious determination while unpeeling right down to her G-string and most pretty ear rings."[78]

Lili St. Cyr, however, was the most famous of the strippers to appear in Las Vegas in the 1950s. She was a regular performer at the El Rancho Vegas, often on the bill with comic Joe E. Lewis, who once told a man attending the dinner show, "I saw you eating while Lili St. Cyr was working. I hope I never get that hungry in my life."[79] Known for a number of seductive routines, the finale to her 1955 performances was best described by Katharine Best and Katharine Hillyer, who described "the stripper de luxe" in their popular book *Las Vegas: Playtown U.S.A.* They wrote that St. Cyr "appears on stage in such radiant undress that audiences are rendered not only speechless but gaspless. Her appeal is particularly demonstrated by the finale of an act called 'Bird in a Gilded Cage,' in which she soars out over the audience in a gilded cage dropping beaded panties, frilly garters, and sequined bras on the hands-outstretched spectators below."[80]

The emergence of topless dancers in production shows in several Strip hotels in the late 1950s weakened the appeal of the strippers. In 1957, unable to compete with the more established hotels like the Sands, Desert Inn, and Flamingo for expensive headliners in their showroom, the owners of the Dunes Hotel offered *Minsky Goes to Paris*. Minsky's shows, featuring danceline, striptease, and comedy acts, had been hits in New York for years until barred in 1939. Harold Minsky found new venues for his shows in Chicago and New Orleans and produced tamer versions of them on a national circuit, including several stops in Las Vegas in the early 1950s. However, the 1957 Dunes show, according to an ad in the local papers, promised "24 Girls—24 Feathers (More or Less)." The response to the show with topless dancers was remarkable. The hotel's publicist claimed that it "created an instant bedlam of activity and business." Indeed, *Minsky Goes to Paris* consistently played to at or near capacity crowds for each of its three nightly shows. This success prompted several hotels and nightclubs over the next two years to book what Ralph Pearl called "Naked Chest revues." Barry Ashton, the stage director at the El Rancho Vegas, even proclaimed, "All the showgirls along the Strip are going to be replaced by nudes."[81]

Led by the Sands Hotel, some of the hotels opposed this trend, and it triggered a debate not just among the Las Vegas hotels, but also among religious leaders and local and state politicians. The Nevada legislature even debated, but ultimately failed to pass, a bill to ban nude shows.[82] Magazines like *Time, Sports Illustrated, Life,* and *Playboy,* as well as newspapers from the major media markets, all covered the story extensively. By summer 1959, *Time* magazine was even telling its national reading audience, "Bare bosoms are almost as commonplace on Las Vegas nightclub stages as snake eyes on the craps tables."[83] Indeed, nudity became an expected part of the production shows through the early twenty-first century, with some, like the *Folies Bergere* at the Tropicana and *Jubilee* at Bally's, running successfully for more than three decades. Producer Bill Moore explained in the late 1980s, "I always think you have to give the people what they expect," and tourists "come to Las Vegas and want to see nudity onstage. There's something sensuous about the whole thing."[84]

A character in Steve Brewer's 2003 novel *Bullets* noted that some cocktail waitresses revealed almost as much as the dancers: "All the waitresses look like they've forgotten their pants. A woman's got to dress like a hooker to compete."[85] The standard line in most of the fiction on Las Vegas argued that young women had to be gorgeous to become "the cocktail girls."[86] In his stinging indictment of Las Vegas, Sid Meyers argued that these scantily clad waitresses were critical to the success of the casino in limiting gamblers' wins. For example, "when a player enjoys a winning streak at the crap table," within seconds, the pit boss will summon a cocktail waitress, who "taps the player on the shoulder and informs him the house would like to buy him a drink." If the gambler accepts the offer, he soon "is drinking freely and being hustled into proposition bets." The cocktail waitress continues to bring drinks, and the man begins to make "large, reckless wagers" and "now has been captivated by greed and drink."[87] Journalists and authors argued that many cocktail waitresses were willing to do much more. Syndicated columnist Bob Considine told his many readers in 1955 that some of the waitresses could "be talked into working after hours at their apartments." Mario Puzo agreed. In 1976, he wrote that in "earlier days they were expected to become bedmates to favored gamblers if a Pit Boss gave them the word."[88]

Briefly in the 1990s there was a retreat from all these carnal temptations with attractions for families. Hotels began to resemble theme parks, with roller coasters, an amusement park, and a Nile barge ride inside the gigantic Luxor hotel and casino. Treasure Island even staged a fiery battle between pirates and the British navy out front in Buccaneer Bay alongside the street. Although there were still some topless shows, in 1994, *Time* magazine claimed that the tourist areas were essentially sanitized; indeed, the streets were "hookerless."[89] After discovering that few tourists came with small children, the hotels fairly swiftly reverted back to the sensuous lures. When *Time* magazine returned in 2004 for another detailed examination of the tourist business in Las Vegas, their reporter, Joel Stein, proclaimed that the movers and shakers in the city had discovered that "sex has proved to be far more profitable than wholesome fun."[90]

By the early years of the twenty-first century, there was a rapid proliferation (forty by one count in 2004) of so-called gentlemen's clubs not far from the Strip hotels. As one Las Vegas guidebook explained, "If you have even the slightest interest in viewing naked, or semi-naked, women dancing and prancing onstage, you hit the jackpot."[91] Many customers also opted for up close and personal lap dances at these clubs. The local Dancers Alliance estimated "that patrons spend $25 million on them annually."[92] Some of the clubs were enormous. Sapphire, for example, could hold 2,000 customers and 250 dancers.[93] Another, called Cheetah's, was featured in the movie *Showgirls*. To accommodate the rapidly growing demand for this kind of entertainment, the county sheriff's office, according to one account, issued over 15,000 cards for women "to dance either topless or totally nude in Las Vegas strip joints."[94] Because the Strip hotels could not offer "exotic dancing," they quickly opened explicitly themed shows like *Skin Tight, Midnight Fantasy, Crazy Girls, Zumanity,* and *Le Femme,* all of which were quite successful. Many hotels also opened lounges and clubs with alluring names like Tabu, Pure, and Rain to attract the young adult crowd.[95] Commentators struggled to find the right metaphor to describe the new atmosphere of the tourist city. On *ABC News,* correspondent John Quinones called it "a mythical land of fantasy adult entertainment." On NBC's *Today Show,* Matt Lauer concluded, "In the wee small hours this town seems so sexually charged you think everyone needs a cold shower."[96]

The collective portrait for the reader and viewer of images of women in Las Vegas is pretty coherent over time. Conveniently, women there are to be used. For the impulsive man, there is the quick, kitschy wedding. For the man eager to end a marriage, there is the quick, often sleazy, divorce. For the voyeuristic man, there is a multitude of strippers and topless dancers. For the man seeking an assignation, prostitutes are easily obtained. Whether they are the bride, the divorcée, the exotic dancer, or the prostitute, Las Vegas women in popular culture are gorgeous and available. Yet none of this should be surprising. A recent study has demonstrated that women fairly consistently, in most media formats, have been "portrayed in stereotypically negative ways."[97] Film, advertising, and literature focused on women's bodies and their sexuality, but it was most apparent in the pulp magazines of the 1930s and 1940s and in the post–World War II hard-boiled detective novels. Lascivious covers featuring women in torn blouses and strapless gowns, erotic themes, and a liberal sprinkling of sexual innuendoes presented women as objects for men.[98] The Las Vegas setting differed only in degree; it offered a ramped-up objectification of women. Perhaps a Las Vegas dancer best explained this perspective in an interview with *ABC News* in 2002. She said that it was all "about the sexy, edgy entertainment and looking at beautiful women and having a great cocktail with your buddies and having a hot night of fun."[99]

Beyond all the other images of women in print and on film, as Myram Borders, one of the city's veteran journalists, explained, "Showgirls were the Las Vegas image."[100] Most readers and viewers encountered a remarkably predictable iconic figure in Las Vegas showgirls. They were tall (usually 5′8″ to 5′10″) and slender, even statuesque. Adorned in colorful costumes with rhinestones, sequins, and feathers, the showgirls had huge headdresses often weighing more than thirty pounds. In G-strings, fishnet tights, and beaded brief skirts, on four-inch heels, and often wearing extravagant feather-covered backpacks, they were always smiling as they moved gracefully about the stage. They did little of the dancing. Instead, showgirls, sensuous and often topless, added elegance to production shows. Although Las Vegas hotels had dance lines in the 1940s that functioned essentially as bookend acts around the show's headliner, offering a couple of numbers before and after the headliner's act, in the 1950s, the showgirls joined the dance lines and increasingly replaced the headliner.

Movies of the 1950s contributed to the emerging image of the glamorous showgirls. In 1955, *Girl Rush,* starring Rosalind Russell, included several numbers for the dance line at the Flamingo Hotel, and a year later, *Meet Me in Las Vegas,* with Dan Dailey and Cyd Charisse, featured the Copa Girls at the Sands. In 1960, *Ocean's Eleven,* with Frank Sinatra and his Rat Pack, offered showgirls from the Desert Inn, Flamingo, Riviera, Sahara, and Sands hotels. Pulp magazines and novels spilled much ink on the lure of showgirls, a "curvy parcel of the world's most gorgeous gals."[101] Television contributed

Showgirls in the Folies Bergere at the Tropicana Hotel, ca. 1977. Source: UNLV Libraries, Special Collections.

to the image as well, particularly the three-year run of *Vega$* (1979–1982), starring Robert Urich. At the end of many episodes, his character, detective Dan Tanna, would relax watching a performance of showgirls at the Desert Inn, Tropicana, or Stardust. Most documentaries on Las Vegas included segments on showgirls, and in the early twenty-first century, the drama *Nikki* (2000–2002) and the reality show *Vegas Showgirls: Nearly Famous* (2002) kept them before the nation's viewers.

Yet it was the effusive coverage in the press, particularly in the 1950s and 1960s, that introduced most Americans to the Las Vegas showgirl. Entertainment columnists rarely restrained themselves in their accounts. In 1957, Lloyd Shearer, in *Parade*, the widely distributed Sunday magazine, boldly claimed that there were more "chorus girls" in Las Vegas "than in any other city—200 to 300 out of a national total of fewer than 900." Indeed, he wrote, "chorines from everywhere long have held Vegas to be the garden spot in the world" because the city's hotels have "the most publicized and photographed chorus girls in the country."[102] *Life* magazine added to the luster of the Las Vegas showgirls in several issues. In June 1960, the magazine described three of the

Strip's floor shows—"'Folies-Bergère' at the Tropicana, the 'Lido de Paris' at the Stardust, and 'Le Parisienne' at the Dunes"—showgirl extravaganzas with "some girls gaudily overdressed, others blatantly underdressed." All three were remarkably popular, "drawing 30,000 customers a week." Along with its brief narrative, the article included full-color photos of the girls in the three shows.[103] Five years later, *Life* published a lengthy article with numerous photos of the Las Vegas showgirls modeling new swimsuits and offering a short history of their many shows. "There are now," it explained, "a dozen shows of varying degrees of splendor and spectacle, in which girls are the main feature." It was also clear that the gambling city had become the center for the showgirl spectacle: "The American guild of Variety Artists lists more working chorus girls in Las Vegas (362) than any other place in the world."[104]

The periodicals' interest in showgirls shifted with the opening of new hotels. Soon after the Sands opened in 1952, there were several articles on that hotel's Copa Girls. Six years later, there were dozens of articles on the showgirls at the premiere of the *Lido de Paris* show at the new Stardust. In 1959, when the Tropicana imported the *Folies Bergere*, that hotel's showgirls grabbed the greatest attention. Regardless of the hotel, there was great interest in the origins of the showgirls. When the Lido show opened in 1958, many journalists ran stories on the Bluebell Girls. Europe's most famous dancers, the Bluebells were part of a dance company formed in 1933 by English dancer Margaret Kelly. Entertainment columnist Bob Thomas proclaimed after their opening at the Stardust that "the Bluebell Girls have captured Las Vegas." An impressed columnist, Hedda Hopper, described these English imports as "tall and willowy" women who "walk as if they are queens."[105] Young women came from many locales to make it as a Las Vegas showgirl, "from England, Australia, France, Germany and plain old Paducah, U.S.A.," according to *Life* magazine.[106]

Readers were eager to learn more about the showgirls than their origins, and journalists obliged. There were many stories about how normal the showgirls' lives were. Many stuck "together, sharing lodgings, sandwich snacks and dreams of stardom." Others spent their days shopping, gardening, or pursuing other careers. For many journalists, they were just like the girl next door. Yet not all portrayed showgirls as women of virtue. In the films *Where It's At* (1969) and *Grasshopper* (1970) and a 1985 made-for-television film called *Stark,* showgirls willingly became prostitutes. In the almost universally panned 1995 film *Showgirls,* the women are mean-spirited, heartless hustlers who stop at nothing, even serious injury to rivals, to gain a starring role at the Stardust. In his novel *Lost in Las Vegas,* novelist Monty Jones described some showgirls as hustlers. They were willing to escort a high roller, hoping he "would share part of his winnings. . . . It was amazing how generous a middle-aged man could be with a beautiful showgirl on his arm."[107]

The temptation to hustle the guests developed, in part, because in the 1950s and early 1960s, several hotels required the showgirls to fraternize with guests. They had to mingle with customers between and after shows. It was a way to dress up the casino, "to make gambling attractive."[108] Ed Reid and Ovid Demaris argued that the hotels wanted the "girls to be ogled by the customers who saw them nude or seminude on the stage just a moment before. It is another lure to bring in business."[109] Fortunately, by the mid-1960s, hotels had largely dropped this condition of employment for showgirls.[110]

Occasionally, journalists and novelists focused on one showgirl in their stories. In 1954, for example, Kim Smith, a Copa Girl at the Sands Hotel, was on the cover of *Life* magazine, a publication that dubbed her the "Prettiest Chorus Girl in Las Vegas." Smith said that she loved her job: "The work is steady, the pay good and the recreation plentiful." She made $128 each week "for dancing in two shows nightly." There were several photos of her working, as well as having a good time at the hotel pool, horseback riding, water skiing on Lake Mead, playing slot machines, and enjoying the snow on nearby Mt. Charleston. In this bubbly story, Smith claimed, "I am having more fun than anyone else in the whole world."[111] Famed author Larry McMurtry, after completing his massive novel *Lonesome Dove* about the cowboy as a dying breed, decided to write a story about the dying craft of the showgirl. His *The Desert Rose* is about a Las Vegas showgirl named Harmony. She "had always been thought to be one of the most glamorous showgirls in Las Vegas, she got to do all the publicity shots for the Stardust and met all the celebrities that came to town if management wanted them to meet a showgirl."[112] She loved her job and was always an optimist despite having the worst luck with men. But now thirty-eight, Harmony learns that she is being fired, to be replaced by her daughter, Pepper. This bittersweet tale of the struggles involved in the lives of showgirls was, according to one critic, "perhaps the best book about ordinary day-to-day life in Las Vegas." It revealed "people as they are, working, rushing their coffee breaks between shows, trying to get their cars fixed and do their household chores, having fast friendships like fast food, the daily round set against the non-stop glitz of the Strip casinos, which are not, for these people, places of entertainment but places of work."[113]

McMurtry was right about the plight of showgirls. From the early 1970s, journalists began to note that they were "a diminishing species." Several factors played a role in their apparent demise. Hotels again sought to lure headliners into the showrooms instead of the lavish production shows, and the remaining production shows were opting for faster-moving dance numbers over the glittering allure of the slower-moving showgirls with heavy head-dresses and high heels.[114] By the early twenty-first century, the *New York Times*, noting that only two shows, *Jubilee* and *Folies Bergere*, remained, found experts claiming that the showgirls were simply "too tame." As more and more tourists went to the strip clubs, the showgirls, even in their "topless costumes," were little more than "a tease."[115]

Ultimately, it is unclear how most readers and viewers, who had never been to the city, understood and interpreted the showgirls of Las Vegas. As historian Linda Chase suggested, some might see the showgirl "as a sad, degraded creature, a piece of meat paraded before the mostly male audience." At the same, she could "be celebrated as a protofeminist, freely expressing her sexuality and making good money doing it."[116] Regardless of that ambiguity, the chamber of commerce, the Las Vegas convention and visitors' authority, and Mayor Oscar Goodman continued to use showgirls in the promotion of the city well into the twenty-first century. They remained persuaded that most Americans still saw the showgirl as the preeminent female face of Las Vegas—indeed, as one of the city's most iconic figures.

"So Much Luxury in the Middle of the Desert"

Images of Luxury and Amenities in Las Vegas

A lavish and refined luxury hard to match anywhere.
Chicago Daily Tribune, 1945

The dining rooms, the shops, the casino, the spacious bars and lounges, the ultra-thick carpets, and a nightclub that makes Agua Caliente's seem as ordinary as a juke box.
Script, 1948

I know of few hotels in the world that can match it for taste in decoration, impeccable service and pleasant atmosphere.
Washington Post and Times Herald, 1956

For years the big casinos—hotels along the Strip—the Sands, the Flamingo, the Thunderbird, the Stardust—have vied with each other in degrees of opulence. Now comes Caesars Palace in an attempt to dominate them all—an enormous fourteen-story confection of white stone and concrete set down in thirty-four acres of Vegas desert.
New Yorker, 1966

If Irving Thalberg were still alive, and he wanted to produce a contemporary remake of MGM's star-studded "Grand Hotel," he would have no choice but to change the locale from Berlin to Las Vegas, and use the plush new Bellagio as the epicenter of his Academy Award–winning drama.
Chicago Tribune, 1998

In late summer 1955, Dorothy Kilgallen and her husband, Richard Kollmar, brought their live talk show to the Sands Hotel for a three-day run. Their daily *Breakfast with Dorothy and Dick* on New York's WOR had become one of the most popular radio programs along the East Coast in its ten-year run. These two Broadway sophisticates—Kilgallen was a popular entertainment columnist and Kollmar was a producer—were intrigued by the extraordinary popularity of Las Vegas and its around-the-clock action. Even though they were broadcasting before 6:00 A.M., Kilgallen noted that there were women in gowns and men in dinner jackets still milling around the hotel. The lavish hotels, however, most amazed her. "It's just incredible," she said; "there is so much luxury in the middle of the desert."[1] Kilgallen was not alone. From the 1930s, journalists and novelists spilled a great deal of ink, and movie and television producers shot many reels of film, all depicting, often with hyperbole, the sumptuous gambling clubs, casinos, and ever-larger hotels offering luxurious accommodations, fine restaurants, spas, spectacular showrooms, and art galleries. By the early twenty-first century, Las Vegas had emerged, at least in periodicals, films, and novels, as a luxurious resort destination, not just a gambling center.

Shortly after Nevada legalized gambling in spring 1931, the Cornero brothers, noted California bootleggers, opened the Meadows just outside Las Vegas. According to the *Las Vegas Review-Journal*, the Corneros intended "to attract persons of taste and refinement." The Meadows casino and cabaret, "designed in desert and Spanish architecture," featured gaudy interiors. There were red curtains and "flashy red chairs" in the cabaret, blue velour drapes in the casino, and gold-and-red curtains in the lobby. The ceiling had a number of Native American motifs, including arrowheads.[2] As the community's "first swank night club," the "ornate" Meadows quickly gained renown and attracted many Southern Californians.[3] In 1932, Las Vegas gained its first impressive hotel. Hailed as a "modern palace," the three-story air-conditioned Apache Hotel, at the corner of Second and Fremont, quickly gained a reputation as one of "the finest of western hotels." Owner Pietro Silvagni and the company that operated the hotel sunk as much money into furnishing the property as it cost to build it. Local newspaperman and booster Charles "Pop" Squires raved about the "expensive furnishings," with the rooms decorated "in the glory of the old west," and the casino, which was "a veritable gem in the beauty of its appointments." The *Los Angeles Times* agreed. It described the Apache as "sumptuously furnished."[4]

The town fathers licensed only a handful of casinos other than the Apache in the 1930s. The Northern Club, Frontier Club, Las Vegas Club, and Boulder

Club were in two-story brick and stucco buildings that looked, other than their neon signs, little different from "contemporary main streets nationwide."⁵ Although there were many naysayers who saw them as "honky-tonks" or "sawdust" joints, these casinos, hotels, and restaurants collectively presented a positive impression. Las Vegas offered the visitor air-conditioned, comfortable, reasonably priced establishments. Some journalists described them as luxurious, with their "attractive, inviting fronts."⁶ In his 1942 book *Desert Challenge*, Richard Lillard, an English professor at Los Angeles City College, even called Las Vegas a "sophisticated cosmopolis."⁷

In April 1941, Thomas Hull opened the El Rancho Vegas, the first of the casino resorts on what would later be dubbed the Strip. At the time, the highway just outside Las Vegas had little more than billboards, small gambling clubs, and an occasional gas station. One club, the Pair-O-Dice, had become a popular spot for dining, dancing, and gambling. When Guy McAfee, a former vice squad commander in Los Angeles, bought the property in 1939, he renovated the building and changed the name to Club 91. McAfee hoped to attract wealthy Southern Californians, the folks who had found the illegal gambling at his Clover Club on the Sunset Strip in Los Angeles so enticing. Most of the clubs, however, were forgettable dives. Actor and entertainer Peter Lind Hayes, for example, described the Red Rooster, which his mother, Grace, purchased in 1947, as little more than a saloon in "an adobe hut."⁸

The El Rancho Vegas truly added luster to Highway 91. Besides a casino and restaurants, it offered entertainment, retail shops, a swimming pool and sundeck, and nicely landscaped grounds. Guests found accommodations in a series of bungalows connected by covered walkways. These "luxury units" featured kitchens, porches, and fireplaces. The theme throughout was western, with wood fences, wagon wheels, and hitching posts.⁹ If Pop Squires had been excited about the opening of the Apache Hotel a decade earlier, he could scarcely restrain himself over the impending opening of the El Rancho Vegas. He predicted that it would "provide a most attractive place for wealthy tourists with all the pleasures, amusements and entertainments which the great resort hotels of the country offer elsewhere."¹⁰ This elaborate resort quickly became a favorite spot for Hollywood celebrities to elope, to meet the residence requirement for divorce, or simply to escape for a vacation.¹¹

One of Hull's guests in 1941 was R. E. Griffith, who owned a chain of movie theaters in the Southwest. He had consulted with "hotel people" in Los Angeles and learned that there was great promise for the hotel-casino business in Las Vegas. Griffith decided to improve on Hull's western-type design with a more overtly themed hotel. As William J. Moore, Griffith's nephew and architect, explained, his uncle wanted it "to be as near western as we could make it." For example, "the ceilings were of hewn timbers—logs—rough—sawed boards antiqued in such a way as to look many years old."[12] The hotel also had wood railings in the lobby, a trophy room, wagon wheel chandeliers, bar stools with saddles, and a Gay Nineties bar. Outside there was a split rail fence, a corral around the swimming pool, and stables. It was so extravagantly western that, according to historian Eugene Moehring, "visitors gasped at the splendor."[13] Beyond giving them a pseudo-western adventure, Moore and Griffith wanted a luxurious experience for their guests. Locating the hotel just south of the El Rancho Vegas on the Los Angeles highway and surrounded by sand, Griffith and Moore had over 3,700 trees and shrubs planted on the property to create "an oasis in the desert." Besides the casino, showroom, and restaurants, there was also a gift shop specializing in western jewelry. All the rooms were air-conditioned, and throughout were amenities expected in a resort hotel, like thick towels in the rooms and sterling silver service in the restaurant. They sought, Moore later claimed, "in every way possible to create . . . luxury."[14]

Several other developers joined Griffith and Hull in the 1940s to offer more appealing hotels and clubs. Marion Hicks, who had been involved in illegal gambling in California, partnered with John Grayson to build the El Cortez Hotel-Casino downtown in 1941. The fifty-nine-room hotel was a Spanish colonial revival style with Moorish arches along one side. Besides a casino, the El Cortez offered a floor show and restaurants.[15] Bob Brooks, a Hollywood restaurateur, opened the Nevada Biltmore the following summer. The Biltmore had a pool and over one hundred bungalows, all with three bedrooms. Its Tahitian-themed casino and bar were richly appointed with carpets and leather upholstery.[16] Nola Hahn, like Guy McAfee, was heavily involved in illegal gambling in Los Angeles, notably at the Clover Club, and decided to open a legal operation in Las Vegas, the Colony Club. McAfee's Golden Nugget, however, was the most impressive of the casinos located off the Los Angeles highway. Opened in August 1946, the Golden Nugget featured "the western vernacular of urban Gold Rush San Francisco, the Barbary Coast style."[17] The Golden Nugget was not only the largest casino in Las Vegas (the local press called it the largest in the world), it was also the most elaborate, with mahogany bars, "early Monterey oak paneling," floors of thick carpet, "inlaid tile" and "Italian marble," upholstery of red leather, and a host of murals and paintings, mostly nudes.[18]

Journalists visiting in the early 1940s found this array of hotels, nightclubs, and casinos enticing, and they could not avoid hyperbole in describing them. They called them "gaudy," "handsome," and "cool and elegant." Most often, however, journalists loved to use the word "swank" when describing Las Vegas enterprises.[19] In his 1942 *Saturday Evening Post* article, Wesley Stout was particularly taken with the new Colony Club, which had opened in July. Stout described it "as modernistic, as chi-chi, as sophisticated in décor as anything in New York."[20] Such places became a natural draw for the Hollywood crowd. As columnist Erskine Johnson explained, "The swank, million-dollar hotels—El Rancho Vegas, Last Frontier, El Cortez and Nevada Biltmore—are jammed. Movie stars, millionaires, socialites, and plain John Does are standing two deep at the roulette and dice tables."[21] It was the general view in the press that Las Vegas had quickly produced truly fine resorts. Indeed, one could find "a lavish and refined luxury hard to match anywhere," particularly in the "tony joints" along the Los Angeles highway, a road quickly becoming better known as the Strip.[22] Four feature films, *Las Vegas Nights, Moon over Las Vegas, Flight to Nowhere,* and *Lady Luck,* released between 1941 and 1946, likewise portrayed Las Vegas hotels as luxurious places with stylish floor shows.

Postcards from the resorts reinforced these upbeat accounts and depictions. Cards from the El Rancho Vegas and the Hotel Last Frontier revealed beautifully landscaped grounds with palm trees and swimming pools. There were well-dressed patrons gambling in the casinos as well as dining and enjoying lavish floor shows in the Round Up Room at the El Rancho and in the Ramona Room at the Last Frontier. The two resorts also had attractive modern cocktail lounges like the Carrillo Room at the Last Frontier. They were more than oases in the desert. The El Rancho Vegas claimed it was "Western America's Finest" hotel, and the Hotel Last Frontier offered travelers "The Early West in Modern Splendor."[23]

Yet the hotel-casinos of the early 1940s were only precursors of what was to come. Over the next six decades, Las Vegas offered its visitors ever-greater luxury in its resort hotels. Beginning with the opening of the Flamingo, Las Vegas experienced a remarkable growth spurt, as a dozen hotel-casinos opened along the Strip in as many years. In the view of newspaper columnists, the Flamingo set the standard for others to emulate. The casino opened on December 26, 1946, and the hotel the following March. The completed project, a spacious, rambling, and elaborate property, was, as architecture historian Alan Hess has pointed out, "conceptually similar to El Rancho and the Last Frontier," yet "stylistically it was dramatically different."[24] Rather than the western themes of its predecessors, the Flamingo projected a more sophisticated look, one that appealed to Southern Californians. Billy Wilkerson, with an assist from Bugsy

Siegel, developed the resort to resemble nightclubs like Mocambo, Ciro's, and Café Trocadero, and to give the feel of the "newest drive-in restaurants" with its "horizontal, sharp, and modern" lines.[25]

Once the Flamingo Casino opened, journalists, many of whom had trumpeted the luxury of earlier Las Vegas resorts, competed furiously for the most apt superlatives. In his nationally syndicated column, Erskine Johnson noted the great expense sunk into creating the most lavish property in Las Vegas. Each room had "custom-built furniture," and the landscaping alone cost a million dollars. It was, he contended, using the most familiar superlative of the era, the "swankiest" facility in Las Vegas.[26] Aline Mosby, a columnist for United Press International, went much further in her column, struggling to find the most appropriate comparison or label. She called the Flamingo both a "junior size Taj Majal" and "modernistic-modernistic" in design. She was particularly fascinated by the bar, with its "green leather walls, a black ceiling, and tomato red furniture." The Flamingo, Mosby proclaimed, was "the world's most super-colossal saloon."[27] However, screenwriter and columnist Jimmy Starr wrote the most enthusiastic description of the new casino. Starr told his readers that the Flamingo was a "magnificent spa." Anticipating the characterizations of Las Vegas common in the 1990s, Starr called the casino an adult "fairyland." Indeed, Starr, nearly a decade before the opening of Disneyland, saw the casino as "a place that might have been dreamed up by Walt Disney." The gardens and the structures "are lush, plush and fantastic." Starr went beyond the hyperbole linked with many casino openings in claiming that the Flamingo truly was "the most fabulous gambling casino . . . ever constructed."[28]

When Bugsy Siegel opened the hotel portion of the Flamingo on March 1, 1947, its modern design and vivid colors produced more breathless prose. One reporter, reflecting on the money spent on each guest room, the "handmade leather wastebaskets," and the pink-and-green color scheme, concluded, "The west has never seen anything like it." To help the reader grasp the opulence of the swanky hotel, the reporter likened it to "an M-G-M movie set."[29] Syndicated columnist Bob Considine carried that luxurious fantasy theme even further. The hotel, bar, casino, and lobby were built, he claimed, "from blueprints taken from a chorus girl's dream of heaven. It has everything but mink covers for its dice tables."[30] Edward Churchill, in *Script* magazine, favorably compared the Flamingo to the famed Mexican gambling resort Agua Caliente. Everything about the property impressed Churchill—"the dining rooms, the shops, the casino, the spacious bars and lounges, the ultra-thick carpets, and a nightclub that makes Agua Caliente's seem as ordinary as a

Flamingo pool in the early 1950s. Source: UNLV Libraries, Special Collections.

juke box." Churchill was also amazed at the amount of money that "went into the swimming pool, ponds, shrubbery, and the green lawn."[31]

Postcards of the Flamingo, particularly those featuring photographs taken by commercial photographer Burton Frasher, reveal how far the troubled partnership of Wilkerson and Siegel had advanced the quality of the Las Vegas resort. Their architects and designers George Vernon Russell, Tom Douglas, and Richard Stadelman had produced a genuinely upscale property. The postcard images include a handsome lobby with deeply cushioned chairs; a bar with upholstered stools overlooking the pool; and a dignified-looking casino with three blackjack tables, three roulette tables, two craps tables, and several slot machines. Throughout the spacious property are thick carpeting and luxurious drapes. The pool area is an oasis of beautifully landscaped lawns and palm trees.[32] Such images gained wider circulation in a number of films between 1947 and 1955. Although not identified as the Flamingo, the property gained great exposure in *The Lady Gambles* in 1949 and *The Las Vegas Story* three years later. It is also in an episode of the television series *Racket Squad* in 1951. It is featured in *The Invisible Wall*, a 1947 mystery film; the Jerry Lewis and Dean Martin comedy *My Friend Irma Goes West* (1950); and the Rosalind Russell musical *Girl Rush* (1955). Novelists also portrayed the Flamingo in glowing terms. Octavus Roy Cohen, for example, described it as "a big, sprawling, elaborate hotel" with "a lovely garden and the biggest swimming pool west of anywhere." He pointed out "that it might fit Palm Beach better than it does Nevada."[33] The image of the Flamingo in films and fiction is that of a resort offering all that the discriminating patron would seek: beautiful people at its enormous pool, a glittering casino, fabulous floor shows, sumptuous suites, and elegantly dressed guests. As the narrator in the documentary *Vegas Nights* proclaims, the Flamingo is a "dazzling" establishment "resplendent" with "beautiful gardens."[34]

The Desert Inn, Sahara, Sands, Riviera, and Tropicana were the most posh of the other hotel-casinos of the 1950s. They offered the "rich sleekness of modern design that suggests suavity and impermanence" and "scenes of undreamed color and glamor." In the view of several journalists, the Sands ultimately surpassed the luxury of the Flamingo. "For the plushest plush," Journalist Dick Pearce claimed, "stay at The Sands."[35] John Gunther agreed. "I know of few hotels in the world," he wrote, "that can match it for taste in decoration, impeccable service and pleasant atmosphere."[36] Collectively, the Strip properties, according to *Oakland Tribune* journalists, "rank among the wonders of the ultramodern world."[37] They offered similar appealing features: extensively landscaped grounds, swimming pools, luxurious suites, fine dining, and big-name entertainment in beautiful showrooms. The spectacular Sky Room at the Desert Inn, the fabulous Copa Room at the Sands, the Italian marble in the lobby of the Riviera, and the mahogany walls and crystal chandelier at the Tropicana all attracted the notice of journalists. When these properties opened, columnists focused on their opulence. Entertainment columnist Louella Parsons, for example, gushed about the Tropicana, which was "something you can't even dream about, it's so lavish and, well, elegant."[38] They also fared well in several movies of the era like *Meet Me in Las Vegas* (1956), but most notably in *Ocean's Eleven*. As a journalist in the *New York Times* explained, the film depicts the "flashy casinos . . . in vivid, full-toned style."[39]

The *Oakland Tribune* correctly gauged the successful strategy crafted by these properties when it described the newly opened Desert Inn as "one of the swank spas dedicated to the proposition that anyone can enjoy luxury at modest rates."[40] This egalitarian notion, Las Vegas's appeal for Middle America, became a common claim of journalists. For example, Julian Halevy explained in *Nation* magazine in 1958: "You live in a luxury world where the fact of money seems beneath notice: a world of Olympic swimming pools, hanging gardens, waitresses beautiful as movie stars, marble baths and bars a block long, air conditioning, deep carpets, royal buffets and obsequious waiters offering free drinks. The illusion is created that we are all rich."[41]

Wilbur Clark's Desert Inn, opened in 1950, was one of the posh hotels in midcentury Las Vegas. Source: UNLV Libraries, Special Collections.

Although all these hotel-casinos truly had luxurious touches, they were, in reality, all glorified motels, as Alan Hess described the Flamingo.[42] Post–World War II Americans had become familiar with these roadside properties. They may have been reminiscent of Miami or Beverly Hills with vivid colors, neon signs, casinos, and fabulous floor shows, but they were essentially one- and two-story properties, some with bungalows, and the obligatory swimming pool. They were, as historian David Schwartz has pointed out, "comfortable but hardly breathtaking."[43] There was more than a little hyperbole in the gushing descriptions of the press, and on occasion, a journalist would offer a more unfavorable assessment. In *Harper's* in 1969, Margot Hentoff argued, "The luxury hotels are most alike in that they are not luxurious. Massive brass turns into polystyrene at a touch. Thick shags are made from synthetic fibers."[44]

In 1963, Jay Sarno, builder of Cabana hotels in Atlanta, Dallas, and Palo Alto, California, came to Las Vegas on a gambling junket. Although he stayed at the Flamingo, Sarno visited the other hotels as well. He acknowledged the developers' efforts to make their properties attractive, but he saw the overall

Luxury suite at Sands Hotel, ca. 1963. Source: UNLV Libraries, Special Collections.

result as unimaginative. "The Flamingo was sick," he said, "like an old storage room. The D.I. (Desert Inn) was a stable." Sarno argued, "Las Vegas in the early '60s had done the Wild Western motif to death. What it needed was a little true opulence."[45] Sarno envisioned a fantasy hotel, a place of refinement with a "Roman–Grecian motif."[46] The flamboyant Sarno had built a version of his Roman fantasy in Palo Alto. His Cabana Hotel had an Italian theme with a long driveway, Italian cypress trees, fountains, and statues of Winged Victory and Michelangelo's David, waitresses in togas, and a Nero's bar.[47] The Palo Alto Cabana was a mere dress rehearsal for Sarno's grand Las Vegas vision, which he decided to call Caesars Palace. He purposely left out the apostrophe to emphasize that this was to be everyman's bacchanalian fantasy. "We wanted to create the feeling," he explained, "that everybody in the hotel was a Caesar."[48]

Sarno set Caesars Palace, a crescent-shaped fourteen-story tower, back from the Strip, which permitted him to have a 135-foot driveway lined with cypress trees, eighteen fountains, and statuary. Notable among them was a facsimile of Gian de Bologna's *Rape of the Sabine Women* near the entrance. Far beyond any of the other Las Vegas properties, Caesars evoked a sense of grandeur upon entry onto the property. As architecture historian Alan Hess explained,

"The focus was on a monumental structure with symmetrical wings reaching out to embrace the limousines cruising up to the porte cochere."[49] Once inside, visitors saw a lobby with Brazilian rosewood and white marble paneling in the foyer. Walking into the casino with twenty black-and-gold marble pillars, patrons' eyes were drawn to a massive chandelier made from German crystal illuminating the table games and slot machines. Sarno and his designer, Jo Harris, extended the Roman theme throughout the property. Patrons could see performances in the Circus Maximus Theatre, have a drink at the Cleopatra Barge Nightclub, a snack at the Noshorium Coffee Shop, or a gourmet meal in the Bacchanal Room. Cocktail waitresses (called Goddesses) wore short togas and desk clerks wore tunics. There was even stationary simulating aged Roman parchment.[50] Sarno's evocation of Roman splendor was timely. Americans had become familiar with images of ancient Rome through popular films like *Quo Vadis* (1951), *The Robe* (1953), *Demetrius and the Gladiators* (1954), *Ben-Hur* (1959), *Spartacus* (1960), *Cleopatra* (1963), and *The Fall of the Roman Empire* (1964). Although some of these films emphasized a decadent Rome, many viewers came away from them with a sense of ancient Rome as a locale of extraordinary luxury and conspicuous consumption, a perception Sarno capitalized on. As he told one reporter, "Complete authenticity we don't have. . . . My approach is to guess what the public will like."[51]

The opening of Caesars Palace captured the attention of the national press. From New York to Iowa and Wisconsin, readers learned about the hotel's huge casino, the "elegantly appointed rooms" with "a veritable swarm of visiting celebrities" and "big time gamblers" attending an opening that became an "orgy of excitement."[52] The *New York Times,* in describing the "massively garish" hotel "with its fountains, colonnades and rococo statuary" and employees "swathed in elaborate golden robes," dutifully reported the gaggle of celebrities on hand: David Janssen, Adam West, Robert Cummings, Eva Gabor, Maureen O'Hara, and Andy Griffith.[53] "For years," the *New Yorker* reported, "the big casinos—hotels along the Strip—the Sands, the Flamingo, the Thunderbird, the Stardust—have vied with each other in degrees of opulence. Now comes Caesars Palace in an attempt to dominate them all."[54]

For years, television and movie production companies shooting in Las Vegas most often had done so at the Sands or the Flamingo, but from its opening, Caesars Palace became the signature Las Vegas locale for most productions for over three decades.[55] The property received its most extensive positive exposure in two feature films, *Where It's At* (1969) and *Rain Man* (1988), and in the 1980 CBS TV film *Pleasure Palace.* There are multiple exterior shots of Caesars Palace in *Where It's At,* featuring the long driveway

Caesars Palace, which opened in 1966, was the first of the fully themed resort hotels in Las Vegas. Source: UNLV Libraries, Special Collections.

lined with Italian cypress, statutes, and fountains, as well as the enormous swimming pool. In *Rain Man*, Dustin Hoffman and Tom Cruise portray brothers who win thousands at blackjack because Hoffman's character is an autistic savant who is extraordinary at card counting. Because of their good fortune, they book a dazzling two-level suite with a spectacular view of the Strip. *Pleasure Palace* stars Omar Sharif as an international playboy and gambler who helps a character, portrayed by Hope Lange, retain ownership of Caesars Palace from a takeover by an international syndicate led by a wealthy Texan. Virtually all of the film was shot at the hotel, showcasing luxurious suites, a spa, upscale shopping, exquisite dining, the beautifully landscaped pool area, a wonderful lounge, high-stakes gambling, high rollers, beautiful women, and Omar Sharif in a tuxedo. The images for the viewer all evoke luxury and refinement, a hotel-casino that resembles the plush European casinos depicted early in the film.[56]

Caesars Palace has remained a symbol of the lavish themed resorts. It has been the subject of numerous documentaries on Las Vegas. In the 1996 A&E production entitled *The Real Las Vegas*, there is a long shot from the east illustrating the grandeur of the fountains and the hotel. As the viewer sees the long, beautifully landscaped driveway with fountains flowing, narrator Richard Crenna notes, "It was the city's most elaborate theme resort created on a scale that would have awed Caesar himself." As the camera focuses on the pool area, he notes that the enormous swimming pool is "designed in the shape of a Roman shield."[57] Coffee-table books, brimming with color photos, also contributed to Caesars' glittering image. These volumes revealed the "decadent Roman entertainment spa," with shots of the impressive architecture, flashy casino, fountains, "tons of Italian marble and stone," and the "elegant and enormous pools."[58]

A year after Caesars Palace opened, construction began on a massive new hotel that further redefined the Las Vegas hotel experience for visitors. The International, which opened in 1969, was the first megaresort. Owner Kirk Kerkorian had been coming to Las Vegas since the 1940s, first as a pilot bringing gamblers to the casinos. He then established a charter air service and invested in Las Vegas property—the Dunes in 1955, and then eighty acres across the street from the Flamingo. He first rented the land, then sold it to the owners of Caesars Palace. Kerkorian bought the Flamingo in 1967 to train a staff for his massive new hotel project off the Strip.[59] He employed Beverly Hills architect Martin Stern to design his big hotel. Stern had developed a reputation in Southern California as a practitioner of the so-called googie style of architecture, with its bold angles and cantilevered roofs. He had considerable experience in Las Vegas, where he had designed both a low-rise and high-rise addition to the Sahara Hotel in the 1950s, a tower for the Sands Hotel in 1964, a low-rise addition for the Flamingo in 1967, and a twenty-six-story addition to the downtown Mint Hotel.[60] The International Hotel, the world's largest resort hotel at its opening with over 1,500 rooms, cost Kerkorian $60 million. The hotel featured architect Stern's major innovation in Las Vegas hotel design: the Y-shaped triform tower. As historian David Schwartz explained, "It was an adaptation to the need to fit over 1,000 hotel rooms on a square plot in a way that would afford each room a decent view."[61] It became the model for many subsequent Strip properties. Everything about the International, decked out in white marble, imported crystal chandeliers, and "nude friezes running along the walls of the casino," was massive.[62] The hotel's publicists claimed not only that the thirty-story structure was the largest hotel in the world, but also that it had the largest casino and largest swimming pool. The showroom accommodated 2,000, and the opening act was Barbra Streisand, backed by a forty-piece orchestra, soon to be followed by the return of Elvis Presley to live performances. To some journalists, it quite simply was "a sight to behold." "The casino," one wrote in the *Oakland Tribune*, "is the most beautiful in the state and the entire complex is engulfed in elegance."[63] *Time* magazine proclaimed that Las Vegas, with the opening of this gigantic hotel, had "reached a new pinnacle of preposterousness."[64] Movie fans got to see

First MGM Grand Hotel in Las Vegas, 1979. It is now Bally's Las Vegas. Source: UNLV Libraries, Special Collections.

the property towering above the Las Vegas skyline, with its large casino and huge, sumptuously furnished suites, in the 1971 James Bond film *Diamonds Are Forever* and in the 1993 film *Indecent Proposal*.

Kerkorian had truly raised the ante. Tourists would expect a resort of fantastic proportions. Four years later, the developer delivered with the opening of the MGM Grand. Those covering the event called the twenty-six-story, 2,100-room hotel the city's "newest, biggest and most expensive pleasure palace."[65] As with his International Hotel, Kerkorian included six restaurants in the $100 million hotel, and there were statues throughout the property—forty-four, to be exact—plus many shops and a casino larger than a football field. This self-contained resort seemed to be a "city within a city."[66] Kerkorian had purchased majority stock in the Metro Goldwyn Mayer film studio and sought to remind his hotel guests of the movie company's glory. There were photos of stars that had appeared in MGM movies throughout the property, there were suites bearing the names of MGM characters, and there was even a movie theater featuring classic MGM films. One journalist was stunned by "the splendor and sheer numerical wonder of it all."[67] After suffering a deadly fire in November 1980 and the attendant national news coverage, the rebuilt MGM Grand got great positive exposure in the 1982 film *Lookin' to Get Out*. Starring Jon Voight and Ann-Margret, the movie offered several scenes of the MGM's gargantuan casino and huge suites.

Inevitably, a developer came along who combined the megaresort with the concept of a themed hotel. Jay Sarno, who died in 1984, befriended a young man who dramatically extended the idea of a lavishly themed casino resort. Steve Wynn, who had first visited Las Vegas in 1952 at age ten, moved to the gambling center in 1967. Son of a bingo parlor operator, Wynn drew on his father's gambling connections and the assistance of prominent Las Vegas banker Parry Thomas to invest in the Frontier Hotel, to obtain a liquor distributorship, and ultimately, to gain sufficient stock ownership in the downtown Golden Nugget to become its CEO.[68] Wynn transformed a property that had become timeworn. Wynn not only expanded the Golden Nugget dramatically with a hotel tower and parking garage, but he also completely renovated the property with a focus on elegance. Besides brass, marble, a plethora of plants, and smoked mirrors throughout the property, he added gourmet restaurants and luxury suites. Wynn even signed Frank Sinatra to perform in the showroom.[69]

In transforming the Golden Nugget, Wynn was drawing on the collective wisdom of many of the city's pioneer developers. As historians Eugene Moehring and Michael Green explained, "Wynn met all the gaming legends from the town's salad days: Benny Binion, Sam Boyd, Jackie Gaughan, Jay Sarno, and others, all of whom gave Wynn valuable insights on hotel and casino operations."[70] Sarno, who had the greatest influence, often chatted with Wynn while gambling at the Golden Nugget. Besides the obvious message to offer a luxurious experience that was accessible for ordinary folks, Wynn understood that there should be a hook for the customers to come into one's property. At Caesars Palace, "the show started on the sidewalk," and a principal element in the show involved water—Sarno's spectacular fountains.[71] In 1989, when the International Gaming Exposition posthumously inducted Jay Sarno into its Gamblers Hall of Fame, Wynn related a conversation he had with Sarno. Wynn had taken his mentor to the see a spectacular new sign for the Golden Nugget. "Jay looked at me," Wynn explained, "and sighed. Jay said, 'Steve, Steve, ya gotta nice sign, but Steve, Steve, Steve, ya gotta do something with waaater.'" Wynn looked heavenward and proclaimed, "Jay, Jay! I Got the Message!"[72]

Indeed he did. Wynn used water as a key feature in his sidewalk show for three of the properties he developed—the Mirage, Treasure Island, and the Bellagio. The larger inspiration Wynn drew from Sarno's work was the allure of a themed luxury megaresort. His massive Mirage Hotel, just north of Caesars Palace, which opened in late 1989, dwarfed even the International and MGM Grand hotels. Wynn incorporated a South Seas theme throughout the property. Guests arrived along a palm-lined driveway, and when registering, they could gaze at a 20,000-gallon aquarium holding a myriad of sea species, including sharks. Not far from the lobby, guests could walk through a domed atrium with ninety-foot tall palm trees, a waterfall, orchids, and bougainvillea. Upon entering the casino, they could gamble at tables with thatched roofs. Near the southeast entrance to the hotel, guests could gaze at white tigers behind a glass barrier and enjoy watching a school of bottle-nosed dolphins outside. The lushly landscaped eighty-eight-acre property included over 1,000 palm trees. To lure those on the sidewalk inside, Wynn offered lagoons, waterfalls, and a fifty-five-foot volcano that erupted every few minutes. The twenty-nine-story Martin Stern–designed triform hotel had over 3,000 rooms, including 260 penthouse suites on the top five floors. Wynn wanted visitors to have, as Sarno had sought with Caesars Palace, an experience beyond just gambling and shows.[73] The creative, frenetic, and always hyperbolic Wynn told a reporter for *Business Week*, "What we want is for our guests to enter into another world, a better and safer world."[74] Novelist Robert Parker, in his 1996 mystery *Chance*, certainly pleased Wynn in describing the Mirage as a haven in the midst of the Mojave Desert: "The lobby of the Mirage was positively sylvan. There were jungle plants and waterfalls, and a small bridge over a stream."[75] In all, the extraordinary property cost over $600 million and quickly surpassed Hoover Dam as the state's most visited place. More important, the Mirage revolution, as historians Eugene Moehring and Michael Green called Wynn's achievement, truly transformed the Las Vegas Strip as developers' Disneyfied, heavily themed megaproperties proliferated over the next decade: Excalibur (1990); a new, larger MGM Grand (1993); Luxor (1993); Monte Carlo (1993); Treasure Island (1993); Mandalay Bay (1996); New York–New York (1997); Paris (1999); and Venetian (1999).[76]

The Bellagio was the quintessential example of this remarkable trend in hotel development. Journalists covering the 1998 opening of Steve Wynn's property, the "most opulent pleasure palace in Vegas," demonstrated little restraint in their descriptions.[77] Modeled on the structures in the small northern Italian town of the same name on Lake Como, the Bellagio tantalized journalists. The lobby, with its mosaic tile and Dale Chiluly–designed multicolored glass ceiling sculpture entitled "Fiori di Como," first caught their imagination. Then it was on to the 13,000-square-foot conservatory, maintained by a staff of over 100 botanists. There were tony stores like Gucci, Hermès, and Prada along Via Bellagio, modeled on Milan's iron-and-glass Galleria arcade, and a host of world-class restaurants. In the art gallery, one could find "three-hundred-million dollars' worth of masterpieces" by Picasso, Matisse, Monet, Renoir, and Cezanne. Outside, along the Strip, over 1,000 fountain jets in the nearly nine-acre lake provided a spectacular water show coordinated with classical and popular music every half hour. The rooms in the 3,000-room hotel, with Italian marble and beautiful fabrics, were the most luxurious in the city.[78] The *Los Angeles Times* proclaimed that the Bellagio, at $1.6 billion, was "the most expensive hotel in the world." A journalist for the *Chicago Tribune* concluded, "If Irving Thalberg were still alive, and he wanted to produce a contemporary remake of MGM's star-studded 'Grand Hotel,' he would have no choice but to change the locale from Berlin to Las Vegas, and use the plush new Bellagio as the epicenter of his Academy Award–winning drama."[79]

Long after its opening, viewers of documentaries and readers of magazines frequently saw photos and stories about the spectacular, elegant hotel, but it gained its widest exposure in the popular 2001 remake of *Ocean's Eleven*. The scene introducing the Bellagio is an aerial one at night featuring a fountain show, then a shot from street level. Numerous exterior and interior shots follow: the long, tree-lined driveway approaching the property, the wrought-iron and glass porte cochere, the Dale Chiluly glass sculpture in the lobby, cut flowers throughout the property, the tastefully decorated, colorful casino, attractive patrons, beautiful cocktail waitresses, innumerable colorful slot and video poker machines, beautiful rooms, some high rollers, the art museum, and lovely restaurants with elegantly dressed diners. Near the film's end, there is a long, beautiful shot of the Bellagio fountain show with "Clair de Lune" playing in the background.[80]

Other developers, seeing the success of Wynn's Bellagio, likewise offered upscale properties to attract "the Ritz crowd."[81] Two themed megaresorts, the Venetian and the Paris, drew particular attention. Besides a replica of the Grand Canal coursing its way through the property, the $1.2 billion Venetian offered reproductions of Italian frescoes on the ceilings and "recreations of St. Mark's Square, the Doge's Palace and the Rialto Bridge." The $800 million Paris, with its half-scale replica of the Eiffel Tower and Arc de Triomphe, was "a sprawling homage to the City of Lights."[82] More important, the properties offered luxurious accommodations, great restaurants, and spas. Fine art, as with the Bellagio Art Gallery, also became an important amenity. One could come to Las Vegas and see impressionists and the early masters. The Rio Hotel, for example, put on display the "Treasures of Russia," with pieces from the era of Peter the Great to Nicholas II, and the Venetian exhibited great artwork in its Guggenheim–Hermitage Museum, which was the product of collaboration with the Solomon R. Guggenheim Foundation and the State Hermitage Museum in Russia.[83]

To journalists and novelists, properties like the Bellagio and Venetian represented a remarkable trend, where "the hotels only get more extravagant and opulent" in the city's effort to lure the wealthy with "a world of perks and privileges" and "palatial villas."[84] It was in many ways, television viewers and readers learned, a new Las Vegas. The highbrow sought to supplant the lowbrow. One could see it in the architecture, the rooms, the restaurants, and the upscale shops: "Mannequins are draped with expertly cut Versace suits and romantic Escada dresses, not tacky rhinestone-studded jackets and leather-trimmed gowns. Window displays would not look out of place on Rodeo Drive or Fifth Avenue."[85] Readers of Andres Martinez's *24/7: Living It Up and Doubling Down in the New Las Vegas* learned developers like Steve Wynn were hoping to attract the nation's "most sophisticated and pampered travelers." Wynn was "betting that by plopping down the greatest hotel ever built in the middle of the Strip, one packed with prestigious restaurants, luxury retailers, and the most spectacular live show anywhere, he can pull this crowd away from Palm Springs, Scottsdale, and Aspen."[86]

An economic reality drove this extraordinary investment in luxurious properties. From the late 1970s, Las Vegas lost its near monopoly on gambling. In 1976, New Jersey citizens approved casino gambling in Atlantic City through a referendum, and casinos were flourishing there within two years. Over the next two decades, several states approved lotteries, and there was a rapid proliferation of Native American casinos and bingo halls, including Foxwoods Resort Casino in Ledyard, Connecticut, the world's largest casino. Additionally, beginning in Iowa, several state governments, eager for new sources of revenue, approved riverboat gambling. Finally, there was the slowly growing challenge of gambling on the Internet.[87] Several Las Vegas entrepreneurs like Kirk Kerkorian, Terry Lanni, and Sheldon Adelson understood the economic threat these developments posed to Las Vegas and embraced the idea of offering spectacle and luxury to set their city apart from other gaming locales. Yet Steve Wynn was the most aggressive and most creative among them. He had concluded in the 1980s that "Las Vegas had a terrible kind of sameness to it. Boxes of rooms on top of rooms filled with slot machines." Given the growing number of locales offering just the same, he believed that tourists would ask of Las Vegas properties, "What is there to *do* besides gaming?"[88] Moreover, he understood that there were increasing numbers of sophisticated travelers who would not consider a place like Las Vegas without the luxurious amenities they had come to expect. Thus, Jon Jerde, Wynn's architect for the Bellagio, explained that Wynn wanted him to design "the greatest spa resort in the world."[89]

In 2000, Wynn sold the Mirage Resorts—Mirage, Treasure Island, and

Bellagio (along with the Golden Nugget in Laughlin and Las Vegas and the Beau Rivage in Mississippi)—to Kirk Kerkorian and began planning another opulent hotel. The Wynn Hotel opened in spring 2005 with all the luxurious amenities Las Vegas tourists had come to expect. The fifty-story, curved, copper-colored tower had rooms with king-sized beds, flat-screen televisions, floor-to-ceiling windows, motorized drapes, and bathrooms with marble floors and televisions. There were great restaurants; an art gallery with works by Rembrandt, Vermeer, Monet, Matisse, Degas, and Van Gogh; and upscale shops like Cartier and Dior. Wynn also added a new exclusive luxury element to the shopping—a Ferrari–Maserati dealership. Outside, there was a spectacular, exclusive golf course, a swimming pool with television-equipped cabanas, and a three-acre Lake of Dreams.[90] In a dramatic break from his other hotels, which had spectacular water features outside to entice visitors into the property, the Wynn featured a 140-foot man-made mountain, covered by pine trees, out front, providing a barrier between the hotel and the hubbub of the Strip.

To gain maximum publicity for his $2.7 billion hotel, Wynn made a spectacular, widely seen commercial telecast during the Academy Awards show, standing atop the structure featuring his signature, saying, "I'm Steve Wynn. This is my new hotel, the only one I've signed my name to." He also had NBC's *Today* show team on the property on opening day for an extended interview. *Time* magazine did a feature article on Wynn, and he permitted Nina Munk to follow him around for three days, gathering material for a lengthy article in *Vanity Fair*. The media response, predictably, was enthusiastic, although a few journalists carped that Wynn had done little more than mimic the Bellagio in his interior design. Still, the innovative developer remained the darling of most. An article in *USA Today*, for example, claimed that the Wynn promised "to out-luxury even the most luxurious properties."[91] More important, they gave Wynn a venue to make remarkable claims about his new property. In *Vanity Fair*, he said that his property represented "a humanist piece of Renaissance architecture," and on the *Today* show, he asserted that he was creating "a new paradigm, a new level of elegance and fun."[92] Within a year of its opening, Wynn proclaimed he had created the most exclusive of the resort city's properties: "This place is clearly elitist. We are not after everybody; we are the top end hotel in Las Vegas."[93]

Besides the properties journalists described to readers and viewers, several novelists and screenwriters from the late 1990s imagined a number of fictitious themed hotels and contributed to the image of Las Vegas as a locale of luxurious megaresorts. The Golden Calf and the Acropolis had ancient

Greek themes, with huge pillars and "white marble statues of famous Greek heroes, poets and philosophers."[94] The designers of the Ivory Coast tried to give guests "the impression of stepping into the antiquated days of British imperialism."[95] Some, like the Transylvania, with its Halloween motif, were satirical creations poking fun at the mammoth themed resort hotels. The Titanic was the most outrageous, "a carefully re-created beached version of the fabled ocean liner." The ship sat in an ice floe with "a passageway that led into an iceberg that was the main area for gambling."[96] The millions of viewers of the popular television series *Las Vegas* weekly saw the spectacular Montecito Hotel and Casino. Modeled on the real Mandalay Bay, the fictitious South Seas–themed hotel had a huge waterfall out front, large, sumptuously furnished suites, a huge, well-appointed casino, and upscale shopping and restaurants. The collective impression of the real and the imagined Las Vegas hotels was one of extraordinary luxury and surreal themes, often replicas of decadent distant places and times.

Great food was an increasingly important element in the impression of a luxury experience in Las Vegas hotels, although for most of the post–World War II period, journalists and authors of guidebooks focused on the inexpensive but bountiful meals one could find along the Strip and on Fremont Street. Twenty-four-hour coffee shops with late-night specials and chuck wagon buffets were the chief gustatory lures in the 1940s and 1950s. Loss leaders for the casinos, coffee shops, like the one in the El Cortez, offered fourteen-ounce steaks for $1.95 in 1957.[97] Most observers acknowledge that the chuck wagon buffet began at the El Rancho Vegas.[98] For just a dollar, a patron could have "every possible variety of hot and cold entrees to appease the howling coyote in your innards in the late night-pre-dawn hours" at the Buckaroo Chuck. For the same price, one could enjoy the Buckaroo Buffet breakfast and lunch.[99] By the mid-1950s, all the Strip hotels had a chuck wagon buffet, and one, the Caravan Room in the Sahara, remained in operation for over fifty years. Some, like the Sands Hotel, offered a fancy Sunday Brunch, which included champagne, and the Last Frontier promoted a Sunday English Hunt Breakfast.[100] In their popular book *Las Vegas: Playtown U.S.A.,* Katharine Best and Katharine Hillyer explained that beyond mountains of cold cuts, cheeses, salads, and desserts, the chuck wagon buffets had become upscale enough to tempt "gourmets" with "stone crabs from Florida, Maine lobster in aspic, imported Danish ham, *prosciutto* in melon, odorful Liederkranz gently warm from the oven."[101] In his novel *Muses of Ruin*, William Pearson launched into a most extraordinary description of the inexpensive bountiful midnight buffets as "the eighth wonder of the world, the phagomaniac's nirvana, the one true art form this androgynous harlot of cities has delivered herself of."[102]

Dinner theaters with the fabulous headliner entertainers were also popular in the postwar years, with several hundred people dining on steaks, lamb chops, lobster, and prime rib while listening to great singers and comedians. There were also some efforts to provide a gourmet dining experience for visitors. "Every casino," the *Los Angeles Times* not quite accurately claimed in 1998, "has always had expensive restaurants where the winners (and losers) could order Dom Perignon and Cristal and get something vaguely continental but there weren't serious restaurants."[103] Gourmet restaurants actually emerged in the 1950s and 1960s. The Tropicana opened Perino's in 1957. Alexander Perino, who had a gourmet room in Los Angeles, opened a Las Vegas version with chef Martin Appelt, whose experience included a stint at the Waldorf Astoria. Four years later, the Dunes had the Top O' the Strip restaurant with Beverly Hills chef Jean Bertraneau.[104] The Flamingo had the Candlelight Room, the first restaurant to offer live lobster flown in from Boston daily. There were others: the Delmonico at the Riviera, the Regency Room at the Sands, the Monte Carlo at the Desert Inn, and the House of Lords at the Sahara.[105]

The Bacchanal at Caesars Palace, however, was the most spectacular restaurant of the 1960s. Opening in August 1966, the restaurant's menu read, "I, Caesar ... welcome you to the most resplendent arena of gustatory delights ... the Bacchanal! Here you shall embark upon an adventure in gourmet dining unparalleled outside my empire." It featured a serving staff all in costume to contribute to the image of a hedonistic ancient Rome. Bacchanal guests encountered a maître' d dressed in white with a gold sash, waiters in purple outfits, and serving girls (meant to evoke slave girls) in "the flimsiest of veiling." The room, which simulated a Roman villa with murals of the ancient city, featured a marble staircase, pillars and statues, flaming torches, a fountain, and luxurious leather chairs. Guests, usually about 400 each evening, enjoyed "an endless supply" of food and wine. There were multiple courses with hors d'oeuvres, soups, salads, stuffed lobster, fettuccine, pheasant, chicken, rack of lamb, fruit and cheese, and strawberry–banana jubilee. Slave girls capped the excess by feeding the guests peeled grapes and offering massages of necks and back. Franco Borghese, in *Diners Club* magazine, called it "a vast dinner with great variety enough to please any palate."[106] It fell to the 1996 edition of *Frommer's* Las Vegas guidebook to offer readers the most expansive description of Bacchanal, categorizing its cuisine as "Roman Orgy Continental." Author Rena Bulkin promised readers an extraordinary culinary experience, "an imperial Roman feast with comely 'wine goddesses' in harem-girl attire performing sinuous belly dances, decanting wine from shoulder height into ornate silver chalices."[107]

Still, for most people, Las Vegas remained a destination known more for cheap all-day breakfasts and buffets. That perception did not begin to change until the early 1990s. Wolfgang Puck, a James Beard Award–winning chef who had had great success with his Spago restaurant on the Sunset Strip in West Hollywood, brought that franchise establishment to Caesars Palace in 1992. Puck's incredible popularity led several hotels to seek other celebrity chefs by "offering as incentives near-perfect dining and kitchen facilities, generous percentages of the restaurants' profits and, in some cases, six-figure salaries."[108] The MGM Grand, for example, lured Emeril Lagasse from New Orleans, Mark Miller from Santa Fe, and Charlie Trotter from Chicago, in addition to persuading Wolfgang Puck to open a second restaurant in Las Vegas. These signings opened the floodgates, and a host of famous chefs established restaurants in Strip hotels: Alain Ducasse, Thomas Keller, Charlie Palmer, Todd English, Alex Stratta, Julian Serano, Daniel Boulud, Bobbie Flay, Mario Batali, and Michael Mina. The MGM even brought Joel Robuchon, named the chef of the century by the French restaurant guide *Gault Millau*.

With so many "acclaimed chefs" establishing "copies of their well-known restaurants in Las Vegas," food critics in the late 1990s began calling the city "one of the top fine-dining destinations in the country."[109] American Public Media's radio program *Marketplace Morning Report* in 2000 noted that *Gourmet* magazine concluded that Las Vegas had the "best dining establishment between the two coasts" and quoted Mitch Consentino, a Napa Valley winemaker, who argued that "it is definitely one of the main places in this country for fine cuisine."[110] This remarkable transformation in image—from a city whose "culinary landscape" formerly was, according to the famed *Zagat* guide, "as barren as the desert that surrounds" it to one widely regarded as a premier fine dining destination—was truly rapid. Remarkably, there was almost no dissent from this assessment in the newspapers and magazines. When the Bellagio opened in 1998, the *Chicago Tribune* noted its wide array of "world-class restaurants," and six years later, Joel Stein wrote in *Time* magazine that "Vegas dining has become so high-end it employs more master sommeliers than any other U.S. city."[111]

From the Flamingo and Caesars Palace to the Bellagio and the Wynn, Las Vegas properties offered accommodations that increasingly appeared in the nation's media outlets and in film and on television as truly luxurious. By the late twentieth century, the appeal of properties like the Bellagio was to the wealthiest of tourists, those who normally vacationed in traditional luxury destinations like Palm Springs. The descriptions and images of opulent, themed hotels, large suites, plush furnishings and decor, spas, art galleries, upscale restaurants, and spectacular showrooms created an image of, as the *Boston Globe* described it in 2005, "the new Las Vegas of super deluxe megahotels, five-star restaurants, upscale shopping, and entertainment extravagances."[112] The impression of Las Vegas as a premier luxury destination had become fixed in the popular images of the city by the early twenty-first century.

"An Awful Place"

The Negative Images of Las Vegas

It's an awful place on the Union Pacific Railroad with only one decent hotel and no class at all.

Edwin Corle, 1934

When you enter Las Vegas you set foot in a catacomb of hell.

Sid Meyers, 1958

This Las Vegas is a jet-age Sodom.

Time, 1969

It's a place built on greed, representing the absolute worst in our culture. I won't put one nickel in a slot machine while I'm here. . . . The ethic that built this city is horrendous.

Jane Fonda, 1978

This is the worst money-grubbing place in the world.

Lost in America, 1985

No matter how much they tried to dress her up with neon and family entertainment, she was still a whore.

Michael Connelly, 1998

On January 29, 1960, CBS Television aired an episode of the *Twilight Zone* entitled "The Fever." As the story begins, the viewer hears series creator Rod Serling explain, "Mr. and Mrs. Franklin Gibbs, three days and two nights, all expenses paid, at a Las Vegas hotel, won by virtue of Mrs. Gibbs' knack with a phrase. But unbeknownst to either Mr. or Mrs. Gibbs is the fact that there's a prize in their package neither expected nor bargained for. In just a moment, one of them will succumb to an illness worse than any virus can produce, a most inoperative, deadly, life-shattering affliction known as The Fever."[1]

Franklin Gibbs, a straitlaced bank teller from Elgin, Kansas, firmly believes that gambling is immoral, and when his wife tries to play a nickel in a slot machine, he chides her: "Why don't you take handfuls of nickels and throw them out in the street." However, when a drunk gives Franklin a dollar and forces him to put it into another machine, the respectable banker wins $10. In Serling's short story version of the episode, he explains that Franklin, as he retrieves the coins, has "a strange, warm sensation . . . an odd excitement that he had never experienced before."[2] "Now," he tells Flora, "you'll see the difference between a normal, mature thoughtful man and these wild idiots around here. We'll put this in our room and take it home with us. Not these baboons around here. They'd throw it away. They'd compulsively put it back in the machine. Not the Gibbs, they know the value of money." Yet Franklin fondles the money, and as they leave the casino, he believes someone is calling his name. Back in their room, as his wife sleeps, Franklin keeps hearing someone or something calling his name.

Flora awakens, and Franklin tells her, as he leaves their room, that he must feed the money back into the machine because it is tainted. She later goes to the casino, only to find him gambling wildly, having already cashed three checks. He has lost "a great deal of money" and is trying to win it back. Franklin explains to his wife that the machine is "inhuman the way it lets you win a little and then takes it all back. It teases you. It holds out promises and wheedles you and sucks you in." As Flora tries to stop him, a crowd gathers, and two employees watching from a distance note that Franklin has been playing for five hours. One says, "When they get hooked, they really get hooked, don't they." Franklin continues losing and cashing more checks. Exhausted, he asks for a glass of water while uttering, "I've almost got her licked now." It becomes a true marathon, and in the morning Franklin tells Flora, "This machine mocks me. It teases, beckons, mocks me. Put in five, get back four. Put in six, get back five. It's got to pay off sooner or later." The handle on the slot machine sticks when Franklin puts in his last dollar, and he yells at the insidious device, pounds the machine, and knocks it over, yelling, "Give me back my dollar!" Security personnel remove him from the casino. Back in his room, Franklin tells Flora, "That machine, it was ready to pay off and deliberately broke down so it wouldn't have to. It's not even a machine, Flora, it's an entity, it's a thing with a mind and a will of its own. It deliberately broke down." Franklin imagines that he hears the machine's voice and opens the door, fearing that the machine is coming down the hallway. Then, believing it is in the room calling to him, the terrified, hooked gambler runs from it, crashing through the window and falling to his death.

In the closing narration, Serling tells the viewers, "Mr. Franklin Gibbs, visitor to Las Vegas, who lost his money, his reason, and finally, his life to an inanimate machine variously described as a one-armed bandit, a slot machine, or, in Mr. Franklin Gibbs' words, 'a monster with a will all its own.' For our purposes, we'll stick with the latter definition, because we're in the Twilight Zone."[3]

Las Vegas has always had critics. Through the 1930s, many observers found it to be a wide-open relic of the Wild West, a wicked, licentious place of vile liquor and packed gambling dens. To the most cynical journalists of the era, it was a town overrun with prostitutes, drunks, and compulsive gamblers. It was a vacation place for only the most hedonistic of tourists.[4] This fanciful episode of Serling's popular television series added other elements to the critique of Las Vegas, one that developed in popular culture over the decades after World War II. As "The Fever" illustrates, critics were often dismissive of the types of people attracted to Las Vegas, the ways the casinos manipulated people, and the adverse impact that the manipulation had on visitors. Indeed, in the eyes of some, Las Vegas was best understood as a place—as was the case for Franklin Gibbs—of despair and self-destruction. Journalists, novelists, and filmmakers frequently focused on the powerful, addictive qualities of gambling, producing many tales of how destructive compulsive gambling was for some Las Vegas visitors and residents. Compulsive gambling and the other available vices made Las Vegas a depraved place, not a destination for any self-respecting person. Indeed, in a few fictional works, the proper end for Las Vegas was its literal destruction.

The American Psychiatric Association began to include compulsive gambling in its *Diagnostic and Statistical Manual of Mental Disorders* in 1980, labeling it an impulse disorder. Studies by a host of scholars over the subsequent quarter century identified several high-risk groups: adolescents, adults in substance abuse treatment programs, men, African Americans, those who have family members with gambling problems or a family history of the pathology, and the poor.[5] Yet few Americans consulted scholarly studies, instead gaining their understanding of compulsive gambling in Las Vegas and elsewhere from newspapers, popular magazines, movies, television, and novels. Print journalists and those on television and public radio argued that compulsive gambling was a national phenomenon fed not only by illegal gambling, but also by bets on horse races, state lotteries, and legal casino gambling first in Las Vegas and then in Atlantic City where gambling became legal in 1976. Reporters investigated the backgrounds of compulsive gamblers and initially found them to be largely white men who had good jobs and families. Over time, however, following the work of scholars examining the pathology, journalists reported that there were ever more African Americans, women, and teens involved. Because there was no single repository for gambling data, the estimates of how many had become compulsive gamblers varied widely, from one million to between ten and twelve million, or between 1 to 6 percent of all who tossed the dice, bet on horse races, bought lottery tickets, or played the slots. Journalists struggled to explain what led to the destructive behavior. They tossed out simple theories, like compulsive gamblers could not resist the excitement of the play, but also more complex explanations, such as gambling serving as a substitute for love, or people turning to gambling to punish themselves for failures in their lives.[6] Rather than seeking to explain the cause, most journalists focused on how destructive the pathology was for gamblers, citing painful stories of broken families, lost jobs, and people resorting to crime to fund their gambling. They also explained the efforts of Gamblers Anonymous, established in 1957, to assist compulsive gamblers.[7] For many journalists, Las Vegas was a special laboratory to observe the pernicious impact that the gambling fever had on behavior. "Wander through the scores of casinos," syndicated columnist Kenneth L. Dixon reported in 1946, "and you see them by the thousands, palms sweaty from gripping handsful of silver dollars, faces flushed with gambling fever, eyes slitted against cigarette smoke."[8]

Filmmakers and novelists who dealt with compulsive gamblers in Las Vegas characterized those afflicted variously as addicted gamblers, hopeless gamblers, or degenerate gamblers, rather than as pathological or compulsive gamblers; they seldom included those people in real life who are most vulnerable to compulsive gambling. There were few African Americans, adolescents, or people with substance use disorders. Moreover, most fictional compulsive gamblers were not poor, but rather people of some or great means—people with inheritances, an investment broker, a bank teller, an assistant bank manager, a professor, a private investigator, an actor, a lounge singer, a forensic scientist, a detective, a piano player, a manager in a department store, a casino bartender. There is scarce evidence of a family history of gambling. Yet film and fiction has accurately portrayed the gender imbalance among compulsive gamblers; they are overwhelmingly men. Most important, filmmakers and authors have treated the topic as an opportunity for a cautionary tale about the personal risks inherent in challenging the odds in Las Vegas casinos.

Some of the Las Vegas gamblers depicted in film and fiction have long struggled with their compulsive behavior. In the 1955 film *Las Vegas Shakedown*, Mrs. Mabel Dooley, who quickly loses virtually all of her $3,000 at the El Rancho Vegas in a few days, admits she has "gambling fever" and has gambled heavily in the past. Lloyd Rollins is deeply in debt because of his chronic gambling problems in the 1952 film *Las Vegas Story*. Rollins has committed fraud and embezzlement in a desperate effort to recoup his losses before a gambling binge at the fictitious Fabulous casino. Lounge singer Vince Nichols in *Painting the Clouds with Sunshine*, a 1951 film, cannot pass up an opportunity to gamble and admits he always finds it hard to suppress gambling urges he has felt all his life.[9] For others, compulsive gambling is a problem that develops almost instantly, like the "first fatal drop" explanation of alcoholism that was popular during the antebellum temperance crusade. Besides Franklin Gibbs in the *Twilight Zone*, the most notable example of gamblers getting quickly hooked is in the 1949 film *The Lady Gambles*, which features a freelance journalist named Joan Boothe who is working on an article on gambling in that "sink of iniquity," Las Vegas. The casino manager lets her play as a shill, and she instantly finds gambling exciting. After playing only with house money, she quickly loses all her expense money. She asks the casino manager for $100 to try and win back her losses, exhibiting one of the traits of the compulsive gambler—chasing one's losses. She is immediately hooked. She has no control, explaining, "It was like seeing myself on the screen or in a dream." There are several other similar examples. Private detective Laura Holt, in the 1980s television series *Remington Steele*, is on a case in Las Vegas. Because she is not a gambler, Holt studies a book on strategy and promptly starts winning at the Desert Inn. When she is ahead by $60,000, her partner, Remington Steele, has to carry her away from the tables because she is hooked and "willing to risk everything on the next roll." Similarly, Linda Howard, playing roulette in *Lost in America*, and Clark Griswold, playing blackjack in *Vegas Vacation*, become addicted almost instantaneously.[10] This dichotomy on how long it takes to develop the pathology is evident in the research on compulsive gambling. Some indeed are "hooked with their first bet or first win, but for most the disorder is insidious with years of social gambling followed by an abrupt onset usually precipitated by greater exposure to gambling."[11]

Most striking in these various depictions is the powerful attraction of gambling to the compulsive player. Erle Stanley Gardner, writing as A. A. Fair, described Las Vegas "slot-machine addicts" in his 1941 novel *Spill the Jackpot.* "They get a fad for it," one character explains, "just like drinking whiskey or anything else." When they win a jackpot and leave a casino, the proprietor does not worry about the loss. After all, "He's a slot-machine addict, and next day, he'll be back."[12] In some accounts, nothing else matters except getting more money to gamble, as in the 1947 film *The Invisible Wall.* A compulsive gambler named Harry Lane, who is a courier for a Los Angeles bookmaker, is dispatched to the new Flamingo Hotel in Las Vegas to deliver $20,000 to a winning gambler. When the winner is delayed, Lane admits, "The casino drew me like a magnet." He quickly loses money at craps, and, knowing he has to "get away from there," Lane tries swimming at the luxurious pool, horseback riding, and just lounging by the pool. He bumps into a tourist who has a system for beating roulette. Lane joins him and wins in two runs at the table, but then begins to lose heavily. He then proceeds, even knowing how vindictive his boss is, to lose $10,000 of the bookmaker's money, acknowledging the bug has bitten him.[13] As the owner of the El Rancho Vegas, in *Las Vegas Shakedown* explains, "To some people gambling is a disease. It's worse than alcoholism. Win or lose, they can't stay from it."[14] This lack of control is a common theme in the fictional accounts. Joan Boothe, for example, explains, "Something is happening to me and I don't know what it is. It grabs hold of me and I can't shake it off. I see it happening, but I can't stop it."[15] One of the most poignant examples in a commercial film is in *Heat,* released in 1986. Compulsive gambler Nick Escalante has always dreamed of winning it all and leaving Las Vegas to live in Venice. One night he has a remarkable run at blackjack and is up over $100,000. The dealer advises him to leave the table while he is so far ahead. The message is simple. Most gamblers would walk away happy with their winnings. However, Escalante, the compulsive gambler, replies simply, "I can't." He eventually loses all the money on a single hand as a lounge singer ironically croons, "Have yourself a merry little Christmas. From now on our troubles will be out of sight."[16]

Most compulsive gamblers know they will lose. Skye McNally, a character in the 2005 novel *Double Down,* admits, "I don't even think I can beat the system. I know the house always wins."[17] Indeed, there comes a point when compulsive gamblers "know inexorably that you have been numbered for devouring."[18] At that point, "all you know is fear and rage and shame. But mostly fear."[19] Yet there is the remarkable appeal for the addict of simply stepping into a casino. Lloyd Rollins, in *Las Vegas Story,* admits the sounds are "music to my ears." Likewise, for Skye McNally, "The minute I hear that ka-ching, smell the carpeting, see the movements of the croupiers as they hover over the craps tables, their tuxedos crisp, their movements theatrical, feel the energy . . . I'm home. Suddenly the world, which ordinarily zooms by me at this kinetic warp speed, slows down, and I finally relax. I finally breathe."[20] The simple anticipation of the play was the allure for others. For compulsive gambler Steve Hunter in the 1961 novel *The Strip*, "as the ball spun, the old excitement began to churn in him. A quickening of the pulse, a lift of the heart into an aware beat, an embracing heat, a distant approach of climax more thunderous and shattering than any he had ever known."[21]

Just playing the various games produced a remarkable euphoria, perceived as an almost mystical experience, for some of the compulsive gamblers in Las Vegas. Mike Cannon, a character on the television series *Las Vegas*, explains, "I loved it. That sweet feeling. Catching a winning hand. The rush—it was addictive." Linda Howard, in the 1985 film *Lost in America*, tells her husband of the extraordinary sensation gambling gives her: "It was like being on another planet. I didn't care. I didn't need anything. I didn't have any problems. Do you know what that feels like?" With a short successful run at a craps table, a player could conclude "he was the fantasy. Those beautiful steps across the carpet with your pockets bulging with hundred and twenty-five dollar chips and a few random fives."[22] In the 1985 film *Fever Pitch*, gambler Steve Taggert explains that when he is gambling "time is suspended." A high roller in the same movie argues that gambling to him is "like Easter to the Pope." It is the resurrection, the ultimate pleasure.[23] At the end of the 2003 film *Owning Mahowny*, a psychiatrist asks gambler Dan Mahowny, on a scale of 1 to 100 percent, what thrill did he get from gambling? Mahowny answers that it was 100 percent. Using the same scale, he asks Mahowny what the biggest thrill outside of gambling produced. Mahowny says only 20 percent. This intoxicating rush even invades some compulsive gamblers' sleep.[24] Steve Hunter, in *The Strip*, dreams of "a vast population of digits, chips and cards, of dice and horses and hundred-dollar bills." For him, "they spun and churned, rolled and thundered across his mind until the redundant fantasy of winning left him weak and spent."[25]

Yet there were often devastating consequences for those suffering from the gambling disorder. At the opening of the 1974 film *The Gambler*, English professor Alex Freed owes $44,000. In a brief moment of introspection, he explains, "I like the threat of losing." Freed truly enjoys the uncertainty and avoids safe bets because there is no "juice" in safe bets. Thus, as soon as he wins $50,000, Freed immediately loses it all. He simply cannot control his urge to gamble. After winning $100,000 in Las Vegas, Freed pays off his debts but quickly starts to bet wildly.[26] Many of the compulsive gamblers depicted in film and fiction bet huge amounts of money, almost at a manic pace. Indebted to loan sharks for $10,000, Dan Mahowny embezzles large amounts of money and bets on horse races and baseball games as he plays blackjack and craps. In the 1950 novel *The Yellow Cat*, Jeff Whitlock, seeking to double or treble his money, "was playing all six hands at a hundred dollars a hand" at blackjack.[27] In Frank Gilroy's 1968 play *The Only Game in Town*, adapted into a movie two years later, musician Joe Grady struggles with his gambling habit. After avoiding gambling for months, hoping to save enough money to leave town, Joe goes to the Sahara, where he wins $2,000, giving him $8,000, which is enough to allow him to start over somewhere else. However, he cannot resist one more night at the tables, and he loses it all. For the next two years, Joe saves what he can from his modest income and builds another stake of $3,600. Yet as before, he again goes on a gambling binge. First, he goes to the Sands, where he loses "five hundred bucks in ten minutes. From the Sands I went to the Riviera. Lose seven straight bets." Joe continues losing at the Tropicana and then on to the Dunes, where he loses his remaining $300 on one roll of the dice. He even sells his watch to a washroom attendant.[28] These examples reflect the research that indicates "there is a general progression in the frequency of gambling, the amount wagered, and the preoccupation with gambling and money with which to gamble."[29]

Frequently, the gamblers in novels and films have "a compulsion to lose." Indeed, they are willing to commit "a sort of symbolic suicide."[30] In his 1996 novel *Chance*, Robert Parker uses his characters to explain this belief: "With many people for whom gambling is an obsession, there's a lot of guilt. They know it's obsessive, and destructive. They see it as a vice. And they are angry with themselves for doing it." They liken it to alcoholism and contend "the vice becomes its own punishment." Indeed, one character argues that they "lose to punish themselves."[31] This line of argument is most extensively offered in the 1965 novel *Muses of Ruin*. Novelist William Pearson has a character admit to the compulsion with the following explanation about his brethren who cannot stop:

He has a subconscious desire to lose, and his losing is a deliberate self-punishment; he seeks this self-punishment because he has been conditioned largely through childhood experiences, to expect that punishment or failure will be followed by excessive attention from those whose love he most desires; he probably had an overprotective mother who used affection and its abrupt withdrawal as a manipulative device; he is obsessed by undefined feelings of guilt and worthlessness; he fears impotency and frequently is in fact impotent; he has a surface charm which makes it easy for him to find new acquaintances and an instability which makes it difficult for him to maintain close friendships; he is therefore often nomadic socially as well as occupationally; and his compulsive behavior is most likely to erupt at moments of emotional or financial stress.[32]

The fictional portrayals clearly reveal the trap that gambling in Las Vegas was for some. David Boothe, trying to come to terms with his wife's behavior, calls the city a "cockeyed oasis," a place of "quick money won and lost." Although he acknowledges that gambling there is fun for most, "for some it's a trap. It grabs down deep and won't let go."[33] The 2004 film *Losing Ground*, adapted from a New York stage play, is a story of seven people who come into a video poker bar in Las Vegas. It is a case study of people who live sad, unfulfilled lives and who are looking for hope in video poker; indeed, they are looking for the big one. One player named James has lost $3,000 the night before and is seeking to recoup his losses. During the course of the evening, he argues with his girlfriend, Reagan, over his losses, and he then proceeds to lose an additional $800. Another player named Marty, who sells crystal meth on the side, diligently seeks a royal flush to help her son afford college. Michelle is the key character in this film of desperation. She has the sense that she will win a hand of four aces, worth $2,000. Michelle has a brief moment of triumph when she collects $400 on one hand, and the win enhances her hopes, "The aces are next. I can feel it." However, she quickly loses all the money, the ATM will give her no more, and the bartender refuses to extend her any credit. She is reduced to begging the other players for money. One man, who has just hit a big jackpot, gives her $200, but Michelle quickly loses that as well. In desperation, Michelle trades sex for more money to play video poker. She is a hopeless, compulsive gambler. Nothing but the gambling matters to her. Her boyfriend no longer cares about her, and she does not even know the day or the time. The film vividly portrays how addictive the game of video poker is to many.[34]

The most lasting image of the compulsive gambler is the pathetic old lady, who is usually playing the slots. In novels, as well as newspaper and magazine articles, she is poor, solitary, haggard, forlorn, poorly or oddly dressed, shod in tennis shoes, and wearing gloves to prevent further wear and tear on sore hands. These women spend ten to twenty hours a day in a grim, determined battle with slot machines, usually playing more than one machine at a time. With paper cups of change in one hand and either pulling the handle or depressing the buttons of the machines with the other, these women become territorial, claiming machines as their own and assuming that their luck is about to turn.[35] She is "an old woman engaged in a strange ritual" in John D. McDonald's *The Only Girl in the Game.* Dressed in "a bright red sweater, a powder-blue skirt far too short for her," and "a conical coolie hat in venomous green," the woman "teetered on reedy old legs as she fed the dime slot machine" and used both hands to pull the lever. Unable to watch the outcome, the woman turned away "in a tension of waiting for the payoff."[36] Lloyd Biggle Jr., in *A Hazard of Losers,* includes, among all the other gamblers, "a little old lady in tennis shoes" playing "three slot machines in rapid succession." She carries the coins in a plastic cup and runs "back and forth, inserting money and jerking the handle of each machine as she passed it." The woman was so caught up in the play that she didn't bother to check the outcome.[37] Ian Fleming was particularly dismissive when describing these women. In his novel *Diamonds Are Forever,* Fleming has a character telling special agent James Bond, "Wait till you see the little old ladies in gloves working those slots." The women had essentially become, in Fleming's view, automatons: "The droves of them stood at the banks of machines like hens in an egg battery, conditioned by the delicious coolness of the room and the music of the spinning wheels, to go on laying it on the line until their wad was gone." Fleming has Bond observing the women and thinking they resembled "Dr. Pavlov's dogs, the saliva drooling down from their jaws at the treacherous bell that brought no dinner, and he shuddered at the thought of the empty eyes of these women and their skins and their wet half-opened mouths and their bruised hands."[38]

A number of documentaries also dealt with compulsive gambling in Las Vegas. In the 1996 *The Real Las Vegas,* there is a brief mention of the problem. Veteran comedian Shecky Greene argues that Las Vegas is negatively defining the nation by promoting gambling: "It's the destruction of mankind." "We're creating in this country, compulsive gamblers."[39] Nine years later, in *Las Vegas: An Unconventional History,* a documentary made for the PBS series *American Experience,* viewers not only see a short segment at a Gamblers Anonymous chapter in Las Vegas, but they also hear how compulsive gambling destroyed one Las Vegas resident. Identified only as Randy, the man explains that he gambled before and after work and sometimes did not even go to work. "You know," he says, "I got to the point where I was gambling my whole check and I was borrowing from whoever, family, whoever to cover, cover my butt and I finally ran out of people to borrow from and, well, I didn't want my fiancée to leave me so I guess in a panic you could say, I figured I had no other alterna-

Robert Culp and Bill Cosby in an episode of the television series I Spy *confronting an elderly slot player who is protecting her machine. Source: UNLV Libraries, Special Collections.*

tive other than to rob a bank."⁴⁰ *Dreamland*, released in 2000, is the most extensive documentary look at compulsive gambling in Las Vegas. It follows the challenges of Las Vegas residents struggling with compulsive gambling. One explains, "Sometimes I gamble not knowing when to stop." Another admits that she "forgot the bills and responsibilities." The slot machines became her "happiness." A third acknowledges that gambling "stopped being a choice" in her life: "It just became the only thing I knew how to do. I didn't have a normal response to life anymore." For her, gambling was "the solution to everything." While acknowledging that most people visiting or living in Las Vegas do not have gambling problems, the filmmaker emphasizes how bleak life has become for those enmeshed in compulsive gambling.⁴¹

Even when not dealing with compulsive gamblers, authors and filmmakers frequently exhibit a jaded view of the millions attracted to Las Vegas, seeing them as parasites or as clueless or desperate working-class people. Hank McCain, driving down Fremont Street in the movie *Machine Gun McCain*, was amazed at the allure that the casinos had for "sad, fat businessmen" and "for hustlers, thieves, and pimps." A young character named Frisbee in the movie *Rafferty and the Gold Dust Twins*, after arriving in Las Vegas, tells her mother, "Vegas sucks. Just the same as L.A. Bunch of hookers, pimps, and part-time movie stars." Indeed, grifters, hustlers, prostitutes, and con artists are all stock characters in fictional accounts of Las Vegas.[42] In his 1958 novel *No House Limit,* Steve Fisher describes a "seedy crowd . . . wearing dungarees and work clothes; women seemed dowdy, and older, and the men somehow more forlorn."[43] In the early 1990s, novelist Edward Allen claimed Las Vegas was "a good town to be ugly in," as few cared how they dressed.[44] Mystery writer Robert Parker agreed. To him, the people walking the Strip "looked like they'd just arrived on a freight car, pink shorts, small plastic mesh baseball hats, small children, Instamatic cameras, white boots, large bellies, plaid shirts, high top sneakers."[45] More important, to some observers like novelist Gerald Petievich, Las Vegas attracted some of life's worst people:

> Maitre d's with the slickest palms west of the Mississippi, gamblers who wore Stetson hats, whores who looked like movie stars, professional stick men, fixers, pickpockets, keno addicts, gallery spies, confidence men from all parts of the world, businessmen and their girlfriends in for the weekend, amateur and professional card counters, dice mechanics, and all manner of stage entertainers, those at the top of the show-biz circuit and those on their way down the drain.[46]

In sum, a host of observers offered a sharply dismissive and patronizing interpretation of the millions who came to Las Vegas and the thousands who lived there. They were the clueless and morally bankrupt masses. According to novelist Robert Parker, tourists generally were profoundly disappointed with their Las Vegas experience. All had not turned out the way it should have in glittering Sin City:

> The Strip was choked with people in dogged search of fun, looking for the promise of Vegas that had brought them all from Keokuk and Presque Isle and North Platte. It wasn't like it was supposed to be. It wasn't the adventure of a lifetime, but it had to be. You couldn't admit that it wasn't. You'd come too far, expected too much, planned too long. If you stayed up later, played harder, gambled bigger, looked longer, saw another show, had another drink, stretched out a little further.[47]

As a character in the movie *This Is My Life* explains, "Las Vegas is a place where people with empty lives and no values go to have fun."[48]

In every decade in the press, in fiction, and in film, the upright condemned the city and urged respectable folks to stay away. "Some of the West Coast dailies," Dick Pearce wrote in *Harpers* in 1955, "call Las Vegas a desert Babylon." He claimed it was "only a matter of time until some prophet comes out of the Nevada wastelands and curses the whole glittering shebang as a modern Gomorrah destined for destruction."[49] Indeed, some religious leaders in the early 1960s condemned the city as a "flowering cancer" and "a horrifying preview of future civilization." The famed evangelist Billy Graham made revival trips to Las Vegas, and the Southern Baptist Convention met there in 1989 because it "offered a unique opportunity for evangelism."[50] The preachy conservative columnist James J. Kilpatrick complained, "What Vegas asks of tourists—and what the tourists willingly provide—is a suspension of belief in the old conventional values: in the value of money, in the meaning of work, in concepts of worth that can be measured in usefulness or beauty or need."[51] Prominent public figures also occasionally joined in the condemnation. For example, in 1983, U.S. Supreme Court chief justice Warren Burger, upon learning that the American Bar Association had scheduled its annual meeting in Las Vegas, proclaimed he would not attend because the gambling center was an "unsavory and unsuitable" place for a justice to speak.[52]

The 1955 movie *Las Vegas Shakedown* reflected the reluctance of respectable people to travel to such a sinful city. In one scene, a woman riding a bus learns that the passenger beside her is heading to Las Vegas. The woman chides her companion for traveling to such a "disgraceful" place with "open gambling day and night." It was such a depraved place that "anything can happen to you" while you are there. There is also an elderly banker and his wife from a small town in Nebraska who travel to Las Vegas. The banker is tired of being a pillar of small-town society and wishes to have a little fun, but his wife worries about folks back home learning about their trip: "Do you realize what it would mean if anybody in North Point found out that Mr. Earnest Raff, the president of the bank, was in Las Vegas? Our life has been rich and full, you don't want to ruin our reputation by spending a weekend in a place like that." Yet she relents when her husband persists, but when the banker's wife places a long-distance telephone call from the hotel, she asks the operator not to say that the call is originating in Las Vegas.[53]

Articles dealing with racism and segregation were also a part of the negative images of Las Vegas, particularly in the decade of the 1950s. There had been few African Americans in Las Vegas until World War II, when the massive Basic Magnesium plant opened in nearby Henderson, attracting hundreds of African American workers and their families. By 1955, there were more than

15,000 African American residents. They faced a city ruled by Jim Crow regulations. Beyond the indignity of restrictive housing covenants, segregated schools, and a substandard infrastructure in the Westside housing district, virtually all hotels and casinos barred African Americans from their gaming areas, restaurants, and showrooms. The racism that prompted the discrimination was common across the nation, a condition exacerbated by the reluctance of white tourists from the South to mix with African Americans in the commercial properties.[54] African American entertainers from the mid-1940s scarcely experienced better treatment. Most, including Eartha Kitt, Dorothy Dandridge, Sammy Davis Jr., Pearl Bailey, Lena Horne, Nat King Cole, and Harry Belafonte, could not stay at the hotels where they performed, dine in the restaurants, gamble in the casinos, or mix with the white audiences until the mid-1950s. Instead, they usually had to stay at rooming houses in the city's Westside.[55] The mainstream media only occasionally devoted space to the rampant discrimination, as in their coverage of the 1955 opening of the Moulin Rouge, the first major interracial hotel-casino.[56] African American newspapers did provide regular coverage of the conditions facing blacks in Las Vegas. For example, readers of *The Crisis,* the official publication of the NAACP, in 1946 learned that Las Vegas "might just as well be in southwestern Alabama as far as jim crow is concerned." Eight years later, the same paper reported that nearly three-fourths of African Americans lived "in substandard housing" with unpaved streets in Las Vegas's Westside.[57]

The darkest images of Las Vegas, however, are in the bleak stories of despair and doom. "The town's dark, seamy underbelly," novelist Jennifer Speart wrote in 1988, "makes it the perfect spot in which to self-destruct." "After all," she asked, "where else can you develop an overnight addiction, get instantly married or divorced, and commit financial suicide all in the same weekend?"[58] Speart's novel reflects a large body of material from television, movies, and fiction focused on the underbelly of Las Vegas—a gritty, dismal, dangerous, lonely, and dispiriting place of cheap apartments, dark and threatening streets, thugs, hustlers, and corrupt policemen and politicians, where robberies, drug deals, assault, rape, murder, frustration, and failure are commonplace and people live desolate lives.[59]

Filmmakers turned frequently to the theme of Las Vegas as a place of despair, particularly for young women. In the 1957 film *Eighteen and Anxious,* Judy Graham is an eighteen-year-old in Los Angeles secretly married to a high school sweetheart who dies in a car race, leaving her pregnant. After she rejects an abortion, her stepfather labels her a tramp and sends her away to have the child, but her parents eventually adopt the baby. Eager to leave all

Moulin Rouge Casino, 1956, the first integrated hotel-casino in Las Vegas. Source: UNLV Libraries, Special Collections.

this behind her and hoping to get "what she wants," Judy goes to Las Vegas with a trumpet player who will perform at the Dunes Hotel. Amid the glitter of the city, her life becomes progressively worse. When the musician ultimately rejects Judy, she drinks heavily and, ever more disillusioned, takes a car on a wild drive that ends with a head-on collision. Although Judy survives the crash, "she had made a mess of everything."[60] Similarly, the 1969 film *The Grasshopper* portrays the plight of nineteen-year-old Christine Adams from British Columbia. She lands a job as a showgirl in the *Casino de Paris* show at the Dunes. Christine's life, split between Las Vegas and Los Angeles, spirals downward rapidly after she marries Tommy Marcott, a retired football star who does public relations work for the hotel. Shortly after a wealthy guest at the hotel assaults her, Christine's husband beats the man savagely, which prompts associates of the man to murder Tommy. Christine turns to drugs and becomes, in turn, a high-priced Las Vegas prostitute, a mistress to a Southern California millionaire, and a prostitute again to raise money for a rock band. When the band leader takes off with the money she has raised, Christine gets high on marijuana and hires a skywriter to write "f***" in the air. The film ends with her arrest.[61]

Joan Didion's 1970 novel *Play It as It Lays*, made into a film two years later, is the sordid chronicle of actress Maria Wyeth. She is thirty-one years old with a faltering career, a failing marriage, and an institutionalized four-year-old daughter; her husband has just forced her to have an abortion. Emotionally unstable (she ends up in a mental hospital), Maria drinks to excess, experiments with drugs, and has a number of casual sexual liaisons. With no significant links to family or community, Maria spends a great deal of time aimlessly driving the Southern California freeways. Maria, author Didion explains, "never understood friendship, conversation, the normal amenities of social exchange."[62] Maria replicates this hopeless pattern of existence in a trip to Las Vegas, which is presented as an arid, empty place:

> For the rest of the time Maria was in Las Vegas she wore dark glasses. She did not decide to stay in Vegas: she only failed to leave. She spoke to no one. She did not gamble. She neither swam nor lay in the sun. She was there on some business but she could not seem to put her finger on what that business was. All day, most of every night, she walked and she drove. Two or three times a day she walked in and out of all the hotels on the Strip and several downtown. She began to crave the physical flash of walking in and out of places, the temperature shock, the hot wind blowing outside, the heavy frigid air inside. She thought about nothing.[63]

In all three of these examples, Las Vegas is a destination of despair, but for some, it is a locale of doom. In "Liebestod," a short segment of a 1987 compilation of films based on operatic music entitled *Aria*, director Franc Roddam portrays Richard Wagner's tragic love story of *Tristan and Isolde* in Las Vegas. In this vignette, a young couple drive through the desert and into Las Vegas, first down Fremont Street and then down the Strip. They gaze in apparent wonder at the sights—the Stardust, Dunes, Flamingo, Sands, and a wedding chapel. Back down on Fremont Street, they go to a hotel, make love, breaking a bottle in the process, and then use the shards to slit their wrists while sitting in a bathtub.[64] The desperation so dramatically exemplified in "Liebestod" is also the theme in the 1998 film *Falling Sky*. The story involves an alcoholic single mother named Reese Nicholson and her daughter, Emily, who move to Las Vegas hoping Reese will make it as a singer in the nightclubs. They move into a trailer park, and though they are near the elegance of the Strip, its promise is always out of reach. After losing a number of jobs because of her drinking problem, Reese commits suicide, leaving only a taped message, which is a metaphor for Las Vegas: "I'm in a dark corner and I can't find my way out."[65]

Leaving Las Vegas is the most searing portrayal of hopelessness in the gambling city. Ben Sanderson, who has lost both his family and his job in the movie industry, is profoundly addicted to alcohol. He travels from Los Angeles to Las Vegas, where he meets a prostitute named Sera who asks, "What brings you to Las Vegas?" Ben responds, "I came here to drink myself to death." Ben and Sera develop a relationship that lasts only as long as Ben's unrelenting quest reaches its inevitable end. Ben stays for a time in a sleazy motel called the Whole Year Inn (which he imagines as the Hole You're In), and then with Sera in her apartment. He sells his Rolex watch and car for virtually nothing because he will soon need no money, drinks during most of his waking moments, eats little, and becomes "a smelly, bloated, exhaustible, sick, self-indulgent man."[66] Because of his drinking, Ben causes scenes in casinos and gets into a bar fight. All the while, he does not want to become too close to Sera, who is ever more solicitous, steadfast in his wish "to die as a stranger in Las Vegas."[67] He does not succeed. Sera remains with him when he dies after refusing medical help.

Reviews of *Leaving Las Vegas,* after praising the acting of Nicolas Cage, who portrayed Ben and Elizabeth Shue, who portrayed Sera, typically launched into a discussion of how appropriate it was for filmmaker Mike Figgis to choose Las Vegas for the saga of a doomed man. What better place for such a dark story than the seedy and decadent Sin City? "Las Vegas," Caryn James wrote in the *New York Times,* "is not the only place in which this harsh, dead-end love affair could have happened, but it is certainly the most likely. For Ben and Sera it is a place of no past and no guilt." Christopher Sharrett, in *USA Today Magazine,* was more direct: "Vegas is a dead end, a graveyard, the logical place to go when one wants to die. It is filled with rapacious, callous people who are there to feed off of carrion. The city's glitter is merely a cover for its very manifest decay."[68]

To some, such a deplorable city, a place of unrelenting despair and hopelessness, deserved destruction. Several films dealt with the partial or complete devastation of Las Vegas. From the 1957 film *The Amazing Colossal Man* to *Mars Attacks* nearly four decades later, filmmakers and novelists subjected Las Vegas to varying degrees of destruction, including Stephen King, in *The Stand,* who has God detonate an atomic bomb, destroying Las Vegas.[69] The hotel-casinos seemed legitimate targets for the righteous. It was as if, as Edward Baldwin has written, "Las Vegas is getting what it deserves when it is attacked."[70]

Although some of these dark images, particularly the depictions of the doomed Franklin Gibbs, Reese Nicholson, and Ben Sanderson, are vivid, even memorable, they do not represent the preponderance of images of Las Vegas in film, fiction, and periodicals, as the previous chapters have demonstrated. Nonetheless, they are part of the rich mosaic of images Americans saw and read about Las Vegas, and it is likely that these cautionary tales and negative images persuaded some to avoid the resort city in southern Nevada.

Conclusion

The Ultimate Attraction of Las Vegas

*All super casinos have much in common. They are never-never lands
in which those who come to Las Vegas can lose themselves for a few
larger-than-life days.*

Peter Earley, 2001

In late spring 1953, Gladwin Hill, the Los Angeles bureau chief for the *New
York Times,* traveled to Las Vegas, and in the June 7 issue of his paper, he told
his readers about the "Klondike in the Desert." Hill, who covered Las Vegas
for almost two decades for the *New York Times,* provided readers with a spirited account of the "unique boom town" a "surprising oasis in the mountain-
ridged Nevada desert." In journeying to Las Vegas, a weary visitor could leave
behind "the world of reality" and find "a strange mirage" that, to Hill, most
resembled "a sun-baked neo-Klondike, as the Klondike might be depicted
in a Hollywood musical with palm trees substituted for snow." There were
many elements in this fantasy land. Along the fabulous Strip, "the traveler
plunges into a never-never land of exotic architecture, extravagant vegetation, flamboyant signery and frenetic diversion." The resort hotels all had
"lavish restaurant–night clubs" and "elaborately furnished salons." Hill noted
that one could have "sumptuous accommodations"—indeed, "Park Avenue
luxury"—for as little as "$7.50 a day" and "enjoy a Broadway-style evening
(for two) within the limits of a $10 bill." The most important appeal, how-
ever, was the town's "unusual atmosphere of do-as-you-please," which made
Las Vegas "unlike where anybody ever came from." Whatever "home-town
tensions and inhibitions" tourists brought to the southern Nevada resort
town, Hill assured readers they would "fall away like overcoats under the desert sun."[1]

Six years after Hill's article, Herb Lyon, entertainment columnist for the *Chicago Daily Tribune*, offered his take on a visit to Las Vegas: "Every time I chance into gawdy, bawdy, naughty Las Vegas, I get the uneasy, queasy feeling it's all a mirage." Like Hill, Lyon reminded readers that the city offered "round-the-clock revelry," a place where one could have breakfast at 6 P.M. and a chuck wagon buffet at 6 A.M. It was all part of the Las Vegas escape formula: "elegant, richly adorned, restful guest rooms and suites, a splash swimming pool, moderate priced dining rooms and finally a fabulous night club, right off the casino." Yet Lyon was writing at the time when Las Vegas had made national news because a number of the hotels had begun to offer topless shows, adding a bit of Sodom and Gomorrah to the city's appeal as an escape destination. Arguing that nudity had become the top attraction, Lyon told his readers about "the dozen lush, plush hotels that comprise the Vegas strip" that "exude a glittering, bacchanalian glamor and clamor, and the nude and spicy floor shows seemingly run free and unfettered." One hotel host explained to Lyon, "People who come to Vegas expect spice and glamor. They want the biggest, the most, and the best in food and fun and entertainment. We have long since learned to give them what they want." Beyond the appeal of the topless shows, Lyon argued that "the whole wonderful, wild, wacky scene" presented by Las Vegas was most intriguing because it offered a visitor "a thousand personal dramas." Once in the casinos, one can "feel the electricity of gayety, tragedy, neuroticism, uncertainty, and hope in the milling, restless throngs."[2]

In fall 1969, Charles Champlin, the arts editor for the *Los Angles Times*, made a pilgrimage to Las Vegas to research a piece for the *Times* magazine. As the nation neared the end of a tumultuous decade of assassinations of key leaders and seemingly unending riots over free speech, civil rights, and the Vietnam war, Champlin argued that Las Vegas was a "tonic" for the country because "it declares a moratorium on ordinary reality and suspends customary belief." He thus took issue with the cynics who concluded that the city lacked "redeeming social merit." Arriving visitors clearly had a sense that they were in "a different place" as soon as the desert heat hit them, but more so when they heard "the tinkling thrum of the slot machines in the airport," which prompted "a kind of electric tension and starts a run-don't-walk excitement. It is probably Pavlovian, but it invigorates every time." One of the leading "restorative qualities" of this unique city was the absence of clocks. "The divorce from mundane reality, and the release from mundane cares," Champlin argued, "is never so dramatic as when you don't know what the hell time it is, and could care less." It is also a place that invited excess. Champlin knew of no other locale "where one can see two major shows and three or four lounge acts, get some sun and pool-time and have at least one gourmet quality meal, and thus cram a week's worth of vacation pleasures into an overnight stay." Behind all these allures, Champlin speculated that there was a crucial underlying therapeutic element. "I suspect," he wrote, "that is the tingle of *feeling* faintly wicked without actually or necessarily being wicked."[3]

Famous because of his remarkably successful novel *The Godfather* and the award-winning films based on that work, Mario Puzo, in 1976, published *Inside Las Vegas,* which he called "a book about Vegas as a dream world of pleasure, supplying one of the basic needs of human nature."[4] The Las Vegas chamber of commerce could not have produced a more favorable invitation to their city. Puzo enticed the world-weary with his characterization of Las Vegas as "a dream." He pointed out that the city had "nothing to do with reality. It is a sanctuary from the real world, real troubles, real emotion, and it's somehow fitting and proper that the city of Las Vegas is surrounded by a vast desert. A desert which acts as a *cordon sanitaire.*"[5] Puzo claimed that Las Vegas offered a unique vacation opportunity, one that could transform a visitor if he were willing to think about vacations in a very different way. "On a three-day visit to Vegas," he argued, "you can have one of the best times of your life. To do that you have to forget about great museums, the pleasure of reading, great theater, great music, stimulating lectures by great philosophers, great food, great wine, and true love. Forget about them. Just for three days. Believe me, you won't miss them. Ye shall be as little children again."[6] Obviously drawing on his own experiences as a self-proclaimed degenerate gambler, Puzo promised that tourists would be enchanted by the magic they would experience in casinos, which "have a mistlike, fairytale quality about them."[7]

In 1991, the idea of Las Vegas as the perfect, magical escape destination got the stamp of approval from the National Geographic Society in its *Traveler* magazine. Building on the work of journalists like Charles Champlin, Rob Schultheis began by describing the remarkable sense of anticipation one experiences driving toward the Strip from the airport. "It makes you think," he wrote, "despite yourself, of broken rules, risky business, licentiousness. Dangerous stuff." In the course of his article, Schultheis described going to Caesars Palace and dancing "on a floating cocktail lounge/disco called Cleopatra's Barge," dropping in at Circus Circus to watch "aerialists fly, jugglers juggle, ponies canter," seeing a show at the Tropicana with "voluptuous show girls in various degrees of dishabille, hoofers, blues singers, rock and roll choruses, acrobats, smoke and lasers," and touring the Liberace Museum, where he saw not only the famed pianist's "16-foot-long, $300,000 white fox cape," but also his "million-dollar Rolls-Royce Phantom V with a wet bar." It all persuaded him that in Las Vegas, "the far-fetched is commonplace, and anything can happen." He found that the myth about Las Vegas as a truly magical place was true:

> We all know it, whether we have been here before or not: Las Vegas, the City of Sin, the Oasis of Unimaginable Delights, of Instant Riches (and Ruin), where everyone's dreams, however foolish and reprehensible, have a chance of coming true. It is a potent myth, the Mother Lode, Carnival, and the Great White Way all rolled into one, and the energy it generates makes Las Vegas perhaps the only truly nonstop city on earth, a 24-hours-a-day, 365-days-a-year Metropolis of the Midnight Sun that never, ever quits.[8]

Although there had been other television series like *Vega$, Crime Story,* and *CSI: Crime Scene Investigation,* as well as a multitude of episodes of a variety of programs on television about Las Vegas, none portrayed the glamor, the excitement, and the fantasy of the city more vividly than *Las Vegas,* which ran for five seasons on NBC. Each week, viewers saw the fast pace, lights, glitz, beautiful people, luxurious megaresorts, huge jackpots, wedding chapels, strip clubs, and prostitutes. Hotel guests interacted with celebrities like Wayne Newton, Paul Anka, Little Richard, Brooks and Dunn, Dennis Hopper, Michael Bublé, and Paris Hilton. Most of the guests at the fictitious Montecito Hotel quickly shed their inhibitions. Indeed, during one episode in the first year, several women had a bachelorette party that featured excessive drinking and male strippers. One of the characters acknowledged, "In Vegas people do things that they would normally not dream of."[9] At the close of the program's pilot, one of the characters is zipping along the Strip in a convertible at night amid the garish lights and frenetic action, and alerted the viewers to the escapist theme of the series: "Vegas. Former mob lawyer is mayor. Legal gambling. Valets with masters' degrees in engineering. Bars that never close. World class food and entertainment. 24/7 action. God, I love this town."[10]

During the city's first century, many perceptions of Las Vegas attracted ever more tourists. They came hoping to experience the last frontier town, to gamble legally, to rub elbows with gangsters, or to see some of the brightest stars of the entertainment world, or to see beautiful women, or to indulge in luxurious accommodations. Yet the most powerful magnet was the sense that Las Vegas would offer the visitor a remarkable escape from their daily lives. The articles, book, and television series above are all helpful in defining the elements that made it a unique destination. Over the decades, a host of other journalists, authors, and filmmakers expanded on those themes of Las Vegas as an extraordinary place, almost a mirage, that would offer a visitor round-the-clock action, luxury that even those with modest means could afford, if only for a couple of nights, a place where one could do things that were unacceptable back home, and, ultimately, a fantasy land, a singular destination that offered a refuge from the mundane.

Early on, authors and journalists portrayed Las Vegas as a round-the-clock town. Americans who picked up a copy of the 1940 Works Progress Administration publication *Nevada: A Guide to the Silver State* learned that Las Vegas is "lively" all night, with "bars, gambling and night clubs" and "some restaurants are crowded till dawn."[11] Subsequent writers embellished this impression. To visiting journalists, every night in Las Vegas seemed like Saturday night. No matter what the hour, they found revelers gambling, dining, or attending shows while exhibiting little interest in resting. Rather, they were enchanted by the round-the-clock fun.[12] The low cost of all the luxury helped fuel this remarkable tempo of excitement. The swank spas succeeded, journalists argued, because developers offered "luxury at modest prices."[13] In 1947, for example, *Life* magazine promised that a guest could stay and "trample the plush carpets at Siegel's $6 million Flamingo Hotel" for only $4 a day.[14] Through the early 1980s, before the emergence of upscale mega-resorts like the Mirage and those that rapidly followed, readers continued to discover that they would pay very little for great entertainment, extraordinary accommodations, and excellent meals. In 1965, novelist William Pearson described the attraction of this "little bit of Eden in the desert":

An ordinary fellow from a place like South Bend, Indiana can't wait to catch the first plane to Vegas. For thirty bucks a day he and his wife can knock on Eden's back door. For thirty bucks a day he gets a room with an air-conditioned view—it would be thirty or more just for the room in Miami, and raining besides—breakfast at noon on a terrace overlooking a Hollywood-sized pool where his favorite Hollywood cutie pie is sun-bathing in a rhinestone swim suit, plus big drinks, big steaks, big evening of watching big movie or TV names shilling for their supper at twenty or thirty grand a week, and a chance at the jackpot on the dollar slots.[15]

Yet the escapist quality of Las Vegas involved much more than an expectation of "opulence, luxury, and obsequious service" for little money.[16] The city offered one a chance to walk on the wild side, if only for a day or two. The normal restraints of family, neighborhood, church, and workplace disappeared when one landed at the airport and entered a city that offered visitors "a montage of the things you have always wanted to do."[17] As one hotel executive explained in 1961, "It's as though you walk through a veil." A local psychologist explained in *Esquire* that a tourist "allows himself to do the things his superego will not permit him to do in his own community."[18] The *New York Times* had a story on such a person in 1973. Their reporter found Mrs. Barbara Gazaway, a respectable "Southern belle, who is executive director of the Mental Health Association back home in Huntsville, Ala.," enthusiastically playing at the craps table at the Flamingo with a dozen men. The reporter explained her exceptional behavior simply: "Things happen to people when they get to Las Vegas." Nonplussed by her first-time experience in being a bit wicked in Las Vegas, Mrs. Gazaway told the reporter that even her "good Methodist" friends back home would understand.[19] As inhibitions melt away, as they had with Mrs. Gazaway, one feels free to pursue any craving. As a tour service operator explained to the *Los Angeles Times* in 1977, "If you're old enough, big enough or can afford it, you can do anything in this town."[20] What other locales would consider immoral is commonplace, whether it be gambling, whoring, or drinking to excess. As *L.A. Weekly* columnist Michael Ventura explained the house rules in Las Vegas, "As long as you don't bother the other customers, you can do *anything*."[21]

More powerful than this hedonistic appeal, Las Vegas represented a place where ordinary folks could escape the mundane. Newspapers and magazine articles, novels, movies, and television programs portrayed people who had fled to Las Vegas because they had argued with their spouses or neighbors or who had had trouble with their boss or were trying to overcome lost love, all commonplace developments that made up part of the daily grind that simply wore people down and induced them to "fall asleep during the 10 o'clock news." But once they get to Las Vegas, "with the adrenalin pumping," the woebegone "stay up all night."[22] Many reveled in being irresponsible, sleeping much of the day and avoiding reading newspapers or watching news programs, turning their back on the world's problems.[23] All could leave their lives' baggage behind and enjoy a little wickedness. Edward Allen, in a *Gentleman's Quarterly* article, explained the particular escape gambling provided him. It "invites me to take an hour's recess from adulthood," he wrote, "to

Gambling in the swimming pool at the Sands Hotel in the 1950s, illustrating Las Vegas as a destination of uninhibited escape. Source: UNLV Libraries, Special Collections.

play in a well-demarked sandbox of irrationality and to look at the world as a magical place, which of course it is when the light hits it at the right angle."[24]

In the end, the consistent overriding image and appeal of Las Vegas, in its first century, is that it provides the world-weary tourist the best escapist fun. Many of the descriptions offered by journalists, novelists, and screenwriters often sounded much like the work of a publicity agent for the city, but it did not matter because the passages resonated with readers and viewers who began to plan their next vacation for the remarkable desert resort city. Caskie Stinnett aptly described the enduring appeal of this singular place in a 1967 issue of *Holiday* magazine. "It is because," she wrote, "there is absolutely nothing else in the world like Las Vegas—nothing so glittering and gay and totally uninhibited—that vast numbers of people find this mirage in the desert so endlessly irresistible. Las Vegas is fun."[25]

Afterword

The Intellectuals' Images of Las Vegas

In July 1969, Kirk Kerkorian brought the quality pop-rock critics from New York out to Las Vegas on his private plane for Elvis Presley's opening show at Kerkorian's new International Hotel. Among them was Margot Hentoff, essayist and reviewer of books and culture, who wrote about the trip in an article in *Harper's* magazine. Hentoff offered a view of Las Vegas widely shared among her circle of friends. "It seemed," she wrote, "only a little more glamorous than Hoboken but, for most of us, equally unknown. No one I know goes to Las Vegas." None of them would purposely go to Sin City for a vacation. "If they have been there at all . . . it has only been out of necessity or passing through from one place to somewhere else." For Easterners of her acquaintance "Las Vegas has always seemed an alien city which rose from the fantasies of gamblers and gangsters whose daydreams were in turn created by movies and dealt with the stuff of superstars, big easy money, and big easy girls." Because of these shared attitudes, she admitted, "I never, for a moment, wanted to go there." When Hentoff and her fellow critics from the Big Apple arrived at the International Hotel, she claimed to have suffered a "cultural shock." As she looked about, Hentoff saw "no clocks, no windows, no seating groups; only a huge cavern filled with slot machines and gaming tables." It was quite cold in the building, and "artificial light flows over everything." As she took it all in, Hentoff said it looked, "quite literally, like Hell."[1] In 1982, Hank Resnik, another native New Yorker who had subsequently moved to San Francisco, shared with readers of *California Living Magazine* a similar bias about Las Vegas. "Sophisticated New York children," he told readers, "knew that Las Vegas was the epitome of bad taste, and bad taste was a cardinal sin." On his first drive through Las Vegas fifteen years earlier, Resnik recollected viewing "the neon signs and the latter-day Xanadus with superiority and contempt." The images triggered his "New Yorker's conception of Las Vegas," and the remembered adjectives came rolling out: "'cheap,' 'tawdry,' 'blatant,' 'materialistic.'"[2]

These two pieces of journalism reveal much about the ways social and cultural critics have viewed Las Vegas. The most hostile critiques invariably come from outsiders, academics or essayists for magazines like *Harper's* and the *Nation,* who have difficulty getting past their preconceptions about the city, a place so unlike where they live. These urban sophisticates invariably are comparing it to New York, Paris, Los Angeles, San Francisco, or Chicago, and in their judgment, Las Vegas does not measure up. They expect to find an ugly, materialistic city with no meaningful history or culture, and they frequently note only what confirms what they already believe about Las Vegas. What results is a shallow elitism, a dismissal of Las Vegas as the worst of modern urban places. As Gary Provost, in his book *High Stakes: Inside the New Las Vegas,* pointed out, "Comparatively speaking, Sodom and Gomorrah got off easy. Las Vegas, it has been written, is a city of shattered dreams, a city where mobsters still pull strings, a city where pathetic showgirls load their tits with silicone to squeeze a few extra years out of their careers before they turn to prostitution. And it is a city where toothless retirees pour their last quarters into soulless slot machines that never pay anybody."[3]

To some critics, Las Vegas is a place no one should ever want to visit. Author and media pundit Dan Savage admitted, before he had a significant change of heart, that he found Las Vegas beneath contempt. "To me," he wrote in *The Seven Deadly Sins and the Pursuit of Happiness,* "Las Vegas was a place where cocktail waitresses went to die, where swag lamps swung, and where gangsters were gunned down in midmassage. Elvis and Frank and Liberace may have left the building, but Vegas was still their cheesy town, not mine." It only appealed to "people who lead lives centered on consumption, devoid of meaning."[4] In one of a series of articles on Las Vegas in the *New York Times* in 2004, journalist John M. Broder focused on its parasitic qualities, arguing that Las Vegas had become "the most efficient machine ever devised to relieve the willing or the weak of their earthly fortunes, whether that weakness is gambling, sex, drink, spectacle or consumption."[5] Crime writer James Ellroy, whose novel *The Cold Six Thousand* dealt with Las Vegas in the 1960s, bluntly agreed. The gambling center, he argued, is "a shit hole. It's a testimony to greed and prostitution and exploitation of women and narcotics and the get-rich-quick fervor that is one of the worst aspects of America."[6]

Other critics went further, characterizing Las Vegas as a hellish place. Celebrated novelist and screenwriter John Gregory Dunne argued that being in a casino just before dawn was tantamount to being in an "anteroom of purgatory," and journalist Nick Tosches claimed, "Dante did not write in the age of malls, but he would have recognized Las Vegas, in any age, for what it is: a religion, a disease, a nightmare, a paradise for the misbegotten."[7] In an article in the *New Republic*, Robert Brustein continued the damnation metaphor. "Nowhere is America's obsession with instant wealth," he wrote, "exploited more efficiently than in these trackless gambling wastes, where thousands of funereal characters, many of them women, huddle over machines like wraiths. I had visions of the damned in one of Dante's circles of Hell."[8] Cultural historian Otto Friedrich described the city as a different kind of hell. "Las Vegas," he wrote, "is what hell might be like if hell had been planned and built by New York gangsters." The city herds a host of tourists "into a row of garish hotels" and encourages them "to squander their money in joyless revelry until it is all gone. Pleasure grimly organized and sold, around the clock, mass produced and mass consumed—what could be more hellish than a gangster vision of paradise?"[9] To James Howard Kunstler, social critic and analyst of urban affairs, it is the hell Americans deserve. "If Las Vegas truly is our city of the future," he wrote in 2002, "then we might as well all cut our own throats tomorrow. I certainly felt like cutting mine after only a few days there, so overwhelming was the sheer anomie provoked by every particular of its design and operation. As a city it's a futureless catastrophe." "As a theosophical matter," he argued, "it presents proof that we are a wicked people who deserve to be punished. In the historical context, it is the place where America's spirit crawled off to die."[10]

Joan Didion, who wrote both a novel dealing with Las Vegas entitled *Play It as It Lays* as well as an essay called "Marrying Absurd," argued that the city was best understood as an alien place. To this resident of Los Angeles, Las Vegas was "bizarre and beautiful in its venality and in its devotion to immediate gratification, a place the tone of which is set by mobsters and call girls and ladies' room attendants with amyl nitrite poppers in their uniform pockets." When visiting Las Vegas, she claimed, there was neither a sense of time nor any "logical sense of where one is." In short, as far as she could tell, Las Vegas seemed to have "no connection with 'real' life."[11] Bruce Begout, a French philosopher and student of contemporary urban life, agreed with Didion in a wide-ranging condemnation of Las Vegas. "It strikes me," he wrote, "that I would not be very far from the truth if I were to answer anyone who happened to ask me what I had learned in Las Vegas with the perfectly simple reply: 'Nothing.'" To Begout, Las Vegas, a city of "pure urban chaos," was essentially a "Zeropolis." Traveling there he found "the degree zero city of urbanity, of architecture and culture, the degree zero city of sociability, art and ideas." After examining the structures, the neon, and the people who inhabited and visited the "superficial, shallow town," a "bottomless pit of excess," Begout concluded:

> When all is said and done, the leisure and social experience offered by Las Vegas, with all its attractions and shows, casinos and cabarets, amounts to practically nothing in anyone's life. A fleeting excitement of the senses, a frenzy of buying and escapism that very quickly borders on persistent nausea.[12]

These pejorative characterizations of the city as a vulgar and repellent place have not gone unchallenged. Defenders argue that Las Vegas attracts a large number of "hip intellectuals," journalists, cultural critics, and essayists, eager to score points with their smug observations on the gambling city, a condescending effort that has produced "an abundance of bad journalism." Indeed, they often offer little more than a pathetic repetition of the condemnation offered by previous critics.[13] David Spanier, a gambler who wrote a great deal about Las Vegas, suggested that being in the city often triggered a "sense of despair" in some critics. "The whole place," he explained, "with its brighter-than-bright exterior concealing a darker-than-dark abyss, offers a perfect 'objective correlative' for personal depression and artistic gloom."[14] Dave Hickey, for many years a professor of art criticism and theory at the University of Nevada, Las Vegas, argued that many of the detractors were elitist academics like the "disconsolate colleagues" of his on the campus. Hickey explained that many of his associates disliked living in a city they believed was "lacking in culture" and one that exploited "people's weaknesses." More important, he suspected that his "unhappy colleagues are appalled by the fact that Vegas presents them with a flat-line social hierarchy." They did not have the same prestige in the resort city that they could claim in traditional university communities like "Cambridge or Bloomington."[15] Hickey went beyond criticizing snooty professors to suggest that the larger challenge for visiting critics is to get beyond the surface qualities of Las Vegas. They might be skilled at uncovering "seamy scandals" in other locales "by getting behind the scenes," but when investigating Las Vegas, social critics too often offered little more than caricature, "writing stories about white people who are so unused to regulating their own behavior that they gamble away the farm, get drunk, throw up on their loafers, and wind up in custody within six hours of their arrival."[16]

John Irsfeld and Hal Rothman, two other professors at UNLV, argued that a larger phenomenon was at work with visiting social critics. In Irsfeld's view, too often authors gave the reader less an analysis of Las Vegas and more "that version of the reality of Las Vegas that each of these artists has experienced."[17] Although Irsfeld gently suggested a fundamental flaw in the perspectives that critics of Las Vegas brought to their work, Rothman hammered them as carpetbaggers. In his view, Las Vegas is a city where "grandstanding writers can project their own neuroses, their fears and needs. But the city these outside observers see is a reflection of themselves."[18] This certainly is evident in one of the most widely read books on Las Vegas, Hunter S. Thompson's *Fear and Loathing in Las Vegas,* an extraordinary example of his gonzo journalism. The book, which became a movie starring Johnny Depp, was Thompson's semiautobiographical account of two trips to Las Vegas in 1971 to find "The American Dream. Horatio Alger gone mad on drugs in Las Vegas."[19] "Every now and then," he contended, "when your life gets complicated and the weasels start closing in, the only real cure is to load up on heinous chemicals and then drive like a bastard from Hollywood to Las Vegas. To *relax,* as it were, in the womb of the desert sun."[20] He takes along "two bags of grass, seventy-five pellets of mescaline, five sheets of high-powered blotter acid, a salt shaker half full of cocaine, and a whole galaxy of multi-colored uppers, downers, screamers, laughers . . . and also a quart of tequila, a quart of rum, a case of Budweiser, a pint of raw ether and two dozen amyls." As a consequence, *Fear and Loathing* is a surreal account described through a series of hallucinogenic trips.[21]

Thompson dropped in at the Circus Circus casino and provided the reader with one of his most vivid images. With its circus acts, twenty-four-hour gambling, merry-go-round bar, and "customers . . . being hustled by every conceivable kind of bizarre shuck," the casino "is what the whole hep world would be doing on Saturday night if the Nazis had won the war. This is the Sixth Reich."[22] He argues that "a week in Las Vegas is like stumbling into a Time Warp, a regression to the late fifties. Which is wholly understandable when you see the people who come here, the Big Spenders from places like Denver and Dallas."[23] This is mainstream America; this is not Thompson's world. "A little bit of this town goes a very long way. After five days in Vegas you feel like you've been here for five years. Some people say they like it—but then some people like Nixon too."[24] Ultimately, Thompson finds Las Vegas to be a depraved incarnation of a failed American culture, one that resisted the 1960s cultural revolution when rebels like him had the "sense of inevitable victory over the forces of Old and Evil."[25]

In the moments between the battles between critics and defenders of Las Vegas, some analysts have pursued a more useful debate, trying to determine whether Las Vegas was a model for America or a reflection of important American trends. Author Tom Wolfe, for example, argued in 1964 that the city had a profound impact on the emerging appearance of suburban America. "Las Vegas," he wrote, "is the only town in the world whose skyline is made up neither of buildings, like New York, nor of trees like Wilbraham, Massachusetts, but signs. One can look at Las Vegas from a mile away on Route 91 and see no buildings, no trees, only signs." The colors Wolfe saw in the signs and structures, the "incredible electric pastels," first evident at the Flamingo, "made Las Vegas one of the few architecturally unified cities in the world" and the symbol of an emerging suburban architectural form.[26] A group of Yale architecture professors and graduate students, led by Robert Venturi, dramatically broadened Wolfe's view in a study entitled *Learning from Las Vegas*, published in 1972. They had gone to the American Southwest in the 1960s "to learn about new forms of urbanism." In Las Vegas, they found "the biggest, brightest strip in the world and we were interested in learning about an architecture of color, decoration, signs, and symbols." They were intrigued to discover in Las Vegas that the "roadside architecture"—that is, the signs—was "more important than buildings." They became advocates of this vernacular, indigenous populist architectural form that made Las Vegas "to the Strip what Rome is to the Piazza." Venturi, along with Denise Scott Brown and Steven Izenour, argued that the Strip architecture should be emulated not just because it offered an effective marketing approach, but also because it was a genuine art form.[27] Architecture historian Alan Hess has extended the Venturi group's argument, pointing out that "the Las Vegas Strip . . . is the ultimate version of the commercial strips found on the fringes of almost all American cities." It is a three-mile highway that "offers a way to study the compelling phenomenon of these populist, sprawling, postindustrial cities. These days, Las Vegas no longer seems like an anomaly."[28]

To observers like Kurt Anderson and Neil Postman, Las Vegas offers a different kind of model. Las Vegas's style of entertainment, they argue, has had a dramatic impact on almost all of show business. As Anderson pointed out in 1994, one can clearly see the influence of the "Vegasy" style where "big rock-'n'-roll concerts nowadays are often as much about wowie-kazowie production values—giant video walls, neon, fireworks, suggestively costumed young men and women, clouds of pastel-colored smoke—as music."[29] For Postman, there is a more insidious Las Vegas influence. A communications professor and media critic, Postman concluded in the mid-1980s that Las

Vegas had become "a metaphor of our national character and aspiration." It was "a city entirely devoted to the idea of entertainment, and as such proclaims the spirit of a culture in which all public discourse increasingly takes the form of entertainment." In his judgment, the nation's "politics, religion, news, athletics, education and commerce" increasingly took their cues from entertainment and, as a "result . . . we are a people on the verge of amusing ourselves to death."[30]

Historian and columnist Hal Rothman argued that Las Vegas led the nation in a more significant way. At the turn of the twenty-first century, he contended that Las Vegas had "become a template for postindustrial, entertainment-driven urbanism" in America. At a time when aging baby boomers and their offspring were pursuing "hedonistic libertarianism," Las Vegas was able to draw on a long experience of offering excess and dramatically enhanced its appeal as a tourist destination. This enabled the city to become, in Rothman's view, the "last Detroit," a place "where relatively unskilled workers" could secure a job with good wages. Because of this remarkable success, Rothman suggested that "Las Vegas offers an economic model to which cities, states, and regions look to create their own economic panacea."[31]

More commonly, however, intellectuals conclude that Las Vegas's evolution simply reflects larger developments in modern America; in other words, it is a microcosm of important national trends. As Dave Hickey argued, "America . . . is a very poor lens through which to view Las Vegas, while Las Vegas is a wonderful lens through which to view America."[32] Or, as Ray Suarez, host of National Public Radio's *Talk of the Nation* program said in 1998, "To understand America, better understand Las Vegas."[33] Many social scientists and social critics agree with Hickey and Suarez and see Las Vegas reflecting the spread of legal gambling across the nation, the increasing number of cities turning to tourism to improve their economies, the rise of the service economy, the ever-greater reliance of cities on boosterism in the Las Vegas mode, the effects of living in a company town, or the inextricable link between corporate and political corruption.[34] Most intriguing, however, is the assertion of a number of critics, notably journalist Marc Cooper, that Las Vegas represents one of the best examples of America's commitment to capitalism. It is, in Cooper's view, the most American of cities because it demonstrates "the American market ethic stripped completely bare, a mini-world totally free of the pretenses and protocols of modern consumer capitalism." Indeed, as Cooper sees it, Las Vegas presents us with the most egalitarian element of free enterprise: "Las Vegas is perhaps the most color-blind, class-free place in America. As long as your cash or credit line holds out, no one gives a damn about your race, gender, national origin, sexual orientation, address, family lineage, voter registration or even your criminal arrest record. Money is the great leveler."³⁵

Likely, Irsfeld, Hickey, and Rothman are correct. These remarkably different takes on Las Vegas may be best understood as a reflection of the observer. What the intellectuals, as well as the journalists, novelists, and screenwriters, have described often tells us more about the writer than the reality of the city they seek to explain. Unlike the assessments of the skeptical and cynical outsiders, most of the thousands of articles about Las Vegas were filed by entertainment and travel columnists who frankly enjoyed covering Las Vegas, a pleasure enhanced by the long tradition of hotels providing them with rooms, meals, and shows. They rarely indulged in muckraking journalism. For some news reporters like Gladwin Hill, Las Vegas became a pleasant part of their beat. Hill established the *New York Times* bureau in Los Angeles right after World War II and headed the bureau for almost two decades. He filed dozens of articles about Las Vegas in the *Times,* notably about the atomic tests, but also about the evolution of the city, and they were invariably positive stories.

In part, that may well explain my effort in this book. Perhaps the traits that I have uncovered in the novels, newspaper and magazine articles, television programs, and movies were ones I was conditioned to see, given my many pleasant research trips to Las Vegas and my familiarity with its history. As Hal Rothman insightfully put it, Las Vegas is a remarkably malleable place. To the outsider, "it has been what they needed it to be—colony, pariah city, place to cast off sins, den of iniquity, locus of opportunity."³⁶ Regardless, Las Vegas is a place that continues to attract ever more tourists and more observers seeking to understand how it has become the most popular of all American tourist destinations. In the end, whether we embrace it or despise it, as Bruce Begout put it, "we are all inhabitants of Las Vegas, however far away we are from southern Nevada. Its name is no longer a fantasy. It lives in our heads."³⁷

NOTES

CHANGING FIRST IMPRESSIONS OF LAS VEGAS

The book's epigraphs are from the following sources: U.S. Army Lt. Joseph Ives quoted in Edward Churchill, "The Truth about Las Vegas," *Script*, March 1948, 9; John Beville, quoted in Brad Peterson, "John Beville Banked on 'Crummiest Little Town,'" *Nevadan*, August 26, 1979, 30J; Robert Kaltenborn Oral History Interview, 1972, Special Collections, Lied Library, University of Nevada, Las Vegas; Harold L. Ickes, *The Secret Diary of Harold L. Ickes,* vol. 2, *The Inside Struggle, 1936–1939* (New York: Simon and Schuster, 1954), 581; Hank Greenspun with Alex Pelle, *Where I Stand: The Record of a Reckless Man* (New York: David McKay, 1966), 68; interview with Herb McDonald, "The Las Vegas I Remember," KNPR, Las Vegas, April 25, 2005; interview with Carl Barschdorf by author, May 10, 2007; Tony Bennett, *The Good Life* (New York: Pocket Books, 1998), 126; Steve Wynn, quoted in John L. Smith, *Running Scared: The Life and Treacherous Times of Las Vegas Casino King Steve Wynn* (1995; New York: Four Walls Eight Windows, 2001), 27; interview with Peter Graves by author, February 28, 2008; Noel Coward, *The Letters of Noel Coward,* ed. Barry Day (New York: Vintage Books, 2009), 585; Jimmy the Greek, *Jimmy the Greek, by Himself* (Chicago: Playboy Press, 1975), 100–101; Helen Morelli Oral History Interview, 1976, Special Collections, UNLV; Esper and Valda Esau, e-mail message to Larry Gragg, February 2007; interview with Jim Seagrave by author, April 1, 2006; interview with Harry Merenda, "The Las Vegas I Remember," KNPR, Las Vegas, July 5, 2005.

PREFACE

1 David G. Schwartz, "Are We Swarmed by the Stupid?," *Las Vegas Weekly,* September 3, 2009, http://www.lasvegasweekly.com/news/2009/sep/03/are-we-swarmed-stupid (accessed July 4, 2012).

INTRODUCTION

1 Bruce Begout, *Zeropolis: The Experience of Las Vegas,* trans. Liz Heron (London: Reaktion Books, 2003), 11.
2 Interview with Donald English by author, August 22, 2005.
3 Eugene P. Moehring and Michael S. Green, *Las Vegas: A Centennial History* (Reno: University of Nevada Press, 2005); Eugene P. Moehring, *Resort City in the Sunbelt: Las Vegas, 1930–2000,* 2nd ed. (Reno: University of Nevada Press, 2000); David G. Schwartz, *Suburban Xanadu: The Casino Resort on the Las Vegas Strip and Beyond* (New York: Routledge, 2003); John M. Findlay, *People of*

Chance: Gambling in American Society from Jamestown to Las Vegas (New York: Oxford University Press, 1986); Hal K. Rothman, *Devil's Bargains: Tourism in the Twentieth-Century American West* (Lawrence: University Press of Kansas, 1998). There are a number of other histories of Las Vegas worth consulting: Thomas "Taj" Ainlay Jr. and Judy Dixon Gabaldon, *Las Vegas: The Fabulous First Century* (Charleston, S.C.: Arcadia Publishing, 2003); Linda Chase, *Picturing Las Vegas* (Salt Lake City: Gibbs Smith, 2009); Gary E. Elliott, *The New Western Frontier: An Illustrated History of Greater Las Vegas* (Carlsbad, Calif.: Heritage Media, 1999); Michelle Ferrari with Stephen Ives, *Las Vegas: An Unconventional History* (New York: Bulfinch Press, 2005); Barbara and Myrick Land, *A Short History of Las Vegas*, 2nd ed. (Reno: University of Nevada Press, 2004); Robert D. McCracken, *Las Vegas: The Great American Playground*, expanded ed. (Reno: University of Nevada Press, 1997); Stanley W. Paher, *Las Vegas: As It Began—As It Grew* (Las Vegas: Nevada Publications, 1971); Ralph J. Roske, *Las Vegas: A Desert Paradise* (Tulsa, Okla.: Continental Heritage Press, 1986); Geoff Shumacher, *Sun, Sin, and Suburbia: An Essential History of Modern Las Vegas* (Las Vegas: Stephens Press, 2004); Joan Burkhart Whitely, *Young Las Vegas, 1905–1931: Before the Future Found Us* (Las Vegas: Stephens Press, 2005).

4 "100,000 Stop Here in 1930," *Las Vegas Age*, May 24, 1931, 1; Katharine Best and Katharine Hillyer, *Las Vegas: Playtown U.S.A.* (New York: David McKay, 1955), 54; Peter Wyden, "How Wicked Is Las Vegas?," *Saturday Evening Post*, November 11, 1961, 17; Connie Paige, "Can Las Vegas Beat the Odds?," *Boston Globe Magazine*, July 25, 1982, 36; "2005 Las Vegas Year-to-Date Executive Summary," Las Vegas Convention and Visitors Authority, http://www.lvcva.com/press/statistics-facts/index.jsp (accessed February 12, 2012).

5 Edward E. Baldwin, "Las Vegas in Popular Culture" (Ph.D. diss., University of Nevada, Las Vegas, 1997); Ingrid Eumann, *The Outer Edge of the Wave: American Frontiers in Las Vegas* (New York: Peter Lang, 2005).

6 One can follow these developments in Larry Gragg, "Selling 'Sin City': Successfully Promoting Las Vegas during the Great Depression, 1935–1941," *Nevada Historical Society Quarterly* 49 (Summer 2006): 83–106; Gragg, "Promoting Post-War Las Vegas: The Live Wire Fund, 1945–1950," *Proceedings*, International Journal of Arts and Sciences Conference for Academic Disciplines (October 2010): 9–16.

7 Interviews Folder, Perry Kaufmann Collection, Box 2, Special Collections, Lied Library, University of Nevada, Las Vegas.

8 Interview with Jim Seagrave by author, April 1, 2006.

9 Earl Wilson, "It Happened Last Night," *Delta* (Greenville, Miss.) *Democrat-Times*, December 26, 1952, 4; "Coast to Coast," *Long Beach* (Calif.) *Press-Telegram*, December 25, 1952, B8.

10 Dixon Gayer to Al Freeman, August 19, 1960, Sands Collection, Box 7, Folder 1, Special Collections, University of Nevada, Las Vegas.

11 Perry Kaufmann Interviews Folder and *Las Vegas Nights*, prod. William LeBaron

and dir. Ralph Murphy, 90 minutes (Paramount, 1941). Griffith was also a key figure in persuading hotel man Thomas Hull to build the El Rancho Vegas, the first hotel on the Strip.

12 Al Freeman to All Departments, June 15, 1970, Sands Collection, Box 50, Folder 2.

13 See Larry Gragg, "Defending a City's Image: Las Vegas Opposes the Making of *711 Ocean Drive*, 1950," *Popular Culture Review* 22 (Winter 2011): 7–9.

14 See Larry Gragg, "Protecting a City's Image: The Death of *Las Vegas Beat*, 1961," *Studies in Popular Culture* 34 (Fall 2011): 1–22.

15 Larry Gragg, "'Never Accorded the Recognition He Deserved': Al Freeman, Sands Hotel Publicist, 1952–1972," *Nevada Historical Society Quarterly* 51 (Spring 2008): 47.

16 Interview with Alan Feldman by author, March 31, 2006.

1. "BRIGHT LIGHT CITY": THE INTRODUCTION TO LAS VEGAS

The epigraphs are from Barbara Samuel, *Lady Luck's Map of Vegas* (New York: Ballantine Books, 2005), 245; Kermit Holt, "Streak of Light Leads to Las Vegas, Desert Oasis," *Chicago Daily Tribune*, February 26, 1961, F9.

1 Mike Weatherford, *Cult Vegas: The Weirdest! The Wildest! The Swingin'est Town on Earth!* (Las Vegas: Huntington Press, 2001), 158. "Viva Las Vegas," lyrics and melody by Doc Pomus and Mort Shuman.

2 Gladwin Hill, "Klondike in the Desert," *New York Times*, June 7, 1953, SM14.

3 Background information largely drawn from Eugene P. Moehring and Michael S. Green, *Las Vegas: A Centennial History* (Reno: University of Nevada Press, 2005), 1–82; Ralph J. Roske, *Las Vegas: A Desert Paradise* (Tulsa, Okla.: Continental Heritage Press, 1986), 52–85.

4 Stanley W. Paher, *Las Vegas: As It Began—As It Grew* (Las Vegas: Nevada Publications, 1971), 97–99; Moehring and Green, *Las Vegas*, 31.

5 Jerome H. Skolnick, *House of Cards: Legalization and Control of Casino Gambling* (Boston: Little, Brown, 1978), 106–107; *Legalized Gambling in Nevada: Its History, Economics and Control* (Carson City: Nevada Gaming Commission, 1963), 10.

6 Magnus White, "The Boom at Boulder," *Saturday Evening Post*, March 23, 1929, 146; Roske, *Las Vegas*, 86; Las Vegas City Commission Minutes, vol. 3, July 2, 1929, 17–18, Special Collections, Lied Library, University of Nevada, Las Vegas.

7 T. M. Carroll, "Las Vegas—From 5,500 to 50,000 and Why," *Las Vegas Age*, July 19, 1930, 6; Eric N. Moody, "Nevada's Legalization of Casino Gambling in 1931: Purely a Business Proposition," *Nevada Historical Society Quarterly* 37 (Summer 1994): 87.

8 Commission Minutes, vol. 3, April 17 and 22, 1931, 162–166; October 4, 1941, 376.

9 Alan Hess, *Viva Las Vegas: After-Hours Architecture* (San Francisco: Chronicle Books, 1993), 22.

10 There are several examples from the 1940s and 1950s: *Las Vegas Nights,* 1941; *The Lady Gambles,* 1949; *Once More My Darling,* 1949; *Painting the Clouds with Sunshine,* 1952; *Las Vegas Story,* 1952; *Meet Me in Las Vegas,* 1955, as well as an episode of the television program *Racket Squad* entitled "Kite High," 1951.

11 See, for example, the Manis Collection, Box 2, Folder 5, Special Collections, University of Nevada, Las Vegas.

12 Moehring and Green, *Las Vegas,* 139; Moehring, *Resort City in the Sunbelt: Las Vegas, 1930–2000,* 2nd ed. (Reno: University of Nevada Press, 2000), 50–51; Frank Wright, *Nevada Yesterdays: Short Looks at Las Vegas History* (Las Vegas: Stephens Press, 2005), 89–90; Katharine Best and Katharine Hillyer, *Las Vegas: Playtown U.S.A.* (New York: David McKay, 1955), 4.

13 "Glitter Gulch," *Las Vegas Review-Journal,* January 7, 1947, 11; Seymour Korman, "Las Vegas: Desert Riviera," *Chicago Daily Tribune,* April 11, 1948, E23.

14 Bob Considine, "Rich Nevada Oasis Must Be Seen to Be Believed, Newsman Says," *Charleston* (W.V.) *Gazette,* January 23, 1955, 1; Sean O'Faolain, "Las Vegas," *Holiday,* September 1956, 57.

15 "Dale Harrison's New York," *Zanesville* (Ohio) *Signal,* April 21, 1938, 4; "Ray Tucker," *Long Beach* (Calif.) *Independent,* April 20, 1949, 14.

16 Richard Prather, *Find This Woman* (1951; reprint, New York: E-reads, 2000), 40.

17 William Pearson, *The Muses of Ruin* (New York: McGraw-Hill, 1965), 115.

18 "Make Las Vegas the Metropolis of Nevada," *Las Vegas Age,* January 19, 1918, 1; "Accommodations Needed," April 29, 1938, 4; "New Las Vegas Hotel to Mark New Era in City," March 31, 1939, 1; Max Stern, "Great Land Frauds at Boulder Dam," *Sheboygan* (Wis.) *Press,* April 18, 1929, 24.

19 "Clark County Solons After Special Session," *Nevada State Journal,* November 19, 1926, 1; "Las Vegas Will Build New Hotel," *Los Angeles Times,* October 15, 1926, A1.

20 "Plans Made for Hotel," *Los Angeles Times,* June 1, 1936, A2.

21 Chris Nichols, *Leisure Architecture of Wayne McAllister* (Layton, Utah: Gibbs Smith, 2007), 126–127; Hess, *Viva Vegas,* 28.

22 David G. Schwartz, *Suburban Xanadu: The Casino Resort on the Las Vegas Strip and Beyond* (New York: Routledge, 2003), 35.

23 George Stamos Jr., "The Great Resorts of Las Vegas: How They Began!," *Las Vegas Sun Magazine,* April 1, 1979, 6–7; Hotel El Rancho Vegas Promotion and Publicity Material, Box 3, Special Collections, University of Nevada, Las Vegas.

24 Moehring and Green, *Las Vegas,* 111.

25 Hotel Last Frontier Promotion and Publicity Material, Box 3, Special Collections, University of Nevada, Las Vegas.

26 The best source to follow in the development of the casino-resort is Schwartz, *Suburban Xanadu,* 77–174.

27 "Coast to Coast," *Long Beach* (Calif.) *Press-Telegram,* December 25, 1952, B8; "Las Vegas: It Wins, It Worries, It Weeps," *Look,* December 27, 1966, 78; Charles Champlin, "Making the World Safe for Frivolity, Las Vegas," *Los Angeles Times, West Magazine,* October 18, 1969, 77.

28 Thomas Perry, *Shadow Woman* (New York: Random House, 1997), 3; Michael Ventura, *The Death of Frank Sinatra* (New York: Holt, 1996), 194.

29 *Rain Main,* prod. Mark Johnson and dir. Barry Levinson, 133 minutes (United Artists, 1988).

30 "The Kingdom of Money," *Crime Story,* prod. Michael Mann and dir. James A. Contner, 60 minutes (Michael Mann Productions, 1987).

31 Marilyn Lynch, *Casino* (New York: Grosset & Dunlap, 1979), n.p.

32 Tom Wolfe, "Las Vegas (What?) Las Vegas (Can't Hear You! Too Noisy) Las Vegas!!!," in *Literary Las Vegas: The Best Writing about America's Most Fabulous City,* ed. Mike Tronnes (New York: Holt, 1995), 3.

33 Best and Hillyer, *Las Vegas,* 76.

34 Steve Fisher, *No House Limit* (New York: E. P. Dutton, 1958), 19.

35 Article in *San Francisco Examiner* reprinted in "Las Vegas 'Horrors' Are Broadcast by Hearst Scribe—Boasts Boulder," *Las Vegas Age,* June 12, 1931, 2; "Boulder Dam and Las Vegas Trip Related by T. A. Nixon," *Greeley* (Colo.) *Daily,* September 1, 1932, 1; Theo White, "Building the Big Dam," *Harper's,* June 1935, 118.

36 Jessica Fletcher and Donald Bain, *Murder She Wrote: You Bet Your Life* (New York: New American Library, 2002), 149.

37 Samuel, *Lady Luck's Map of Vegas,* 246.

38 "Shows and Sun and Scenery," *Oakland Tribune,* February 6, 1972, 5V; Herb Lyon, "Fantastic Las Vegas," *Chicago Daily Tribune,* November 29, 1959, I10; Malcolm Epley, "Beach Combings," *Long Beach* (Calif.) *Press-Telegram,* April 14, 1952, section 2, 1.

39 *Girls' Night,* prod. Bill Boyes and dir. Nick Hurran, 120 minutes (Granada Film Productions, 1998).

40 Edward Allen, *Mustang Sally* (New York: Norton, 1992), 14–15 and 24.

41 Carolyn Thomas, *The Cactus Shroud* (Philadelphia: J. B. Lippincott, 1957), 22.

42 Prater, *Find This Woman,* 14.

43 Frank Gruber, *Honest Dealer* (New York: Rinehart, 1947), 20; A. A. Fair, *Spill the Jackpot* (New York: Dell, 1967), 14; Dick Pearce, "Pleasure Palaces," *Harper's,* February 1955, 80.

44 Hill, "Klondike in the Desert," SM14.

45 Lee Shippey, "Leeside," *Los Angeles Times,* November 30, 1946, A4.

46 Considine, "Rich Nevada Oasis," 1; William W. Yates, "Gambling Life Blood of Colorful, Fabulous Las Vegas," *Chicago Daily Tribune,* January 26, 1958, D1; Edward Collier, "Nevada's Baghdad Vivid, Gaudy Around Clock," *Lancaster* (Ohio) *Eagle-Gazette,* January 30, 1960, 7.

47 I. G. Broat, *The Junketeers* (New York: Pocket Books, 1978), 204.

2. LAS VEGAS: THE LAST FRONTIER TOWN

The epigraphs are from "Emery County Men Back from Nevada," *Standard* (Ogden, Utah), June 29, 1905, 7; Duncan Aikman, "New Pioneers in Old West's Deserts," *New York Times,* October 26, 1930, SM18; Bruce Bliven, "The American Dnieperstroy," *New Republic,* December 11, 1935, 127; Diana Rice, "In the

Field of Travel," *New York Times,* May 9, 1943, X13; Richard S. Prather, *Find This Woman* (1951; reprint, New York: E-reads, 2000), 25.

1 "Wild, Woolly and Wide-Open," *Look,* August 14, 1940, 21–25.

2 Richard G. Lillard, *Desert Challenge: An Interpretation of Nevada* (New York: Knopf, 1942), 316–317.

3 There is a vast literature on this subject. This paragraph, except where otherwise noted, is drawn from Anne M. Butler, "Selling the Popular Myth," in *The Oxford History of the American West,* ed. Clyde A. Milner II, Carol A. O'Connor, and Martha A. Sandweiss (New York: Oxford University Press, 1994), 771–801; Richard White, *"It's Your Misfortune and None of My Own": A History of the American West* (Norman: University of Oklahoma Press, 1991), 613–632; Bernard Drew, "Nevada as the Pulps Saw Her," *Nevadan* in *Las Vegas Review-Journal,* July 23, 1978, 26–27J; Robert V. Hine and John Mack Faragher, *The American West: A New Interpretive History* (New Haven, Conn.: Yale University Press, 2000), 493–510; Patricia Nelson Limerick, *The Legacy of Conquest: The Unbroken Past of the American West* (New York: Norton, 1987); John G. Cawelti, *The Six-Gun Mystique Sequel* (Bowling Green, Ohio: Bowling Green State University Popular Press, 1999); Richard Slotkin, *Gunfighter Nation: The Myth of the Frontier in Twentieth-Century America* (New York: Atheneum, 1992); William W. Savage Jr., *The Cowboy Hero: His Image in American History and Culture* (Norman: University of Oklahoma Press, 1979); Richard W. Slatta, *Cowboys of the Americas* (New Haven, Conn.: Yale University Press, 1990); R. Philip Loy, *Westerns and American Culture, 1930–1955* (Jefferson, N.C.: McFarland, 2001).

4 Hine and Faragher, *American West,* 499.

5 Kristine Fredriksson, *American Rodeo: From Buffalo Bill to Big Business* (College Station: Texas A&M University Press, 1985), 56 and 176; Michael Allen, *Rodeo Cowboys in the North American Imagination* (Reno: University of Nevada Press, 1998), 15–23.

6 Robert G. Athearn, *The Mythic West in Twentieth Century America* (Lawrence: University Press of Kansas, 1986), 160.

7 J. B. Griswold, "Wild West," *American Magazine,* May 1938, 14–15.

8 Anne Martin, "These United States—VIII, Nevada: Beautiful Desert of Buried Hopes," *Nation,* July 26, 1922, 89–90.

9 Harper Leech, "Boulder Dam a Cuss Word in Nevada Peaks," *Chicago Daily Tribune,* April 20, 1928, 17.

10 The *San Francisco Post* article is reprinted in "Nevada and Her Morals," *Las Vegas Age,* May 6, 1905, 3.

11 Eugene P. Moehring and Michael S. Green, *Las Vegas: A Centennial History* (Reno: University of Nevada Press, 2005), 13.

12 "Emery County Men Back from Nevada," 7.

13 A. Weinstock, "Immune from the Desert Lure," *Fresno* (Calif.) *Morning Republican,* November 24, 1907, 3.

14 Ralph J. Roske, *Las Vegas: A Desert Paradise* (Tulsa, Okla.: Continental Heritage Press, 1986), 63; Stanley W. Paher, *Las Vegas: As It Began—As It Grew* (Las Vegas:

Nevada Publications, 1971), 127; "New Arizona Club," *Las Vegas Age*, March 24, 1906, 4; "Shriners See Vegas," May 11, 1907, 5.

15 Ben S. Lemmon, "Lot Sales Keep Las Vegas Busy," *Los Angeles Times*, January 23, 1929, 6; Mildred Adams, "An Untamed Giant Awaits Its Harness," *New York Times*, May 4, 1930, SM4; Duncan Aikman, "New Pioneers in Old West's Deserts," October 26, 1930, SM7 and 18; Duncan Aikman, "Nevada Now Awaits Dam and Dry Regime," *Baltimore Sun*, October 14, 1930, 13.

16 Taylor's article from the *San Francisco Chronicle* is reprinted in "Las Vegas 'Horrors' Are Broadcast by Hearst Scribe—Boosts Boulder," *Las Vegas Age*, June 12, 1931, 3.

17 Zane Grey, *Boulder Dam* (New York: Grosset & Dunlap, 1964), 5.

18 "Las Vegas Poker Game Goes On with Dead Man Sitting at Table," *Los Angeles Times*, April 21, 1939, 1; "Las Vegas–Hoover Dam Area Rich in Tourist Interest," December 15, 1939, B7.

19 Paher, *Las Vegas*, 99; Weinstock, "Immune from the Desert Lure," 3.

20 Joan Burkhart Whitely, *Young Las Vegas, 1905–1931: Before the Future Found Us* (Las Vegas: Stephens Press, 2005), 188; Russell R. Elliott and William D. Rowley, *History of Nevada*, 2nd ed. (Lincoln: University of Nebraska Press, 1987), 257 and 269–270.

21 "Prohibition," *Las Vegas Age*, January 3, 1920, 2; K. J. Evans, "Sam Gay," *The First 100: Portraits of the Men and Women Who Shaped Las Vegas*, ed. A. D. Hopkins and K. J. Evans (Las Vegas: Huntington Press, 1999), 35; Roske, *Las Vegas*, 65.

22 "Boulder Dam and Las Vegas Trip Related by T. A. Nixon," *Greeley* (Colo.) *Daily and Greeley Republican*, September 1, 1932, 1.

23 Whitely, *Young Las Vegas*, 188; "Officials Freed in Liquor Case," *Los Angeles Times*, June 26, 1929, 7.

24 "Raider Rush Shuts Dives in Las Vegas," *Salt Lake Tribune*, May 19, 1931, 1; "Drys Raid Las Vegas, Jail 56, Seize Liquor Supplies," *Oakland Tribune*, May 19, 1931, 3.

25 R. A. Kelly, *Liberty's Last Stand* (San Francisco: Pioneer Publishing, 1932), 10.

26 "'Wild West' Town Near Boulder Dam," *New York Times*, August 23, 1936, X10; Theo White, "Building the Big Dam," *Harper's*, June 1935, 118; Bliven, "American Dnieperstroy," 127.

27 Martin, "Nevada," 90.

28 Chapin Hall, "Los Angeles Gets Fill of Sensations," *New York Times*, February 24, 1929, 52.

29 Lillard, *Desert Challenge*, 327.

30 Dale L. Morgan, *The Humboldt: Highroad of the West* (Freeport, N.Y.: Farrar and Rinehart, 1943), 343.

31 Whitely, *Young Las Vegas*, 5 and 183; Moehring and Green, *Las Vegas*, 31–32; Lillard, *Desert Challenge*, 328; Roske, *Las Vegas*, 62–63.

32 Max Stern, "Great Land Frauds at Boulder Dam," *Sheboygan* (Wis.) *Press*, April 18, 1929, 24.

33 Ruth Rosen, *The Lost Sisterhood: Prostitution in America, 1900–1918* (Baltimore: Johns Hopkins University Press, 1982), 78–79.

34 Mara L. Keire, *For Business and Pleasure: Red-Light Districts and the Regulation of Vice in the United States, 1890–1933* (Baltimore: Johns Hopkins University Press, 2010), 89–113.

35 "Report of Grand Jury," *Las Vegas Age*, November 30, 1912, 1.

36 White, "Building the Big Dam," 119; James Adam, "Las Vegas Has Clean-up Drive in Boom Plans," *Coshocton* (Ohio) *Tribune*, January 17, 1929, 13; *San Francisco Chronicle*, quoted in "Las Vegas 'Horrors,'" *Las Vegas Age*, June 12, 1931, 3; Lillard, *Desert Challenge*, 328; Paul Ralli, *Nevada Lawyer: A Story of Life and Love in Las Vegas* (Culver City, Calif.: Murray & Gee, 1949), 38.

37 Bliven, "American Dnieperstroy," 127.

38 Victor Castle, "Well, I Quit My Job at the Dam," *Nation*, August 26, 1931, 207.

39 Courtney Ryley Cooper, *Designs in Scarlet* (Boston: Little, Brown, 1939), 309.

40 The quote from the *Las Vegas Review-Journal* is in Annie Blachley, *Pestilence, Politics, and Pizzazz: The Story of Public Health in Las Vegas* (Reno, Nev.: Greasewood Press, 2002), 32.

41 "Wild, Woolly and Wide-Open," 23.

42 Moehring and Green, *Las Vegas*, 103–104; Anne M. Butler, *Daughters of Joy, Sisters of Misery: Prostitutes in the American West, 1865–1890* (Urbana: University of Illinois Press, 1985), 9; Sarah Hall Washburn, "Changing Images: The End of Legalized Prostitution in Las Vegas" (M.A. thesis, University of Nevada, Las Vegas, 1999), 60.

43 Richard English, "The Boom Came Back," *Collier's*, August 22, 1942, 49.

44 Moehring and Green, *Las Vegas*, 9–10; "Nevada Is the Guiding Star," *Nevada State Journal*, March 11, 1905, 7.

45 "Writes of His Trip from the West," *Lowell* (Mass.) *Sun*, June 3, 1905, 9; "Saloons and Gambling," *Las Vegas Age*, July 29, 1905, 1; "Leave to Buy Desert Lots," *Los Angeles Times*, May 14, 1905, II, 1; "What's Doing in Las Vegas," *Los Angeles Times*, May 23, 1905, II, 6; "Emery County Men Back from Nevada," 7.

46 *Los Angeles Examiner* article reprinted in "Examiner Write-up," *Las Vegas Age*, December 23, 1905, 1.

47 Moehring and Green, *Las Vegas*, 9–75.

48 James Adam, "Las Vegas Goes Land Crazy as Dam Boom Hits," *Coshocton* (Ohio) *Tribune*, January 10, 1929, 5; "Land Boom Caused in Desert Country," *Charleston* (W.V.) *Daily Mail*, January 23, 1929, 5; Magner White, "The Boom at Boulder," *Saturday Evening Post*, March 23, 1929, 10; Stern, "Great Land Frauds at Boulder Dam," 24.

49 Stern, "Great Land Frauds at Boulder Dam," 24; Lemmon, "Lot Sales Keep Las Vegas Busy," 6; Al H. Martin, "Las Vegas Awaits Start of Work on Huge Power Dam," *Appleton* (Wis.) *Post-Crescent*, July 25, 1929, 17; R. E. Baldwin, "Boulder Dam Has Started a Boom," *Altoona* (Pa.) *Mirror*, March 26, 1929, 3.

50 "Las Vegas Has Hope for Boom in Boulder Dam," *Huntingdon* (Pa.) *Daily News*, January 21, 1929, 5.

51 White, "Boom at Boulder," 146; Al H. Martin, "Real Estate Boom Hits Nevada Town," *North Adams* (Mass.) *Evening Transcript*, January 23, 1929, 8.

52 Stern, "Great Land Frauds at Boulder Dam," 24; Lemmon, "Lot Sales Keep Las Vegas Busy," 6; Martin, "Real Estate Boom Hits Nevada Town," 16.

53 Adam, "Las Vegas Goes Land Crazy as Dam Boom Hits," 5; Lemmon, "Lot Sales Keep Las Vegas Busy," 6; White, "Boom at Boulder," 146; Stern, "Great Land Frauds at Boulder Dam," 24; "On the Boom," *Salt Lake Tribune*, February 25, 1929, 6; Hall, "Los Angeles Gets Fill of Sensations," 52.

54 Martin, "Real Estate Boom Hits Nevada Town," 16; Martin, "Las Vegas Awaits Start of Work on Huge Power Dam," 17; Baldwin, "Boulder Dam Has Started a Boom," 3; "Las Vegas Has Hope for Boom in Boulder Dam," 5.

55 English, "Boom Came Back," 36; "Las Vegas Gambling," *Life*, December 21, 1942, 91.

56 Moehring and Green, *Las Vegas*, 101–104.

57 Wesley Stout, "Nevada's New Reno," *Saturday Evening Post*, October 31, 1942, 12.

58 Ibid., 68.

59 English, "Boom Came Back," 49.

60 Stout, "Nevada's New Reno," 69.

61 Moehring and Green, *Las Vegas*, 92; Larry Gragg, "Selling 'Sin City': Successfully Promoting Las Vegas During the Great Depression, 1935–1941," *Nevada Historical Society Quarterly* 49 (Summer 2006): 94; "Helldorado Is in Full Swing on Second Nite," *Las Vegas Age*, April 26, 1935, 1.

62 "Las Vegas Ready to Go 'Wild West,'" *Washington Post*, April 25, 1935, 4; "'Old Timers' Hold Center of Stage at Rip-Roarin' 'Helldorado' Doin's," *Salt Lake Tribune*, April 27, 1935, 2; Rice, "In the Field of Travel," X13.

63 Macy H. Lapham, *Crisscross Trails: Narrative of a Soil Surveyor* (Berkeley, Calif.: W. E. Berg, 1949), 217.

64 *Heldorado*, prod. Edward J. White and dir. William Witney, 70 minutes (Republic Pictures, 1946). Other films that had scenes incorporating Helldorado events into their story lines include *Painting the Clouds with Sunshine*, prod. William Jacobs and dir. David Butler, 87 minutes (Warner Bros., 1951), and *Sky Full of Moon*, prod. Sidney Franklin and dir. Norman Foster, 73 minutes (MGM, 1952). There was also an episode from the 1950s television series *State Trooper* that had an extended scene involving the Helldorado parade, "Fury on Fremont Street," *State Trooper*, dir. D. Ross Lederman, 30 minutes (Revue Studios, 1957).

65 Prather, *Find This Woman*, 15–25.

66 Lynn Rogers, "Desert Wasteland Now Famed Tourist Mecca," *Los Angeles Times*, September 5, 1948, E5; Tom Wynn, "Las Vegas Exciting Desert Resort City," *Long Beach* (Calif.) *Press Telegram*, September 16, 1951, B3.

67 Drew Pearson, "Washington Merry-Go-Round," *Long Beach* (Calif.) *Independent*, November 2, 1943, 2; Bob Thomas, "Hollywood Today," *Kingsport* (Tenn.) *Times*, December 31, 1946, 4.

68 Richard Foster, *Blonde and Beautiful* (New York: Popular Library, 1955), 5; Carolyn Thomas, *The Cactus Shroud* (Philadelphia: J. B. Lippincott, 1957), 31; Octavus Roy Cohen, *A Bullet for My Love* (New York: Macmillan, 1950), 3.

69 Lillard, *Desert Challenge,* 307.

70 Ibid., 308–327.

71 Ralli, *Nevada Lawyer,* 3, 4, 37, and 38; Paul Ralli, *Viva Vegas* (Hollywood: House-Warven, 1953), 1 and 11.

72 Gragg, "Selling 'Sin City,'" 98.

73 *Las Vegas Nights,* prod. William LeBaron and dir. Ralph Murphy, 90 minutes (Paramount Pictures, 1941); *Moon Over Las Vegas,* prod. and dir. Jean Yarbrough, 90 minutes (Universal Pictures, 1944); *Flight to Nowhere,* prod. William B. David and dir. William Rowland, 79 minutes (Golden Gate Pictures, 1946); *Heldorado; Lady Luck,* prod. Warren Duff and dir. Edwin L. Marin, 97 minutes (RKO Radio Pictures, 1946); *The Invisible Wall,* prod. Sol M. Wurtzel and dir. Eugene Forde, 72 minutes (Sol M. Wurtzel Productions, 1947); *Dark City,* prod. Hal Wallis and dir. William Dieterle, 98 minutes (Paramount, 1950); *My Friend Irma Goes West,* prod. Hal Wallis and dir. Hal Walker, 91 minutes (Paramount, 1950); *The Groom Wore Spurs,* prod. Howard Welsch and dir. Richard Whorf, 80 minutes (Fidelity Pictures, 1951); *Painting the Clouds with Sunshine; Sky Full of Moon; Girl Rush,* prod. Frederick Brisson and dir. Robert Pirosh, 85 minutes (Paramount, 1955); *Las Vegas Shakedown,* prod. William F. Broidy and dir. Sidney Salkow, 79 minutes (William F. Broidy Pictures, 1955); *Meet Me in Las Vegas,* prod. Joe Pasternak and dir. Roy Rowland, 112 minutes (MGM, 1956).

74 George N. Fenin and William K. Everson, *The Western: From Silents to Cinerama* (New York: Orion Press, 1962), 210–218.

75 "District Court," *Las Vegas Age,* October 30, 1909, 1 and 8.

76 Basil Woon, *Incredible Land: A Jaunty Baededker to Hollywood and the Great Southwest* (New York: Liveright, 1933), 264–268.

77 Bliven, "American Dnieperstroy," 127.

78 White, "Building the Big Dam," 118 and 120.

79 Jules Archer, "Paris of the Desert," *In Short,* 1946, reprinted in *Las Vegas Review-Journal,* August 5, 1990, 3T.

80 Chamber of Commerce Monthly Report, April 1939, Walter Bracken/Las Vegas Land and Water Company Files, Box 11, Chamber of Commerce Folder, Union Pacific Collection, Special Collections, Lied Library, University of Nevada, Las Vegas.

81 Athearn, *Mythic West,* 157.

82 Bernard De Voto, "The Anxious West," *Harper's,* December 1946, 484.

83 Ann Fabian, "History for the Masses: Commercializing the Western Past," in *Under an Open Sky: Rethinking America's Western Past,* ed. William Cronon, George Miles, and Jay Gitlin (New York: Norton, 1992), 223–238; Marguerite S. Shaffer, "'The West Plays West': Western Tourism and the Landscape of Leisure," in *A Companion to the American West,* ed. William Deverell (Malden, Mass.: Blackwell, 2004), 375–389; Butler, "Selling the Popular Myth," 799.

84 Tourism jumped from scarcely more than 100,000 in 1930 to 800,000 in 1941. See Larry Gragg, "The Risk in Using Gambling to Create 'America's Playground': Las Vegas, 1905–1960," in *Gambling, Space, and Time: Shifting Boundaries and*

Cultures, ed. Paulina Raento and David G. Schwartz (Reno: University of Nevada Press, 2011), 149.

3. BUGSY SIEGEL AND THE FOUNDING OF LAS VEGAS

The epigraphs are from Tom Wolfe, "Las Vegas (What?) Las Vegas (Can't Hear You! Too Noisy) Las Vegas!!!," in *Literary Las Vegas: The Best Writing about America's Most Fabulous City,* ed. Mike Tronnes (New York: Holt, 1995), 8; Stephen Birmingham, *"The Rest of Us": The Rise of America's Eastern European Jews* (Boston: Little, Brown, 1984), 293; Michael Herr and Guy Peeleart, *The Big Room* (New York: Summit Books, 1986), 20; James F. Smith, "Ben Siegel: Father of Las Vegas and the Modern Casino-Hotel," *Journal of Popular Culture* 25 (Spring 1992): 1; Pete Hamill, "Bugsy Siegel's Fabulous Dream," *Playboy,* February 1992, 130.

1 Warren Robert Hull, *Family Secret* (Tucson, Ariz.: Hats Off Books, 2004), 149–174.

2 "The 'Inside' on Bugsy," *Time,* July 7, 1947, 59.

3 Robert Lacey, *Little Man: Meyer Lansky and the Gangster Life* (Boston: Little, Brown, 1991), 451; Otto Friedrich, *City of Nets: A Portrait of Hollywood in the 1940s* (1986; reprint, Berkeley: University of California Press, 1997), 259. See also Thomas Reppetto, *American Mafia: A History of Its Rise to Power* (New York: Holt, 2004), 279.

4 "'Inside' on Bugsy," 59.

5 Hamill, "Bugsy Siegel's Fabulous Dream," 130.

6 Wolfe, "Las Vegas," 9.

7 Robert Warshow, *The Immediate Experience: Movies, Comics, Theatre and Other Aspects of Popular Culture* (1962; reprint, Cambridge, Mass.: Harvard University Press, 2001), 102.

8 "Bugsy Siegel: Gambling on the Mob," *Biography,* prod. Pamela Wolfe and Andrew D. Berg and dir. Bill Harris, 50 minutes (A&E Television Networks, 1995); Martin A. Gosch and Richard Hammer, *The Last Testament of Lucky Luciano* (Boston: Little, Brown, 1975), 23; Friedrich, *City of Nets,* 257.

9 Hamill, "Bugsy Siegel's Fabulous Dream," 130.

10 *Mobsters,* prod. Stephen J. Roth and dir. Michael Karbelnikoff, 104 minutes (Universal Pictures, 1991); "Gambling on the Mob"; Don H. Wolfe, *The Black Dahlia Files: The Mob, the Mogul, and the Murder that Transfixed Los Angeles* (New York: Regan Books, 2005), 180.

11 Dean Jennings, *We Only Kill Each Other* (1967; reprint, New York: Pocket Books, 1992), 23.

12 Daniel Eisenberg, Uri Dan, and Eli Landau, *Meyer Lansky: Mogul of the Mob* (New York: Paddington Press, 1979), 57 and 56; *Lansky,* prod. Fred C. Caruso and dir. John McNaughton, 93 minutes (Frederick Zollo Productions, 1999).

13 Gosch and Hammer, *Last Testament,* 23.

14 Ibid., 25.

15 Ibid., 73; George Carpozi Jr., *Bugsy* (New York: Pinnacle Books, 1973), 21; *Gangster Wars*, prod. Stephen Cohen and dir. Richard C. Sarafian, 121 minutes (Universal TV, 1981).

16 Gus Russo, *The Outfit: The Role of Chicago's Underworld in the Shaping of Modern America* (New York: Bloomsbury, 2001), 99; Stephen Fox, *Blood and Power: Organized Crime in Twentieth-Century America* (New York: Penguin, 1989), 25–26 and 109; Reppetto, *American Mafia*, 84 and 103.

17 David Pietrusza, *Rothstein: The Life, Times, and Murder of the Criminal Genius Who Fixed the 1919 World Series* (New York: Carroll & Graf, 2003), 196–202; Reppetto, *American Mafia*, 107; Virgil W. Peterson, *The Mob: 200 Years of Organized Crime in New York* (Ottawa, Ill.: Green Hill, 1983), 136; George Wolf with Joseph DiMona, *Frank Costello: Prime Minister of the Underworld* (New York: Morrow, 1974), 38.

18 *Mobsters; Gangster Wars; Lansky; Don't Call Me Bugsy*, prod. Greg Newman, 70 minutes (MPI Media Group, 1992).

19 Hamill, "Bugsy Siegel's Fabulous Dream," 150; *Bugsy*, prod. Warren Beatty, Mark Johnson, and Barry Levinson and dir. Barry Levinson, 136 minutes (Tri-Star Pictures, 1991). Millicent Rosen, Siegel's eldest daughter, explains that the family lived in the Waldorf Astoria before moving to the Scarsdale home. Interview with Millicent Rosen by author, May 19, 2010.

20 *Mobsters;* "Gambling on the Mob"; David Hanna, *Ice Picks and Coffins: The Killers of Murder, Inc.* (New York: Leisure Books, 1974), 166; Hamill, "Bugsy Siegel's Fabulous Dream," 150; Earl Wilson, *The Show Business Nobody Knows* (Chicago: Cowles Book Company, 1971), 139.

21 *Mobsters.*

22 "Gambling on the Mob"; *Bugsy.*

23 Hanna, *Ice Picks and Coffins,* 168; Russo, *The Outfit,* 290.

24 Millicent Rosen explained that her aunt and uncle had moved to California before her father's move there. Interview by author, May 19, 2010.

25 Andy Edmunds, *Bugsy's Baby: The Secret Life of Mob Queen Virginia Hill* (New York: Carol Publishing Group, 1993), 76; Wolfe, *Black Dahlia,* 183; Birmingham, *Rest of Us,* 263.

26 Carpozi, *Bugsy,* 53, 55, and 68; Edmunds, *Bugsy's Baby,* 76; Wolfe, *Black Dahlia,* 186; Friedrich, *City of Nets,* 259.

27 Carpozi, *Bugsy,* 66 and 68; Wolfe, *Black Dahlia,* 194.

28 Estimates from Hanna, *Ice Picks and Coffins,* 168; Jennings, *We Only Kill Each Other,* 39; Gus Russo, *Supermob: How Sidney Korshak and His Criminal Associates Became America's Hidden Power Brokers* (New York: Bloomsbury USA, 2007), 199.

29 Marcia Winn, "Bioff's Shadow Is Still a Cloud on Hollywood," *Chicago Daily Tribune,* July 28, 1943, 8; Thomas M. Pryor, "Noting Some Major Battle Scars," *New York Times,* December 28, 1941, X4.

30 W. T. Ballard, *Chance Elson* (New York: Pocket Books, 1959), 105; Carpozi, *Bugsy,* 67.

31 Hamill, "Bugsy Siegel's Fabulous Dream," 151; Albert Fried, *Rise and Fall of*

the Jewish Gangster in America, rev. ed. (New York: Columbia University Press, 1993), 245–246.

32 Carpozi, Bugsy, 47–48; Friedrich, City of Nets, 259.

33 Kevin Starr, The Dream Endures: California Enters the 1940s: Americans and the California Dream (1997; reprint, New York: Oxford University Press, 2002), 192.

34 Don't Call Me Bugsy.

35 Kitty Kelly, His Way: The Unauthorized Biography of Frank Sinatra (New York: Bantam Books, 1987), 121.

36 For example, see The Real Las Vegas: The Complete Story of America's Neon Oasis, prod. MPH Entertainment and dir. Jim Milio and Melissa Jo Peltier, 200 minutes (A&E Television Networks, 1996).

37 Jennings, We Only Kill Each Other, 48.

38 Ed Reid and Ovid Demaris, The Green Felt Jungle (Cutchogue, N.Y.: Buccaneer Books, 1963), 16.

39 Hamill, "Bugsy Siegel's Fabulous Dream," 151.

40 La Cosa Nostra, The Mafia: An Expose, 450 minutes (Madacy Records, 1997).

41 Edmunds, Bugsy's Baby, 48, 84, 85, and 95; Wolfe, Black Dahlia, 194; Don't Call Me Bugsy; Rogues Gallery, prod. Susan F. Walker and Rob Goubeaux and dir. Greg Vines, 65 minutes (Andrew Solt Productions, 1997).

42 Rogue's Gallery.

43 Carpozi, Bugsy, 43; Edmunds, Bugsy's Baby, 76.

44 Carpozi, Bugsy, 56–57; Jennings, We Only Kill Each Other, 9 and 47; Rogues Gallery; La Cosa Nostra.

45 Wolfe, Black Dahlia, 189–191; Carpozi, Bugsy, 78–80.

46 Carpozi, Bugsy, 95; Henry A. Zeiger, The Hit Parade (New York: Berkley, 1976), 134.

47 Paul Harrison, "Gangsters," Lowell (Mass.) Sun and Citizen Leader, November 6, 1941, 18.

48 Jennings, We Only Kill Each Other, 149; Sam Ross, Solomon's Palace (New York: Dell, 1974), 273; Max Allan Collins, Neon Mirage (New York: Bantam Books, 1991), 180; Las Vegas: An Unconventional History, prod. Amanda Pollak and dir. Stephen Ives, 180 minutes (Paramount Home Entertainment, 2005).

49 James Toback, Bugsy: An Original Screenplay (New York: Carol Publishing Group, 1991), 99 and 102.

50 Ross, Solomon's Palace, 274–275. See also Ralph Pearl, Las Vegas Is My Beat (New York: Bantam Books, 1974), 18.

51 "Reinvention of Bugsy Siegel," Bugsy, extended cut, prod. and dir. Charles Kiselyak, 90 minutes (Sony Pictures, 2006).

52 The Neon Empire, prod. Richard Maynard and dir. Larry Peerce, 122 minutes (Fries Entertainment, 1990); Ballard, Chance Elson, 173; Morris Renek, Las Vegas Strip (New York: Avon Books, 1976), 9.

53 Ross, Solomon's Palace, 287.

54 Bugsy; "Reinvention of Bugsy Siegel."

55 Chapin Hall, "What Goes On?," Los Angeles Times, March 7, 1939, 2.

56 Hubbard Keavy, "Gaming and Divorce Outdraw Boulder Dam at Las Vegas Says Special News Writer," *Reno Evening Gazette,* June 11, 1941, 4; "Gamblers' Luck," *Time,* April 9, 1945, 20; "Las Vegas Gambling," *Life,* December 21, 1942, 94; Wesley Stout, "Nevada's New Reno," *Saturday Evening Post,* October 31, 1942, 69.

57 Alex Small, "Nevada—Fabulous State," *Chicago Daily Tribune,* September 9, 1945, C2.

58 Richard English, "The Boom Came Back," *Collier's,* August 12, 1942, 36.

59 Stout, "Nevada's New Reno," 12.

60 Samuel Wallace, "Gambling Top Attraction in Las Vegas, Nev." *Chicago Daily Tribune,* September 7, 1947, G12; Jack Goodman, "Desert Attractions," *New York Times,* March 16, 1947, X14.

61 Kenneth L. Dixon, "Assignment America," *Port Arthur* (Tex.) *News,* June 13, 1946, 7; Erskine Johnson, "In Hollywood," *Daily Kennebec* (Augusta, Maine) *Journal,* June 11, 1946, 6; Henry McLemore, "Sports Prospector Hits on Rich Vein When He Discovers Las Vegas," *Dunkirk* (N.Y.) *Evening Observer,* December 8, 1937, 12; "Las Vegas Gambling," 94.

62 "Bonanza Fashions," *Life,* November 12, 1945, 97.

63 Newspapers across the nation, especially the *New York Times* and *Los Angeles Times,* covered celebrity marriages and divorces in Las Vegas.

64 Erskine Johnson, "In Hollywood," *Lima* (Ohio) *News,* July 5, 1946, 19.

65 "Wild, Woolly and Wide-Open," *Look,* August 14, 1940, 21–25.

66 Ovid Demaris, *The Last Mafioso: The Treacherous World of Jimmy Fratianno* (New York: Times Books, 1981), 43.

67 John Scarne, *The Odds Against Me: An Autobiography* (New York: Simon & Schuster, 1966), 369.

68 "'Bugsy' Siegel Ends Career as Gangster," *Life,* July 7, 1947, 73.

69 Eisenberg, Dan, and Landau, *Meyer Lansky,* 225–226.

70 Frank Rose, *The Agency: William Morris and the Hidden History of Show Business* (New York: HarperCollins, 1995), 92–93. However, not all Lansky biographers agree that he had a genuine interest in developing Las Vegas in the 1940s. See Lacey, *Little Man,* 152.

71 Susan Berman, *Easy Street* (New York: Dial Press, 1981), 1; for Davie Berman's relationship with Siegel, see 19–24.

72 W. R. Wilkerson III, *The Man Who Invented Las Vegas* (Bellingham, Wash.: Ciro's Books, 2000), 10, 11, 21, and 26.

73 Ibid., 43–44 and 49.

74 Ibid., 39–62, 108, 120, and 121. It is not entirely clear when Wilkerson gained control of the property. A title search of the Flamingo property reveals that Margaret Folsom sold it to Moe Sedway on September 13, 1945; he in turn transferred the deed to Greg Bautzer two months later. Betty Waters, *Flamingo Hilton Hotel and Casino, Las Vegas, Nevada: Title Search* (Clark County Title Service, 1992).

75 Wilkerson, *Man Who Invented Las Vegas,* 81, 85, and 86. In a July 14 radio broadcast, Walter Winchell was reporting "that a prominent West Coast racketeer was attempting to 'muscle' a prominent West Coast newspaper publisher out of his

interest in a hotel." Bugsy Siegel FBI File, 62-81518-10. On September 10, syndicated columnist Hedda Hopper reported that Bugsy Siegel was building a "huge night club [sic]" called the Flamingo. Hedda Hopper, "Looking at Hollywood," *Chicago Daily Tribune,* September 10, 1946, 23.

76 Wilkerson, *Man Who Invented Las Vegas,* 132.

77 Ibid., 72.

78 Harris Gaffen, *The Man Who Invented Las Vegas* (Los Angeles, 1992), n.p.

79 Paul Ralli, *Nevada Lawyer: A Story of Life and Love in Las Vegas* (Culver City, Calif.: Murray & Gee, 1949), 278 and 280.

80 Jamie Coughtry, ed., *John F. Cahlan: Fifty Years in Journalism and Community Development* (Reno: University of Nevada Oral History Program, 1987), 327.

81 "The Las Vegas I Remember: Interview with Herb McDonald," KNPR, Las Vegas, April 25, 2005; Marian Betran Decaro Oral History Interview, Special Collections, Lied Library, University of Nevada, Las Vegas.

82 Curtis O. Lynum, *The FBI and I: One Family's Life in the FBI during the Hoover Years* (Bryn Mawr, Pa.: Dorrance, 1988), 84–85.

83 Quoted in Fox, *Blood and Power,* 82.

84 Rose Marie, *Hold the Roses* (Lexington: University Press of Kentucky, 2002), 110.

85 Liberace, *Liberace: An Autobiography* (New York: G. P. Putnam's Sons, 1973), 175.

86 Susan Berman, *Lady Las Vegas: The Inside Story Behind America's Neon Oasis* (New York: TV Books, 1996), 68.

87 Erskine Caldwell, *With All My Might: An Autobiography* (Atlanta: Peachtree, 1987), 240–241.

88 Richard Hammer, *Playboy's Illustrated History of Organized Crime* (Chicago: Playboy Press, 1975), 217–223.

89 Joan E. Vadeboncoeur, "Levinson, Beatty Aim Straight in 'Bugsy,'" *Syracuse Herald-Journal,* December 20, 1991, C4.

90 Janet Maslin, "Sure, He Had His Faults, but the Man Had Vision!," *New York Times,* December 13, 1991, C12; Doug Brode, "Beatty's Best," *Syracuse Post-Standard,* December 21, 1991, E2.

91 Toback, *Bugsy,* 8–11.

92 Roger Ebert, "Bugsy," *Chicago Sun-Times,* December 20, 1991, http://rogerebert.suntimes.com/apps/pbcs.dll/article?AID=/1001122 (accessed June 20, 2010); David Thompson, ed., *Levinson on Levinson* (London: Faber and Faber, 1992), 122.

93 *La Cosa Nostra, The Mafia.* Millicent Rosen repeated her admiration for her father several times in an interview with me. Interview with Millicent Rosen by author, May 19, 2010.

94 For example, see Carpozi, *Bugsy,* 76–77.

95 Renek, *Las Vegas Strip,* 10. See also the Warren Beatty version of this hope in *Bugsy.*

96 David G. Schwarz is typical of historians who give little credit to Siegel for the development of the resort casino in Las Vegas. See his *Suburban Xanadu: The*

Casino Resort on the Las Vegas Strip and Beyond (New York: Routledge, 2003), 51–55. See also John M. Findlay, *People of Chance: Gambling in American Society from Jamestown to Las Vegas* (New York: Oxford University Press, 1986), 163–164. The Rothman quote appears in A. D. Hopkins and K. J. Evans, eds., *The First 100: Portraits of the Men and Women Who Shaped Las Vegas* (Las Vegas: Huntington Press, 1999), 148.

97 Bob Considine, "Bugsy Was Slain Bucking the 'Syndicate,'" *Charleston* (W.V.) *Gazette*, January 25, 1955, 20; *Neon Empire*; Hamill, "Bugsy Siegel's Fabulous Dream," 154; John L. Smith, "The Ghost of Siegel," in *The Players: The Men Who Made Las Vegas*, ed. Jack Sheehan (Reno: University of Nevada Press, 1997), 91.

4. ORGANIZED CRIME IN LAS VEGAS

The epigraphs are from "Racketeers Plan Invasion of California," *Oakland Tribune*, January 12, 1950, 1; Jack Lait and Lee Mortimer, *U.S.A. Confidential* (New York: Crown, 1952), 189; "Capone Gang Operations in Nevada Bared," *Chicago Daily Tribune*, December 1, 1954, A2; Sid W. Meyers, *The Great Las Vegas Fraud* (Chicago: Mayflower Press, 1958), 35; Wallace Turner, "Las Vegas: Gambling Take Creates New Force in U.S.," *New York Times*, November 18, 1963, 1; Ed Reid and Ovid Demaris, *The Green Felt Jungle* (Cutchogue, N.Y.: Buccaneer Books, 1963), 5; Bob Wiedrich, "If Bets Are On, the Mob Is In," *Chicago Tribune*, December 6, 1979, B3; Trip Gabriel, "From Vice to Nice: The Suburbanization of Las Vegas," *New York Times*, December 1, 1991, SM79; *This Week with David Brinkley*, ABC News, March 20, 1994.

1 "Gambling Is Hit at Meeting by Speakers Here," *Reno Evening Gazette*, February 5, 1931, 12; "Opponents Voice Gambling Bill at Hearing," February 17, 1931, 2.

2 "Nevada's Two False Steps," *Los Angeles Times*, March 22, 1931, A4.

3 "Racketeer Murders in Los Angeles," *Nevada State Journal*, May 22, 1931, 4.

4 See, for example, "Safe Deposit Box Found in L.A. Murders," *Oakland Tribune*, May 26, 1931, D2.

5 Richard Rayner, *A Bright and Guilty Place: Murder, Corruption, and L.A.'s Scandalous Coming of Age* (New York: Doubleday, 2009), 157, 205, and 208; Jules Tygiel, *The Great Los Angeles Swindle: Oil, Stocks, and Scandal During the Roaring Twenties* (New York: Oxford University Press, 1994), 177; Joe Domanick, *To Protect and To Serve: The LAPD's Century of War in the City of Dreams* (New York: Pocket Books, 1994), 46–47.

6 Rayner, *Bright and Guilty Place*, 160; "Former Deputy District Attorney Charged with Two California Murders," *Lowell* (Mass.) *Sun*, May 22, 1931, 1; "Murder Clue Leads to Cell of Former L.A. Vice Ruler," *Oakland Tribune*, May 24, 1931, 2; "Racketeer Murders in Los Angeles," 4; "Quiz Alleged Underworld King," *Oxnard* (Calif.) *Daily Courier*, August 19, 1931, 1; "Gamblers in Exodus from L.A., Report," *Los Angeles Evening Herald and Express*, May 16, 1941, A2.

7 Kevin Starr, *The Dream Endures: California Enters the 1940s* (New York: Oxford University Press, 1997), 168.

8 "Los Angeles . . . 'America's Wickedest City,'" *Look,* September 26, 1939, 31; George Creel, "Unholy City," *Collier's,* September 2, 1939, 13.

9 Frank Wright, *Nevada Yesterdays: Short Looks at Las Vegas History* (Las Vegas: Stephens Press, 2005), 50–51; "Gamblers Go to Las Vegas," *Los Angeles Times,* June 1, 1939, A.

10 Stephen Fox, *Blood and Power: Organized Crime in Twentieth-Century America* (New York: Penguin Books, 1990), 36–37; Charles Rappleye and Ed Becker, *All American Mafioso: The Johnny Rosselli Story* (New York: Doubleday, 1991), 39–40; John Buntin, *L.A. Noir: The Struggle for the Soul of America's Most Seductive City* (New York: Three Rivers Press, 2009), 27; Kevin Starr, *Material Dreams: Southern California through the 1920s* (New York: Oxford University Press, 1990), 169.

11 "Raiders Seize Rum, Nab Four," *Los Angeles Times,* March 12, 1925, A3; "Clean-up Begun in Liquor Feuds," *Los Angeles Times,* April 13, 1926, A22; "Rum Baron of Southland Flees Police Dry Drive," *Los Angeles Times,* August 8, 1926, 3; Albert Nathan, "Death, Sudden and Mysterious, Is Fate of Hijacker," *Los Angeles Times,* August 15, 1926, B7; "Cornero Fined as Gun Toter," *Los Angeles Times,* September 22, 1926, A5; "Cornero Slips Law's Clutch," *Los Angeles Times,* April 30, 1927, A2; "Tony Cornero Often Involved with Police," *Los Angeles Times,* February 10, 1948, 2; "38 Indicted in Rum Ring," *Nevada State Journal,* December 23, 1926, 1; "Tony Cornero Dead; Is Stricken at Dice," *New York Times,* August 1, 1955, 38; "Police Arrest 8 in Warfare of Gangsters," *San Mateo* (Calif.) *Times,* July 26, 1928, 1; "Gangster Keeps Promise to Give Coast Officer Machine Gun," *Salt Lake Tribune,* December 24, 1929, 4.

12 Fox, *Blood and Power,* 36; Earl Warren, *The Memoirs of Earl Warren* (Garden City, N.Y.: Doubleday, 1977), 132.

13 Fox, *Blood and Power,* 36–37; Domanick, *To Protect and To Serve,* 47–48; Rappleye and Becker, *All American Mafioso,* 41–42; "Tony Cornero Gives Self Up," *Los Angeles Times,* October 29, 1929, A5; "Cornero Given Two-Year Term," *Los Angeles Times,* November 13, 1929, A5.

14 Wright, *Nevada Yesterdays,* 49–50; Alan Balboni, *The Peoples of Las Vegas* (Reno: University of Nevada Press, 2005), 146.

15 Jim Newton, *Justice for All: Earl Warren and the Nation He Made* (New York: Riverhead Books, 2006), 107; Ed Cray, *Chief Justice: A Biography of Earl Warren* (New York: Simon & Schuster, 1997), 101; Bruce Henstell, *Sunshine and Wealth: Los Angeles in the Twenties and Thirties* (San Francisco: Chronicle Books, 1984), 67–69; "Hoses Turned on Officers," *Los Angeles Times,* August 2, 1939, 1; "Cornero Surrenders to Sheriff's Deputies," *Los Angeles Times,* August 11, 1939, 1; "Gambling Ship Owner Still Blocks Raiders," *New York Times,* August 3, 1939, 3; "Warren Gets New Writs for Raids on Ships," *San Mateo* (Calif.) *Times,* August 2, 1939, 1.

16 Alan Balboni, "Tony Cornero," in *The First 100: Portraits of the Men and Women Who Shaped Las Vegas,* A. D. Hopkins and K. J. Evans, eds. (Las Vegas: Huntington Press, 1999), 107–108.

17 Creel, "Unholy City," 13.

18 "Las Vegans Open Fight for Boulder Dam Park," *Nevada State Journal*, March 8, 1939, 8.

19 Westbrook Pegler, "Fair Enough," *Times Record* (Troy, N.Y.), June 28, 1947, 4. Other good examples include "Million Dollar Dope Ring Headed by 'Bugsy' Siegel, Police in Mexico Reveal," *Nevada State Journal*, June 28, 1947, 3; Seymour Korman, "Las Vegas: Desert Riviera," *Chicago Daily Tribune*, April 11, 1948, E23; Jack Lait, "Hollywood and Elsewhere," *Brownsville* (Tex.) *Herald*, August 13, 1948, 4.

20 James Phelan, "Memory of Bugsy Stains Pitch for Respectability," *Long Beach* (Calif.) *Press-Telegram*, February 22, 1955, B3.

21 William Howard Moore, *The Kefauver Committee and the Politics of Crime* (Columbia: University of Missouri Press, 1974), 29; "Manners and Morals," *Time*, November 28, 1949, 11.

22 "Racketeers Plan Invasion of California," 1. Evidence of the community "cringing" is in Edward Churchill, "The Truth about Las Vegas," *Script*, March 1948, 10.

23 David G. Schwartz, *Cutting the Wire: Gaming Prohibition and the Internet* (Reno: University of Nevada Press, 2005), 50; Virgil Peterson, *Gambling: Should It Be Legalized?* (Springfield, Ill.: Charles C. Thomas, 1951); Moore, *Kefauver Committee*, 38; "Charge Al Capone Mob in Las Vegas," *Independent* (Long Beach, Calif.), December 1, 1954, 6.

24 "Cities Bid Attorney General Curb Crime Syndicates' Political Aims," *New York Times*, September 22, 1949, 36. A consortium of fourteen national newspapers agreed to pool stories on racketeering and gambling. See Moore, *Kefauver Committee*, 41.

25 "U.S. Crime Parley Plans Study of Slot Machines," *New York Times*, February 13, 1950, 6.

26 "Text of Address by President Truman to Law Enforcement Officers," *New York Times*, February 16, 1950, 2; "Senate Group Approves a $100,000 Inquiry of Interstate Crime, Its Corruption of Cities," *New York Times*, February 28, 1950, 3.

27 Edwin A. Lahey, "Senate Crime Investigators Head for West Coast After Election Day," *Corpus Christi* (Texas) *Times*, November 7, 1950, 14.

28 "Underworld Links with Nevada's Legal Gambling Shocks Senate Investigators," *Lima* (Ohio) *News*, November 16, 1950, 5; "U.S. Opens Probe of Gangland; Mickey Cohen on Solon's List," *Oakland Tribune*, November 16, 1950, 1; "Gamblers are Gamblers," *Chicago Daily Tribune*, November 21, 1950, 16; "Disposition of Siegel Hotel under Inquiry," *Galveston* (Tex.) *News*, November 16, 1950, 8.

29 Jack Gould, "Millions Glued to TV for Hearing; Home Chores Wait, Shopping Sags," *New York Times*, March 20, 1951, 1 and 28; Lee Bernstein, *The Greatest Menace: Organized Crime in Cold War America* (Amherst: University of Massachusetts Press, 2002), 62.

30 David Halberstam, *The Fifties* (New York: Ballantine Books, 1994), 191.

31 Thomas Doherty, *Cold War, Cool Medium: Television, McCarthyism, and American Culture* (New York: Columbia University Press, 2003), 115–116; "Kefauver-casts Prove Real Tele Bargain," *Billboard*, March 31, 1951, 1; "Who's a Liar," *Life*,

April 2, 1951, 22. A year earlier, *Life* published a lengthy article about gambling across the nation and Kefauver's probe into its connections to organized crime; Ernest Havemann, "Gambling in the U.S.," *Life,* June 19, 1950, 96–121.

32 Joseph Bruce Gorman, *Kefauver: A Political Biography* (New York: Oxford University Press, 1971), 78.

33 Bernstein, *Greatest Menace,* 61–78; Gorman, *Kefauver,* 102.

34 Estes Kefauver, "What I Found in the Underworld," *Saturday Evening Post,* April 7, 1951, 71; Sen. Estes Kefauver, "Crime in America," *Kingsport* (Tenn.) *News,* July 31, 1951, 3; Estes Kefauver, *Crime in America* (Garden City, N.Y.: Doubleday, 1951), 229–237; *The Kefauver Committee Report on Organized Crime* (New York: Didier, 1951), 71–75.

35 *Kefauver Committee Report,* 74; Kefauver, *Crime in America,* 229.

36 Eugene P. Moehring, *Resort City in the Sunbelt: Las Vegas, 1930–2000,* 2nd ed. (Reno: University of Nevada Press, 2000), 89; David G. Schwartz, *Suburban Xanadu: The Casino Resort on the Las Vegas Strip and Beyond* (New York: Routledge, 2003), 75.

37 Peter Wyden, "How Wicked Is Las Vegas?," *Saturday Evening Post,* November 11, 1961, 18.

38 Fox, *Blood and Power,* 321.

39 Arthur M. Schlesinger Jr., *Robert Kennedy and His Times* (Boston: Houghton-Mifflin, 1978), 168.

40 Robert F. Kennedy, *The Enemy Within* (New York: Harper & Row, 1960), 240 and 265.

41 "Excerpts from the Testimony of Robert Kennedy before Senate Panel," *New York Times,* January 14, 1961, 8.

42 Ronald Goldfarb, *Perfect Villains, Imperfect Heroes: Robert F. Kennedy's War against Organized Crime* (Sterling, Va.: Capital Books, 1995), 77.

43 *Hang Tough! Grant Sawyer: An Activist in the Governor's Mansion* (Reno: University of Nevada Oral History Program, 1993), 89–91.

44 "FBI Agents Scrutinize Nevada Gambling for U.S. Attorney General," *Nevada State Journal,* August 20, 1961, 6.

45 "Bob Kennedy's Vegas Probe Called 'Fishing,'" *Los Angeles Times,* November 7, 1961, C11.

46 Ibid.; "Officials Say Clark Gaming Probe Story 'Distorted,'" *Reno Evening Gazette,* November 7, 1961, 1.

47 Meyers, *Great Las Vegas Fraud,* 47, 68, and 85.

48 Ibid., 53 and 79.

49 Wallace Turner, *Gamblers' Money: The New Force in American Life* (New York: Signet Book, 1966), 28, 121, and 123.

50 Ibid., 130.

51 Ibid., 83–103 and 198–207.

52 Ibid., 132.

53 Display ad, *Los Angeles Times,* December 6, 1963, D20; "'Open End' Lists Crime Discussion," *New York Times,* February 24, 1964, 49.

54 Reid and Demaris, *Green Felt Jungle,* 5 and 53–81.

55 Ibid., 44. Reid's characterization of casino security as "psychopathic" likely is a consequence of being beaten up by two men at the Desert Inn in 1954 while he was doing research for magazine articles detailing how "Las Vegas is swarming with unsavory characters." See "Crime Reporter Is Beaten in Las Vegas," *Galveston* (Tex.) *News*, March 22, 1954, 10.

56 Reid and Demaris, *Green Felt Jungle*, 154–176.

57 Ibid., 5 and 51–52.

58 Ibid., 193.

59 Other examples include a four-part series by Casey Shawhan and James Bassett in the *Oakland Tribune* in 1953 and "Inside Las Vegas," a three-part series in the *Washington Post and Times Herald* in 1956 by John Gunther, widely known for his "Inside" books on foreign locales and the United States.

60 Dan Fowler, "What Price Gambling in Nevada?," *Look*, June 15, 1954, 49–52.

61 Lester Velie, "Las Vegas: The Underworld's Secret Jackpot," *Reader's Digest*, October 1959, 138.

62 Fred J. Cook, "Treasure Chest of the Underworld: Gambling, Inc.," *Nation*, October 22, 1960, 301.

63 "Nevada Lieut. Governor Grilled in Gaming Probe," *Oakland Tribune*, October 27, 1954, 10; Bob Considine, "Pierre Lafitte Got 'Tape' to Trip Nevada Racketeers," *Charleston* (W.V.) *Gazette*, January 27, 1955, 1 and 7; "'Mike Fright' Seizes Nevada," *Long Beach* (Calif.) *Independent*, February 23, 1955, 4; Robert Lacey, *Little Man: Meyer Lansky and the Gangster Life* (Boston: Little, Brown, 1991), 218.

64 "Police Link Costello to a Nevada Casino," *New York Times*, June 12, 1957, 1; Wayne Phillips, "Costello's Stake in Nevada Sifted," *New York Times*, June 13, 1957, 25; "Nevada to Sift Link to Costello, Tropicana," *Los Angeles Times*, June 13, 1957, 2.

65 "Wealthy Gambler and Wife Slain," *Chicago Daily Tribune*, December 4, 1958, A1; "Las Vegas Hotelman, Wife Slain," *Independent* (Long Beach, Calif.), December 4, 1958, A11; "Vegas Hotel Man, Wife Found Slain," *Los Angeles Times*, December 4, 1958, 2.

66 Phelan, "Memory of Bugsy," B3.

67 Robbins E. Cahill, *Recollections of Work in State Politics, Government, Taxation, Gaming Control, Clark County Administration, and the Nevada Resort Association* (Reno: University of Nevada Oral History Program, 1977), 294, 943–945, and 1412–1415; Gary E. Elliott, *Senator Alan Bible and the Politics of the New West* (Reno: University of Nevada Press, 1994), 22; Jerome Skolnick, *House of Cards: The Legalization and Control of Casino Gambling* (Boston: Little, Brown, 1978), 110–124; Ronald A. Farrell and Carole Case, *The Black Book and the Mob: The Untold Story of the Control of Nevada's Casinos* (Madison: University of Wisconsin Press, 1995), 23–31.

68 Joseph F. McDonald, "Nevada Blocks Mobs but Gets Dregs," *Washington Post*, May 25, 1950, B13; John Gunther, "Inside Las Vegas," *Washington Post and Times Herald*, August 12, 1956, AW5; Seymour Korman, "Nevada Gaming Bonanza Keeps State Solvent," *Chicago Daily Tribune*, June 26, 1950, B1; William S. Fair-

child, "Las Vegas: The Sucker and the Almost-Even Break," *Reporter*, June 9, 1953, 16–17; Bob Considine, "Nevada Keeps Its Gambling Honest, but Realizes It Is Major Industry," *Charleston* (W.V.) *Gazette*, January 28, 1955, 2; Dick Pearce, "Pleasure Palaces," *Harper's*, February 1955, 81.

69 Phelan, "Memory of Bugsy," B3; John Gunther, "Inside Las Vegas," *Washington Post and Times Herald*, August 19, 1956, AW16; "Las Vegas Balks at Gangster Visit," *Los Angeles Times*, January 17, 1953, 2.

70 Kenneth Rudeen, "Gambling's Adult Western," *Sports Illustrated*, May 11, 1959, 94.

71 Guy Shipler, "Nevadan Raps Critics of Gambling in State," *Los Angeles Times*, May 1, 1962, 32.

72 Katharine Best and Katharine Hillyer, *Las Vegas: Playtown U.S.A.* (New York: David McKay, 1955), 85; Rudeen, "Gambling's Adult Western," 94.

73 "FBI 'Bugged' Las Vegas Gambling Casinos for Two Years," *Syracuse Herald-Journal*, June 29, 1966, 31; "FBI Agent Faces Trial in Wiretap," *New York Times*, July 1, 1966, 19.

74 Sandy Smith, "How Top Gangsters Siphon Off $6 Million a Year at Las Vegas," *Chicago Sunday Sun-Times*, July 10, 1966, 1.

75 *American White Paper*, NBC News, August 25, 1966.

76 "Casinos Face Crackdown in Nevada Probe," *Chicago Tribune*, August 13, 1966, D16; Gene Blake, "Las Vegas Takes Gaming Probe with Its Usual Aplomb," *Los Angeles Times*, August 14, 1966, B; Wallace Turner, "Inquiry into Las Vegas Gambling Opens Today," *New York Times*, August 9, 1966, 14; "U.S. Bars Testimony in Nevada Inquiry," *New York Times*, August 28, 1966, 36.

77 "Nevada Governor and Hoover Clash," *New York Times*, October 28, 1966, 28. Casino executive Edward Levinson filed suit against the FBI, charging it with violating state law in wiretapping his offices at the Fremont Hotel. See "U.S. Summons 16 in Nevada Suit," *New York Times*, September 14, 1966, 54.

78 Jim Barrows, "State 'Skim' Probers Fire Back—Most Casinos 'Clean,'" *Las Vegas Sun*, August 25, 1966, 1.

79 "FBI Harassment Charged in Nevada," *New York Times*, September 2, 1966, 1 and 32; Peter R. Kann, "Nevada Agency Denies Casinos in Las Vegas 'Skimmed' Large Sums," *Wall Street Journal*, September 2, 1966, 1.

80 "Nevada Panel Urges Tighter Gaming Law," *New York Times*, September 21, 1966, 32.

81 "U.S. Jury Probe of Las Vegas Gaming Opens," *Chicago Tribune*, November 26, 1966, 8; "Sinatra Subpoenaed in 'Skimming' Inquiry," *Los Angeles Times*, January 20, 1967, 21; Wallace Turner, "7 Nevada Gaming Figures Indicted on Tax Charges," *New York Times*, May 12, 1967, 1.

82 Caskie Stinnett, "Las Vegas: Where Anything Is Forgivable Except Restraint," *Holiday*, May 1967, 35.

83 Sandy Smith, "The Mob," *Life*, September 8, 1967, 98.

84 Michael Drosnin, *Citizen Hughes* (1985; reprint, New York: Broadway Books, 2004), 106.

85 Ibid., 119.

86 Anthony Burton, "Hughes Eases Hoods Out of Vegas' Strip," *Chicago Tribune*, September 27, 1967, n.p., Howard Hughes Collection, Box 93, Special Collections, Lied Library; "Hughes Brings New Image to Glittering Las Vegas," *Houston Chronicle*, August 29, 1967, 1; Wallace Turner, "Howard Hughes Captures Imagination of Las Vegas as He Fashions Nevada Empire," *New York Times*, January 14, 1968, 69; Bob Considine, "Desert Develops Skyline," *Lowell* (Mass.) *Sun*, January 15, 1968, 5.

87 "Nevada May Bar Spilotro from Clubs," *Chicago Tribune*, June 26, 1978, 6.

88 Lee Dembart, "Teamster Pension Loans Linked to Associates of Crime Figures," *New York Times*, October 28, 1976, 85.

89 Louis M. Kohlmeier, "Teamster Loan Strange Indeed," *Salt Lake Tribune*, November 5, 1976, 16.

90 "$7 Million Vegas Loss Under Probe," *Chicago Tribune*, July 1, 1976, 6; "Nevada Agency Audits A. Glick's Argent Corp.; Embezzling Suspected," *Wall Street Journal*, July 2, 1976, 2; "Argent Discloses Advances of $10 Million to Its Owner, Allen Glick, and His Firms," *Wall Street Journal*, September 2, 1976, 9.

91 Bill Phillips, "Gaming Hassle: Former Hot Dog Stand Owner Sends Shock Waves through Nevada," *Nevada State Journal*, December 26, 1976, 1.

92 Ibid., 1 and 3; Al Delugach, "Panel Denies Casino Post for Ex-Bookie," *Los Angeles Times*, January 23, 1976, D13.

93 "Las Vegas Financier Denies Gangland Link," *Nevada State Journal*, November 25, 1975, 3.

94 Wallace Turner, "Reputed Organized Crime Heads Named in Casino Skimming Case," *New York Times*, October 12, 1983, B8.

95 "Blood Threat," *Time*, February 3, 1986, 22.

96 Ibid. For background on the Civellas, see Kenneth J. Peak and William N. Ousley, "The FBI's 'Strawman': Breaking the Kansas City Mob's Connection to Las Vegas," *Missouri Historical Review* 104 (January 2010): 97–99.

97 "Shaking the Mob's Grip," *Time*, October 24, 1983, 37; "Blood Threat," 22; "Ex–Casino Owner Says He Sold after Threats," *New York Times*, November 9, 1985, 33. DeLuna told Glick, "Do what you got to do, boy. Make your public announcement . . . for whatever ——— reason you want to pick, and get out." Quote in Peak and Ousley, "FBI's 'Strawman,'" 101.

98 "Possible New Owners of Argent May Have Crime Ties, FBI Says," *Wall Street Journal*, September 10, 1979, 40; Al Delugach, "Nevada Board OKs New Operators for 3 Casinos," *Los Angeles Times*, November 16, 1979, E17. Sachs and partner Herb Tobman also faced an order to sell (plus a $3 million fine) five years later when the Nevada Gaming Commission ruled that they had failed to stop the skim. See Wallace Turner, "Nevada to Move Ahead on Forcing Casinos' Sale," *New York Times*, January 28, 1984, A9.

99 Ronald Koziol, "'Lefty' Marked for Mob 'Hit,'" *Chicago Tribune*, October 8, 1982, 14.

100 "Bodies of Missing Crime Figures Found Buried on Indiana Farm," *New York Times*, June 24, 1986, A22.

101 "Mob Control of Casino Alleged," *Los Angeles Times*, May 24, 1979, B1 and B28.

For an account of these prosecutions see Peak and Ousley, "FBI's 'Strawman,'" 106–107.

102 The following are just a sample of the wave of articles produced by the investigations: Wallace Turner, "Nevadans Recall Caution to Jersey: Casinos Draw Trouble," *New York Times,* March 21, 1980, B7; George Lardner Jr. and Mary Thornton Washington, "Impact on Mob–Teamster Links Seen in Vegas Skimming Case," *Washington Post,* October 13, 1983, A9; "Glick Faces Gaming License Loss," *Los Angeles Times,* May 31, 1979, E14; Ronald Koziol, "Nevada Seizes Stardust Casino," *Chicago Tribune,* June 24, 1979, 8; "The Mob Taps Out in Vegas," *Newsweek,* October 24, 1983, 93; "The Bookkeeper Who Did His Job Too Well," *Fortune,* November 10, 1986, 31. Harry Reid, in his autobiography, emphatically pointed out that an independent investigation into his chairmanship of the Nevada Gaming Commission found no evidence of his complicity with organized crime figures. See Harry Reid with Mark Warren, *The Good Fight: Hard Lessons from Searchlight to Washington* (New York: G. P. Putnam's Sons, 2008), 236–272.

103 "Torello on Trial," *Crime Story,* prod. Michael Mann and dir. Gary Sinese, 60 minutes (Michael Mann Productions, 1987).

104 *Ocean's Eleven,* prod. and dir. Lewis Milestone, 127 minutes (Warner Bros., 1960).

105 W. T. Ballard, *Chance Elson,* 2nd ed. (New York: Pocket Books, 1959), 59.

106 See Chapter 3 for a full discussion of Siegel's role in Las Vegas.

107 *Las Vegas Shakedown,* prod. William F. Broidy and dir. Sidney Salkow, 79 minutes (William F. Broidy Pictures, 1955); Jack Waer, *Murder in Las Vegas* (New York: Avon, 1955), 8; William R. Cox, "Las Vegas Trap," in *The Hardboiled Lineup,* ed. Harry Widmer (New York: Lion Book, 1956), 7; John D. McDonald, *The Only Girl in the Game* (Greenwich, Conn.: Fawcett, 1960), 31.

108 Ian Fleming, *Diamonds Are Forever* (1956; reprint, New York: Penguin Group, 2003), 19; William R. Cox, *Murder in Vegas* (New York: New American Library, 1960), 100.

109 David Chandler, *Father O'Brien and His Girls* (New York: New American Library, 1964), 41; Richard Rayner, *The Devil's Wind* (New York: HarperCollins, 2005), 88.

110 McDonald, *Only Girl,* 31; Charles Fleming, *The Ivory Coast* (New York: St. Martin's Press, 2002), 146; Arthur Moore and Clayton Matthews, *Las Vegas* (New York: Pocket Books, 1974), 115.

111 Richard Foster, *Blonde and Beautiful* (Toronto: Popular Library, 1955), 17; Cox, "Las Vegas Trap," 7; Arelo Sederberg, *Casino* (1974; reprint, New York: Dell, 1977), 38; Patrick Quentin, *Suspicious Circumstances* (New York: Simon & Schuster, 1957), 149 and 182.

112 Moore and Matthews, *Las Vegas,* 122.

113 Gerald Petievich, *Shakedown* (New York: Simon & Schuster, 1988), 66.

114 Waer, *Murder in Las Vegas,* 8; Ovid Demaris, *Candyleg* (Greenwich, Conn.: Fawcett, 1961), 104–105.

115 Irving Shulman, *The Big Brokers* (1951; reprint, New York: Lorevan Publishing, 1986), 257–258; William Pearson, *The Muses of Ruin* (New York: McGraw-Hill, 1965), 178; Elliot Paul, *The Black and the Red* (New York: Random House, 1956), 22.

116 *The Real Las Vegas: The Complete Story of America's Neon Oasis,* prod. MPH Entertainment and dir. Jim Milio and Melissa Jo Peltier, 200 minutes (A&E Television Networks, 1996); *A&E American Justice: Vegas and the Mob,* prod. Matt Palm, 100 minutes (History Channel, 1992); *Las Vegas: The Money and the Power,* prod. and dir. Julie Harman, 93 minutes (A&E Television Networks, 2002); *La Cosa Nostra, The Mafia: An Expose,* 43 minutes (Madacy Entertainment Group, 2004); *Las Vegas: An Unconventional History,* prod. Amanda Pollak and Stephen Ives and dir. Stephen Ives, 180 minutes (Paramount Home Entertainment, 2005).

117 Michael Corleone's father, Don Vito Corleone, had used a similar line in the earlier film. *The Godfather,* prod. Albert S. Ruddy and dir. Francis Ford Coppola, 175 minutes (Paramount Pictures, 1972); *The Godfather, Part II,* prod. and dir. Francis Ford Coppola, 200 minutes (Paramount Pictures, 1974).

118 Mario Puzo, *Inside Las Vegas* (New York: Grosset & Dunlap, 1977), 54.

119 Mario Puzo, *The Last Don* (New York: Random House, 1996).

120 David Thompson and Ian Christie, *Scorsese on Scorsese* (London: Faber and Faber, 1990), 202.

121 *Casino,* prod. Barbara De Fina and dir. Martin Scorsese, 178 minutes (Universal Pictures, 1995).

122 Janet Maslin, "A Money-Mad Mirage from Scorsese," *New York Times,* November 22, 1995, C14.

123 "Shaking the Mob's Grip," *Time,* October 24, 1983, 37.

124 Gabriel, "From Vice to Nice," SM72.

125 *This Week with David Brinkley,* ABC News, March 20, 1994. There certainly are other explanations for the mob's demise. In 1997, Katie Couric on NBC's *Today* show asked FBI special agent Bob Siller, "What happened to the mob? I mean, some people say that Howard Hughes . . . bought it out when he came here in 1966 and snatched up six hotels. That was the beginning of the end. Would you say he deserves some credit in this?" Predictably, Siller focused on the role of his agency, "No, I think what really ran them out is effective law enforcement, and particularly the FBI." *Today,* NBC News, April 7, 1997.

126 Michael Green, "Las Vegas Mob," *ONE: Online Nevada Encyclopedia,* http://www.onlinenevada.org/las_vegas_mob (accessed November 23, 2009).

127 Wilbur Shepperson, *Mirage Land: Images of Nevada* (Reno: University of Nevada Press, 1992), 145.

128 Steve Lopez, "A Lawyer to Wiseguys Would Rule Sin City," *Time,* May 10, 1999, 8.

129 "Anybody but Oscar," *Las Vegas Review-Journal,* March 9, 1999, B6; Steve Friess, "Rolling Lucky Sevens," *U.S. News and World Report,* May 10, 1999, 30; Connie Bruck, "They Love Me!," *New Yorker,* August 16, 1999, 31.

130 James Rainey, "California and the West: Las Vegas Set to Take Its Chances on Next Mayor," *Los Angeles Times,* June 6, 1999, 14.

131 Bruck, "They Love Me!," 31–32.

132 Interview with Oscar Goodman by author, March 14, 2008.

133 Interview with Don Payne by author, August 2, 2005.

5. IMAGES OF GAMBLING IN LAS VEGAS

The epigraphs are from Chapin Hall, "What Goes On?," *Los Angeles Times,* May 24, 1939, A; Mario Puzo, *Inside Las Vegas* (New York: Grosset & Dunlap, 1977), 102; Ron Abell, *Tap City* (Boston: Little, Brown, 1985), 28; Brian Rouff, *Dice Angel* (Las Vegas: Hardway Press, 2001), 135.

1 Puzo, *Inside Las Vegas,* 16, 25, and 243–245.

2 *Pepe,* prod. and dir. George Sidney, 195 minutes (Columbia Pictures, 1960).

3 Irving Shulman, *The Big Brokers* (1951; reprint, New York: Lorevan Publishing, 1986), 130–131, 139, and 147.

4 Hall, "What Goes On?," A.

5 Mildred Seydell obituary, *Santa Fe New Mexican,* February 22, 1988, A4.

6 Seydell's article in the *Atlanta Georgian* reprinted in "Mildred Seydell Writes of Las Vegas Gaming; Says Dignified," *Las Vegas Review-Journal,* January 13, 1938, 5.

7 Wesley Stout, "Nevada's New Reno," *Saturday Evening Post,* October 31, 1942, 68. See also "Las Vegas Gambling," *Life,* December 21, 1942, 91–94; "Ray Tucker," *Long Beach* (Calif.) *Independent,* April 20, 1949, 14.

8 Hubbard Keavy, "Gambling Is Key to Boom in Las Vegas, Says Writer after Visit to Nevada City," *Reno Evening Gazette,* June 12, 1941, 10.

9 Gladwin Hill, "Why They Gamble: A Las Vegas Survey," *New York Times,* August 25, 1957, 27; Betty Logan, "Pearls of Wisdom Mid Roulette Wheels," *Centralia* (Wash.) *Chronicle Advertiser,* August 7, 1936, 5.

10 "'What a Gal' Ma Preaches to Raw Men of Desert," *Oakland Tribune,* August 9, 1931, 1–2; "'Ma' Visits Her Ex-Mate; Talks to Gamblers," *Chicago Daily Tribune,* August 9, 1931, 3.

11 "Notes on People," *New York Times,* February 2, 1978, C2; Kenneth A. Briggs, "Billy Graham's Latest Crusade: The Gospel in Las Vegas," February 3, 1978, B1; John Dart, "Of Two Minds in Las Vegas," *Los Angeles Times,* January 31, 1978, B3.

12. "Gambling Goes Legit," *Time,* December 6, 1976, 65.

13 Hall, "What Goes On?," A.

14 Richard English, "The Boom Came Back," *Collier's,* August 22, 1942, 49.

15 Frank Gruber, *The Honest Dealer* (New York: Rinehart, 1947), 102; Seymour Korman, "Nevada—Where the Sky Is the Limit and Gold Is Raked Off Tables," *Chicago Daily Tribune,* January 17, 1955, 6. See also Shulman, *Big Brokers,* 131.

16 John Gunther, "Inside Las Vegas," *Washington Post and Times Herald,* August 12, 1956, AW5.

17 Puzo, *Inside Las Vegas,* 102.

18 "Our Gambling Habits," *New York Times,* November 28, 1938, 14; "Gambling Goes Legit," 56.

19 Quoted in Denise von Herrmann, *The Big Gamble: The Politics of Lottery and Casino Expansion* (Westport, Conn.: Praeger, 2002), 108.

20 Wade Goodwin, *All Things Considered,* National Public Radio, June 24, 1999.

21 Bruce Bliven, "The American Dnieperstroy," *New Republic,* December 11, 1935, 127.

22 Frank Gruber, *The French Key* (1939; reprint, Anstey, England: Linford, 1990), 291–293.

23 Writers' Program, *Nevada: Guide to the Silver State* (1940; reprint, Portland, Ore.: Binfords & Mort, 1957), 183.

24 Keavy, "Gambling Is Key to Boom," 10.

25 Logan, "Pearls of Wisdom," 5. Historian David Schwartz has argued that casinos then and now are not that democratic. Rather, the "casino floor" is "brutally segmented," distinguishing the ordinary players from the high rollers. *Suburban Xanadu: The Casino Resort on the Las Vegas Strip and Beyond* (New York: Routledge, 2003), 4.

26 Examples of newspapers continuing to reflect this egalitarian image include Seymour Korman, "Las Vegas: Desert Riviera," *Chicago Daily Tribune,* April 11, 1948, E7; Jack Goodman, "Jackpot Jamboree," *New York Times,* August 15, 1948, SM30. One can also see it in novels like Gruber's *The Honest Dealer,* 60; Octavus Roy Cohen, *A Bullet for My Love* (New York: Macmillan, 1950), 3; Carolyn Thomas, *The Cactus Shroud* (Philadelphia: J. B. Lippincott, 1957), 45.

27 *Las Vegas Nights,* prod. William LeBaron and dir. Ralph Murphy, 90 minutes (Paramount Pictures, 1941); *Moon Over Las Vegas,* prod. and dir. Jean Yarbrough, 90 minutes (Universal Pictures, 1944); *Flight to Nowhere,* prod. William B. David and dir. William Rowland, 79 minutes (Golden Gate Pictures, 1946); *Lady Luck,* prod. Warren Duff and dir. Edwin L. Marin, 97 minutes (RKO Radio Pictures, 1946); *The Invisible Wall,* prod. Sol M. Wurtzel and dir. Eugene Forde, 72 minutes (Sol M. Wurtzel Productions, 1947); *The Lady Gambles,* prod. Michael Kraike and dir. Michael Gordon, 99 minutes (Universal International Pictures, 1949); *Las Vegas Story,* prod. Robert Sparks and dir. Robert Stevenson, 88 minutes (RKO Radio Pictures, 1952); *Las Vegas Shakedown,* prod. William F. Broidy and dir. Sidney Salkow, 79 minutes (William F. Broidy Pictures, 1955); *The Girl Rush,* prod. Frederick Brisson and dir. Robert Pirosh, 85 minutes (Paramount, 1955); *Ocean's Eleven,* prod. and dir. Lewis Milestone, 127 minutes (Warner Bros., 1960).

28 "Kite High," *Racket Squad,* prod. Hal Roach Jr. and dir. William Beaudine, 30 minutes (Showcase Productions, 1951).

29 "Topper Goes to Las Vegas," *Topper,* prod. Bernard Schubert and dir. Lew Landers, 30 minutes (CBS, 1954); "The Fever," *The Twilight Zone,* prod. Buck Houghton and dir. Robert Florey, 30 minutes (CBS, 1960).

30 "Lori," *I Spy,* prod. Morton Fine and David Friedkin and dir. Paul Wendkos, 60 minutes (3F Productions, 1966); "The Rabbit Who Ate Las Vegas," *The A-Team,* prod. John Ashley and Patrick Hasburgh and dir. Bruce Kessler, 60 minutes (Universal TV, 1983); "Diced Steele," *Remington Steele,* prod. Kevin Inch and dir. Don Weis, 60 minutes (MTM Enterprises, 1985); "Cool Change," *CSI: Crime Scene Investigation,* prod. Cynthia Chvatal, Ron Mitchell, and William Petersen

and dir. Michael W. Watkins, 60 minutes (CBS Paramount Network Television, 2000); "Jokers and Fools," *Las Vegas,* prod. Daniel Arkin and dir. Timothy Busfield, 60 minutes (Gary Scott Thompkins Productions, 2003).

31 "A Role of the Dice," *Arrest and Trial,* prod. Arthur H. Nadel and dir. David Lowell Rich, 75 minutes (Revue Studios, 1964).

32 *Viva Las Vegas,* prod. and dir. George Sidney, 85 minutes (MGM, 1964); *Diamonds Are Forever,* prod. Albert R. Broccoli, Harry Saltzman, and Alan Silvers and dir. Guy Hamilton, 120 minutes (Eon Productions, 1971); *The Electric Horseman,* prod. Ray Stark and dir. Sydney Pollack, 122 minutes (Columbia Pictures, 1979); *Going in Style,* prod. Tony Bill and Fred T. Gallo and dir. Martin Brest, 97 minutes (Warner Bros., 1979); *Rain Man,* prod. Mark Johnson and dir. Barry Levinson, 133 minutes (United Artists, 1988); *Honeymoon in Vegas,* prod. Mike Lobell and dir. Andrew Bergman, 96 minutes (Castle Rock Entertainment, 1992); *Casino,* prod. Barbara De Fina and dir. Martin Scorcese, 178 minutes (Universal Pictures, 1995); *Vegas Vacation,* prod. Jerry Weintraub and dir. Stephen Kessler, 93 minutes (Warner Bros., 1997); *Ocean's Eleven,* prod. Jerry Weintraub and dir. Stephen Soderbergh, 116 minutes (Warner Bros., 2001); *The Cooler,* prod. Sean Furst and Michael A. Pierce and dir. Wayne Kramer, 101 minutes (Content Films, 2003).

33 *Hollywood or Bust,* prod. Hal B. Wallis and dir. Frank Tashlin, 95 minutes (Paramount Pictures, 1956).

34 *Vegas Vacation.*

35 *Las Vegas Nights; Meet Me in Las Vegas,* prod. Joe Pasternak and dir. Roy Rowland, 112 minutes (MGM, 1956).

36 *Las Vegas Shakedown.*

37 *Starman,* prod. Larry J. Franco and dir. John Carpenter, 115 minutes (Columbia Pictures, 1984).

38 *Girls' Night,* prod. Bill Boyes and dir. Nick Hurran, 102 minutes (Granada Film Productions, 1998).

39 *Rain Man;* Walter Goodman, "The Casino as a Movie Setting and Metaphor," *New York Times,* January 16, 1989, C13–C14.

40 *Going in Style.* There are many other examples of novice and sympathetic players winning jackpots: "Vacation in Las Vegas," *Gomer Pyle, U.S.M.C.,* prod. Sheldon Leonard and dir. Coby Ruskin, 30 minutes (Ashland Productions, 1966); "The Las Vegas Strangler," *Starsky and Hutch,* prod. Joseph T. Narr and dir. George McCowen, 120 minutes (Spelling-Goldberg Productions, 1976); *The Vegas Casino War,* prod. Michael Greenburg and dir. George Englund, 96 minutes (George Englund Productions, 1984); *Honeymoon in Vegas; Money Plays,* prod. Wayne Rogers and William Tannen and dir. Frank D. Gilroy, 92 minutes (Money Plays Company, 1997); *The Cooler.*

41 Gunther, "Inside Las Vegas," *Washington Post and Times Herald,* August 19, 1956, AW18.

42 Casey Shawhan and James Bassett, "Lowdown on Vegas—It's Fairly Pure," *Oakland Tribune,* July 19, 1953, A27.

43 Katharine Best and Katharine Hillyer, *Las Vegas: Playtown U.S.A.* (New York: David McKay, 1955), xi and 12.

44 Gunther, "Inside Las Vegas," August 12, 1956, AW7.

45 Arelo Sederberg, *Casino* (New York: Dell, 1977), 30.

46 "Role of the Dice."

47 Michael Connelly, *Trunk Music* (New York: St. Martin's Paperbacks, 1998), 108. Also helpful is *All Things Considered,* National Public Radio, June 24, 1999.

48 Gary Phillips, *Shooter's Point* (New York: Kensington, 2002), 173.

49 *Las Vegas: American Boomtown,* MSNBC, 2001.

50 Rouff, *Dice Angel,* 135.

51 Sean O'Faolain, "Las Vegas," *Holiday,* September 1956, 59; Robert Nathan, *The Rancho of Little Loves* (New York: Knopf, 1956), 70.

52 *Meet Me in Las Vegas.*

53 Gary Phillips, *High Hand* (New York: Kensington, 2001), 107.

54 "Boulder Dam and Las Vegas Trip Related by T. A. Nixon," *Greeley* (Colo.) *Daily and Greeley Republican,* September 1, 1932, 1.

55 Michael Connelly, *Void Moon* (New York: Warner Vision Books, 2001), 107.

56 Louise Wener, *The Perfect Play* (New York: Harper, 2005), 312.

57 John Goodger, *The Druperman Tapes* (New York: St. Martin's Minotaur, 2005), 23.

58 Julian Halevy, "Disneyland and Las Vegas," *Nation,* June 7, 1958, 511.

59 Frank Kane, *A Short Bier* (New York: Dell, 1960), 70; Abell, *Tap City,* 28; Gerald Petievich, *Shakedown* (New York: Simon & Schuster, 1988), 143.

60 *Casino.*

61 Ian Fleming, *Diamonds Are Forever* (1956; reprint, New York: Penguin, 2003), 135–136.

62 Red Smith, "Sin and Sand in the Desert," *Mansfield* (Ohio) *News-Journal,* March 2, 1960, 21.

63 Bob Whearley, "The Truth about Las Vegas," *Denver Post,* August 12, 1963, 1.

64 William Pearson, *Muses of Ruin* (New York: McGraw-Hill, 1965), 185.

65 Norma Lee Browning, "The Two Faces of Vegas," *Chicago Daily Tribune,* October 7, 1962, C50; Steve Allen, *Murder in Vegas* (New York: Kensington, 1991), 9; Ovid Demaris, *Candyleg* (Greenwich, Conn.: Fawcett, 1961), 50.

66 Tim Underwood, *Ringers* (New York: Penguin Books, 1992), 7.

67 Al Alvarez, *The Biggest Game in Town* (Boston: Houghton Mifflin, 1983), 14–15.

68 Michael Ventura, *The Death of Frank Sinatra* (New York: Holt, 1996), 22.

69 Dave Hickey, *Air Guitar: Essays on Art and Democracy* (Los Angeles: Art Issues Press, 1997), 24.

70 Diane Wakoski, *The Emerald City of Las Vegas* (Santa Rosa, Calif.: Black Sparrow Press, 1995), 155–156.

71 Alma Whitaker, "Sugar and Spice," *Los Angeles Times,* April 28, 1929, 26.

72 Hill, "Why They Gamble," 60.

6. THE ENTERTAINMENT CAPITAL OF THE WORLD

The epigraphs are from Westbrook Pegler, "Fair Enough," *Charleston* (W.V.) *Gazette,* June 26, 1947, 6; Seymour Korman, "Nevada, Where the Sky Is the Limit and Gold Is Raked Off Tables," *Chicago Daily Tribune,* January 19, 1955, 3; Nicholas Naff, "Las Vegas—Town that Doesn't Mind Making Change," *Los Angeles Times,* September 26, 1965, N21; Perry Phillips, "The Las Vegas Boom Continues," *Oakland Tribune,* February 6, 1972, 2V.

1 Chet Sobsey, "Hotelmen Spend Millions to Lure Las Vegas Trade," *Charleston* (W.V.) *Gazette Magazine,* April 25, 1954, 19.

2 John P. Cahlan, "Opening of the Meadows Draws Monster Crowd," *Las Vegas Review-Journal,* May 4, 1931, 3; Bill Willard, "The Entertainment Capital," *Nevada,* December 1988, 15.

3 "Las Vegas Made Safe," *Time,* June 1, 1931, 13.

4 "'Wild West' Town Near Boulder Dam," *New York Times,* August 23, 1936, XX10.

5 "El Borracho: Café Society Likes Its Old Gags," *Life,* February 17, 1947, 60; "Night Clubs: In Wartime They Are More Lavish," *Life,* February 9, 1942, 86.

6 Robert Sylvester, *No Cover Charge: A Backward Look at the Night Clubs* (New York: Dial Press, 1956); Susan Waggoner, *Nightclub Nights: Art, Legend, and Style, 1920–1960* (New York: Rizzoli International, 2001); Burton W. Peretti, *Nightclub City: Politics and Amusement in Manhattan* (Philadelphia: University of Pennsylvania Press, 2007), 1–27 and 164–231; Lewis Erenberg, "Impresarios of Broadway Nightlife," in *Inventing Times Square: Commerce and Culture at the Crossroads,* ed. William R. Taylor (1991; reprint, Baltimore: Johns Hopkins University Press, 1996), 171–175.

7 "Night Clubs: They Are Enjoying the Greatest Boom in Their History," *Life,* May 10, 1943, 69.

8 George Stamos Jr., "The Great Resorts of Las Vegas: How They Began," *Las Vegas Sun Magazine,* April 1, 1979, 8.

9 "$7,000,000 in Hotel Showbiz," *Billboard,* February 10, 1945, 28.

10 "Fifi D'Orsay Is New Ranch Star," *Las Vegas Review-Journal,* November 18, 1942, 3; "New Show Opens at El Rancho," February 24, 1943, 9.

11 David Fluke Collection, Box 1, Folder 23, Special Collections, Lied Library, University of Nevada, Las Vegas.

12 Ibid.; "Frontier Hotel Spends 100G for Talent in Year; Plans Expansion," *Billboard,* October 16, 1943, 5.

13 *The Billboard 1943 Music Year Book* (Cincinnati: Billboard, 1943), 124.

14 Wesley Stout, "Nevada's New Reno," *Saturday Evening Post,* October 31, 1942, 69.

15 "Paris of the Desert," *In Short* (1946), reprinted in "Stories Touted City in Early Tourism Days," *Las Vegas Review-Journal,* August 5, 1990, 5T.

16 Clair C. Stebbins, "Daytime Sun and Nighttime Fun; That's the Routine at Las Vegas," *Sunday Times Signal* (Zanesville, Ohio), February 11, 1951, section 2, 8.

17 Steve Schickel, "Around 'n' About," *Suburbanite Economist* (Chicago), July 1, 1959, 20G.

18 Peter Wyden, "How Wicked Is Las Vegas?," *Saturday Evening Post,* November 11, 1961, 20.

19 Fluke Collection, Box 2.

20 "Las Vegas, Nev. Hotel Expands Name Policy," *Billboard,* January 27, 1945, 27; "$7,000,000 in Hotel Showbiz," February 10, 1945, 28.

21 Al Fischler, "Las Vegas as Showbiz Mint," *Billboard,* August 31, 1946, 3 and 43.

22 Frank Gruber, *The French Key* (1939; reprint, Anstey, U.K.: F. A. Thorpe, 1990), 290–291.

23 *Las Vegas Nights,* prod. William Le Baron and dir. Ralph Murphy, 90 minutes (Paramount Pictures, 1941).

24 This is evident also in the films *Flying Blind* (1941) and *Lady Luck* (1946).

25 Richard English, "Million-Dollar Talent War," *Saturday Evening Post,* October 24, 1953, 69; George Stamos Jr., "The Great Resorts of Las Vegas: How They Began!," *Saturday Evening Post,* April 22, 1979, 8.

26 "Five-Million-Dollar Flamingo Resort Hotel Opens," *Las Vegas Review-Journal,* December 26, 1946, 3. The FBI reported that Siegel met with Sinatra on December 18, 1946. See Tom Kuntz and Phil Kuntz, eds., *The Sinatra Files: The Secret FBI Dossier* (New York: Three Rivers Press, 2000), 109.

27 Bob Thomas, "Las Vegas Is Transformed into New Barbary Coast," *Laredo* (Tex.) *Times,* December 31, 1946, 14.

28 "Las Vegas Strikes It Rich," *Life,* May 26, 1947, 99; Hy Gardner, "Las Vegas Marriages Lead Divorces 6 to 1," *Oakland Tribune,* October 1, 1952, 30; Seymour Korman, "Las Vegas Now a Year Round Desert Resort," *Chicago Daily Tribune,* July 27, 1952, F9; Stebbins, "Daytime Sun and Nighttime Fun."

29 Octavus Roy Cohen, *A Bullet for My Love* (New York: Macmillan, 1950), 11.

30 Maxine Lewis Oral History Interview, 1987; Maxine Lewis Flamingo Bookings, 1948–1951, Special Collections, Lied Library.

31 Lee Zhito, "Las Vegas Set to Spend Big on Top Names," *Billboard,* June 10, 1950, 3, 44, and 47.

32 Erskine Johnson, "When Stars Collect in Nevada These Days It Is No Gamble," *Fresno* (Calif.) *Bee,* April 10, 1953, 3B; Fluke Collection, Box 2; "TV Competish Cues Movie Relief Bill," *Billboard,* January 10, 1953, 3.

33 Gladwin Hill, "Klondike in the Desert," *New York Times,* January 7, 1953, SM14; James Bacon, "Las Vegas New Nightlife Capital," *Syracuse Herald-American,* August 30, 1953, 1; English, "Million-Dollar Talent War," 68.

34 Mort Cathro, "Las Vegas: Don't Mention Gambling around Here," *Oakland Tribune,* January 28, 1962, FL3.

35 Caskie Stinnett, "Las Vegas: Where Anything Is Forgivable Except Restraint," *Holiday,* May 1967, 35.

36 Dick Pearce, "Pleasure Palaces," *Harper's,* February 1955, 81.

37 John Gunther, "Inside Las Vegas," *Washington Post and Times Herald,* August 19, 1956, AW18.

38 Elliot Paul, *The Black and the Red* (New York: Random House, 1956), 275. See also Steve Fisher, *No House Limit* (New York: E. P. Dutton, 1958), 109.

39 *Wide, Wide World*, NBC, December 4, 1955, script, 60–64 and 64a, Box 51, Folder 8, Sands Collection, Special Collections, Lied Library.

40 Larry Gragg, "'Never Accorded the Recognition He Deserved': Al Freeman, Sands Hotel Publicist, 1952–1972," *Nevada Historical Society Quarterly* 51 (Summer 2008): 37–39.

41 Ibid., 32.

42 Television History—The First 75 Years, http://tvhistory.tv/facts-stats.htm (accessed May 24, 2011); Bob Thomas, "Hollywood Scene," *Fitchburg* (Mass.) *Sentinel*, September 20, 1957, 10; Bob Thomas, "Old TV Stars Find Vegas Good Pension," *Ada* (Okla.) *Evening News*, July 5, 1959, 9.

43 Lewis Oral History Interview.

44 Stan Irwin Oral History Interview, 2003, Special Collections, Lied Library.

45 Pierre Cossette, *Another Day in Showbiz* (Toronto: ECW Press, 2002), 47–49.

46 "Vegas Bounces Wally Cox," *Reno Evening Gazette*, July 16, 1955, 1; Bob Thomas, "Some Stars Fail in Las Vegas," *Austin* (Tex.) *Daily Herald*, February 7, 1956, 7; John Crosby, "One Can Always Write and Talk about Weather," *Oakland Tribune*, March 13, 1956, 18.

47 Roland L. Bessette, *Mario Lanza: Tenor in Exile* (Portland, Ore.: Amadeus Press, 1999), 159–167; Derek Mannering, *Mario Lanza: Singing to the Gods* (Jackson: University Press of Mississippi, 2005), 127–130; Armando Cesari, *Mario Lanza: An American Tragedy* (Fort Worth, Tex.: Baskerville, 2004), 190–196.

48 Casey Shawhan and James Bassett, "Costly Floor Shows Frost Las Vegas Gambling Cake," *Oakland Tribune*, July 21, 1953, D10; James Bacon, "Las Vegas Takes Over as Top Spot in U.S. Show Biz," *Panama City* (Fla.) *News-Herald*, August 16, 1953, 10.

49 Bob Thomas, "Las Vegas Talent War Skyrockets Salaries," *Newport* (R.I.) *Daily News*, December 30, 1954, 7; Vernon Scott, "Las Vegas' Richest Year Sees 3 Plush Gambling Palaces Fold," *Sun* (Yuma, Ariz.), January 17, 1956, 16.

50 "Ladies Man," *Time*, July 11, 1969, 54; "Big Stars Demand Big Money," *Iowa City-Press Citizen*, October 10, 1970, 3B; Murray Olderman, "Dolly Parton—Queen of Las Vegas Earners," *Indiana* (Pa.) *Evening Gazette*, February 20, 1980, 30; Annette John-Hall, "Celine Dion Wins Crowd, Loses Shoes," *Philadelphia Inquirer*, March 27, 2003, D2.

51 Mike Weatherford, *Cult Vegas: The Weirdest! The Wildest! The Swingin'est Town on Earth!* (Las Vegas: Huntington Press, 2001), 45–83; Erskine Johnson, "Closing 3 Las Vegas Casinos Wrecks Gravy Train for Stars," *Sun* (Yuma, Ariz.), February 9, 1956, 17; Richard Joseph, "Las Vegas Now Bigger and Brassier Than Ever," *Chicago Tribune*, January 31, 1965, F6.

52 Mike Doan, "Top Shows Finding Topless Competition," *Chronicle Telegram* (Elyria, Ohio), June 29, 1969, B10; Donn Knepp, *Las Vegas: The Entertainment Capital* (Menlo Park, Calif.: Land Publishing, 1987), 146–147.

53 Joseph, "Las Vegas Now Bigger and Brassier Than Ever," F6. See also Stinnett, "Las Vegas," *Holiday*, 37; Dick Schaap, "Las Vegas: The Greatest Show-off on Earth," *Holiday*, December 1968, 50.

54 Su Kim Chung, "Glamour, Glitz, and Girls: The Donn Arden Papers," *Journal*

of American and Comparative Cultures 25 (March 2002): 181–184; Peter Michel, "Showgirls," Digital Collections, October 2006, Special Collections, Lied Library.

55 Andres Martinez, *24/7: Living It Up and Doubling Down in the New Las Vegas* (New York: Dell, 1999), 101.

56 Richard Corliss, "That Old Feeling: The Show at the Casino," *Time,* November 19, 2003, http://www.time.com/time/arts/article/0,8599,546855,00.html (accessed September 12, 2011).

57 Peter Bart, "Celebrating the Celine Machine," *Daily Variety,* March 31, 2003, 3. See also Corliss, "That Old Feeling"; Dylan Callaghan, "Sin City Spectacular! Las Vegas Ups the Ante with Multimillion-Dollar Stage Extravaganzas," *Hollywood Reporter,* December 2, 2003, 27. *The Beatles Love, CRISS Angel Believe,* and *Viva ELVIS* are Cirque du Soleil shows that have opened since 2005.

58 Doan, "Top Shows Finding Topless Competition," B10.

59 Dick Kleiner, "Vegas Hotels Feature New Stage Show Trend," *Post* (Frederick, Md.), May 30, 1980, A7.

60 The best sources for the extraordinary richness of Las Vegas entertainment are the Fluke Collection at University of Nevada, Las Vegas, and Donn Knepp's *Las Vegas.*

61 Gary Dretzka, "The Magic of Las Vegas," *Chicago Tribune,* July 7, 1996, section 8, 1.

62 Seymour Korman, "Las Vegas Bets a Stack on Women Guests," *Chicago Tribune,* January 16, 1966, A1; Schaap, "Las Vegas," 53.

63 Charles Champlin, "Making the World Safe for Frivolity, Las Vegas," *Los Angeles Times West Magazine,* October 19, 1969, 75.

64 Tom Wolfe, "Las Vegas (What?) Las Vegas (Can't Hear You! Too Noisy) Las Vegas!!!," in *Literary Las Vegas: The Best Writing about America's Most Fabulous City,* ed. Mike Tronnes (New York: Holt, 1995), 18.

65 *Destiny Turns on the Radio,* prod. Gloria Zimmerman and dir. Jack Baran, 102 minutes (Rysher Entertainment, 1995).

66 Phil Gallo, "Dion Ends 'Day' in Vegas with $400 mil," *Daily Variety,* December 14, 2007, 4; Steve Friess and Lorraine Ali, "'She's Just Not Vegas,'" *Newsweek,* March 17, 2003, 62.

67 Bart, "Celebrating the Celine Machine," 3.

68 Gallo, "Dion Ends 'Day,'" 4.

69 The best biography of the pianist is Darden Asbury Pyron, *Liberace: An American Boy* (Chicago: University of Chicago Press, 2001). Unless otherwise indicated, the source for Liberace's life is this book.

70 Ibid., 261.

71 Blatz advertisement, *Life,* October 15, 1951, 59. The Pabst Brewing Company purchased Blatz in 1959.

72 "Kidding on the Keys," *Life,* December 7, 1953, 88.

73 Liberace, *An Autobiography* (New York: G. P. Putnam's Sons, 1973), 175.

74 Leslie Bennetts, "Liberace Out to 'Top Himself' at Music Hall Show," *New York Times,* April 13, 1984, C7.

75 Holly Miller, "All That Glitters," *Saturday Evening Post,* December 1978, 66.
76 Richard Corliss, "The Evangelist of Kitsch," *Time,* November 3, 1986, 96; William A. Henry III, "Show Business: A Synonym for Glorious Excess," *Time,* February 16, 1987, 82.
77 Lewis Funke, "The Theatre: Liberace," *New York Times,* April 22, 1957, 29.
78 Corliss, "Evangelist of Kitsch," 96.
79 Liberace, *Autobiography,* 181.
80 The best sources on Prima's life are Garry Boulard, *Louis Prima* (Urbana: University of Illinois Press, 2002); Tom Clavin, *That Old Black Magic: Louis Prima, Keely Smith, and the Golden Age of Las Vegas* (Chicago: Chicago Review Press, 2010); *Louis Prima: The Wildest,* prod. Joe Lauro and dir. Don McGlynn, 90 minutes (Blue Sea Productions, 1999); David Kamp, "They Made Vegas Swing," *Vanity Fair,* December 1999, 346–378.
81 Clavin, *Old Black Magic,* 80.
82 Quoted in ibid., 84.
83 Dorothy Kilgallen, "The Voice of Broadway," *Weirton* (W.V.) *Daily Times,* February 10, 1955, 6; Johnson, "Closing 3 Las Vegas Casinos Wrecks Gravy Train for Stars," 17; "Desert Inn Plans Entertainment Politics," *San Mateo* (Calif.) *Times,* August 12, 1960, 10; Russ Wilson, "Accident Brought Primas to the Top," *Oakland Tribune,* September 30, 1959, 52D; Kamp, "They Made Vegas Swing," 351.
84 Kamp, "They Made Vegas Swing," 373.
85 Ibid., 374.
86 Johnson, "Closing 3 Las Vegas Casinos Wrecks Gravy Train for Stars," 17.
87 Scott Shea quoted in Clavin, *Old Black Magic,* 85.
88 "Nightclubs: The Wages of Vulgarity," *Time,* September 7, 1959, 50.
89 Quoted in Boulard, *Louis Prima,* 111–112.
90 James Bacon, "Rock 'n' Roll Bandleader, Singing Wife Tops in Popularity," *Waterloo* (Iowa) *Sunday Courier,* May 22, 1960, 34.
91 "Nightclubs: The Wages of Vulgarity," 50.
92 Boulard, *Louis Prima,* 120.
93 Don Rickles with David Ritz, *Rickles' Book* (New York: Simon & Schuster, 2007), 83.
94 Ron Rosenbaum, "Do You Know Vegas?," *Esquire,* August 1982, 62.
95 Ibid., 68.
96 Ibid.
97 Ibid., 73.
98 Wayne Newton with Dick Maurice, *Once Before I Go* (New York: Avon Books, 1991), 25–26.
99 Burke Johnson, "Wayne Newton," *Arizona Days and Ways Magazine* in *Arizona Republic,* June 12, 1966, 5; Robert Windeler, "The Most Successful Performer in Vegas History? Not Frank, Not Elvis—It's Wayne Newton," *People Weekly,* April 30, 1979, 89; Henry Allen, "Wayne Newton?," *Washington Post,* January 13, 1980, M1; John Denier, "Wayne's World," August 25, 2002, E1.
100 Betsy Carter and Peter S. Greenberg, "King of the Strip," *Newsweek,* January 12, 1976, 63; Rosenbaum, "Do You Know Vegas?," 64.

101 Newton, *Once Before I Go*, 53.
102 Carter and Greenberg, "King of the Strip," 64; Windeler, "Most Successful Performer in Vegas History," 88; Allen, "Wayne Newton?," M1; Denier, "Wayne's World," E1; Howard Reich, "Newtonian Principles: King of Las Vegas, A Consummate Entertainer in Drury Lane Show," *Chicago Tribune*, March 1, 1996, Tempo section, 1; Bill Kohlhaase, "Moving Las Vegas: the Lounge Show," *Los Angeles Times*, February 9, 1998, F2.
103 Windeler, "Most Successful Performer in Vegas History," 89.
104 "Show Business: What Ever Happened to Baby Wayne?," *Time*, June 29, 1970, 55.
105 Allen, "Wayne Newton?," M1.
106 Robert Kerwin, "The Very Hot, Very Happy Wayne Newton," *Chicago Tribune*, August 20, 1978, G20.
107 Denier, "Wayne's World," E1.
108 Allen, "Wayne Newton?," M1.
109 Kerwin, "Very Hot, Very Happy," G20.
110 Windeler, "Most Successful Performer in Vegas History," 88.
111 Carter and Greenberg, "King of the Strip," 63.
112 Rosenbaum, "Do You Know Vegas?," 73.
113 Kerwin, "Very Hot, Very Happy," G20; Windeler, "Most Successful Performer in Vegas History," 89; Mark Biakczak, "Wayne Newton Proud of Musical Legacy," *Syracuse Post-Standard*, November 19, 1999, 18.
114 Kerwin, "Very Hot, Very Happy," G20.
115 *Vegas Vacation*, prod. Jerry Weintraub and dir. Stephen Kessler, 93 minutes (Warner Bros., 1997).
116 "Wayne Newton Gets First TV Special Next Season," *Arizona Republic*, May 28, 1967, M7; Kerwin, "Very Hot, Very Happy," G20; Windeler, "Most Successful Performer in Vegas History," 87–88; Peter B. King, "Wayne Newton," *Hutchinson* (Kans.) *News*, May 1, 1985, 18; Alan Montgomery, "Wayne Newton Closes Out Grandstand Attractions," *Hutchinson* (Kans.) *News*, September 16, 1990, 8; Nancy Spiller, "What *Is* It about Wayne?," *USA Weekend* in *Salina* (Kans.) *Journal*, February 14–16, 1992, 6; Wayne Newton, Entertainer, The Gaming Hall of Fame, Center for Gaming Research, University of Nevada, Las Vegas, http://gaming.unlv.edu/hof/2000_newton.html (accessed June 6, 2011).
117 Spiller, "What *Is* It about Wayne?," 6.
118 Carol Cling, "Newton Reminds Audience of Golden Age in Las Vegas," *Las Vegas Review-Journal*, March 17, 2000, 4J; Reich, "Newtonian Principles," 1.
119 Rick Kogan, "Wayne Newton Brings Las Vegas Along," *Chicago Tribune*, January 25, 1989, 16.
120 Reich, "Newtonian Principles," 1.
121 Les Devor, "Vegas Vagaries," *Las Vegas Review-Journal*, April 24, 1956, 5.
122 The best biographies of Presley are by Peter Guralnick, *Last Train to Memphis: The Rise of Elvis Presley* (Boston: Little, Brown, 1994); Charles L. Ponce De Leon, *The Life of Elvis Presley: Fortunate Son* (New York: Hill and Wang, 2007).
123 "Music: Teeners' Hero," *Time*, May 14, 1956, 55.

124 Devor, "Vegas Vagaries," *Las Vegas Review-Journal*, April 25, 1956, 5; "Show Review: New Frontier," *Las Vegas Sun*, April 28, 1956, 6.

125 Guralnick, *Last Train to Memphis*, 271.

126 Thelma Coblentz Oral History, 1980, Special Collections, Lied Library.

127 "Show Review," 6.

128 Devor, "Vegas Vagaries," *Las Vegas Review-Journal*, April 25, 1956, 5.

129 Ralph Pearl, "Vegas Daze and Nights," *Las Vegas Sun*, May 1, 1956, quoted on Elvis Presley Museum site, http://www.elvispresleymuseum.com/1956_New_Frontier _Hotel.html. (accessed June 14, 2011).

130 Quoted in Guralnick, *Last Train to Memphis*, 273.

131 "Man, Dig That Presley," *Chicago Daily Tribune*, June 17, 1956, G39.

132 "Music: Teeners' Hero," 55.

133 Both quoted in Guralnick, *Last Train to Memphis*, 274.

134 "Elvis Presley Headlines at New Frontier," *Los Angeles Times*, April 24, 1956, 20.

135 Pete Martin, "I Call on Bing Crosby," *Saturday Evening Post*, May 11, 1957, 119.

136 Quoted in Guralnick, *Last Train to Memphis*, 274.

137 YouTube video of Liberace clowning around with Elvis in Las Vegas in 1956 (accessed June 15, 2011).

138 Ponce De Leon, *Life of Elvis Presley*, 75; Guralnick, *Last Train to Memphis*, 272–273; "Music: Teeners' Hero," 55.

139 Quoted in Guralnick, *Last Train to Memphis*, 274.

140 Peter Guralnick, *Careless Love: The Unmaking of Elvis Presley* (Boston: Little, Brown, 1999), 76–77, 80, 115–116, 119, 129, 137–138, and 166–168.

141 "Viva Las Vegas," *Variety*, December 31, 1963, http://www.variety.com/review VE1117796144?refcatid=31 (accessed June 15, 2011); "Cinema: The Way-Out West," *Time*, May 29, 1964, 94; Howard Thompson, "Elvis Presley Teams with Ann-Margret," *New York Times*, May 21, 1964, 42.

142 "Elvis and Ann-Margret Are a Smash Combo in 'Viva Las Vegas,'" *Deming* (Ariz.) *Headlight*, May 28, 1964, 7.

143 "Cinema: The Way-Out-West," 94; Thompson, "Elvis Presley Teams with Ann-Margret," 42.

144 "Viva Las Vegas," *Variety*, December 31, 1963.

145 Margaret Harford, "Presley, Ann-Margret Sing, Dance in 'Vegas,'" *Los Angeles Times*, July 3, 1964, D6; Thompson, "Elvis Presley Teams with Ann-Margret," 42.

146 Richard Goldstein, "A White Boy with Black Hips," *New York Times*, August 10, 1969, D11.

147 Ponce De Leon, *Life of Elvis Presley*, 162–163.

148 Goldstein, "White Boy with Black Hips," D22.

149 Ponce De Leon, *Life of Elvis Presley*, 171.

150 "Rock 'n' Roll: Return of the Big Beat," *Time*, August 15, 1969, 65; Goldstein, "White Boy with Black Hips," D22.

151 Ralph Pearl, "Vegas Daze and Nites," *Las Vegas Sun*, August 2, 1969, 15.

152 "Rock 'n' Roll: Return of the Big Beat," 65; Goldstein, "White Boy with Black

Hips," D22. There were many similar reviews. For example, see Eliot Tiegel, "Elvis Retains Touch in Return to Stage," *Billboard*, August 16, 1969, 47.

153 Robert Hilburn, "Third Vegas Stint for Elvis Presley," *Los Angeles Times*, August 12, 1970, H13; Hilburn, "Fan to Fan: What's Happened to Elvis," *Los Angeles Times*, February 6, 1972, Y44.

154 Mary Manning, "Elvis Has Yet to Leave the Building," *Las Vegas Sun*, February 14, 2010, http://www.lasvegassun.com/news/2008/may/15/elvis-has-yet-leave-building/ (accessed June 22, 2011).

155 See Guralnick, *Careless Love*, 63. See also Ponce De Leon, *Life of Elvis Presley*, 123.

156 "Idols Team Up on TV," *Life*, May 16, 1960, 103; "Television: One of the Worst," *Time*, May 23, 1960, 63; Murray Schumach, "Money No Object in Sinatra Show," *New York Times*, May 13, 1960, 63.

157 "Elvis Returns Sinatra Blast on Rock-Roll," *Daily Review* (Hayward, Calif.), October 31, 1957, 28.

158 Quoted in Guralnick, *Careless Love*, 62.

159 Tom Allen, "Inside Sinatra's Clan," *Chicago Daily Tribune*, October 16, 1960, B16.

160 Albert Auster, "Frank Sinatra: The Television Years—1950–1960," *Journal of Popular Film and Television* 26 (Winter 1999): 166–174.

161 Sands advertisement, *Las Vegas Sun*, January 19, 1960, 5.

162 Ralph Pearl, "Vegas Daze and Nites," *Las Vegas Sun*, January 22, 1960, 4.

163 Ibid.

164 Ralph Pearl, *Las Vegas Is My Beat* (Toronto: Bantam Books, 1974), 59 and 61.

165 Interview with Carl Barshchdorf by author, May 10, 2007; Weatherford, *Cult Vegas*, 20.

166 Hedda Hopper, "Film Companies Rock Desert City," *Los Angeles Times*, February 8, 1960, C10.

167 Cecil Smith, "Nothing Serene at Summit Meeting," *Los Angeles Times*, January 25, 1960, A8.

168 There is a short clip shot by a tourist of Kennedy at the filming of *Ocean's Eleven* available on YouTube (accessed July 11, 2011).

169 "Demo Hopeful Kennedy in Brief Vegas Visit," *Las Vegas Sun*, January 30, 1960, 1.

170 Allen, "Inside Sinatra's Clan," B16.

171 Forest Duke, "The Visiting Fireman," *Las Vegas Review-Journal*, August 4, 1960, 3; Ralph Pearl, "Vegas Daze and Nites," *Las Vegas Sun*, August 5, 1960, 4; Philip K. Scheuer, "Sinatra Premieres 'Ocean's Eleven,'" *Los Angeles Times*, August 5, 1960, A7; Monique Van Dooren, "Actress Prefers 'Quiet' New York to Vegas," *Daily Reporter* (Dover, Ohio), August 24, 1960, 11.

172 Bosley Crowther, "The Screen: 'Ocean's 11,'" *New York Times*, August 11, 1960, 19.

173 John L. Scott, "The Clan Cuts Up at Sands Outing," *Los Angeles Times*, April 16, 1966, 20.

174 There are many biographies of Sinatra. Two of the best are Arnold Shaw, *Sinatra: Twentieth-Century Romantic* (New York: Pocket Books, 1969), and, particularly

for his early years, James Kaplan, *Frank: The Voice* (New York: Doubleday, 2010). His daughter, Nancy Sinatra, published a useful book that provides a detailed time line of her father's life: *Frank Sinatra: An American Legend* (Pleasantville, N.Y.: General Publishing Group, 1998). My biographical sketch, unless otherwise indicated, is largely drawn from these sources.

175 Louis Calta, "News of Night Clubs," *New York Times*, October 10, 1943, X5; "Radio: That Old Sweet Song," *Time*, July 5, 1943, 76.

176 Shaw, *Sinatra*, 124.

177 Quoted in ibid., 134.

178 Quoted in Kaplan, *Frank*, 437.

179 Ibid., 378.

180 Sinatra biographer Anthony Summers contends Paul "Skinny" D'Amato intervened for the singer, calling Moe Dalitz, the Cleveland mobster who financed and ran the Desert Inn, to secure the booking. See Summers, *Sinatra: The Life* (New York: Knopf, 2005), 177. The quote is in Weatherford, *Cult Vegas*, 11.

181 Jack Cortez, "Curtain," *Fabulous Las Vegas Magazine*, July 26, 1952, 18.

182 Kaplan, *Frank*, 656.

183 Richard Gehman, *Sinatra and the Rat Pack* (New York: Belmont Productions, 1961), 9 and 10.

184 Charles Champlin, " . . . and a Very Good Sinatra," *Los Angeles Times*, January 11, 1966, C10.

185 "Cinema: The Kid from Hoboken," *Time*, August 29, 1955, 52.

186 Ibid., 59.

187 Gay Talese, "Frank Sinatra Has a Cold," *Esquire*, April 1966, http://www.esquire .com/features/ESQ1003-OCT_SINATRA_rev_ (accessed May 15, 2011).

188 "Sinatra Denies Luciano Friendship," *Oakland Tribune*, February 23, 1947, 1; "Cuba: Hoodlum on the Wing," *Time*, March 3, 1947, 36.

189 "Nevada Ties Sinatra to Chicago Hoodlum," *Chicago Tribune*, September 12, 1963, 1; Richard Oulahan and Thomas Thompson, "Frank Sinatra v. Nevada," *Life*, September 27, 1963, 93–95.

190 "Sinatra Subpoenaed in 'Skimming' Inquiry," *Los Angeles Times*, January 20, 1967, 1.

191 "Press: Ol' Black Eyes Doonesbury v. Sinatra," *Time*, June 24, 1985, 66.

192 "Crime: Mixing Business and Pleasure," *Time*, May 30, 1977, 16.

193 "Cinema: The Kid from Hoboken," 52.

194 Aline Mosby, "Crooner's Next Round May 27," *Tucson* (Ariz.) *Daily Citizen*, April 10, 1947, 1 and 4.

195 Peter Bart, "Sinatra Involved in Brawl in Bar," *New York Times*, June 11, 1966, 45.

196 Jerry Cohen, "Sinatra Bows Out at Sands the Hard Way—Gets Socked," *Los Angeles Times*, September 12, 1967, 1.

197 Quoted in Summers, *Sinatra*, 245.

198 Weatherford, *Cult Vegas*, 147.

199 Richard Lacayo, "Ring-a-Ding Ding," *Time*, May 25, 1998, 73.

200 Max Rudin, "Fly Me to the Moon: Reflections on the Rat Pack," *American Heritage* 49 (December 1998): 54.

201 *The Story of Las Vegas: An Overview,* prod. Gardner Monks and Lynn M. Zook, 51 minutes (2007).

7. "BEAUTIFUL WOMEN WERE AS COMMONPLACE IN LAS VEGAS AS POKER CHIPS": IMAGES OF LAS VEGAS WOMEN IN POPULAR CULTURE

The chapter's title is from Sharon Sala, *Lucky* (1955; reprint, New York: Avon Books, 2002), 5. The epigraphs are from "Wild Women of Las Vegas: Morals Take a Back Seat Amid Sizzling Desert Sin," *Pose,* April 1955, 16–17; "As Nevada Went, So Goes the Nation?," *Forbes,* September 1, 1973, 28; Mario Puzo, *Inside Las Vegas* (New York: Grosset & Dunlap, 1976), 176; Bob Sehlinger, *The Unofficial Guide to Las Vegas* (New York: Prentice Hall Travel, 1994), 244–245.

1 Wallace Turner, *Gamblers' Money: The New Force in American Life* (New York: New American Library, 1966), 21; Garson Kanin, *Where It's At* (New York: New American Library, 1969), 35; Wallace Turner, "Las Vegas: Trickery at Casinos Goes on Despite Close Scrutiny," *New York Times,* November 19, 1963, 34.

2 Stephanie James, *Gambler's Woman* (New York: Silhouette Books, 1984), 11.

3 "Wild, Woolly and Wide-Open," *Look,* August 14, 1940, 24; Richard English, "The Boom Came Back," *Collier's,* August 22, 1942, 48; Seymour Korman, "Nevada, Where the Sky Is the Limit and Gold Is Raked Off Tables," *Chicago Daily Tribune,* January 18, 1955, 6; Hank Kovell, "In Las Vegas, Gaming May be Down, but One Big Gamble Still Thrives—Matrimony," February 13, 1983, I3.

4 English, "The Boom Came Back," 37; "Wild, Woolly and Wide-Open," 24; Hubbard Keavy, "Gambling Is Key to Boom in Las Vegas, Says Writer after Visit to Nevada City," *Reno Evening Gazette,* June 12, 1941, 2.

5 "Railroad Station for Elopers," *New York Times,* March 11, 1940, 12.

6 Jim Marshall, "To Vegas, Darling," *Collier's,* October 25, 1941, 72.

7 *Flight to Nowhere,* prod. William B. David and dir. William Rowland, 79 minutes (Golden Gate Pictures, 1946).

8 Erskine Johnson, "Gay City of Gold," *Daily Kennebec* (Maine) *Journal,* June 11, 1946, 6; Marshall, "To 'Vegas,' Darling," 72.

9 Hy Gardner, "Las Vegas Marriages Lead Divorces 6 to 1," *Oakland Tribune,* October 1, 1952, 30; Katharine Best and Katharine Hillyer, *Las Vegas: Playtown U.S.A.* (New York: David McKay, 1955), 37; Kovell, "In Las Vegas, Gaming May be Down," I3.

10 Lola Ogunnaike, "Britney Spears, After a Dip into Marriage, Is Free for Whatever Future May Hold," *New York Times,* January 6, 2004, E3.

11 "Love, Las Vegas Style," *Love Chronicles,* prod. Susan Hoenig, 45 minutes (A&E Television Networks, 1999).

12 "New Rival for Reno," *New York Times,* August 29, 1911, 1.

13 "Reno Copes with Twin Evils, Divorce and Gambling," *New York Times,* January 8, 1911, SM4.

14 Mella Rothwell Harmon, "Getting Renovated: Reno Divorces in the 1930s," *Nevada Historical Society Quarterly* 42 (Spring 1999): 50; Paul Ralli, *Nevada Law-*

yer: A Story of Life and Love in Las Vegas (Culver City, Calif.: Murray & Gee, 1949), 6 and 27.

15 "Film Star's Wife, Lured by Sunshine, Sports, Scenic Wonders Seen as Pied Piper for Nation's Top-Flight Divorce Colony," *Las Vegas Review-Journal,* March 7, 1939, 5; Jamie Coughtry, ed., *John F. Cahlan: Fifty Years in Journalism and Community Development* (Reno: University of Nevada Oral History Program, 1987), 309–310.

16 "Divorce Awaited by Mrs. Gable," *Oakland Tribune,* January 23, 1939, 3; Gladys Rowley, "Reno Revue," *Nevada State Journal,* January 31, 1939, 3.

17 May Mann, "Going Hollywood," *Ogden* (Utah) *Standard-Examiner,* February 13, 1939, 3.

18 Ibid.

19 "Wild, Woolly and Wide-Open," 21.

20 Ibid.

21 Hubbard Keavy, "Gambling and Divorce Outdraw Boulder Dam at Las Vegas, Says Special News Writer," *Reno Evening Gazette,* June 11, 1941, 4; Johnson, "Gay City of Gold," 6.

22 Richard Prather, *Find This Woman* (1951; reprint, New York: E-reads, 2000), 102; Jane L. Sears, *Las Vegas Nurse* (New York: Avon Books, 1963), 56.

23 Paul Ralli, *Viva Vegas* (Hollywood: House-Warven, 1953), 100; Carolyn Thomas, *Cactus for a Shroud* (Philadelphia: J. B. Lippincott, 1957), 34; Sears, *Las Vegas Nurse,* 56; Ed Reid and Ovid Demaris, *The Green Felt Jungle* (Cutchogue, N.Y.: Buccaneer Books, 1963), 94

24 William Pearson, *The Muses of Ruin* (New York: McGraw-Hill, 1965), 42.

25 Keavy, "Gambling and Divorce Outdraw Boulder Dam," 4; "Reno Challenged," *Business Week,* July 14, 1945, 26; Seymour Korman, "Las Vegas: Desert Riviera," *Chicago Daily Tribune,* April 11, 1948, E7.

26 A. A. Fair, *Spill the Jackpot* (1941; reprint, New York: Dell, 1967), 56; Prather, *Find This Woman,* 28; Frank Gruber, *The Honest Dealer* (New York: Rinehart, 1947), 21; Octavus Roy Cohen, *A Bullet for My Love* (New York: Macmillan, 1950), 4; Thomas, *Cactus for a Shroud,* 12. Also, there is a character in the 1955 movie *Las Vegas Shakedown* awaiting a divorce.

27 Fair, *Spill the Jackpot,* 56.

28 Alice Denham, "The Deal," in *Great Tales of City Dwellers,* ed. Alex Austin (New York: Manvis, 1955), 76.

29 "Wild Women of Las Vegas," 16–17.

30 Roe Richmond, "Assignment at Las Vegas," *Mike Shayne Mystery Magazine,* October 1957, 99. Similarly, see "Dateline Las Vegas," a 1957 episode of the television series *Wire Service.*

31 Cohen, *Bullet for My Love,* 1; Jack Waer, *Murder in Las Vegas* (New York: Avon, 1955), 11; William R. Cox, "Las Vegas Trap," *The Hardboiled Lineup,* ed. Harry Widmer (New York: A Lion Book, 1956), 8; Al Fray, *The Dame's the Game* (New York: Popular Library,1960), 13.

32 "Sex Lures of Las Vegas," *Brief,* January 1955, 52–70.

33 "The Belles of Las Vegas," *Real Men,* December 1958, 26–29.

34 In the novel *Casino,* a woman named Teddy Knight did have a 40 percent share of the Silverado Hotel Casino. Marilyn Lynch, *Casino* (New York: Ace Books, 1979), 5.

35 Edward E. Baldwin is particularly helpful in discussing this. See his "Las Vegas in Popular Culture" (Ph.D. diss., University of Nevada, Las Vegas, 1997), 20, 41, 45–46, and 81.

36 Ovid Demaris, *Candyleg* (Greenwich, Conn.: Fawcett, 1961), 18.

37 Brad Curtis, *The Golden Greed* (New York: Tower, 1965), 9, 12, and 13.

38 Arthur Moore and Clayton Matthews, *Las Vegas* (New York: Pocket Books, 1974), 15.

39 Steve Fisher, *No House Limit* (New York: E. P. Dutton, 1958), 52–53.

40 Denham, "The Deal," 70–82.

41 M. Gottdiener, Claudia C. Collins, and David R. Dickens, *Las Vegas: The Social Production of an All-American City* (Malden, Mass.: Blackwell, 1999), 73

42 *Sir! A Magazine for Males,* quoted in Jack Sheehan, *Skin City: Uncovering the Las Vegas Sex Industry* (Las Vegas: Stephens Press, 2004), 23; Cox, "Las Vegas Trap," 10; Moore and Matthews, *Las Vegas,* 57.

43 Richard B. Taylor and Patricia Howell, *Las Vegas, City of Sin?* (San Antonio, Tex.: Naylor, 1963), 51.

44 Emily Elliot, *Midnight Memories* (New York: Dell, 1983), 29.

45 Norman Herries, *My Private Hangman* (New York: Ace Books, 1956), 65–66.

46 *Casino,* prod. Barbara De Fina and dir. Martin Scorsese, 178 minutes (Universal Pictures, 1995). When Frank Rosenthal, model for the character Ace Rothstein, met his wife, Geri McGee, on whom the character of Ginger was based, she was a chip hustler.

47 Monty Joynes, *Lost in Las Vegas* (Charlottesville, Va.: Hampton Roads, 1998), 113.

48 Quoted in Sheehan, *Skin City,* 23.

49 Harvey Hardy, "Las Vegas before Neon," *True West,* May–June 1970, 74.

50 Gordon Gassaway, "Southern Nevada Picturesque Paradise for the Wandersome," *Los Angeles Times,* February 24, 1918, VI2.

51 Michael Johnson, "Transforming the 'Old West' into 'Modern Splendor': The Suppression of Brothel Prostitution in Las Vegas," paper presented at the Biennial Conference on Nevada History, Las Vegas, May 24, 2006.

52 Eugene P. Moehring and Michael S. Green, *Las Vegas: A Centennial History* (Reno: University of Nevada Press, 2005), 104 and 118; Jamie Coughtry and R. T. King, eds., *George L. Ullom, Politics and Development in Las Vegas, 1930s–1970s* (Reno: University of Nevada Oral History Program, 1989), 48.

53 "Three Operators of Vegas Bawdy House Found Guilty of Transporting Prostitutes," *Nevada State Journal,* August 1, 1954, 7; Bob Considine, "The Inside Story of Las Vegas," *PIC,* July 1955, 70–71.

54 "New Nevada Law Bars Brothels in Las Vegas," *New York Times,* February 26, 1971, 30; Hank Greenspun, "Where I Stand," *Las Vegas Sun,* January 23, 1960, 2.

55 Reid and Demaris, *Green Felt Jungle,* 99 and 92.

56 George Reasons and Al Delugach, "Sheriff Lamb: The Lion of Las Vegas," *Los Angeles Times,* April 14, 1977, B3; "What Gambling Does For—And To—Las

Vegas," *U.S. News and World Report,* March 9, 1981, 66. In 1982, police arrested 13,000 prostitutes; Deke Castleman, *Las Vegas,* 8th ed. (New York: Compass American Guides, 2004), 188.

57 Carole Nelson Douglas, *Crystal Days* (New York: Bantam Books, 1990), 24.

58 Casey Shawhan and James Bassett, "Costly Floor Shows Frost Las Vegas Gambling Cake," *Oakland Tribune,* July 21, 1953, D10.

59 Reid and Demaris, *Green Felt Jungle,* 93–95; Taylor and Howell, *Las Vegas,* 52; Lynch, *Casino,* 158.

60 Puzo, *Inside Las Vegas,* 193.

61 Taylor and Howell, *Las Vegas,* 51.

62 *The Whole Las Vegas Catalog* (Las Vegas: Creel Printing, 1977), 56.

63 The first ad was in 1971. See Castleman, *Las Vegas,* 189.

64 Jerry Cohen, "Vegas Meets an Insatiable U.S. Demand," *Los Angeles Times,* April 17, 1977, 3; Alfred A. Alvarez, *The Biggest Game in Town* (Boston: Houghton Mifflin, 1983), 84–85; Marc Cooper, *The Last Honest Place in America* (New York: Nation Books, 2005), 70.

65 *Dateline,* NBC News, September 14, 2003.

66 Hank Kovell, *Poor Man's Guide to Las Vegas* (Glendale, Calif.: Economy Self-Publishing, 1981), 75–77.

67 Joyce Wiswell, *Fielding's Las Vegas Agenda* (Redondo Beach, Calif.: Fielding Worldwide, 1995), 155.

68 For example, see *Highway Dragnet,* prod. Jack Jungmeyer and dir. Nathan Juran, 70 minutes (William F. Broidy Productions, 1954); *The Grasshopper,* prod. Jerry Belson and Garry Marshall and dir. Jerry Paris, 98 minutes (National General Pictures, 1969); *Corvette Summer,* prod. Hal Barwood and dir. Matthew Robbins, 105 minutes (MGM, 1978); *Vegas Casino War,* prod. Michael Greenburg and dir. George Englund, 96 minutes (George Englund Productions, 1984); *Fever Pitch,* prod. Freddie Fields and dir. Richard Brooks, 96 minutes (MGM, 1985); *Stark,* prod. David H. Balkan and dir. Rod Holcomb, 94 minutes (CBS Entertainment Production, 1985); *Hard Vice,* prod. and dir. Joey Travolta, 86 minutes (A-Pix Entertainment, 1994). Several television series had prostitutes in some of their story lines: *Vega$,* prod. Philip D. Fehrle and Larry Forrester, 60 minutes (Aaron Spelling Productions, 1978–1981); *Crime Story,* prod. Stuart Cohen, Gail Morgan Hickman, and Michael Jaffe, 60 minutes (Michael Mann Productions, 1986–1988); *CSI: Crime Scene Investigation,* multiple producers (CBS Paramount Network Television, 2000–2012); *Las Vegas,* multiple producers (NBC Universal Television, 2003–2008).

69 W. T. Ballard, *The Seven Sisters* (New York: Pocket Books, 1962), 48 and 59.

70 Lynch, *Casino,* 1978, 35, and 112.

71 John H. Irsfeld, "Stop, Rewind, and Play," in *Radio Elvis and Other Stories* (Fort Worth, Tex.: TCU Press, 2002), 59 and 64–66.

72 John O'Brien, *Leaving Las Vegas* (1990; reprint, New York: Grove Press, 1995), 135, 144, 148, and 181.

73 Mike Weatherford, *Cult Vegas: The Weirdest! The Wildest! The Swingin'est Town on Earth* (Las Vegas: Huntington Press, 2001), 219.

74 "Jimmy Fidler in Hollywood," *Joplin* (Mo.) *Globe,* August 18, 1946, 11; "Strip 'Artist' Lili Just a Nuisance at Desert Resort," *Independent* (Long Beach, Calif.), October 16, 1952, 8.

75 These three examples of ads are from *Las Vegas Review-Journal,* September 27, 1953, 12.

76 Weatherford, *Cult Vegas,* 222.

77 Ralph Pearl, "Vegas Daze and Nites," *Las Vegas Sun,* August 3, 1958, 9.

78 Ibid., October 7, 1957, 4.

79 Quoted in Kelly DiNardo, *Gilded Lili: Lili St. Cyr and the Striptease Mystique* (New York: Backstage Books, 2007), 97–98.

80 Best and Hillyer, *Las Vegas,* 74.

81 Dunes Hotel ad, *Las Vegas Sun,* January 8, 1957, 5; Ralph Pearl, "Vegas Daze and Nites," *Las Vegas Sun,* July 11, 1958, 4; "Battle of Bare Bosoms Stirs Resort Hotel Producers," *Las Vegas Sun,* July 31, 1958, 1.

82 For a thorough discussion of the controversy, see Larry Gragg, "'A Big Step to Oblivion for Las Vegas?' The 'Battle of the Bare Bosoms,' 1957–1959," *Journal of Popular Culture* 43 (October 2010): 1004–1022.

83 "Big Week in Vegas," *Time,* August 17, 1959, 60. Herb Lyon, in the *Chicago Daily Tribune,* agreed, claiming that nudity had emerged as the top attraction of the Strip. See his "Fantastic Las Vegas," *Chicago Daily Tribune,* November 29, 1959, I9.

84 Quoted in Jefferson Graham, *Vegas—Live and in Person* (New York: Abbeville Press, 1989), 158.

85 Steve Brewer, *Bullets* (Denver: Speck Press, 2003), 2.

86 W. T. Ballard, *Three for the Money* (New York: Pocket Books, 1963), 14.

87 Sid Meyers, *The Great Las Vegas Fraud* (Chicago: Mayflower Press, 1958), 234–235.

88 Bob Considine, "Rich Nevada Oasis Must Be Seen to Be Believed, Newman Says," *Charleston* (W.V.) *Gazette,* January 23, 1955, 2; Puzo, *Inside Las Vegas,* 176.

89 Kurt Andersen, "Las Vegas, U.S.A.," *Time,* January 10, 1994, 45. See also Betsy Streisand, "Las Vegas Gamboling," *U.S. News and World Report,* January 31, 1994, 61–63.

90 Joel Stein, "The Strip is Back!," *Time,* July 26, 2004, 24.

91 Mary Herczog, *Las Vegas for Dummies,* 3rd ed. (Hoboken, N.J.: Wiley, 2005), 278–279.

92 William L. Fox, *In the Desert of Desire: Las Vegas and the Culture of Spectacle* (Reno: University of Nevada Press, 2005), 120.

93 Cooper, *Last Honest Place,* 72.

94 Sheehan, *Skin City,* 24.

95 *20/20 Downtown,* ABC News, April 24, 2002.

96 Ibid; NBC, *Today Show,* April 29, 2005.

97 Kimberly A. Neuendorf, Thomas D. Gore, Amy Dalessandro, Patricie Janstova, and Sharon Snyder-Suhy, "Shaken and Stirred: A Content Analysis of Women's Portrayals in James Bond Films," *Sex Roles* 62 (2010): 748.

98 Katherine Fishburn, *Women in Popular Culture: A Reference Guide* (Westport,

Conn.: Greenwood Press, 1982); Steven Heller, "Pulp Fiction," *Prints,* September/October 2003, 108–113; Geoffrey O'Brien, *Hardboiled America: Lurid Paperbacks and the Masters of Noir,* expanded ed. (New York: Da Capo, 1997); Julie M. Stankiewicz and Francine Rosselli, "Women as Sex Objects and Victims in Print Advertisements," *Sex Roles* 58 (2008): 579–589; Doug Stewart, "Guys and Molls," *Smithsonian Magazine,* August 2003, 54–59; Kathryn Weibel, *Mirror Mirror: Images of Women Reflected in Popular Culture* (Garden City, N.Y.: Anchor Books, 1977).

99 *20/20 Downtown,* ABC News, April 24, 2002.
100 "Love, Las Vegas Style."
101 "Belles of Las Vegas," 26–29. See also novels like Frank Kane, *A Short Bier* (New York: Dell, 1960), 58; Don Pendleton, *The Executioner: Vegas Vendetta* (1971; reprint, Los Angeles: Pinnacle Books, 1975), 55; Marne Davis Kellogg, *Birthday Party* (New York: Bantam Books, 2000), 79.
102 Lloyd Shearer, "Chorus Girls," *Parade Magazine* in *Independent-Press-Telegram* (Long Beach, Calif.), June 2, 1957, 27.
103 "Paris Come-on in Vegas," *Life,* June 6, 1960, 51–52, 54, and 57.
104 "The Audacious New Swimsuits," *Life,* January 8, 1965, 46–55 and 57.
105 Bob Thomas, "Bluebird Girls Have Captured Las Vegas and Vice Versa," *Indiana* (Pa.) *Evening Gazette,* July 11, 1958, 14; Hedda Hopper, "English Lovelies in Las Vegas," *Odessa* (Tex.) *American,* August 15, 1958, 15.
106 "Audacious New Swimsuits," 46–55 and 57.
107 Joynes, *Lost in Las Vegas,* 66.
108 Aline Mosby, "Las Vegas Has Eight Pawn Shops; 107 Cops Keep Peace," *San Mateo* (Calif.) *Times,* July 13, 1954, 10; Shearer, "Chorus Girls," 28; David Chandler, *Father O'Brien and His Girls* (New York: New American Library, 1964), 22.
109 Reid and Demaris, *Green Felt Jungle,* 93.
110 "Audacious New Swimsuits," 57.
111 "Showgirl Shangri-L.A.," *Life,* June 21, 1954, 47.
112 Larry McMurtry, *The Desert Rose* (New York: Simon & Schuster, 1983), 13.
113 David Spanier, *The Hand I Played: A Poker Memoir* (Reno: University of Nevada Press, 2001), 192.
114 Murray Olderman, "Girls Off-Duty Entrepreneurs," *Lima* (Ohio) *News,* January 31, 1971, C6; "Search Is On for Ultimate Showgirl," *Indiana* (Pa.) *Gazette,* March 31, 1983, 6.
115 Rick Bragg, "The Era of Showgirls Is Leaving Las Vegas," *New York Times,* March 22, 2001, A1. The *Folies Bergere* closed in 2008.
116 Linda Chase, *Picturing Las Vegas* (Layton, Utah: Gibbs Smith, 2009), 92–93.

8. "SO MUCH LUXURY IN THE MIDDLE OF THE DESERT": IMAGES OF LUXURY AND AMENITIES IN LAS VEGAS

The chapter's title is from *Breakfast with Dorothy and Dick,* August 31, 1955, Sands Collection, Box 60, Special Collections, Lied Library, University of Nevada, Las Vegas. The epigraphs are from Alex Small, "Nevada—Fabulous State,"

Chicago Daily Tribune, September 9, 1945, C2; Edward Churchill, "The Truth about Las Vegas," *Script,* March 1948, 10; John Gunther, "Inside Las Vegas," *Washington Post and Times Herald,* August 26, 1956, AW12; *New Yorker,* quoted in Ing, "Buzz of the Burg," *Idaho* (Pocatello) *State Journal,* August 30, 1966, 4; Gary Dretzka, "Anti-Vegas Bellagio, the Strip's Latest and Greatest, Puts Emphasis on Elegance and Romance," *Chicago Tribune,* November 22, 1998, Travel, 1.

1 *Breakfast with Dorothy and Dick,* August 31, 1955, Special Collections, Lied Library.

2 "The Meadows Formally Opens," *Las Vegas Review-Journal,* May 1, 1931, 1. There is a sketch of Cornero's life in Alan Balboni, "Tony Cornero," in *The First 100: Portraits of the Men and Women Who Shaped Las Vegas,* ed. A. D. Hopkins and K. J. Evans (Las Vegas: Huntington Press, 1999), 106–108.

3 "Meadows Razed Last Night by Big Conflagration," *Las Vegas Review-Journal,* February 9, 1943, 1; Basil Woon, *Incredible Land: A Jaunty Baedeker to Hollywood and the Great Southwest* (New York: Liveright, 1933), 267–268; "Clara Bow, Rex Sued for Gaming Debt," *Oakland Tribune,* December 3, 1931, 1.

4 "Hostelry Leases Made," *Los Angeles Times,* January 17, 1932, D3; "Las Vegas Seeking Share of Reno Divorce Business," January 24, 1932, 6; "Resort and Hotel Notes," April 3, 1932, E4; "Hotel Apache Opens Today," *Las Vegas Age,* March 19, 1932, 1 and 2. The structure is now known as Binion's Hotel and Casino.

5 Alan Hess, *Viva Las Vegas: After-Hours Architecture* (San Francisco: Chronicle Books, 1993), 21–22.

6 G. E. Richerson, "Many Interesting Things Seen on Week End Trip to North," *Casa Grande* (Ariz.) *Dispatch,* July 26, 1940, 2; "Las Vegas Ideal Trip," *Los Angeles Times,* December 20, 1935, A13; "Las Vegas, Nevada, 'Bright Spot,' Still Typical Frontier Town," *Los Angeles Times,* December 23, 1938, B6; Chapin Hall, "What Goes on?," *Los Angeles Times,* May 23, 1939, A; Chapin Hall, "What Goes On?," *Los Angeles Times,* May 24, 1939, A; "Las Vegas–Hoover Dam Area Rich in Tourist Interest," *Los Angeles Times,* December 15, 1939, B7; Hubbard Keavy, "Gaming and Divorce Outdraw Boulder Dam at Las Vegas Says Special News Writer," *Reno Evening Gazette,* June 11, 1941, 4.

7 Richard Lillard, *Desert Challenge: An Interpretation of Nevada* (New York: Knopf, 1942), 307.

8 Hess, *Viva Las Vegas,* 26; Eugene P. Moehring and Michael S. Green, *Las Vegas: A Centennial History* (Reno: University of Nevada Press, 2005), 111; Peter Lind Hayes and Mary Healy, *Moments to Remember with Peter and Mary: Our Life in Show Business from Vaudeville to Video* (New York: Vantage Press, 2004), 209.

9 David G. Schwartz, *Suburban Xanadu: The Casino Resort on the Las Vegas Strip and Beyond* (New York: Routledge, 2003), 34–36, Chris Nichols, *The Leisure Architecture of Wayne McAllister* (Layton, Utah: Gibbs Smith, 2007), 129.

10 "Pop" Squires, "The Bright Future," *Las Vegas Age,* February 21, 1941, 6.

11 For example, see "Judy Garland Married in Airplane Elopement Today," *Mansfield* (Ohio) *News Journal,* July 28, 1941, 1

12 *An Interview with William J. Moore* (Reno: University of Nevada Oral History Program, 1985), 2 and 5.

13 Hess, *Viva Las Vegas*, 31–32; Schwartz, *Suburban Xanadu*, 44–45; Eugene Moehring, *Resort City in the Sunbelt: Las Vegas, 1930–2000*, 2nd ed. (Reno: University of Nevada Press, 2000), 46.

14 *Interview with William Moore*, 11, 15, and 28.

15 Michael Green, "El Cortez Hotel-Casino," *ONE: Online Nevada Encyclopedia*, October 6, 2010; Hess, *Viva Las Vegas*, 34.

16 Wesley Stout, "Nevada's New Reno," *Saturday Evening Post*, October 31, 1942, 69; Nevada Biltmore Scrapbook and Clippings, Jewell Brooks Collection, Special Collections, Lied Library.

17 Hess, *Viva Las Vegas*, 42 and 59.

18 "Spirit of Old West Revived in Golden Nugget Gambling Hall," *Las Vegas Review-Journal*, August 29, 1946, 5.

19 "Las Vegas Gambles," *Life*, December 21, 1942, 94; "Gamblers' Luck," *Time*, April 9, 1945, 20; Richard English, "The Boom Came Back," *Colliers*, August 22, 1942, 36; Wesley Stout, "Nevada's New Reno," *Saturday Evening Post*, October 31, 1942, 12; Lillard, *Desert Challenge*, 352.

20 Stout, "Nevada's New Reno," 69.

21 Erskine Johnson, "Gay City of Gold," *Daily Kennebec* (Augusta, Maine) *Journal*, June 11, 1946, 6.

22 Small, "Nevada—Fabulous State," C2.

23 Frasher Foto Postcard Collection, Pomona Public Library, Pomona, California, http://content.ci.pomona.ca.us/index_frasher.php (accessed November 4, 2011); Hotel El Rancho Postcards, Center for Gaming Research, Lied Library, http://gaming.unlv.edu/ElRanchoVegas/postcards.html (accessed November 4, 2011).

24 Hess, *Viva Las Vegas*, 44. The casino briefly closed in February 1947 but reopened with the opening of the hotel portion of the property.

25 Ibid., 38.

26 Erskine Johnson, "Hollywood Chatter," *Statesville* (N.C.) *Daily Record*, January 1, 1947, 4.

27 Aline Mosby, "$5,000,000 Super-Colossal Saloon Opens in Las Vegas," *Los Angeles Daily News*, January 1, 1947; Bugsy Siegel FBI File, 62-2837-5.

28 "Daily Diary," *Los Angeles Herald Express*, January 6, 1947; Bugsy Siegel FBI File, 62-2837-570.

29 Erskine Johnson, "In Hollywood," *Evening Observer* (Dunkirk, N.Y.), March 15, 1947, 5.

30 Bob Considine, "Las Vegas a Paradox of Rotary and Roulette," *Washington Post*, April 13, 1947, B3.

31 Churchill, "Truth about Las Vegas," 10.

32 Frasher Foto Postcard Collection.

33 Octavus Roy Cohen, *A Bullet for My Love* (New York: Macmillan, 1950), 9.

34 *Vegas Nights*, prod. J. D. Kendis, 45 minutes (1948). See also the description of the Flamingo in the mystery novel by Carolyn Thomas, *The Cactus Shroud* (New York: J. B. Lippincott, 1957), 120.

35 Malcolm Epley, "Beach Combing," *Long Beach* (Calif.) *Press-Telegram*, April 14, 1952, section 2, 1; Dick Pearce, "Pleasure Palaces," *Harper's*, February 1955, 81.

36 Gunther, "Inside Las Vegas," AW12.

37 Casey Shawhan and James Bassett, "Lowdown on Vegas—It's Fairly Pure," *Oakland Tribune*, July 19, 1953, 27.

38 Louella O. Parsons, "Louella Parsons in Hollywood," *Daily Review* (Hayward, Calif.), April 8, 1957, 20.

39 Bosley Crowther, "Pictorial Quality," *New York Times*, August 14, 1960, X1.

40 "It's Worth Seeing: Las Vegas, Desert Town, Flowers into Resort City," *Oakland Tribune*, August 20, 1950, B8.

41 Julian Halevy, "Disneyland and Las Vegas," *Nation*, June 7, 1958, 511. See also Al Alvarez, *The Biggest Game in Town* (Boston: Houghton Mifflin, 1983), 11.

42 Hess, *Viva Las Vegas*, 40.

43 David G. Schwartz, *Roll the Bones: The History of Gambling* (New York: Gotham Books, 2006), 407.

44 Margot Hentoff, "Absolutely Free," *Harper's*, November 1969, 32.

45 Quoted in Jefferson Graham, *Vegas: Live and In Person* (New York: Abbeville Press, 1989), 53.

46 Gary E. Elliott, *The New Western Frontier: An Illustrated History of Greater Las Vegas* (Carlsbad, Calif.: Heritage Media, 1999), 133; George Stamos Jr., "The Great Resorts of Las Vegas, How They Began," *Las Vegas Sun Magazine*, October 14, 1979, 6.

47 "Silicon Valley's Campy Cabana Hotel to Receive Face-Lift," *Knight Ridder Tribune*, June 30, 1997; Hotel Cabana, http://www.paloaltohistory.com/hotelcabana .html (accessed February 21, 2009).

48 Quoted in Barbara Land and Myrick Land, *A Short History of Las Vegas* (Reno: University of Nevada Press, 1999), 159.

49 Hess, *Viva Las Vegas*, 84.

50 Stamos, "Great Resorts of Las Vegas," 8; A. D. Hopkins, "Jay Sarno," in Hopkins and Evans, *First 100*, 287; Olga Curtis, "Being a Goddess No Easy Life," *Burlington* (N.C.) *Daily Times-News*, August 30, 1966, 10A; Myram Borders, "$25 Million Las Vegas Caesars Palace Opens Casino with Lavish Roman Theme," *Nevada State Journal*, August 4, 1966, 14; Margaret Malamud and Donald T. McGuire Jr., "Living Like Romans in Las Vegas," in *Imperial Projections: Ancient Rome in Modern Popular Culture*, ed. Sandra R. Joshel, Margaret Malamud, and Donald T. McGuire Jr. (Baltimore: Johns Hopkins University Press, 2001), 256–257.

51 Quoted in Malamud and McGuire, "Living Like Romans," 262.

52 Peter Bart, "48-Hour Party Opens Newest Las Vegas Hotel," *New York Times*, August 8, 1966, 22; Florabel Muir, "Hollywood," *Cedar Rapids* (Iowa) *Gazette*, August 15, 1966, 14; "Lavish Party Opens Las Vegas Hotel," *Wisconsin State Journal*, August 8, 1966, 8.

53 Bart, "48-Hour Party," 22; Peter Bart, "Vexation Time in Vegas," *New York Times*, August 14, 1966, 101.

54 Ing, "Buzz of the Burg," 4.

55 Several of these productions are listed in "Special Events Held at Caesars Palace, 1966–2001," Promotional and Publicity Material: Caesars World Inc., Box

1, Special Collections, Lied Library. Films like *Flareup* (1969), *Hell's Angels '69* (1969), *The Gambler* (1974), *The Electric Horseman* (1979), *History of the World, Part I* (1981), *Oh God! You Devil* (1984), *You Ruined My Life* (1987), *Fools Rush In* (1997), and *Intolerable Cruelty* (2003); episodes of television programs like *Starsky and Hutch* (1976), *McMillan and Wife* (1976), *Charlie's Angels* (1977), *Knight Rider* (1983), *Return of the Man from U.N.C.L.E.* (1983), *Will and Grace* (1998), *Friends* (1999), *The Strip* (1999–2000), and *Caesars 24/7* (2005); television specials like those of Ed Sullivan (1968), Steve Lawrence and Eydie Gorme (1973), Alan King (1974), Merv Griffin (1980), Lily Tomlin (1981), and Celine Dion (2003); as well as a host of boxing and tennis matches and awards shows provided viewers frequent reminders of the elegance and spectacle of Caesars Palace.

56 *Where It's At,* prod. Frank Ross and dir. Garson Kanin, 106 minutes (Frank Ross Productions, 1966); *Rain Man,* prod. Mark Johnson and dir. Barry Levinson, 133 minutes (United Artists, 1988); *Pleasure Palace,* prod. Norman Rosemont and dir. Walter Grauman, 97 minutes (Marble Arch Productions, 1980).

57 *The Real Las Vegas,* prod. MPH Entertainment and dir. Jim Milio and Melissa Jo Peltier, 200 minutes (A&E Television Networks, 1996).

58 Graham, *Vegas: Live and In Person,* 50–55; Rick Browne and James Marshall, *Planet Vegas: A Portrait of Las Vegas by 20 of the World's Leading Photographers* (San Francisco: Collins, 1995), 146–147; Su Kim Chung, *Las Vegas Then and Now* (San Diego: Thunder Bay Press, 2002), 96–97; Carol M. Highsmith and Ted Landphair, *Las Vegas: A Photographic Tour* (New York: Crescent Books, 2003), 56–59; Michelle Ferrari with Stephen Ives, *Las Vegas: An Unconventional History* (New York: Bulfinch Press, 2005), 181–183; Giovanna Franci, *Dreaming of Italy: Las Vegas and the Virtual Grand Tour* (Reno: University of Nevada Press, 2005), 68–98.

59 K. J. Evans, "Kirk Kerkorian," in Hopkins and Evans, *First 100,* 241–244. See also Dial Torgerson, *Kerkorian: An American Success Story* (New York: Dial Press, 1974), 157–166.

60 See the articles in the Martin Stern Collection, Special Collections Web site, Lied Library, http://librarynevada.edu/speccol/martinstern.html (accessed October 12, 2011).

61 Schwartz, *Suburban Xanadu,* 152.

62 Steven B. Roberts, "Nevada Gets World's Biggest Resort Hotel," *New York Times,* July 4, 1969, 25.

63 "New Skyline for Vegas," *Nevada State Journal,* July 1, 1969, 7; "New Vegas Hotel State's Tallest," *Nevada State Journal,* August 24, 1969, 49; Perry Phillips, "Night Sounds," *Oakland Tribune,* July 4, 1969, 31.

64 "Las Vegas: The Game Is Illusion," *Time,* July 11, 1969, 32.

65 "Gambling on Las Vegas," *Newsweek,* December 17, 1973, 80.

66 Perry Phillips, "Night Sounds," *Oakland Tribune,* December 14, 1973, 31.

67 Alice Holman, "Here 'n There," *Daily Review* (Hayward, Calif.), November 30, 1973, 25.

68 John L. Smith, *Running Scared: The Life and Treacherous Times of Las Vegas*

Casino King Steve Wynn (1995; reprint, New York: Four Walls Eight Windows, 2001), 27–83; A. D. Hopkins, "Steve Wynn," in Hopkins and Evans, *First 100*, 350–351; William N. Thompson, "Steve Wynn: 'I Got the Message,'" in *The Maverick Spirit: Building the New Nevada*, ed. Richard O. Davies (Reno: University of Nevada Press, 1999), 199–203; Mark Seal, "Steve Wynn: King of Wow!," in *The Players: The Men Who Made Las Vegas*, ed. Jack Sheehan (Reno: University of Nevada Press, 1997), 174–177.

69 Smith, *Running Scared*, 87; Moehring and Green, *Las Vegas*, 207.

70 Moehring and Green, *Las Vegas*, 207.

71 Quote from Malamud and McGuire, "Living Like Romans," 263.

72 Quoted in Thompson, "Steve Wynn," 210.

73 Richard W. Stevenson, "Golden Nugget's Roll of the Dice," *New York Times*, November 16, 1989, D1; William Murray, "Las Vegas: Day for Night," October 21, 1990, SMA95; Robert Macy, "A Volcano in Front, Sharks at the Desk," *Cedar Rapids* (Iowa) *Gazette*, November 24, 1989, 6B; T. R. Reid, "In Roll of the Dice, Las Vegas Offers Family Fare," *Washington Post*, January 12, 1990, A3.

74 Quoted in Ronald Grover, "Tigers, a Volcano, Dolphins, and Steve Wynn," *Business Week*, November 20, 1989, 71.

75 Robert Parker, *Chance* (New York: Berkley Books, 1997), 91. See also Michael Connelly, *Trunk Music* (New York: St. Martin's Press, 1998), 87–88.

76 Moehring and Green, *Las Vegas*, 210.

77 Susan Spano, "Luxe Vegas: The Splashy New Bellagio Spent Megabucks to Lure Sophisticates to Sin City. Will It?," *Los Angeles Times*, October 25, 1998, L1.

78 Dretzka, "Anti-Vegas Bellagio," Travel, 1; *Upfront Tonight*, CNBC, October 20, 1998.

79 Spano, "Luxe Vegas," L1; Dretzka, "Anti-Vegas Bellagio," Travel, 1.

80 *Ocean's Eleven*, prod. Jerry Weintraub and dir. Steven Soderbergh, 116 minutes (Warner Bros., 2001).

81 David Segal, "With Loopy Bellagio, Vegas Raises the Stakes—And the Tab," *Washington Post*, May 2, 1999, E1.

82 Ibid.; Carol Higgins Clark, *Popped* (New York: Pocket Books, 2004), 179.

83 Lisa Snedeker, "Las Vegas Casinos Gamble on Art as a Crowd Pleaser," *Los Angeles Times*, June 10, 2001, B2; *Sunday Morning*, CBS News, September 19, 2004.

84 Joel Stein, "The Strip Is Back!," *Time*, July 26, 2004, 26; *20/20 Downtown*, ABC News, April 24, 2002.

85 Jeannine Stein, "All This and Shopping; No Longer Just Casinos, Smorgasbords and Sequins, Las Vegas Has Become a Shrine to Designer Boutiques and Themed Malls," *Los Angeles Times*, April 29, 1998, E2.

86 Andres Martinez, *24/7: Living It Up and Doubling Down in the New Las Vegas* (New York: Dell, 2000), 96.

87 Schwartz, *Roll the Bones*, 428–446 and 488–494.

88 Seal, "Steve Wynn," 178 and 173.

89 Inga Saffron, "Steve Wynn Uses Art in His Las Vegas Gamble Because a Hotel for High Rollers Is Serious Business," *Philadelphia Inquirer*, October 22, 1998, 1.

90 Tom Gorman, "Weekend Escape: At Wynn's Namesake, He's on a Par with Him-

self," *Los Angeles Times,* July 10, 2005, L4; *Today,* NBC News, April 29, 2005; "Check In/Check Out: Las Vegas: Wynn Las Vegas," *New York Times,* July 17, 2005, D4; Joel Stein, "Wynn's Big Bet," *Time,* May 2, 2005, 43–46; Nina Munk, "Steve Wynn's Biggest Gamble," *Vanity Fair,* June 2005, 170–172 and 211–215.

91 Steve Sloan, "Wynn Plunks Down $2.7 Billion on Vegas Strip," *USA Today,* April 22, 2005, D1.

92 Munk, "Steve Wynn's Biggest Gamble," 215; *Today,* NBC News, April 29, 2005.

93 Elizabeth Weiss, "There's Something about Wynn," *Travel Agent,* March 6, 2006, 12.

94 Diane Davidson, *Deadly Gamble* (Huntington Station, N.Y.: Rising Tide Press, 1997), 18–19; Angela Winters, *High Stakes* (Washington, D.C.: BET Publications, 2004), 15.

95 Brian Hodge, *Wild Horses* (New York: Morrow, 1999), 5.

96 William Bernhardt, *Dark Eye* (New York: Ballantine Books, 2005), 40; Gary Phillips, *Shooter's Point* (New York: Kensington, 2002), 175–176.

97 Su Kim Chung, "Menus: The Art of Dining," Digital Collections, Special Collections, Lied Library, http://digital.library.unlv.edu/collections/menus (accessed January 5, 2012).

98 The consensus is that Herb McDonald, the hotel's publicity and entertainment director, through serendipity, developed the chuck wagon. Hungry late one night, he brought cold cuts, cheese, and bread from the kitchen and made a sandwich at the bar. Casino guests saw him and asked if they could get a quick snack. Thus was born the late-night buffet.

99 David G. Schwartz, "Fifty Years of Dining on the Las Vegas Strip," Center for Gaming Research, Lied Library, http://gaming.unlv.edu/dining/early.html (accessed January 5, 2012).

100 Chung, "Menus"; Roland L. Hill, *In Las Vegas I Recommend* (Long Beach, Calif.: Hillsway, 1950), 31.

101 Katharine Best and Katharine Hillyer, *Las Vegas: Playtown U.S.A.* (New York: David McKay, 1955), 112–113.

102 William Pearson, *Muses of Ruin* (New York: McGraw-Hill, 1965), 114.

103 S. Irene Virbila, "Las Vegas: Betting on Good Taste," *Los Angeles Times Magazine,* September 13, 1998, 26.

104 George Stamos Jr., "The Great Resorts of Las Vegas: How They Began," *Las Vegas Sun Magazine,* August 26, 1979, 8, and July 15, 1979, 8–9.

105 Schwartz, "Fifty Years"; Chung, "Menus"; "Vegas Diner Has Wide Choice," *Van Nuys* (Calif.) *News,* June 25, 1971, Dining, 1 and 5.

106 Kay Loring, "Roman Orgy—Las Vegas Style," *Chicago Tribune,* October 19, 1969, n.p.; Stanton Delaplane, "Postcard from Las Vegas," *San Francisco Chronicle,* August 9, 1969, n.p.; "It's the Way It's Poured that Counts," *Hospitality,* July 1968, n.p.; Franco Borghese, "Dining Out in America," *Signature: The Diners Club Magazine,* November 1967, n.p., all in Nat Hart Scrapbook, Nat Hart Collection, Special Collections, Lied Library.

107 Rena Bulkin, *Frommer's '96: Las Vegas* (New York: Macmillan, 1996), 113.

108 Phil Vettel, "A Taste of Las Vegas: Great Food Is No Longer a Gamble, but Bring Lots of Money to the Table," *Chicago Tribune,* February 7, 1999, Travel Section, 1.

109 Ibid.

110 *Marketplace Morning Report,* Minnesota Public Radio, December 12, 2000.

111 Dretzka, "Anti-Vegas Bellagio," Travel Section, 1; Stein, "The Strip Is Back!," 26.

112 Christina Tree and William A. Davis, "From Gambling to Galleries in Vegas," *Boston Globe,* November 30, 2005, C7.

9. "AN AWFUL PLACE": THE NEGATIVE IMAGES OF LAS VEGAS

The title and the first epigraph are from Edwin Corle, "Apache Bar," *Mojave: A Book of Stories* (New York: Liveright, 1934), 223–224. The other epigraphs are from Sid Meyers, *The Great Las Vegas Fraud* (Chicago: Mayflower Press, 1958), 19; "Las Vegas: The Game Is Illusion," *Time* July 11, 1969, 32; Jane Fonda quoted by Lee Grant, "'The Electric Horseman'—A Big Deal in Las Vegas," *Los Angeles Times,* December 24, 1978, M1; *Lost in America,* prod. Marty Katz and dir. Albert Brooks, 92 minutes (Geffen, 1985); Michael Connelly, *Trunk Music* (New York: St. Martin's Press, 1998), 87.

1 "The Fever," *The Twilight Zone,* prod. Buck Houghton and dir. Robert Florey, 25 minutes (Cayuga Productions, 1960).

2 Rod Serling, *Stories from the Twilight Zone* (New York: Bantam Books, 1960), 89–90.

3 Evidently Serling's inspiration for this story, which he wrote, was his own experience in Las Vegas losing at a slot machine. See Gordon F. Sander, *Serling: The Rise and Twilight of Television's Last Angry Man* (New York: E. P. Dutton, 1992), 147.

4 A typical example is an article by Bruce Bliven, "The American Dnieperstory," *New Republic,* December 11, 1935, 127.

5 Commission on Behavioral and Social Sciences and Education, *Pathological Gambling: A Critical Review* (Washington, D.C.: National Academies Press, 1999), 107–155; Marc N. Potenza, Thomas R. Kosten, and Bruce J. Rounsaville, "Pathological Gambling," *Journal of the American Medical Association* 286 (July 11, 2001): 141–144; Stephanie Stucki and Margret Rihs-Middel, "Prevalence of Adult Problem and Pathological Gambling between 2000 and 2005: An Update," *Journal of Gambling Studies* 23 (2007): 245–257.

6 "Profile of a Gambler: Beginner's Luck Fuels an Impulsiveness that Ignores Wins, Losses," *Los Angeles Times,* December 24, 1984, C9; "More Women Are Gambling," *New York Times,* June 10, 1985, C20; "Link to Gambling?," *Los Angeles Times,* December 8, 1985, NJ31.

7 The following is just a sample of the many stories published about how destructive compulsive gambling can be: Ronald Grover, Andrew Osterland, and Paula Dwyer, "Sure There's a Price, but It Pays to Play," *Business Week,* June 21, 1999, 76; Joseph Epstein, "You Bet Your Life," *Chicago Tribune,* October 8, 1972, H24; Alexandra Marks, "More Problem Gamblers Seek Help," *Christian Science Monitor,* July 23, 1996, 14; "Nevadans Biggest Gamblers, Study Finds," *Los Angeles Times,* July 22, 1976, A25; Ellen Mitchell, "Upsurge in Gambling Arouses Concern," *New York Times,* April 10, 1983, LI1; Gary Logan, "Overcoming the Gambling Compulsion," *Washington Post,* January 24, 1986, D5.

8 Kenneth L. Dixon, "Assignment America," *Port Arthur* (Tex.) *News,* June 13, 1946, 7.

9 *Las Vegas Shakedown,* prod. William F. Broidy and dir. Sidney Salkow, 79 minutes (William F. Broidy Pictures, 1955); *Las Vegas Story,* prod. Robert Sparks and dir. Robert Stevenson, 88 minutes (RKO Radio Pictures, 1952); *Painting the Clouds with Sunshine,* prod. William Jacobs and dir. David Butler, 87 minutes (Warner Bros., 1951).

10 *The Lady Gambles,* prod. Michael Kraike and dir. Michael Gordon, 99 minutes (Universal International Pictures, 1949); "Diced Steele," *Remington Steele,* prod. Kevin Inch and dir. Don Weis, 60 minutes (MTM Enterprises, 1985); *Lost in America: Vegas Vacation,* prod. Jerry Weintraub and dir. Stephen Kessler, 93 minutes (Warner Bros., 1997).

11 *Compulsive Gambling in Kentucky,* Research Report 316 (Frankfort, Ky.: Legislative Research Commission, 2003): 18.

12 A. A. Fair, *Spill the Jackpot* (New York: Dell, 1967), 53 and 54.

13 *The Invisible Wall,* prod. Sol M. Wurtzel and dir. Eugene Forde, 72 minutes (Sol M. Wurtzel Productions, 1947).

14 *Las Vegas Shakedown.*

15 *Lady Gambles.*

16 *Heat,* prod. Cassian Elwes, George Pappas, and Keith Rotman and dir. Dick Richards, 92 minutes (Escalante, 1986).

17 Tess Hudson, *Double Down* (Ontario: MIRA Books, 2005), 20.

18 Aben Kandel, *The Strip* (New York: New American Library, 1961), 53.

19 William Pearson, *The Muses of Ruin: A Novel about Las Vegas* (New York: McGraw-Hill, 1965), 8.

20 *Las Vegas Story;* Hudson, *Double Down,* 22.

21 Kandel, *Strip,* 20.

22 "Decks and Violence," *Las Vegas,* prod. Daniel Arkin and D. Howard Grigsby and dir. Guy Norman Bee, 60 minutes (Gary Scott Thompson Productions, 2003); *Lost in America;* Kandel, *Strip,* 103.

23 *Fever Pitch,* prod. Freddie Fields and dir. Richard Brooks, 95 minutes (MGM, 1986).

24 *Owning Mahowny,* prod. Alessandro Camon and dir. Richard Kwietniowsky, 104 minutes (Alliance Atlantis Communications, 2003).

25 Kandel, *Strip,* 35.

26 *The Gambler,* prod. Robert Chartoff and Irwin Winkler and dir. Karel Reisz, 111 minutes (Paramount Pictures, 1974).

27 *Owning Mahowny;* Clifford Knight, *The Yellow Cat* (New York: E. P. Dutton, 1950), 55.

28 Ironically, Joe Grady, after selling his car for $200, goes on an amazing winning streak. Frank Gilroy, *The Only Game in Town* (New York: Random House, 1968), 29, 32–33, and 90–92.

29 *Compulsive Gambling in Kentucky,* 18.

30 John D. McDonald, *The Only Girl in the Game* (Greenwich, Conn.: Fawcett, 1960), 103.

31 Robert B. Parker, *Chance* (New York: Berkley Books, 1997), 122.

32 Pearson, *Muses of Ruin,* 130. On gamblers wanting to lose, see *CBC News Online* (November 18, 2003), http://www.cbc.ca/news/background/gambling/addiction .html (accessed November 21, 2010). Whatever the cause of their behavior, surprisingly, the end is not always a sad one for the compulsive gambler in film and fiction. In some cases, suicides are averted, estranged spouses reunite, and gamblers renounce their gaming. These benign conclusions prompted Jeffrey W. Dement to criticize most Hollywood depictions of compulsive gambling as irresponsible for their unrealistic ends. Dement, *Going for Broke: The Depiction of Compulsive Gambling in Film* (Lanham, Md.: Scarecrow Press, 1999).

33 *Lady Gambles.*

34 *Losing Ground,* prod. and dir. Bryan Wizemann, 90 minutes (Ballast Films, 2005).

35 Katharine Best and Katharine Hillyer, *Las Vegas: Playtown U.S.A.* (New York: David McKay, 1955), 25; Jerry Klein, "Las Vegas: A Desert Disneyland for Adults," *Journal Star* (Peoria, Ill.), March 4, 1979, D1–D2; Stephanie James, *Gambler's Woman* (New York: Silhouette Books, 1984), 11–12. These are just three of the many examples of the numerous accounts of little old ladies who have become compulsive gamblers.

36 McDonald, *The Only Girl in the Game,* 52–53.

37 Lloyd Biggle Jr., *A Hazard of Losers* (Tulsa, Okla.: Council Oaks Books, 1991), 23.

38 Ian Fleming, *Diamonds Are Forever* (1956; reprint, New York: Penguin Books, 2003), 122, 136, and 137.

39 *The Real Las Vegas,* prod. MPH Entertainment and dir. Jim Milio and Melissa Jo Peltier, 200 minutes (A&E Television Networks, 1996).

40 *Las Vegas: An Unconventional History,* prod. Amanda Pollak and dir. Stephen Ives, 180 minutes (Paramount Home Entertainment, 2005).

41 *Dreamland,* prod. Greg Little and dir. Lisanne Skyler, 71 minutes (Caldera Productions, 2000).

42 *Machine Gun McCain,* prod. Bino Cicogna and Marco Vicario and dir. Giuliano Montaldo, 96 minutes (Euro International Film, 1969); *Rafferty and the Gold Dust Twins,* prod. Michael Gruskoff and Art Linson and dir. Dick Richards, 91 minutes (Gruskoff-Venture-Linson, 1975). Two typical novels dealing with such types of characters are Richard Foster, *Blonde and Beautiful* (Toronto: Popular Library, 1955), 5; Sue Grafton, *A Is for Alibi* (1982; reprint, New York: St. Martin's Paperbacks, 2005), 126.

43 Steve Fisher, *No House Limit* (New York: E. P. Dutton, 1958), 42.

44 Edward Allen, *Mustang Sally* (New York: Norton, 1992), 71.

45 Parker, *Chance,* 98. See also Dan Barton, *Heckler* (New York: Thomas Dunne Books, 2001), 21.

46 Gerald Petievich, *Shakedown* (New York: Simon & Schuster, 1988), 60.

47 Parker, *Chance,* 287.

48 *This Is My Life,* prod. Lynda Obst and dir. Nora Ephron, 105 minutes (Twentieth Century-Fox, 1992).

49 Dick Pearce, "Pleasure Palaces," *Harper's,* February 1955, 80.

50 Norma Lee Browning, "The Two Faces of Vegas," *Chicago Daily Tribune,* October 7, 1962, C50; Ari Goldman, "Southern Baptists Meeting at Las Vegas after Revivals on Strip," *New York Times,* June 13, 1989, A16.

51 James J. Kirkpatrick, "Vegas Booms as Never Before," *Syracuse Herald-Journal,* November 16, 1976, 15.

52 "'Burger Remark' Infuriates Nevada," *San Francisco Chronicle,* February 11, 1983, 22. Burger ultimately relented and not only attended, but also spoke. See "Burger to Las Vegas," *Pittsburgh Post-Gazette,* February 10, 1984, 19.

53 *Las Vegas Shakedown.* A character in the 1955 film *Girl Rush* similarly calls Las Vegas a "depraved" place. *Girl Rush,* prod. Frederick Brisson and Robert Emmett Dolan and dir. Robert Pirosh, 85 minutes (Paramount, 1955).

54 Eugene P. Moehring, *Resort City in the Sunbelt: Las Vegas, 1930–2000,* 2nd ed. (Reno: University of Nevada Press, 2000), 173–183; Trish Geran, *Beyond the Shimmering Lights: The Pride and Perseverance of African Americans in Las Vegas* (Las Vegas: Stephens Press, 2006).

55 See, for example, Eartha Kitt, *Confessions of a Sex Kitten* (New York: Barricade Books, 1989), 55; James Gavin, *Stormy Weather: The Life of Lena Horne* (New York: Atria Books, 2009), 242–243; Donald Bogle, *Dorothy Dandridge* (New York: Boulevard Books, 1998), 170–176; Daniel Mark Epstein, *Nat King Cole* (Boston: Northeastern University Press, 2000), 232–233; Harry Belafonte with Michael Shnayerson, *My Song: A Memoir* (New York: Knopf, 2011), 105–109.

56 "Las Vegas Pushes Its Luck," *Life,* June 20, 1955, 20; Gladwin Hill, "The 'Sure Thing' Boom at Las Vegas," *New York Times,* January 30, 1955, X29.

57 Verlene Stevens, "Race in Las Vegas," *Crisis,* September 1946, 271; Franklin H. Williams, "Sunshine and Jim Crow," *Crisis,* April 1954, 205–206. Other examples include James Goodrich, "Negroes Can't Win in Las Vegas," *Ebony,* March 1954, 5; "Vegas Clubs Drop 'Unwritten' Color Bars," *Jet,* April 14, 1960, 8.

58 Jessica Speart, *Tortoise Soup* (New York: Avon Books, 1998), 119.

59 Several television series reflected this "reality": *Vega$* (1978–1981), *Crime Story* (1986–1988), *The Strip* (1999–2000), and *CSI: Crime Scene Investigation* (2000–present). A sample of the many movies that portrayed a gritty Las Vegas include: *Dark City,* prod. Hal B. Wallis and dir. William Dieterle, 98 minutes (Paramount Pictures, 1950); *Guns, Girls, and Gangsters,* prod. Robert E. Kent and dir. Edward L. Cahn, 70 minutes (Edwin Small Productions, 1959); *Heat* (1986); *Queen of Diamonds,* prod. and dir. Nina Menkes, 77 minutes (independent film, 1991); *Hard Vice,* prod. and dir. Joey Travolta, 86 minutes (A-Pix Entertainment, 1994); *Night of the Running Man,* prod. Dana Dubovsky, Mark L. Lester, and George W. Perkins and dir. Mark L. Lester, 93 minutes (American World Pictures, 1995); *Very Bad Things,* prod. Cindy Cowan, Diane Nabatoff, and Michael Schiffer and dir. Peter Berg, 100 minutes (Initial Entertainment Group, 1998); *Luckytown,* prod. and dir. Paul Nicholas, 101 minutes (A Plus Entertainment, 2000). Hundreds of novelists also contributed to this grim image. A sample of them includes: W. T. Ballard, *Dealing Out Death* (Philadelphia: David McKay, 1948); Octavus Roy Cohen, *A Bullet for My Love* (New York: Macmillan,

1950); Elliot Paul, *The Black and the Red* (New York: Random House, 1956); Mc-Donald, *The Only Girl in the Game;* Brad Curtis, *The Golden Greed* (New York: Tower, 1965); Arelo Sederberg, *Casino* (New York: Dell, 1974); Ian Anderson, *The Big Night* (New York: Simon & Schuster, 1979); Ovid Demaris, *The Vegas Legacy* (New York: Dell, 1983); Steve Allen, *Murder in Vegas* (New York: Kensington, 1991); Harold Robbins, *The Raiders* (New York: Simon & Schuster, 1995); Connelly, *Trunk Music* (1998); James Ellroy, *The Cold Six Thousand* (New York: Knopf, 2001); Elizabeth Lowell, *Running Scared* (New York: Morrow, 2002); William Bernhardt, *Dark Eye* (New York: Ballantine Books, 2005).

60 *Eighteen and Anxious,* prod. Edmond Chevie and dir. Joe Parker, 93 minutes (AB-PT Pictures, 1957).

61 *The Grasshopper,* prod. Jerry Belson and Garry Marshall and dir. Jerry Paris, 98 minutes (National General Pictures, 1969).

62 Joan Didion, *Play It as It Lays* (1970; reprint, New York: Farrar, Straus and Giroux, 1990), 13.

63 Ibid., 169–170.

64 "Leibestod," *Aria,* prod. Don Boyd and dir. Franc Roddam, 6 minutes (RVP Productions, 1987).

65 *Falling Sky,* prod. Gary Shar and Mark Burnham and dir. Brian J. De Palma and Russ Brandt, 96 minutes (Shar Visions, 1999).

66 *Leaving Las Vegas,* prod. Lila Cazes and Annie Stewart and dir. Mike Figgis, 111 minutes (Lumiere Pictures, 1995); John O'Brien, *Leaving Las Vegas* (1990; reprint, New York: Grove Press, 1995), 162.

67 O'Brien, *Leaving Las Vegas,* 150.

68 Caryn James, "American Dreamland, a Neon Mirage," *New York Times,* November 26, 1995, H24; Christopher Sharrett, "Filming Las Vegas," *USA Today Magazine,* July 1996, http://news-business.vlex.com/vid/filming-vegas-53599486 (accessed February 1, 2012).

69 *The Amazing Colossal Man,* prod. and dir. Bert I. Gordon, 80 minutes (Malibu Productions, 1957); *Mars Attacks,* prod. and dir. Tim Burton, 106 minutes (Warner Bros., 1996); *Con Air,* prod. Jerry Bruckheimer and dir. Simon West, 115 minutes (Touchstone Pictures, 1997); *The Stand,* prod. Mitchell Galen and dir. Mike Garris, 336 minutes (Greengrass Productions, 1994).

70 Edward E. Baldwin, "Las Vegas in Popular Culture" (Ph.D. diss., University of Nevada, Las Vegas, 1997), 192.

CONCLUSION: THE ULTIMATE ATTRACTION OF LAS VEGAS

The epigraph is from Peter Earley, *Super Casino: Inside the "New" Las Vegas* (New York: Bantam Books, 2001), 32.

1 Gladwin Hill, "Klondike in the Desert," *New York Times,* June 7, 1953, SM14, 65 and 67.

2 Herb Lyon, "Fantastic Las Vegas," *Chicago Daily Tribune,* November 29, 1959, I9–10.

3 Charles Champlin, "Making the World Safe for Frivolity," *Los Angeles Times West Magazine,* October 19, 1969, 68, 74, and 75.

4 Mario Puzo, *Inside Las Vegas* (New York: Grosset & Dunlap, 1976), 18.

5 Ibid., 24.

6 Ibid., 20.

7 Ibid., 16 and 55.

8 Rob Schultheis, "Yes!! It's . . . Las Vegas!!!!! An Unabashed Frolic in the City Where Dreams Work Overtime and Inhibitions Take a Holiday," *National Geographic Traveler,* May/June 1991, 107–114.

9 *Las Vegas,* "Year of the Tiger," prod. Daniel Arkin and dir. Perry Lang, 60 minutes (Gary Scott Thompson Productions, 2003).

10 Ibid., "Pilot."

11 Writers' Program, *Nevada: Guide to the Silver State* (1940; reprint, Portland, Ore.: Binfords & Mort, 1957), 183.

12 Alex Small, "Nevada—Fabulous State," *Chicago Daily Tribune,* September 9, 1945, C2; Seymour Korman, "Las Vegas," April 11, 1948, E7; Edward Churchill, "The Truth about Las Vegas," *Script,* March 1948, 9.

13 "It's Worth Seeing: Las Vegas, Desert Town, Flowers into Resort City," *Oakland Tribune,* August 20, 1950, 8B.

14. "Las Vegas Strikes It Rich," *Life,* May 26, 1947, 99.

15 William Pearson, *The Muses of Ruin* (New York: McGraw-Hill, 1965), 116–117.

16 Alfred A. Alvarez, *The Biggest Game in Town* (Boston: Houghton Mifflin, 1983), 10.

17 Paul Ralli, *Viva Vegas* (Hollywood: House-Warven, 1953), 2.

18 Peter Wyden, "How Wicked Is Las Vegas?," *Saturday Evening Post,* November 11, 1961, 20; Arthur Steuer, "Playground for Adults Only," *Esquire,* August 1961, 44.

19 Judy Klemesrud, "Women Gambling in Las Vegas Don't Hide in Corner Any More," *New York Times,* September 26, 1973, 36.

20 Jerry Cohen, "Vegas Meets an Insatiable U.S. Demand," *Los Angeles Times,* April 17, 1977, 3.

21 Michael Ventura, "Las Vegas: The Odds on Anything," in *Literary Las Vegas: The Best Writing about America's Most Fabulous City,* ed. Mike Tronnes (New York: Holt, 1995), 177.

22 John Handley, "Las Vegas," *Chicago Tribune,* June 13, 1976, C3; "Kite High," *Racket Squad,* prod. Carroll Case and Hal Roach Jr. and dir. William Beaudine, 30 minutes (Showcase Productions, 1951); *Swingers,* prod. Victor Simpkins and dir. Doug Lyman, 96 minutes (Independent Pictures, 1996).

23 Pearson, *Muses of Ruin,* 39.

24 Edward Allen, "Penny Ante," reprinted in Tronnes, *Literary Las Vegas,* 315.

25 Caskie Stinnett, "Las Vegas: Where Anything Is Forgivable Except Restraint," *Holiday,* May 1967, 32.

1 Margot Hentoff, "Absolutely Free," *Harper's*, November 1969, 28 and 30.

2 Hank Resnik, "Cheer and Loathing in Las Vegas," *California Living Magazine* in *San Francisco Sunday Examiner and Chronicle*, November 28, 1982, 4.

3 Gary Provost, *High Stakes: Inside the New Las Vegas* (New York: Truman Talley Books, 1994), 10–11.

4 Dan Savage, *The Seven Deadly Sins and the Pursuit of Happiness in America* (New York: E. P. Dutton, 2002), 19.

5 John M. Broder, "When a City Discovers the Virtues of Vice. And Vice Versa," *New York Times,* June 4, 2004, A20.

6 Quoted in Geoff Schumacher, *Sun, Sin and Suburbia: An Essential History of Modern Las Vegas* (Las Vegas: Stephens Press, 2004), 25.

7 John Gregory Dunne, *Vegas: Memoir of a Dark Season* (New York: Warner Books, 1975), 68; Nick Tosches, "Holy City," in *Literary Las Vegas: The Best Writing about America's Most Fabulous City,* ed. Mike Tronnes (New York: Holt, 1995), xv.

8 Robert Brustein, "The Las Vegas Show," *New Republic,* January 4–11, 1999, 27.

9 Otto Friedrich, *City of Nets: A Portrait of Hollywood in the 1940s* (1986; Berkeley: University of California Press, 1997), 289.

10 James Howard Kunstler, *The City in Mind: Meditations on the Urban Condition* (New York: Free Press, 2001), 142–143.

11 Joan Didion, "Marrying Absurd," in Tronnes, *Literary Las Vegas,* 171–172

12 Bruce Begout, *Zeropolis: The Experience of Las Vegas,* trans. Liz Heron (London: Reaktion Books, 2003), 11, 22, 29, and 84.

13 Hal Rothman used the label "hip intellectuals." See *The Grit Beneath the Glitter: Tales from the Real Las Vegas,* ed. Hal K. Rothman and Mike Davis (Berkeley: University of California Press, 2002), 13. David Spanier characterized much of the criticism of Las Vegas as "bad journalism." Spanier, *The Hand I Played: A Poker Memoir* (Reno: University of Nevada Press, 2001), 209.

14 Spanier, *Hand I Played,* 185.

15 Dave Hickey, *Air Guitar: Essays on Art and Democracy* (Los Angeles: Art Issues Press, 1997), 20–21. Ironically, Hickey left the University of Nevada, Las Vegas, and one of his parting shots revealed his own elitism. The university is, he claimed, "a very small place in which a relatively small faculty serves a relatively unprepared student body. And I think they do as good as they can do, but they're certainly not concerned with turning out rocket scientists. They want the kind of students that Nevada business needs. . . . So if I'm up there trying to turn out students with a certain level of excellence and that's totally out of tune with the school's mission, then I'm going to be in the way. And I was in the way there for 20 years." Phil Hagen, "How Wrong Was He?," *Vegas Seven,* May 20, 2010, http://weeklyseven.com/news/2010/may/20/how-wrong-was-he (accessed May 12, 2012).

16 Hickey, *Air Guitar,* 22.

17 John H. Irsfeld, "Las Vegas: West Egg?," in *East of Eden, West of Zion: Essays on Nevada,* ed. Wilbur S. Shepperson (Reno: University of Nevada Press, 1989), 162.

18 Rothman and Davis, *Grit Beneath the Glitter,* 13–14.

19 Hunter S. Thompson, *Fear and Loathing in Las Vegas: A Savage Journey to the Heart of the American Dream* (1971; reprint, New York: Vintage Books, 1989), 12.

20 Ibid.

21 Ibid., 4.

22 Ibid., 46–47.

23 Ibid., 156.

24 Ibid., 193.

25 Ibid., 68.

26 Tom Wolfe, "Las Vegas (What?) Las Vegas (Can't Hear You! Too Noisy) Las Vegas!!!," in Tronnes, *Literary Las Vegas,* 5 and 9.

27 Robert Venturi, Denise Scott Brown, and Steven Izenour, foreword to Alan Hess, *Viva Las Vegas: After-Hours Architecture* (San Francisco: Chronicle Books, 1993), 7; Robert Venturi, Denise Scott Brown, and Steven Izenour, *Learning from Las Vegas: The Forgotten Symbolism of Architectural Form,* rev. ed. (Cambridge, Mass.: MIT Press, 1977), 18; David Littlejohn, *The Real Las Vegas: Life Beyond the Strip* (New York: Oxford University Press, 1999), 4.

28 Hess, *Viva Las Vegas,* 8.

29 Kurt Anderson, "Las Vegas, U.S.A.," *Time,* January 10, 1994, 46.

30 Neil Postman, *Amusing Ourselves to Death: Public Discourse in the Age of Show Business* (New York: Viking, 1985), 3–4. Journalist Marc Cooper agrees with Postman; see *The Last Honest Place in America: Paradise and Perdition in the New Las Vegas* (New York: Nation Books, 2004), 11.

31 Rothman and Davis, *Grit Beneath the Glitter,* 6; Hal Rothman, *Neon Metropolis: How Las Vegas Started the Twenty-First Century* (New York: Routledge, 2002), xiii, xxiii, and xxvii; Hal Rothman, *Devil's Bargains: Tourism in the Twentieth-Century American West* (Lawrence: University Press of Kansas, 1998), 334.

32 Hickey, *Air Guitar,* 23.

33 *Talk of the Nation,* National Public Radio, November 25, 1998.

34 "As Nevada Went, So Goes the Nation?," *Forbes,* September 1, 1973, 24–28, 32, and 34; M. Gottdiener, Claudia C. Collins, and David R. Dickens, *Las Vegas: The Social Production of an All-American City* (Malden, Mass.: Blackwell, 2000), xi and 254–256; Littlejohn, *Real Las Vegas,* 16–17; Sally Denton and Roger Morris, *The Money and the Power: The Making of Las Vegas and Its Hold on America, 1947–2000* (New York: Knopf, 2001), 10–12.

35 Cooper, *Last Honest Place,* 10–11. See also Peter Earley, *Super Casino: Inside the "New" Las Vegas* (New York: Bantam Books, 2001), 48.

36 Rothman and Davis, *Grit Beneath the Glitter,* 14.

37 Begout, *Zeropolis,* 12.

BIBLIOGRAPHICAL ESSAY

The best introduction to the study of Las Vegas history is Eugene P. Moehring and Michael Greene, *Las Vegas: A Centennial History* (2005). (I use shortened entries in the bibliography for any sources fully cited in the endnotes.) Also useful are Ralph J. Roske, *Las Vegas: A Desert Paradise* (1986), and Gary E. Elliott, *The New Western Frontier: An Illustrated History of Greater Las Vegas* (1999). Helpful studies of particular periods of the city's history include Eugene P. Moehring, *Resort City in the Sunbelt: Las Vegas, 1930–2000*, 2nd edition (2000), David G. Schwartz, *Suburban Xanadu: The Casino Resort on the Las Vegas Strip* (2003), John M. Findlay, *People of Chance: Gambling in American Society form Jamestown to Las Vegas* (1986), and two works by Hal Rothman: *Devil's Bargains: Tourism in the Twentieth-Century American West* (1998) and *Neon Metropolis: How Las Vegas Started the Twenty-First Century* (2002).

There are a few helpful studies of Las Vegas in popular culture: Edward E. Baldwin, "Las Vegas in Popular Culture"; John H. Irsfeld, "Cowboys, Crooks, and Corporations: How Popular Literature Has Treated Las Vegas," in *The Players: The Men Who Made Las Vegas*, edited by Jack Sheehan (Reno, 1997); Candace Kant, "City of Dreams: Las Vegas on Film, 1980–1989," *Nevada Historical Society Quarterly* 33 (1990), 1–12; Francisco Menendez, "Las Vegas of the Mind: Shooting Movies In and About Nevada," in *The Grit beneath the Glitter: Tales from The Real Las Vegas*, edited by Hal K. Rothman and Mike Davis (2002); and David Spainer, "Playing with Words," in *The Hand I Played: A Poker Memoir* (2001).

The place to begin an examination of the images of Las Vegas over the course of the twentieth century is in the nation's newspapers and magazines. A number of databases are remarkably useful in finding newspapers. ProQuest, for example, has archived the *New York Times, Los Angeles Times, Chicago Tribune,* and *Wall Street Journal* from those national newspapers' inception to the early twenty-first century. Similarly, NewspaperArchives.com has digitized hundreds of newspapers from small towns to large cities for all of the twentieth century, and I drew heavily from both these critical sources. I consulted three Las Vegas newspapers—*Las Vegas Age, Las Vegas Review-Journal,* and *Las Vegas Sun*—on microfilm at the Lied Library at the University of Nevada, Las Vegas. At the Lied Library's Special Collections, I also drew on that repository's large collection of newspaper clippings contained in a wide range of manuscript collections. I examined a large number of magazines with wide circulations, notably *Collier's, Harper's, Time, Newsweek, Saturday Evening Post, Look,* and *Life.* As with the newspapers, the Lied Library Special Collections has an impressive number of magazine clippings about Las Vegas. Novels are also an important source for determining the prevailing images of Las Vegas over time. Beyond those at the Lied Library, the staff of the Curtis Laws Wilson Library at Missouri University of Science and Technology was a great help in finding dozens and dozens of novels published from the 1940s through the early twentieth century. I also learned the value of using Amazon for the relatively inexpensive purchase of many hard-to-find titles. Amazon, along with eBay, were also critical in my quest to find films and television programs about Las Vegas after identifying most of the titles in Gary DuVal, *The Nevada Filmography* (Jefferson, N.C.: McFarland, 2002), and the Internet Movie Data Base (http://imdb.com/).

To understand the appeal of Las Vegas as a last frontier town, it is critical to examine America's fascination with the West. A few studies stand out: Clyde A. Milner II, Carol A. O'Connor, and Martha A. Sandweiss, eds., *The Oxford History of the American West* (1994); Richard White, *"It's Your Misfortune and None of My Own": A History of the American West* (1991); Robert V. Hine and John Mack Faragher, *The American West: A New Interpretive History* (2000); Patricia Nelson Limerick, *The Legacy of Conquest: The Unbroken Past of the American West* (1987); John G. Cawelti, *The Six-Gun Mystique Sequel* (1999); Richard Slotkin, *Gunfighter Nation: The Myth of the Frontier in Twentieth-Century America* (1992); William W. Savage Jr., *The Cowboy Hero: His Image in American History and Culture* (1979); and Robert G. Athearn, *The Mythic West in Twentieth Century America* (1986). Anne Martin's "These United States—VIII, Nevada: Beautiful Desert of Buried Hopes," in *Nation,* July 26, 1922, is a good contemporary effort by a native of the state to place early twentieth-century Nevada in the western tradition. Two historians provide a good look at early Las Vegas: Stanley W. Paher, *Las Vegas: As It Began—As It Grew* (1971), and Joan Burkart Whitely, *Young Las Vegas, 1905–1931: Before They Found Us* (2005). There are several contemporary accounts dealing with various aspects of frontier elements in Las Vegas. The widespread violation of Prohibition in Las Vegas is in R. A. Kelly, *Liberty's Last Stand* (1932). Two journalists in the 1930s noted prostitution in Las Vegas: Victor Castle, "Well, I Quit My Job at the Dam," *Nation,* August 26, 1931, and Bruce Bliven, "The American Dnieperstroy," *New Republic,* December 11, 1935. *Standard* (Ogden, Utah), June 29, 1905; Magner White, "The Boom at Boulder," *Saturday Evening Post,* March 23, 1929; Richard English, "The Boom Came Back," *Collier's,* August 22, 1942; Wesley Stout, "Nevada's New Reno," *Saturday Evening Post,* October 31, 1942; and "Las Vegas Gambling," *Life,* December 21, 1942, are good examples of journalists' accounts of the various Las Vegas booms of the first half of the twentieth century. Basil Woon, in *Incredible Land: A Jaunty Baedeker to Hollywood and the Great Southwest* (1933), addresses many of these topics. Frontier themes about Las Vegas are evident in many films of the 1940s and 1950s, notably *Las Vegas Nights* (1941), *Heldorado* (1946), *Sky Full of Moon* (1952), and *Meet Me in Las Vegas* (1955).

Americans have long been fascinated by Benjamin "Bugsy" Siegel and his life, particularly in connection with Las Vegas, and his exploits have attracted a large number of journalists, popular biographers, documentary filmmakers, and movie producers, but few scholars. There are two full-length biographies—Dean Jennings, *We Only Kill Each Other* (1992), and George Carpozi Jr., *Bugsy* (1973)—and several books on organized crime that include significant passages on Siegel, such as David Hanna, *Ice Picks and Coffins: The Killers of Murder, Inc.* (1974), but these works have little or no documentation. The same is true of biographies of Virginia Hill, one of Siegel's paramours: Ed Reid, *The Mistress and the Mafia: The Virginia Hill Story* (New York:

Bantam Books, 1972), David Hanna, *Virginia Hill: Queen of the Underworld* (New York: Belmont Tower Books, 1975), and Andy Edmunds, *Bugsy's Baby: The Secret Life of Mob Queen Virginia Hill* (1993). There are a couple of helpful essays that seek to explain Siegel's significance: James F. Smith, "Ben Siegel: Father of Las Vegas and the Modern Casino-Hotel," *Journal of Popular Culture* (Spring 1992), and Pete Hamill, "Bugsy Siegel's Fabulous Dream," *Playboy,* February 1992. Two biographies of Siegel's lifelong friend Meyer Lansky include considerable discussion of Siegel: Daniel Eisenberg, Uri Dan, and Eli Landau, *Meyer Lansky: Mogul of the Mob* (1979), and Robert Lacey, *Little Man: Meyer Lansky and the Gangster Life* (1991). A number of novelists have written about Siegel. W. T. Ballard, *Chance Elson* (1959), Sam Ross, *Solomon's Palace* (1974), and Max Collins, *Neon Empire* (1991), illustrate the treatment of Siegel in fiction. There are many film depictions of Siegel, notably *Gangster Wars* (1981), *Neon Empire* (1990), *Bugsy* (1991), *Mobsters* (1991), and *Lansky* (1999). Several documentaries detail his life, usually with a focus on his impact on Las Vegas: *Don't Call Me Bugsy* (1992), *Bugsy Siegel: Gambling on the Mob* (1995), *The Real Las Vegas* (1996), *La Cosa Nostra, The Mafia: An Expose* (1997), *Rogues Gallery* (1997), and *Las Vegas: An Unconventional History* (2005). *The Man Who Invented Las Vegas* (2000), by W. R. Wilkerson III, is the best account of the development of the Flamingo Hotel. There are several helpful recollections of Siegel in Las Vegas, including Paul Ralli, *Nevada Lawyer: A Story of Life and Love in Las Vegas* (1949), Erskine Caldwell, *With All My Might* (1987), Jamie Coughtry, ed., *John F. Cahlan: Fifty Years in Journalism and Community Development* (1987), Curtis O. Lynum, *The FBI and I: One Family's Life in the FBI during the Hoover Years* (1988), and Rose Marie, *Hold the Roses* (2002). There is a remarkably frank admission of the creation of a mythical Siegel by screenwriter James Toback, actor Warren Beatty, and director Barry Levinson in "Reinvention of Bugsy Siegel," on *Bugsy: Extended Cut* (2006). Finally, I learned a great deal about Siegel's personal life from his eldest daughter, Millicent Rosen, who kindly consented to two helpful interviews in 2010 and 2011.

There is a mountain of secondary material on organized crime in America. The following are good books to consult: Stephen Fox, *Blood and Power: Organized Crime in Twentieth-Century America* (1989), Richard Hammer, *Playboy's Illustrated History of Organized Crime* (1975), Virgil W. Peterson, *The Mob: 200 Years of Organized Crime in New York* (1983), Thomas Repetto, *American Mafia: A History of Its Rise to Power* (2004), and Gus Russo, *The Outfit: The Role of Chicago's Underworld in the Shaping of Modern America* (2001) and *Supermob: How Sidney Korshak and His Criminal Associates Became America's Hidden Power Brokers* (2007). The work of Estes Kefauver's Senate committee had a large impact on the nation's view of the influence of organized crime in American life. *The Kefauver Committee Report on Organized Crime* (1951), Estes Kefauver, *Crime in America* (1951), Lee Bernstein, *The Greatest Menace: Organized Crime in the Cold War* (2002), Joseph Bruce Gorman, *Kefauver: A Political Biography* (1971), and William Howard Moore, *The Kefauver Committee and the Politics of Crime* (1974), are all important in understanding Kefauver's role. There are three essential sources for Robert Kennedy's view of organized crime and its connection to Las Vegas: Robert F. Kennedy, *The Enemy Within* (1960), *Hang Tough! Grant Sawyer: An Activist in the Governor's Mansion* (1993), and Ronald Goldfarb, *Perfect*

Villains, Imperfect Heroes: Robert F. Kennedy's War against Organized Crime (1995). The three most influential muckraking works on organized crime's influence in Las Vegas are Sid W. Meyers, *The Great Las Vegas Fraud* (1958), Ed Reid and Ovid Demaris, *The Green Felt Jungle* (1963), and Wallace Turner, *Gamblers' Money: The New Force in American Life* (1966). Dan Fowler, "What Price Gambling in Nevada?" *Look*, June 15, 1954; Lester Velie, "Las Vegas: The Underworld's Secret Jackpot," *Reader's Digest*, October 1959; and Fred J. Cook, "Treasure Chest of the Underworld: Gambling, Inc.," *Nation*, October 22, 1960, are representative magazine articles dealing with the city's connection to various mobs. Works that address Nevada's efforts to regulate gambling include Robbins E. Cahill, *Recollections of Work in State Politics, Government, Taxation, Gaming Control, Clark County Administration, and the Nevada Resort Association* (1977), Gary E. Elliott, *Senator Alan Bible and the Politics of the New West* (1994), Jerome Skolnick, *House of Cards: The Legalization and Control of Casino Gambling* (1978), and Ronald A. Farrell and Carole Case, *The Black Book and the Mob: The Untold Story of the Control of Nevada's Casinos* (1995). Although many journalists covered the skim story in Las Vegas in the mid-1960s, crime reporter Sandy Smith's work was critical because the FBI shared information with him. See *Chicago Sun Times*, July 10, 1966, and Sandy Smith, "The Mob," *Life*, September 8, 1967. There are many books on Howard Hughes and his role in Las Vegas, such as Michael Drosnin's *Citizen Hughes* (2004). Researchers will also find helpful the large newspaper clipping collection about Hughes in the Howard Hughes Collection, Special Collections, Lied Library, University of Nevada, Las Vegas. The often convoluted saga of Allen Glick, Frank "Lefty" Rosenthal, and Tony Spilotro is covered extensively in the *New York Times, Chicago Tribune*, and *Los Angeles Times*. Kenneth J. Peak and William N. Ousley's "The FBI's 'Strawman': Breaking the Kansas City Mob's Connection to Las Vegas," *Missouri Historical Review* 104 (January 2010) is a good account of the investigation and prosecution of the Chicago, Kansas City, and Milwaukee mobsters involved in Las Vegas. *Crime Story*, produced by Michael Mann, is the best television depiction of organized crime in Las Vegas. Irving Shulman, *The Big Brokers* (1951), Ian Fleming, *Diamonds Are Forever* (1956), Elliot Paul, *The Black and the Red* (1956), William R. Cox, *Murder in Vegas* (1960), Ovid Demaris, *Candyleg* (1961), William Pearson, *The Muses of Ruin* (1965), Mario Puzo, *The Godfather* (1969), Arthur Moore and Clayton Matthews, *Las Vegas* (1974), Mario Puzo, *The Last Don* (1997), Charles Fleming, *The Ivory Coast* (2002), and Richard Rayner, *The Devil's Wind* (2005), are a good sample of the dozens of novels dealing with the mob in Las Vegas. Four films were particularly important in developing the narrative of a city captured by organized crime: *The Godfather* (1972), *The Godfather, Part II* (1974), *Bugsy* (1991), and *Casino* (1995).

Mario Puzo's *Inside Las Vegas* (1977) is the most passionate defense of gambling in Las Vegas, but there are many others: *Los Angeles Times*, May 24, 1939; *Reno Evening Gazette*, June 12, 1941; *New York Times*, August 25, 1957; "Gambling Goes Legit," *Time*, December 6, 1976; and Wade Goodwin, *All Things Considered*, National Public Radio, June 24, 1999. There are several descriptions of the egalitarian character of gambling crowds: "Pearls of Wisdom Mid Roulette Wheels," *Centralia* (Wash.) *Chronicle Advertiser*, August 7, 1936; Writers' Program, *Nevada: Guide to the Silver*

State (1957); *Viva Las Vegas* (1964); *Honeymoon in Vegas* (1992); *Casino* (1995); *Vegas Vacation* (1997); and *The Cooler* (2003). Yet in earlier films, there is a more exclusive view of gambling crowds: *Las Vegas Nights* (1941), *Flight to Nowhere* (1946), *Las Vegas Story* (1952), and *Ocean's Eleven* (1960), as well as in the episode entitled "Kite High" in the television series *Racket Squad* (1951). Jackpot wins by improbable gamblers is an appealing device used by several filmmakers. See *Las Vegas Nights* (1941), *Meet Me in Las Vegas* (1956), *Going in Style* (1979), *Starman* (1984), *Rain Man* (1988), *Vegas Vacation* (1997), and *Girls' Night* (1998).

One can begin an investigation of the massive topic of entertainment in Las Vegas through a lengthy series entitled "The Great Resorts of Las Vegas" by George Stamos Jr. in the *Las Vegas Sun Magazine* between April 1, 1979, and December 23, 1979, Donn Knepp's *Las Vegas: The Entertainment Capital* (1987), and Mike Weatherford's *Cult Vegas: The Weirdest! The Wildest! The Swingin'est Town on Earth!* (2001). A Las Vegas resident's decades-long hobby of noting headliners at the various casinos is captured in the David Fluke Collection in the Special Collections at Lied Library. The challenge for early entertainment directors to find headliners is detailed in the 1987 Maxine Lewis Oral History Interview and the Maxine Lewis Flamingo Bookings, 1948–1951, both in Special Collections. The 2003 Stan Irwin Oral History Interview in Special Collections and Pierre Cossette's *Another Day in Showbiz* (2002) also explain the challenges for entertainment directors. A series of articles in *Billboard* magazine likewise document the efforts of entertainment directors particularly in the following issues: January 27, 1945; February 10, 1945; August 31, 1946; June 10, 1950; and January 10, 1953. By the early 1950s, many magazines and newspapers were covering the battle to sign headline entertainers. Richard English's article "Million-Dollar Talent War" in the *Saturday Evening Post* on October 24, 1953, is one of the best examples.

There is a substantial body of material on the dominant Las Vegas entertainers. The best biography of Liberace is Darden Asbury Pyron's *Liberace: An American Boy* (2001). Liberace's memoir, *An Autobiography* (1973), is also helpful. Among the many magazine articles over the course of his career, these stand out: "Kidding on the Keys," *Life,* December 7, 1953; Holly Miller, "All That Glitters," *Saturday Evening Post,* December 1978; Richard Corliss, "The Evangelist of Kitsch," *Time,* November 3, 1986; and William A. Henry III, "Show Business: A Synonym for Glorious Excess," *Time,* February 16, 1987. There are a couple of good biographies of Louis Prima that also deal with Keely Smith: Garry Boulard, *Louis Prima* (2002), and Tom Clavin, *That Old Black Magic: Louis Prima, Keely Smith, and the Golden Age of Las Vegas* (2010). There is a helpful DVD entitled *Louis Prima: The Wildest* (1999). Magazine articles that cover his time in Las Vegas include "Nightclubs: The Wages of Vulgarity," *Time,* September 7, 1959, and David Kamp, "They Made Vegas Swing," *Vanity Fair,* December 1999. Beyond his autobiography, written with Dick Maurice, *Once before I Go* (1991), the best introduction to Wayne Newton's popularity in Las Vegas is Ron Rosenbaum, "Do You Know Vegas?," *Esquire,* August 1982. Over the years, many journalists and entertainment columnists have weighed in on Newton's role in the developing entertainment picture in Las Vegas: Burke Johnson, "Wayne Newton," *Arizona Days and Ways Magazine* in *Arizona Republic,* June 12, 1966; Betsy Carter and Peter S. Greenberg, "King of the Strip," *Newsweek,* January 12, 1976; "Show Business: What Ever Happened to Baby Wayne?," *Time,* June 29, 1970; Robert Windeler, "The Most Successful Performer in Vegas History? Not Frank, Not Elvis—It's Wayne Newton," *People Weekly,* April 30, 1979; and Nancy Spiller, "What *Is* It about Wayne?," *USA Weekend* in *Salina* (Kan.) *Journal,* February 14–16, 1992. The movie *Vegas Vacation* (1997) offers a delightful parody of Newton's great popularity among women. A good place to begin an investigation of Elvis Presley's impact on Las Vegas is with the following biographies: Peter Guralnick, *Last Train to Memphis: The Rise of Elvis Presley* (1994) and *Careless Love: The Unmaking of Elvis Presley* (1999), and Charles L. Ponce De Leon, *The Life of Elvis Presley: Fortunate Son* (2007). Presley's unsuccessful first appearance at the New Frontier Hotel in Las Vegas can be followed in several reviews and articles in the *Las Vegas Sun* and *Las Vegas Review-Journal* between April 25 and May 1, 1956. There are many helpful magazine articles on his performances in Las Vegas and his appearance in the iconic film *Viva Las Vegas:* "Music: Teeners' Hero," *Time,* May 14, 1956; "Viva Las Vegas," *Variety,* December 31, 1963; "Cinema: The Way-Out West," *Time,* May 29, 1964; "Rock 'n' Roll: Return of the Big Beat," *Time,* August 15, 1969, 65; and Eliot Tiegel, "Elvis Retains Touch in Return to Stage," *Billboard,* August 16, 1969. Among the hundreds of newspaper articles on Presley in Las Vegas, see Richard Goldstein, "A White Boy with Black Hips," *New York Times,* August 10, 1969; Robert Hilburn, "Third Vegas Stint for Elvis Presley," *Los Angeles Times,* August 12, 1970; Robert Hilburn, "Fan to Fan: What's Happened to Elvis," *Los Angeles Times,* February 6, 1972. Arnold Shaw's *Sinatra: Twentieth-Century Romantic* (1969), and particularly for his early years, James Kaplan's *Frank: The Voice* (2010), are the best of many biographies of Frank Sinatra. There is a detailed time line of her father's life in Nancy Sinatra's *Frank Sinatra: An American Legend* (1998). There are many articles in the nation's press on Sinatra from the late 1930s to his death in 1998. One can follow the changing views of Sinatra in the following magazine articles: "Radio: That Old Sweet Song," *Time,* July 5, 1943; "Cuba: Hoodlum on the Wing," *Time,* March 3, 1947; "Cinema: The Kid from Hoboken," *Time,* August 29, 1955; "Frank Sinatra v. Nevada," *Life,* September 27, 1963; Gay Talese, "Frank Sinatra Has a Cold," *Esquire,* April 1966; "Crime: Mixing Business and Pleasure," *Time,* May 30, 1977; Richard Lacayo, "Ring-A-Ding Ding," *Time,* May 25, 1998; and Chris Morris, "From Hoboken to Hollywood, An Unforgettable Style," *Billboard,* May 30, 1998.

Most of the images of women in Las Vegas are dismissive. The worst are the articles in the pulp magazines of the 1950s like "Sex Lures of Las Vegas," *Brief,* January 1955; "Wild Women of Las Vegas: Morals Take a Back Seat Amid Sizzling Desert Sin," *Pose,* April 1955; and "The Belles of Las Vegas," *Real Men,* December 1958. In many novels and short stories and in some movies, women in Las Vegas are simply there to be used or possessed, as in Alice Denham, "The Deal," in *Great Tales of City Dwellers,* edited by Alex Austin (1955); Ovid Demaris, *Candyleg* (1961); Brad Curtis, *The Golden Greed* (1965); *Honeymoon in Vegas* (1992); and *Indecent Proposal* (1993). Novels like Emily Elliot's *Midnight Memories* (1983) and the movie *Casino* portray women as hustlers. Strippers and dancers in topless production shows are also present. See Kelly DiNardo, *Gilded Lili: Lili St. Cyr and the Striptease Mystique* (2007), and Larry Gragg, "'A Big Step to Oblivion for Las Vegas?' The 'Battle of the Bare Bosoms,'

1957–1959," *Journal of Popular Culture* 43 (October 2010). Prostitutes are ubiquitous in portrayals of Las Vegas: *Highway Dragnet* (1954); Bob Considine, "The Inside Story of Las Vegas," *PIC*, July 1955; W. T. Ballard, *The Seven Sisters* (1962); *The Grasshopper* (1969); Harvey Hardy, "Las Vegas before Neon," *True West*, May–June 1970; Mario Puzo, *Inside Las Vegas* (1977); *Corvette Summer* (1978); "What Gambling Does for—And to—Las Vegas," *U.S. News and World Report*, March 9, 1981; *Vegas Casino War* (1984); *Fever Pitch* (1985); *Stark* (1985); *Hard Vice* (1994); *Leaving Las Vegas* (1995); *Money Plays* (1998); John H. Irsfeld, "Stop, Rewind, and Play," in *Radio Elvis and Other Stories* (2002); and *Dateline*, NBC, September 14, 2003. The iconic glamorous showgirls are the counter to all the negative images of women in Las Vegas, and they appear in newspaper and magazine articles as well as in novels, television series, and movies: *Girl Rush* (1955); *Meet Me in Las Vegas* (1956); Lloyd Shearer, "Chorus Girls," *Parade Magazine* in *Independent-Press-Telegram* (Long Beach, Calif.), June 2, 1957; "Paris Come-on in Vegas," *Life*, June 6, 1960; *Ocean's Eleven* (1960); *Vega$* (1979–1982); Larry McMurtry, *The Desert Rose* (1983); and *Las Vegas* (2003–2008).

The luxurious Las Vegas hotels are nicely captured in color photos in several books: Rick Browne and James Marshall, *Planet Vegas: A Portrait of Las Vegas by 20 of the World's Leading Photographers* (1995); Su Kim Chung, *Las Vegas Then and Now* (2002); Carol M. Highsmith and Ted Landphair, *Las Vegas: A Photographic Tour* (2003); Michelle Ferrari with Stephen Ives, *Las Vegas: An Unconventional History* (2005); and Giovanna Franci, *Dreaming of Italy: Las Vegas and the Virtual Grand Tour* (2005). For some outstanding postcard images of the first three Strip hotels, see the Frasher Foto Postcard Collection in the Pomona Public Library in Pomona, California. Alan Hess's *Viva Las Vegas: After-Hours Architecture* (1993) and David G. Schwartz's *Suburban Xanadu: The Casino Resort on the Las Vegas Strip and Beyond* (2003) are splendid guides to Las Vegas architecture. Also, see Chris Nichols, *The Leisure Architecture of Wayne McAllister* (2007). There was always a considerable press flurry at the opening of each luxurious hotel. For the Flamingo, see *Los Angeles Daily News*, January 1, 1947, and *Los Angeles Herald Express*, January 6, 1947. For the Desert Inn, see "Wilbur's Dream Joint," *Time*, May 8, 1950, and "Gambling in the U.S." *Life*, June 19, 1950. For Caesars Palace, see *Los Angeles Times*, August 3, 1966, and *New York Times*, August 8, 1966. For the International, see "Las Vegas: The Game Is Illusion," *Time*, July 11, 1969. For the MGM Grand, see "Gambling on Las Vegas," *Newsweek*, December 17, 1973. For the Mirage, see *New York Times*, November 16, 1989, and Ronald Grover, "Tigers, a Volcano, Dolphins, and Steve Wynn," *Business Week*, November 20, 1989. For the Bellagio, see *Los Angeles Times*, October 25, 1998, and *Chicago Tribune*, November 22, 1998. For the Wynn, see Joel Stein, "Wynn's Big Bet," *Time*, May 2, 2005, and Nina Munk, "Steve Wynn's Biggest Gamble," *Vanity Fair*, June 2005. Two digital sites at the Lied Library's Special Collections illustrate the evolution of cuisine in Las Vegas hotels: David G. Schwartz, "Fifty Years of Dining on the Las Vegas Strip" and Su Kim Chung, "Menus: the Art of Dining." By the late twentieth century, many journalists were hailing the multitude of gourmet restaurants in Las Vegas. See, for example, S. Irene Virbila, "Las Vegas: Betting on Good Taste," *Los Angeles Times Magazine*, September 13, 1998, and *Marketplace Morning Report*, Minnesota Public Radio, December 12, 2000.

There is no shortage of Las Vegas critics. The most frequent indictment is that the city has created generations of compulsive gamblers. There are scores of newspaper and magazine articles on compulsive gambling and some good novels that deal with this subject, like Aben Kandel's *The Strip* (1961) and Tess Hudson's *Double Down* (2005); however, most people likely became acquainted with compulsive gambling in Las Vegas from depictions in movies and on television: *The Invisible Wall* (1947); *The Lady Gambles* (1949); *Painting the Clouds with Sunshine* (1951); *Las Vegas Story* (1952); *Las Vegas Shakedown* (1955); "The Fever," *The Twilight Zone* (1960); *The Gambler* (1974); *Lost in America* (1985); *Fever Pitch* (1986); *Heat* (1986); *Vegas Vacation* (1997); *Dreamland* (2000); "Decks and Violence," *Las Vegas* (2003); *Lucky* (2003); *Owning Mahoney* (2003); and *Losing Ground* (2005). Several novels are critical of the pathetic tourists who visit Las Vegas: Richard Foster, *Blonde and Beautiful* (1955); Steve Fisher, *No House Limit* (1958); Edward Allen, *Mustang Sally* (1992); Robert B. Parker, *Chance* (1997); Dan Barton, *Heckler* (2001); and Sue Grafton, *A Is for Alibi* (2005). Older women playing slot machines have been a particular target for many authors: Katharine Best and Katharine Hillyer, *Las Vegas: Playtown U.S.A.* (1955); John D. McDonald, *The Only Girl in the Game* (1960); Stephanie James, *Gambler's Woman* (1984); Lloyd Biggle Jr., *A Hazard of Losers* (1991); and Ian Fleming, *Diamonds Are Forever* (2003). The 1955 movie *Las Vegas Shakedown* includes characters discussing it as a city respectable people should avoid. A few journalists, mostly African Americans, described the widespread racism in Las Vegas in the 1940s and 1950s: Verlene Stevens, "Race in Las Vegas," *Crisis*, September 1946; Franklin H. Williams, "Sunshine and Jim Crow," *Crisis*, April 1954; James Goodrich, "Negroes Can't Win in Las Vegas," *Ebony*, March 1954; and "Vegas Clubs Drop 'Unwritten' Color Bars," *Jet*, April 14, 1960. Most novels and several films depict Las Vegas as a gritty, lonely, and dangerous place: *Dark City* (1950), *Guns, Girls, and Gangsters* (1959), *Heat* (1986), *Queen of Diamonds* (1991), *Hard Vice* (1994), *Night of the Running Man* (1995), *Very Bad Things* (1998), and *Luckytown* (2000). Joan Didion's novel *Play It as It Lays* (1990) and the films *The Grasshopper* (1969), "Leibestod," *Aria* (1987), *Falling Sky* (1999), and *Leaving Las Vegas* (1995) reveal Las Vegas as a place of hopelessness, even doom. Intellectuals and social critics have had a field day condemning Las Vegas. The following is a good sampling from the harshest critics: John Gregory Dunne, *Vegas: A Memoir of a Dark Season* (1978); Hunter S. Thompson, *Fear and Loathing in Las Vegas: A Savage Journey to the Heart of the American Dream* (1989); Joan Didion, "Marrying Absurd" and Nick Tosches, "Holy City," in *Literary Las Vegas: The Best Writing about America's Most Fabulous City*, edited by Mike Tronnes (New York: Henry Holt, 1995); James Howard Kunstler, *The City in Mind: Meditations on the Urban Condition* (2001); Dan Savage, *The Seven Deadly Sins and the Pursuit of Happiness in America* (New York: Dutton, 2002); and Bruce Begout, *Zeropolis: The Experience of Las Vegas*, translated by Liz Heron (2003).

Ultimately, the perception of Las Vegas in most of American popular culture has been a positive one as a place of great escape. That sense of the place is in a host of newspaper and magazine articles like these: Alex Small, "Nevada—Fabulous State," *Chicago Tribune*, September 9, 1945; "It's Worth Seeing: Las Vegas, Desert Town, Flowers into Resort City," *Oakland Tribune*, August 20, 1950; Gladwin Hill, "Klondike in the Desert," *New York Times,* June 7, 1953; Herb Lyon, "Fantastic Las Vegas," *Chicago Tribune,* November 29, 1959; Caskie Stinnett, "Las Vegas: Where Anything Is Forgivable Except Restraint," *Holiday,* May 1967; Charles Champlin, "Making the World Safe for Frivolity," *Los Angeles Times West Magazine,* October 19, 1969; Judy Klemesrud, "Women Gambling in Las Vegas Don't Hide in Corner Any More," *New York Times,* September 26, 1973; and Rob Schultheis, "Yes!! It's . . . Las Vegas!!!!! An Unabashed Frolic in the City Where Dreams Work Overtime and Inhibitions Take a Holiday," *National Geographic Traveler,* May/June 1991. Unquestionably, the most enthusiastic booster of Las Vegas was Mario Puzo in his book *Inside Las Vegas* (1977).

INDEX